William W Smith

A Complete Etymology of the English Language

Containing the Anglo-Saxon, French, Dutch, German, Welsh, Danish, Gothic,

Swedish, Gaelic, Italian, Latin, and Greek roots, and the English words derived

therefrom, accurately spelled, accented, and defined

William W Smith

A Complete Etymology of the English Language
Containing the Anglo-Saxon, French, Dutch, German, Welsh, Danish, Gothic, Swedish, Gaelic, Italian, Latin, and Greek roots, and the English words derived therefrom, accurately spelled, accented, and defined

ISBN/EAN: 9783337237059

Printed in Europe, USA, Canada, Australia, Japan

Cover: Foto ©Paul-Georg Meister /pixelio.de

More available books at **www.hansebooks.com**

A COMPLETE

ETYMOLOGY

OF THE

ENGLISH LANGUAGE:

CONTAINING

THE ANGLO-SAXON, FRENCH, DUTCH, GERMAN, WELSH, DANISH, GOTHIC, SWEDISH, GAELIC, ITALIAN, LATIN, AND GREEK ROOTS, AND THE ENGLISH WORDS DERIVED THEREFROM ACCURATELY SPELLED, ACCENTED, AND DEFINED.

BY

WILLIAM W. SMITH,

AUTHOR OF "THE LITTLE SPELLER," "THE JUVENILE DEFINER," "THE GRAMMAR SCHOOL SPELLER," AND THE "DEFINER'S MANUAL."

Hig sprecad niwum tungum.

NEW YORK ·:·CINCINNATI ·:· CHICAGO
AMERICAN BOOK COMPANY

The Sources of Language.

ENGLISH ETYMOLOGY.

By WILLIAM W. SMITH.

Smith's Complete Etymology.
Smith's Condensed Etymology.

These works differ from all others in being etymologies of the whole language. Their predecessors shut themselves up with the Latin and Greek only, and ignore a wide field. The selections in Smith's Etymology are made solely with reference to the importance of the words in our own dialect, *from whatever source.* Thus, Anglo-Saxon furnishes *nearly one-half* of our more common words, while French, Dutch, German, Welsh, Danish, Gothic, Swedish, Gaelic, and Italian, divide the rest with Latin and Greek.

The Condensed Etymology exhibits all the excellent features of the parent volume, with less extensive lists, embracing the really essential words only. Both contain valuable introductory exercises to drill the pupil in the perplexing coincidences and general conformation of the language.

SMITH'S ORTHOGRAPHICAL WORKS.

The same author has given us the following very valuable works to teach Orthography and Definition, by various methods of grouping and classification in several grades.

SMITH'S LITTLE SPELLER. First Round in the Ladder of Learning. Simple words and pictures.

SMITH'S JUVENILE DEFINER. Lessons composed of familiar words grouped with reference to similar signification or use, and correctly spelled, accented, and defined.

SMITH'S GRAMMAR-SCHOOL SPELLER. Familiar words, grouped with reference to the sameness of sound of syllables differently spelled. Also definitions, complete rules for spelling and formation of derivatives, and exercises in false orthography.

SMITH'S SPELLER AND DEFINER'S MANUAL. A complete *School Dictionary* containing 14,000 words, with various other useful matter in the way of Rules and Exercises.

Making a series celebrated for adaptation, elegance, compendiousness, variety, system, eclecticism; and embracing Orthography, Definition, and Etymology.

Copyright 1867, by A. S. BARNES & CO.
Copyright, 1895, by ELIZABETH S. SMITH.

W. P. 2

PREFACE.

ALL the Etymologies of the English Language heretofore published have been confined merely to the words derived from the Latin and Greek—the present one has embraced all the words of the language, or rather, such as it is necessary to teach at home or in school.

"Words," says Bosworth, "are the creation of mind. With the faculty of speech, man was endowed with exalted mental powers, and warm social feelings, but the thoughts of his mind, and the feelings of his heart lay hid within him, and could not be communicated, till by the creative power of his mind, he formed words to express them.

"As words were formed to convey, not only the thoughts of the mind, but the feelings of the heart, they would in the first production of a language, naturally take that shape which would best represent their mental and physical powers. Those sounds would be selected which were adapted to the frame of the organs, and the feeling expressed. A robust conformation of the bodily frame, and great energy of mind, would, therefore, naturally express itself in words of corresponding strength and tone. These are the features which distinguish the languages of Gothic origin, especially the Anglo-Saxon, with its immediate descendant, the modern English; which has the strength of iron, with the gleam and sparkling of burnished steel."

The English Language is eminently a composite language, made up of contributions from other languages: Anglo-Saxon,* Danish, Dutch, Celtic, German, French, Latin, Greek, and some others.

The Anglo-Saxon is a branch of the Low German dialects, and resembles the old Frisic, the parent of the modern Dutch, and once spoken extensively between the Rhine and the Elbe. It is a very ancient language, its origin being completely lost in antiquity; the Latin in comparison, is a mere modern language.

The Anglo-Saxon is the *Mother Tongue* of the English Language, about four-fifths of the words in actual use being from this source. Not only in the number of words, but in their peculiar character and importance, as well as their influence on grammatical forms, (the English Grammar being almost exclusively occupied with what is of Anglo-Saxon origin), Anglo-Saxon constitutes its principal strength.

At the same time that our chief peculiarities of structure and idiom are essentially Anglo-Saxon, from the same copious fountain have sprung words designating the greater part of objects of sense; the terms which occur most frequently in discourse, and which recall the most vivid conceptions; as, *sun, moon, earth, fire, day, night*, &c.; and words expressive of the dearest connections, the strongest and most powerful feelings of nature, from our earliest days; as, *mother, father, sister, brother, wife, home*, &c.

The language of business, of the shop, the market, and of every-day life; our national proverbs; our language of humor, satire, and colloquial pleasantry; the most energetic words we can employ, whether of kindness or invective; in short, words expressive of our strongest emotions and actions in all the most stirring scenes of life, from the cradle to the grave, are derived from the Anglo-Saxon.

Every speaker or writer, then, who would not only convince the under-

* Anglo-Saxon is a general name given to the Teutonic settlers in the island of Great Britain.

standing, but touch the affections, should adopt Anglo-Saxon expressions, which from early use, and the dearest associations, excite emotion, and affect the heart.

Saxon is a name first used by the geographer Ptolemy, to indicate a branch of the German or Teutonic race, whose descendants now occupy the Kingdom of Saxony, the Lusatian districts of Prussia, the Circle of Wittenberg, the old Circle of Westphalia, the British Islands and Colonies, and the United States of America.

The Saxons mentioned by Ptolemy were a small tribe, who, in A. D. 141, dwelt on the north bank of the Elbe, and upon several small islands in the vicinity of the mouth of that river and of the Eider. From their geographical position as far west as the Atlantic coast, it seems probable that they were among the first of the Teutonic tribes which passed across from Asia into Europe.

Very trivial and uncertain are the accounts left us of the conquest of Great Britain by the Jutes, Saxons, and Angles.

It is certain that the invaders came over in small bodies each with a captain at its head, who became the petty king or chief of the new settlement in Britain, by which the Celtic population was either expelled or enslaved; so that in five or six centuries the eastern half of Britain was ruled by numerous petty kings. In the eighth century these petty kingdoms were consolidated into what is known as the Saxon Heptarchy.

Many hundred words in the language, especially those used as names of places, are Danish, introduced during the incursions into and occupation of England by the Danes.

An analysis of the language shows that the Norman French element enters very largely into its composition. This element, which is composed of the Celtic, Latin, and Scandinavian, was first introduced (1066) by the Normans under William the Conqueror.

The Norman conquest almost abolished the use of the Anglo-Saxon language in writing, and for more than a century the prevalent literature of England was either in Latin, or Anglo-Norman.

Norman French was spoken by the superior classes of society in England from the conquest to the time of Edward the Third (1827).

The laws of the realm, the proceedings of Parliament and the courts of justice were in that language, but the "Saxon Chronicle" had been carried on in obscure monasteries, by various annalists, to the year 1154.

In the thirteenth century during the progressive mixture of the two races, a literature sprang up in which the two languages became more or less intermixed. In the fourteenth century the Anglo-Saxon principle seemed to have gained the upper hand. In the fifteenth century the Anglo-Norman element seemed to be gaining the preponderance, but the proportions still continued to vary until it became fixed in the age of Queen Elizabeth.

The contributions of the Latin Language to the English are next in importance and amount to those of the Anglo-Saxon; these contributions come chiefly through the medium of the French or Norman French, in consequence of the Norman Conquest.

The Latin has served not only to refine and polish the English, but to enrich its vocabulary with many necessary and indispensable words.

To the Greek the English Language is indebted for most of its terms in physical science, and indeed for a great part of the terms employed in all the arts and sciences.

NOTE.—The SAXON CHRONICLE is a series of annals of A.-S. affairs, from the earliest times to A. D. 1154, compiled by the Monks.

WORDS OF SIMILAR PRONUNCIATION,

BUT HAVING DIFFERENT MEANINGS.

ABEL, *n.* A man's name.
ABLE, *a.* Strong; skillful.
ACCLAMATION, *n.* A shout of applause.
ACCLIMATION, *n.* Becoming inured to a climate.
ACTS, *n.* Performances.
AXE, *n.* A chopping instrument.
  ADDS, *v. t.* Increases.
  ADZE, *n.* A kind of axe.
ADHERENCE, *n.* Constancy.
ADHERENTS, *n.* Followers.
ADVICE, *n.* Counsel.
ADVISE, *v. t.* To counsel.
AIL, *v. t.* To pain; to trouble.
ALE, *n.* A malt liquor.
  AISLE, *n.* A passage.
  ISLE, *n.* A small island.
  I'LL, *v. t.* Contraction of "I will."
AIR, *n.* The fluid we breathe.
ERE, *adv.* Before.
HEIR, *n.* One who inherits.
ARE,† Plural of the verb BE.
— ALLEGATION, *n.* Affirmation.
- ALLIGATION, *n.* Tying together.
ALL, *a.* The whole.
AWL, *n.* Boring instrument.
ALLEY, *n.* A passage.
ALLY, *n.* A friend.
ALMS, *n.* What is given the poor.
ARMS, *n.* The limbs from the hand to the shoulder.
ALOUD, *a.* With great noise.
ALLOWED, *pp.* Permitted.   [laid.
ALTAR, *n.* A place where offerings are
ALTER, *v. t.* To change.
ANALYZE, *v. t.* To separate.
ANNALIZE, *v. t.* To record.
ANT, *n.* A genus of insects.
AUNT, *n.* A father's or mother's sister.
ANTE, Before.
ANTI. Opposed to.

ARC, *n.* A part of a circle.
ARK, *n.* A kind of boat.
ARCHES, *n.* Parts of a circle.
ARCHERS, *n.* Bowmen.
ARRAIGN, *v. t.* To accuse.
ARRANGE, *v. t.* To put in order.
ASCENT, *n.* Act of rising.
ASSENT, *n.* Consent.
ASPERATE, *v. t.* To make rough.
ASPIRATE, *v. t.* To breathe upon.
ASPERATION, *n.* Act of making rough.
ASPIRATION, *n.* An ardent wish.
ASSISTANCE, *n.* Help; aid.
ASSISTANTS, *n.* Helpers.
ATTENDANCE, *n.* Waiting on.
ATTENDANTS, *n.* Those who attend.
ATE, *pp.* Devoured.
EIGHT, *a.* Twice four.
AUGUR, *v. i.* To predict.
AUGER, *n.* An instrument.
AUSTERE, *a.* Severe.
OYSTER, *n.* A shell fish.
AXES, *n.* Chopping instruments.
AXIS, *n.* The line on which a thing
BAIL, *n.* Security.   [turns.
BALE, *n.* A bundle.
BAIZE, *n.* A kind of cloth.
BAYS, *n.* Portions of the sea.
BAIT, *n.* Food to allure.
BATE, *v. t.* To lessen.
BALD, *a.* Without hair.
BAWLED, *pp.* Cried aloud.
BALL, *n.* A round body.
BAWL, *v. i.* To cry aloud.
BALLAD, *n.* A song.
BALLET, *n.* A dance.
BALLOT, *n.* A ticket for voting.
BANDED, *pp.* United.
BANDIED, *pp.* Tossed to and fro.
BARD, *n.* A poet.
BARRED, *pp.* Fastened with a bar.

BARE, *a.* Naked.
BEAR, *n.* Animal; *v. t.* To carry.
BARK, *n.* The rind of a tree.
BARQUE, *n.* A kind of ship.
BARON, *n.* A degree of nobility.
BARREN, *a.* Not productive.
BARONESS, *n.* A baron's wife.
BARRENNESS, *n.* Sterility.
BASE, *n.* The bottom; *a.* Mean.
BASS, *n.* The lowest part of harmony.
BASS,† *n.* A kind of fish.
BAY, *n.* A portion of the sea.
BEY, *n.* A Turkish title.
BE, *v. n.* To exist.
BEE, *n.* An insect.
BALM, *n.* A plant; balsam.
BARM, *n.* Yeast.
BEACH, *n.* The sea-shore.
BEECH, *n.* A tree.
BEAT, *n.* A stroke.
BEET, *n.* A plant and its root.
BEAU, *n.* A man of dress.
Bow, *n.* An instrument.
Bow,† *n.* An act of respect.
BELL, *n.* A hollow vessel.
BELLE, *n.* A young woman.
BIN, *n.* A cell or chest for grain.
BEEN, *v. n.* The perfect participle of the verb BE.
BEER, *n.* A malt liquor.
BIER, *n.* A carriage for the dead.
BERRY, *n.* A small fruit.
BURY, *v. t.* To cover with earth.
BERTH, *n.* A room in a ship.
BIRTH, *n.* The act of coming into
BETTER, *a.* Superior. [life.
BETTOR, *n.* One who lays wagers.
BILE, *n.* A fluid.
BOIL,† *n.* A tumor; *v. i.* To have a bubbling motion.
BIGHT, *n.* The bend of a rope.
BITE, *v. t.* To crush with the teeth.
BLEW, *v. i.* Drove by the wind.
BLUE, *n.* A color.
BLOAT, *v. t.* To puff up.
BLOTE, *v. t.* To dry by smoke.
BOAR, *n.* The male swine.
BORE, *n.* A hole made by boring.
BOARD, *n.* Timber, broad and thin.
BORED, *pp.* Perforated by an auger.
BORDER, *n.* The outer edge.
BOARDER, *n.* One who has food and lodging with another for a reward.

BOLL, *n.* The pod of a plant.
BOWL, *n.* A vessel to hold liquids.
BOLE, *n.* The trunk of a tree.
BORN, *pp.* Come into life.
BORNE, *pp.* Carried.
BOURN, *n.* A bound.
BOROUGH, *n.* A town.
BURROW, *n.* A hole for rabbits.
BOUGH, *n.* A branch of a tree.
Bow, *n.* An act of respect.
BOY, *n.* A male child.
BUOY, *n.* A float to indicate shoals.
BRAKE, *n.* A drag put to wheels.
BREAK, *n.* An opening; *v. i.* To part
BREACH, *n.* A gap; a break. [in two.
BREECH, *n.* The hinder part of a gun.
BREAD, *n.* Food made of flour.
BRED, *pp.* Brought up from infancy.
BREWS, *v. t.* Makes malt liquor.
BRUISE, *v. t.* To crush by a heavy blow.
BREWED, *pp.* Mixed and fermented.
BROOD, *n.* Offspring; progeny.
BRIDAL, *a.* Belonging to a wedding.
BRIDLE, *n.* An instrument for a horse.
BRUIT, *v. t.* To noise abroad.
BRUTE, *n.* A creature without reason.
BUT, *con.* Except; yet.
BUTT, *n.* A large barrel or cask.
BUY, *v. t.* To purchase.
BY, *prep.* At; in; near.
BYE, *n.* A dwelling.
CACHE, *n.* A hole for hiding goods.
CASH, *n.* Money.
CAIN, *n.* A man's name.
CANE, *n.* A walking-stick.
CALENDAR, *n.* A register of the year.
CALENDER, *n.* A hot press.
CALL, *n.* A vocal address.
CAUL, *n.* A net for the hair.
CALLOUS, *a.* Insensible.
CALLUS, *n.* The hard edge of a wound.
CALK, *v. t.* To stop leaks.
CORK, *n.* The bark of a tree.
GAUK, *n.* A kind of spar.
CAMERA, *n.* An optical machine.
CHIMERA, *n.* A vain, idle fancy.
CANDID. *a.* Fair; open.
CANDIED, *a.* Incrusted with sugar.
CANNON, *n.* A great gun.
CANON, *n.* A rule in churches.
CANON,† *n.* A gorge; a gully.
CANVAS, *n.* Coarse cloth.
CANVASS, *n.* An examination; *v. t.* To solicit.

WORDS OF SIMILAR PRONUNCIATION.   7

CAPITAL, n. The upper part.
CAPITOL, n. An edifice.
  CARAT, n. A weight of four grains.
  CARET, n. A mark in writing.
  CARROT, n. A root.
CASK, n. A hollow wooden vessel.
CASQUE, n. A helmet.
CAST, v. t. To throw.
CASTE, n. A class of people.
  CASTER, n. A frame for small bottles.
  CASTOR, n. A beaver.
  CASTILE, n. A town in Spain.
  CAST-STEEL, n. Refined steel.
CAUSE, n. That which produces.
CAWS, n. The cries of crows.
  CAUF, n. A chest for live fish.
  COUGH, n. An effort of the lungs.
CAUDAL, a. Relating to an animal's tail.
CAUDLE, n. A warm drink of wine.
CEDE, v. t. To yield; to give up.
SEED, n. The reproductive part of a plant.
CEILING, n. The upper surface of a room.
SEALING, n. Act of fastening.
  CELERY, n. A plant.
  SALARY, n. Annual payment.
CELL, n. A small room.
SELL, v. t. To part with for a price.
  CELLAR, n. A room under a house.
  SELLER, n. One who sells.
CENSUS, n. Numbering the people.
SENSES, n. The faculties.
CENT, n. A hundred; a coin.
SENT, pp. Caused to go.
SCENT, n. Odor.
CENTAURY, n. A plant.
CENTURY, n. A hundred years.
  CENTS, n. Copper coins.
  SENSE, n. Feeling; perception.
  SINCE,† a. From the time that.
— CERE, v. t. To cover with wax.
SEER, n. One who foresees.
SEAR, a. Dry; v. t. To burn.
  CESSION, n. Act of giving away.
  SESSION, n. Act of sitting.
CHAGRIN, n. Ill humor.
SHAGREEN, n. The skin of a fish.
  CHAMPAGNE, n. A sparkling wine.
 *CHAMPAIGN, n. An open country.
  CAMPAIGN,† n. The time an army is in the field.
CHANCE, n. Accident.
CHANTS, v. t. Sings.

CHASTE, a. Modest; virtuous.
CHASED, pp. Pursued; hunted.
CHEWS, v. t. Crushes with the teeth.
CHOOSE, v. t. To select; to prefer.
CHOIR, n. A band of singers.
QUIRE, n. Twenty-four sheets.
CHOLER, n. Anger; rage.
COLLAR, n. A ring around the neck
CHORD, n. A musical sound.
CORD, n. A small rope.
CHRONICAL, a. Of long duration.
CHRONICLE, n. A history.
CITE, v. t. To summon to answer.
SITE, n. Situation.
SIGHT, n. Perception by the eye.
CLAUSE, n. A part of a sentence.
CLAWS, n. The nails of a beast or bird.
CLEAVE, v. i. To adhere; to stick.
CLEAVE, v. t. To divide; to split
CLIMB, v. t. To ascend.
CLIME, n. A climate.
  CLOSE, v. t. To shut; to end.
  CLOTHES, n. Garments.
  CLOSE, a. Confined; compact.
COALED, v. t. Supplied with coal.
COLD, a. Not hot; frigid.
  COARSE, a. Not fine; rough.
  COURSE, n. Route; progress.
  CORSE, n. A dead body.
COAT, n. An outside garment.
COTE, n. A cottage; a sheep-cot.
COFFER, n. A chest for money.
COUGHER, n. One who coughs.
COFFIN, n. A box for the dead.
COUGHING, ppr. Expelling from the lungs.
COLONEL, n. A military officer.
KERNEL, n. The seed in a nut.
COLOR, n. Hue; tint.
CULLER, n. One who chooses.
COMITY, n. Courtesy; politeness.
COMMITTEE, n. A body of managers.
COMPLACENT, a. Civil.
COMPLAISANT, a. Seeking to please.
COMPLACENCE, n. Satisfaction.
COMPLAISANCE, n. Condescension.
COMPLIANCE, n. Assent.
COMPLEMENT, n. A complete set.
COMPLIMENT, n. Delicate flattery.
CONCERT, n. A musical entertainment.
CONSORT, n. A companion. [crets.
CONFIDANT, n. One trusted with secrets.
CONFIDENT, a. Having full belief.

CONSEQUENCE, n. That which follows.
CONSEQUENTS, n. Deductions.
CONSONANCE, n. Concord.
CONSONANTS, n. Letters which are sounded with a vowel.
CONVENT, n. A body of monks or nuns.
CONVENT, v. t. To call before a judge.
COQUETTE, n. A vain girl.
COQUET, v. t. To deceive in love.
COROL, n. A corolla.
CORAL, n. A hard substance found in the ocean.
CORE, n. The inner part.
CORPS, n. A body of troops.
CORPSE,† n. A dead body.
CORRESPONDENCE, n. Interchange of letters.
CORRESPONDENTS, n. Those who correspond.
COUNCIL, n. An assembly.
COUNSEL, n. Advice.
COURIER, n. A messenger.
CURRIER, n. A preparer of leather.
COUSIN, n. A relative.
COZEN, v. t. To cheat.
COWARD, n. One without courage.
COWERED, pp. Stooped.
CRANE, n. A bird with a long beak.
CRAYON, n. A kind of pencil.
CREAK, v. i. To make a harsh noise.
CREEK, n. A small inlet.
CREWS, n. The men who manage ships.
CRUISE, n. A voyage.
CRUSE, n. A phial; a cruet.
CURRANT, n. A fruit.
CURRENT, n. A running stream.
CYMBAL, n. A musical instrument.
SYMBOL, n. A representative of something.
CYGNET, n. A young swan.
SIGNET, n. A seal.
CYPRESS, n. A forest tree.
CYPRUS, n. A thin black stuff.
DAM, n. A bank to confine water.
DAMN, v. t. To doom.
DAMMED, pp. Confined by banks.
DAMNED, pp. Doomed.
DANCE, v. i. To move with music.
DAUNTS, v. t. Discourages.
DANE, n. A native of Denmark.
DEIGN, v. i. To condescend.

DAY, n. The time between the rising and setting of the sun.
DEY, n. The title of the governors of Algiers and Tunis.
DEAR, a. Beloved; costly.
DEER, n. Animals of the stag kind.
DECEASE, n. Death.
DISEASE, n. Sickness.
DEMEAN, v. t. To behave.
DEMESNE, n. Land.
DEPRAVATION, n. Corruption.
DEPRIVATION, n. Loss.
DESCENDENT, a. Falling; sinking.
DESCENDANT, n. The offspring of an ancestor.
DESCENT, n. Progress downward.
DISSENT, n. Disagreement.
DESCENSION, n. Descent.
DISSENSION, n. Discord; strife.
DEVICE, n. Design.
DEVISE, v. t. To contrive.
DEVISER, n. A contriver.
DIVISOR, n. A number.
DEW, n. Moisture from the air.
DO, v. t. To perform.
DUE, n. That which belongs to one.
DIE, v. i. To lose life.
DYE, n. A coloring liquor.
DIFFUSE, v. t. To spread.
DIFFUSE, a. Copious.
DIRE, a. Dreadful.
DYER, n. One who dyes.
DISCREET, a. Prudent.
DISCRETE, a. Separate.
DIVERS, a. More than one.
DIVERSE, a. Different.
DOE, n. A she-deer.
DOUGH, n. Paste of bread.
DOME, n. A cupola.
DOOM, v. t. To condemn.
DONE, pp. Performed.
DUN, a. Of a dark color.
DOSE, n. The quantity given.
DOZE, n. A light sleep.
DOST, v. A part of the verb DO.
DUST, n. Earth reduced to powder.
DURST, pret. of the verb DARE.
DRACHM, n. A part of an ounce.
DRAM, n. A small quantity.
DRAFT, n. A bill.
DRAUGHT, n. A potion.
DUAL, a. Expressing the number two.
DUEL, n. A combat.

WORDS OF SIMILAR PRONUNCIATION.

DYING, n. Expiring.
DYEING, n. The act of staining.
EARN, v. t. To gain by labor.
URN, n. A vase.
EITHER, a. One or the other.
ETHER, n. An element supposed to be rarer than air.
ELISION, n. Division.
ELYSIAN, a. Delightful.
EMERSION, n. Act of rising out.
IMMERSION, n. Being in a fluid.
ERRAND, n. A message.
ERRANT, a. Wandering.
ARRANT,† a. Bad in a high degree.
ERUPTION, n. Act of bursting forth.
IRRUPTION, n. A sudden invasion.
EWE, n. A female sheep.
YOU, pro. The person spoken to.
YEW, n. An evergreen.
HUE,† n. Color; tint.
EXERCISE, n. Labor; work.
EXORCISE, v. t. To abjure.
FEINT, n. A false appearance.
FAINT, a. Languid.
FAIN, a. Glad; pleased.
FANE, n. A temple.
FEIGN, v. t. To pretend.
FAIR, a. Beautiful; just.
FARE, n. Price of conveyance; food.
FARTHER, adv. Further.
FATHER, n. A male parent.
FOTHER,† n. A load of lead.
FAT, n. The unctuous part of animal flesh.
VAT,† n. A cistern.
FAWN, n. A young deer.
FAUN, n. A woodland deity.
FEAT, n. A deed.
FEET, n. The plural of foot.
FETE,† n. A feast; a festival day.
FELLOE, n. The rim of a wheel.
FELLOW, n. A companion.
FATED, a. Decreed by fate.
FETED, pp. Honored.
FETID, a. Stinking; rancid.
FILLIP, n. A jerk of the finger.
PHILIP, n. A man's name.
FIND, v. t. To obtain by searching.
FINED, pp. Punished with penalty.
FIR, n. An evergreen.
FUR, n. The finer hair on animals.
FAR,† a. Distant; remote.
FIZZ, v. i. To emit a hissing noise.
PHIZ, n. The face.

FLEA, n. A small agile insect.
FLEE, v. i. To run from danger.
FLEW. The preterit of FLY.
FLUE, n. A passage for smoke.
FLOUR, n. Grain reduced to powder.
FLOWER, n. A blossom.
FORMALLY, adv. Ceremoniously.
FORMERLY, adv. In times past.
FOR, prep. Because of.
FORE, a. Not behind.
FOUR, a. and n. Twice two.
FORT, n. A fortified place.
FORTE, n. A peculiar talent.
FORTH, adv. Forward.
FOURTH, a. The ordinal of four.
FOUL, a. Not clean.
FOWL, n. A winged animal.
FRANC, n. A French silver coin.
FRANK, a. Liberal; generous.
FRAYS, n. Quarrels.
PHRASE, n. Part of a sentence.
FREEZE, v. i. To congeal with cold.
FRIEZE, n. A coarse woolen cloth.
FREES, v. t. Sets at liberty.
GABEL, n. A tax.
GABLE, n. The end of a house.
GAGE, n. A pledge; a pawn.
GAUGE, n. A measure.
GAIT, n. Manner of walking.
GATE, n. A kind of door.
GALA, n. A show.
GAYLY, adv. In a gay manner.
GAMBLE, v. i. To play for money.
GAMBOL, n. A skip; a hop.
GANTLET, n. Military punishment.
GAUNTLET, n. An iron glove.
GOAL, n. The mark set to bound a race.
GAOL,† n. A prison.
GENIUS, n. Intellect; talent.
GENUS, n. A class of things.
GENTILE, n. One not Jewish.
GENTLE, a. Soft; mild.
GILD, v. t. Overlay with gold.
GUILD, n. A corporation.
GILL, n. The organ of respiration in fishes.
GILL,† n. The fourth part of a pint.
GILT, n. Gold laid on the surface.
GUILT, n. A crime.
GLARE, n. A dazzling light.
GLAIR, n. The white of an egg.
GNAW, v. t. To bite off by little.
NOR, conj. A negative particle.
NICE, a. Fine; delicate.
GNEIS, n. A species of granite.

God, *n.* The Supreme Being.
Goad,†*n.* A stick for driving beasts.
Goer, *n.* One who goes. [horn.
Gore, *n.* Blood; *v. t.* To pierce with a
Gored, *pp.* Pierced with a horn.
Gourd, *n.* A plant.
Grate, *n.* An iron frame for fire.
Great, *a.* Important.
Grater, *n.* A kind of coarse file.
Greater, *a.* Larger.
Grease, *n.* Animal fat.
Greece, *n.* A country of Europe.
Groan, *n.* A deep sigh.
Grown, *pp.* Advanced in growth.
Grocer, *n.* A dealer in tea, &c.
Grosser, *a.* More impure.
Grope, *v. t.* To search by feeling.
Group,†*n.* An assembly of figures.
Guana, *n.* A lizard.
Guano, *n.* An excellent manure.
Guessed, *pp.* Conjectured.
Guest, *n.* A visitor.
Guitar, *n.* A stringed instrument.
Catarrh, *n.* A disease of the head.
Hail, *n.* Frozen drops of rain.
Hale, *a.* Healthy; hearty.
Hair, *n.* The covering of the head.
Hare, *n.* A kind of rabbit.
Hall, *n.* A large room.
Haul, *v. t.* To pull; to draw.
Halo, *n.* A circle round the sun or moon.
Hallow, *v. t.* To make holy.
Harsh, *a.* Rough; severe.
Hash, *n.* Minced meat.
Hart, *n.* A he-deer.
Heart, *n.* The seat of life.
Hay, *n.* Dried grass.
Hey, *intj.* An expression of joy.
Heal, *v. t.* To restore.
Heel, *n.* The hind part of the foot.
Hear, *v. t.* To perceive by the ear.
Here, *adv.* In this place.
Heard, *pp.* Did hear.
Herd, *n.* A number of beasts together.
Hew, *v. t.* To cut with an axe.
Hue, *n.* Color; tint.
Hide, *n.* The skin of an animal; *v. t.* To conceal.
Hied, *pp.* Hastened.
Hie, *v. i.* To hasten.
High, *a.* Lofty; tall.
Higher, *a.* More lofty.
Hire, *n.* Wages paid for service.

Him, *pro.* The objective of He.
Hymn, *n.* A song of adoration.
Hoard, *n.* A store laid up.
Horde, *n.* A clan; a tribe.
Hoarse, *a.* Having the voice rough.
Horse, *n.* An animal.
Hoa, *intj.* An exclamation.
Hoe, *n.* A farming instrument.
Ho, *intj.* Stop; cease.
Hoes, *n.* Instruments for farming.
Hose, *n.* Stockings; leather pipes to conduct water.
Hole, *n.* A cavity.
Whole, *n.* All of a thing.
Holy, *a.* Pure; sacred.
Wholly, *adv.* Completely.
Hoop, *n.* A circular binding.
Whoop, *n.* A loud shout.
Hour, *n.* Sixty minutes.
Our, *pro.* Belonging to us.
Huzza, *n.* A shout.
Hussar, *n.* A horse soldier.
Hyperbola, *n.* A conic section.
Hyperbole, *n.* A figure of speech.
I, *pro.* The person speaking.
Eye, *n.* The organ of vision.
Idle, *a.* Doing nothing.
Idol, *n.* An image worshiped.
Impostor, *n.* One who pretends.
Imposture, *n.* Deception; fraud.
In, *prep.* Noting time.
Inn, *n.* A hotel.
Incidence, *n.* A falling on.
Incidents, *n.* Events.
Indict, *v. t.* To declare guilty.
Indite, *v. t.* To dictate.
Indicted, *pp.* Accused.
Indited, *pp.* Composed.
Indicter, *n.* One who indicts.
Inditer, *n.* One who composes.
Indiscreet, *a.* Imprudent.
Indiscrete, *a.* Not separated.
Ingenious, *a.* Witty; inventive.
Ingenuous, *a.* Open; artless.
Intense, *a.* Extreme.
Intents, *n.* Designs.
Invade, *v. t.* To infringe.
Inveighed, *pp.* Uttered censure.
Jam, *n.* A conserve of fruits.
Jamb, *n.* The side of a door.
Jester, *n.* One given to merriment
Gesture, *n.* Action of sentiment.
Key, *n.* An instrument.
Quay, *n.* A wharf.

WORDS OF SIMILAR PRONUNCIATION. 11

KILL, *v. t.* To deprive of life.
KILN, *n.* A stove or furnace.
   KNAG, *n.* A knot in wood.
   NAG, *n.* A small horse.
KNEAD, *v. t.* To work into a mass.
KNEED, *a.* Having knees.
NEED, *n.* Necessity; want.
   KNEW, *v.* Had knowledge of.
   GNU, *n.* An animal of Africa.
   NEW, *a.* Not old.
KNIGHT, *n.* A military attendant.
NIGHT, *n.* The time of darkness.
KNIT, *v. t.* To unite closely.
NIT, *n.* The egg of an insect.
KNOW, *v. t.* To have knowledge of.
NO, *n.* A denial; *a.* None.
   KNOWS, *v. t.* Understands.
   NOSE, *n.* The organ of smell.
KNOT, *n.* A part which is tied.
NOT, *adv.* The word of refusal.
NOTT, *n.* A proper name.
   LACKS, *v. t.* Wants; needs.
   LAX, *a.* Loose; slack.
LADE, *v. t.* To load; to freight.
LAID, *pp.* Placed; produced eggs.
   LANCH, *v. t.* To dart; to let fly.
   LAUNCH, *v. n.* To slide into the water.
LANE, *n.* A narrow way.
LAIN, *pp.* Rested horizontally.
   LATIN, *n.* Language of the Romans.
   LATTEN, *n.* A fine kind of brass.
LAUD, *v. t.* To extol; to praise.
LORD,† *n.* The Supreme Being.
LEA, *n.* A meadow.
LEE, *n.* A sheltered place.
LEACH, *v. t.* To filtrate.
LEECH, *n.* A worm that sucks blood.
LEAD, *n.* A soft, heavy metal.
LED, *pp.* Guided, conducted.
LEAD,† *v. t.* To guide by the hand.
LEAF, *n.* The green part of plants.
LIEF, *adv.* Willingly.
LEAVE, *n.* Permission; *v. t.* To quit.
LEAK, *n.* A hole which lets water in
LEEK, *n.* A plant.   [or out.
LEAN, *a.* Not fat.
LIEN, *n.* A legal claim on property.
   LEASED, *v. t.* Let or hired.
   LEAST, *a.* Smallest.
LEGISLATOR, *n.* A lawgiver.
LEGISLATURE, *n.* The body in a State which makes the laws.
   LENDS, *v. t.* Grants for a time.
   LENS, *n.* A piece of convex glass.

LESSEN, *v. t.* To diminish.
LESSON, *n.* A task.
   LEVEE, *n.* A ceremonious visit.
   LEVY, *v. t.* To collect.
LIAR, *n.* One who tells lies.
LIER, *n.* One who lies down.
LYRE, *n.* A musical instrument.
   LIE, *n.* A falsehood.
   LYE, *n.* Water mixed with wood-ashes.
LIMB, *n.* A branch.
LIMN, *v. t.* To draw.
LINE, *n.* That which has length without breadth.
LOIN, *n.* The back of an animal.
LINEAMENT, *n.* Feature.
LINIMENT, *n.* A wash.
   LINKS, *n.* Divisions of a chain.
   LYNX, *n.* An animal remarkable for sharp sight.
LIVER, *n.* One who lives.
LIVRE,† *n.* A French coin.
   LO, *intj.* Look; see.
   LOW, *a.* Not high; mean.
LOAM, *n.* A rich vegetable mold.
LOOM,† *n.* A frame for weaving.
LOAN, *n.* Any thing lent.
LONE, *a.* Solitary.
LOATH, *a.* Unwilling.
LOATHE, *v. t.* To feel nausea.
LOCK, *n.* An instrument.
LOCH, *n.* A term for lake in Scotland.
LOUGH, *n.* A term for lake in Ireland.
LORE, *n.* Learning.
LOWER, *v. t.* To bring low.
LOWER,† *v. t.* To appear dark.
LOSE, *v. t.* To miss any thing.
LOOSE, *a.* Unbound.
MADE, *pp.* Created; formed.
MAID, *n.* An unmarried woman.
MAIL, *n.* A coat of steel network.
MALE, *n.* The he of any species.
MAIN, *a.* Principal; chief.
MANE, *n.* The hair on the neck of horses.
MAINE, *n.* One of the United States.
   MAIZE, *n.* Indian corn.
   MAZE, *n.* A place of perplexity.
MANTEL, *n.* The beam of a fireplace.
MANTLE, *n.* A kind of cloak.
   MANNER, *n.* Form; method.
   MANOR, *n.* A large landed estate.
   MANNA, *n.* A substance given by the Lord to the Israelites.

MARK, n. A visible line.
MARQUE, n. A license.
MARTEN, n. A large kind of weasel.
MARTIN, n. A sort of swallow.
MARSHAL, n. A chief officer.
MARTIAL, a. Warlike.
MARE, n. A female horse.
MAYOR, n. The chief magistrate of a city.
MEAD, n. A kind of drink.
MEED, n. Reward.
MEAN, a. Wanting dignity.
MIEN, n. Look; aspect.
MESNE, a. Middle.
MEAT, n. Flesh to be eaten.
MEET, a. Suitable; v. t. To come to-
METE, v. t. To measure. [gether.
MEDDLE, v. i. To interfere.
MEDAL, n. A piece stamped in honor of some performance.
MEDLAR, n. A tree.
MEDDLER, n. One who meddles.
MESSAGE, n. Any thing to be told.
MESSUAGE, n. A house and land.
METTLE, n. Spirit; courage.
METAL, n. A mineral insoluble in water and fusible by heat.
METER, n. A measurer.
METER, n. Measure of verse.
MEWL, v. i. To cry as an infant.
MULE, n. An animal of mongrel breed.
MEWS, v. i. Cries as a cat.
MUSE, n. Deep thought.
MILLENARY, a. Consisting of a thousand.
MILLINERY, n. Goods of a milliner.
MINCE, v. t. To cut into small parts.
MINTS, n. Places where money is coined.
MINDS, n. The intelligent faculties.
MINES, n. Subterraneous works.
MINER, n. One employed in mining.
MINOR, n. One under lawful age.
MISSAL, n. The mass book.
MISSEL, n. A singing bird.
MISSILE, n. A weapon thrown.
MISSED, pp. Failed in aim.
MIST, n. A fine, thin rain.
MITE, n. A small insect.
MIGHT, n. Power; strength.
MITY, a. Having insect mites.
MIGHTY, a. Powerful.
MOAN, n. Audible sorrow.
MOWN, pp. Cut down with a scythe.

MOAT, n. A ditch round a castle.
MOTE, n. A small particle.
MORE. A greater quantity.
MOWER, n. One who cuts grass.
MORN, n. The first part of the day.
MOURN, v. i. To grieve; to lament.
MORNING, n. The first part of the day.
MOURNING, n. Grief; sorrow.
MORTAR, n. Cement for bricks.
MORTER, n. A lamp or light.
MOW, n. A compartment for hay.
MOW,† v. t. To cut down.
MUSTARD, n. A genus of plants.
MUSTERED, pp. Assembled.
NAP, n. A short sleep.
KNAP, v. i. To make a sharp noise.
NAVAL, a. Maritime; nautical.
NAVEL, n. The center of the ab-
NAIVE, a. Artless. [domen.
NAVE, n. The center of the wheel.
KNAVE, n. A petty rascal.
NAY, adv. No.
NEIGH, n. The voice of a horse.
NEAL, v. t. To temper by heat.
KNEEL, v. i. To rest on the knee.
NEAR, a. Not far distant.
NE'ER, adv. At no time.
NEITHER, conj. Not either; nor.
NETHER, a. Lower.
NEWS, n. Fresh account.
NOOSE, n. A running knot.
NONE, a. No one.
NUN, n. A female devotee.
OAR, n. A pole with a broad blade.
O'ER, prep. Above; across.
ORE, n. A mineral body.
ODE, n. A lyric poem.
OWED, pp. Under obligation.
OF, prep. Belonging to.
OFF, adv. Noting separation.
OH, intj. Denoting pain.
OWE, v. t. To be indebted to.
OTTAR, n. The oil of roses.
OTTER, n. An amphibious animal.
ONE, n. A single person; a unit.
WON, pp. Gained by conquest.
ORDINANCE, n. A decree; law.
ORDNANCE, n. Cannon.
ORDER, n. Method.
ORDURE, n. Dung; filth.
OUGHT, v. t. To be bound by duty.
AUGHT, n. Any thing.
PACED, pp. Moved slowly.
PASTE, a. Flour and water mixed.

WORDS OF SIMILAR PRONUNCIATION.

PACKED, *pp.* Bound in a bundle.
PACT, *n.* A contract; a bargain.
PAIL, *n.* A wooden vessel.
PALE, *a.* Not ruddy.
PAIN, *n.* Anguish; agony.
PANE, *n.* A square of glass.
PAIR, *n.* Two things suiting one an-
PARE, *v. t.* To peel.   [other.
PEAR, *n.* A fruit.
PALATE, *n.* The organ of taste.
PALLET, *n.* A small bed.
PALETTE, *n.* A painter's board.
PALL, *n.* The covering over the dead.
PAUL, *n.* A man's name.
PARTITION, *n.* That which divides.
PETITION, *n.* A request; entreaty.
PASSABLE, *a.* Tolerable.
PASSIBLE, *a.* That may feel.
PASTOR, *n.* A clergyman.
PASTURE, *n.* Land grazed by cattle.
PATIENCE, *n.* Suffering without complaint.
PATIENTS, *n.* Persons under the care of a doctor.
PAUSE, *n.* A stop; suspense.
PAWS, *n.* The fore-feet of a beast of prey.
PORES,†*n.* Passages for perspiration.
PEACE, *n.* Freedom from war.
PIECE, *n.* A part of the whole.
PEAK, *n.* The top of an eminence.
PIQUE, *n.* A slight resentment.
PEAL, *n.* A succession of loud sounds.
PEEL, *n.* The skin or rind.
PANEL, *n.* A square between other bodies.
PANNEL, *n.* A kind of saddle.
PURL, *v. i.* To flow with a gentle noise.
PEARL, *n.* A white, hard, smooth substance found in a kind of oyster.
PEDAL, *a.* Belonging to the feet.
PEDAL, *n.* A key moved by the foot.
PEDDLE, *v. t.* To carry about to sell.
PEER, *n.* An equal.
PIER, *n.* A column; a wharf.
PENCIL, *n.* A small brush.
PENSILE, *a.* Suspended.
PENDANT, *n.* Something which hangs.
PENDENT, *a.* Hanging.   [woman.
PERSONAL, *a.* Belonging to man or
PERSONNEL, *n.* The persons in a public office.
PILOT, *n.* A guide.
PILATE, *n.* A man's name.

PILLAR, *n.* A column.   [head.
PILLOW, *n.* Something under the
PINT, *n.* Half a quart.
POINT,† *n.* The sharp end.
PISTIL, *n.* Part of a flower.
PISTOL, *n.* The smallest fire-arm.
PLACE, *n.* Locality; situation.
PLAICE, *n.* A sort of flat fish.
PLAIN, *n.* Smooth; clear.
PLANE, *n.* A flat surface.
PLAINTIFF, *n.* One who seeks justice.
PLAINTIVE, *a.* Expressive of sorrow.
PLAIT, *n.* A fold.
PLATE, *n.* A flat piece of metal.
PLEAS, *n.* Arguments.
PLEASE, *v. i.* To give pleasure.
PLUM, *n.* A fruit.
PLUMB, *n.* A perpendicular.
PLUME,† *n.* A feather; a crest.
POLE, *n.* A measure; a long stake.
POLL, *n.* The head.
POOL, *n.* A small collection of water.
POULE, *n.* The stakes played for.
POPLAR, *n.* A tree of the aspen species.
POPULAR, *a.* Pleasing to the people.
POPULACE, *n.* The people.
POPULOUS, *a.* Full of people.
PORE, *n.* A passage for perspiration.
POUR, *v. t.* To let out of a vessel.
PORING, *ppr.* Looking intently.
POURING, *ppr.* Sending as a fluid.
PORT, *n.* A harbor.
PORTE, *n.* The Turkish court.
PORTION, *n.* A part; a share.
POTION,† *n.* A draught of medicine.
PRACTICE, *n.* The habit of doing.
PRACTISE, *v. t.* To exercise.
PRAISE, *n.* Commendation.
PRAYS, *v. i.* Entreats; petitions.
PREYS, *v. i.* Feeds by violence.
PRAY, *v. t.* To supplicate.
PREY, *n.* Rapine; plunder.
PRECEDENT, *n.* A rule or example.
PRECEDENT, *a.* Going before.
PRESIDENT, *n.* One who presides.
PRESENCE, *n.* State of being present.
PRESENTS, *n.* Gifts.
PRIDE, *n.* Self-esteem.
PRIED, *pp.* Moved by means of a lever.
PRIES, *v. i.* To inspect closely.
PRIZE, *n.* A reward gained.
PRINCE, *n.* The son of a king.
PRINTS, *n.* Impressions made.

PRINCIPAL, *a.* Chief; important.
PRINCIPLE, *n.* An element.
PRIOR, *a.* Previous; former.
PRIER, *n.* One who inquires closely.
PROFIT, *n.* Gain; benefit.
PROPHET, *n.* One who foretells events.
PROPHECY, *n.* That which is foretold. [tell.
PROPHESY, *v. i.* To predict; to foretell.
QUARTS, *n.* Fourths of a gallon.
QUARTZ, *n.* Rock crystal.
QUEEN, *n.* The wife of a king.
QUEAN, *n.* A worthless woman.
RABBET, *n.* A joint.
RABBIT, *n.* A small quadruped.
RADICAL, *n.* Of first principles.
RADICLE, *n.* A part of a seed.
RADISH, *n.* An esculent root.
REDDISH, *a.* Somewhat red.
RAIN, *n.* Water from the clouds.
REIGN, *n.* To have royal power.
REIN, *n.* The strap of a bridle.
RAISE, *v. t.* To lift; to erect.
RAYS, *n.* Beams of light.
RAZE, *v. t.* To demolish.
RAISED, *pp.* Lifted; elevated.
RAZED, *pp.* Demolished.
RAISER, *n.* One who raises.
RAZOR, *n.* An instrument for shaving.
RAISIN, *n.* A dried grape.
REASON, *n.* The rational faculty.
RANCOR, *n.* Malice; hate.
RANKER, *a.* Coarser.
RAP, *n.* A quick, smart blow.
WRAP, *v. t.* To roll together.
RAPPING, *ppr.* Striking with quick blows.
WRAPPING, *n.* A cover.
RAPINE,† *n.* Plunder; pillage.
READ, *v. t.* To peruse.
REED, *n.* A hollow, knotted stalk.
READ, *pp.* Perused.
RED, *a.* Having the color like blood.
REAL, *a.* True.
REEL, *n.* A machine for winding.
RESEAT, *v. t.* To seat again.
RECEIPT, *n.* A written acknowledgment.
RELIC, *n.* That which remains.
RELICT, *n.* A widow.
RESIDENCE, *n.* Place of abode.
RESIDENTS, *n.* Those who reside in a
RESIGN, *v. t.* To give up. [place.
RESIGN, *v. t.* To sign again.

REST, *n.* Quiet; ease.
WREST, *v. t.* To twist by violence.
RESTAURATION, *n.* Restoration.
RESTORATION, *n.* Recovery.
RHEUM, *n.* A thin, watery matter.
ROOM, *n.* Space.
RHUMB, *n.* A vertical circle.
RUM, *n.* Spirituous liquor.
RHOMB,† *n.* A quadrilateral figure.
RHYME, *n.* Harmonical sounds.
RIME, *n.* Hoar frost.
RICE, *n.* An esculent grain.
RISE, *n.* Ascent; *v. t.* To ascend.
RIFLE, *n.* A kind of gun.
RIVAL,† *n.* A competitor.
RIGGER, *n.* One who rigs.
RIGOR, *n.* Severity; strictness.
RIGHT, *a.* Direct; proper.
RITE, *n.* Ceremony.
WRIGHT, *n.* A workman.
WRITE, *v. t.* To express by letters formed with a pen.
ROAD, *n.* An open way.
RODE, *pp.* Traveled in a vehicle.
ROWED, *pp.* Impelled by oars.
ROAM, *v. i.* To ramble.
ROME, *n.* A city in Italy.
ROAR, *v. i.* To cry as a lion.
ROWER, *n.* One who manages an oar.
ROE, *n.* A species of deer.
ROW, *v. t.* To impel a boat by oars.
ROW,† *n.* A riotous noise.
ROES, *n.* Female deer; eggs of fishes.
ROWS, *v. t.* Impels by oars.
ROSE, *n.* A well-known flower.
ROOD, *n.* The fourth part of an acre.
RUDE, *a.* Rough; coarse of manners.
ROUSE, *v. t.* To stir up; to provoke.
ROWS, *n.* Riotous disturbances.
ROTE, *n.* Memory of words.
WROTE, *pret.* of WRITE.
ROUGH, *a.* Not smooth; rugged.
RUFF, *n.* A linen ornament.
ROUT, *n.* An evening party; *v. t.* To disperse.
ROUTE, *n.* Road; course.
RUNG, *n.* A step of a ladder; *pp.*
WRUNG, *pp.* Twisted. [Sounded.
RYE, *n.* A species of grain.
WRY, *a.* Crooked.
SAIL, *n.* Canvas of a ship.
SALE, *n.* Act of selling.
SAILER, *n.* That which sails.
SAILOR, *n.* A seaman; a mariner.

WORDS OF SIMILAR PRONUNCIATION. 15

SATIRE, *n.* Ridicule; sarcasm.
SATYR, *n.* A sylvan God.
SAVER, *n.* One who saves.
SAVOR, *n.* A scent; taste.
SCENE, *n.* A view.
SEEN, *pp.* Having viewed.
SEINE, *n.* A net used in fishing.
SCULL, *n.* A short oar.
SKULL, *n.* The case of the brain.
SEA, *n.* A body of salt water.
SEE, *v. t.* To perceive by the eye.
C, *n.* A letter in the alphabet.
SEAL, *n.* An engraved stamp.
SEEL, *v. t.* To close the eyes.
CEIL, *v. t.* To cover the upper surface.
SEAM, *n.* A juncture.
SEEM, *v. n.* To appear.
SEAMED, *pp.* Joined together.
SEEMED, *pp.* Appeared.
SEAR, *a.* Dry; *v. t.* To burn.
SEER, *n.* One who foresees.
SEAS, *n.* Bodies of salt water.
SEES, *v. t.* Perceives by the eye.
SEIZE, *v. t.* To take hold of.
SECTS, *n.* Religious denominations.
SEX, *n.* The distinction between male and female.
SENIOR, *n.* One older than another.
SEIGNIOR, *n.* A title.
SERF, *n.* A slave.
SURF, *n.* The swell of the sea that beats upon the shore.
SERGE, *n.* A kind of woolen cloth.
SURGE, *n.* A rising billow
SET, *v. t.* To place.
SIT,† *v. i.* To repose on a seat.
SEW, *v. t.* To join by the needle.
SOW, *v. i.* To scatter seed.
SO, *adv.* In this manner.
SOWER, *n.* One who sows.
SOAR, *v. i.* To fly aloft.
SORE, *n.* An ulcer; a painful part.
SEWER, *n.* One who uses a needle.
SEWER,† *n.* A passage to convey off water and filth.
SHEAR, *v. t.* To clip with shears.
SHEER, *v. n.* To deviate.
SHIRE, *n.* A county.
SHEATH, *n.* The case of any thing.
SHEATHE, *v. t.* To inclose in a case.
SHOW, *v. t.* To exhibit to view.
SHEW, *v. t.* To exhibit to view.
SHOE, *n.* A protection for the foot.
SHOO, *intj.* Begone.

SHONE, *pp.* Emitted rays of light.
SHOWN, *pp.* Exhibited.
SIDE, *n.* Edge; margin.
SIGHED, *pp.* To emit breath audibly.
SIGHS, *n.* Deep respirations.
SIZE, *n.* Bulk; magnitude.
SIGHER, *n.* One who sighs.
SIRE, *n.* Father.
SIGN, *n.* A token; a signal.
SINE, *n.* The name of a line.
SINK, *v. i.* To go to the bottom.
CINQUE, *n.* The number five.
SLAY, *v. t.* To kill.
SLEY, *n.* A weaver's reed.
SLEIGH, *n.* A vehicle for snow.
SLEW, *pret.* of SLAY.
SLUE, *v. t.* To turn about.
SLIGHT, *n.* Neglect; *a.* Small.
SLEIGHT, *n.* Artful trick.
SLOE, *n.* A fruit.
SLOW, *a.* Not swift.
SLOUGH, *n.* A deep, miry place.
SLOUGH,† *v. i.* To fall off.
SMELT, *n.* A small sea-fish.
SMELT, *v. t.* To melt; *pp.* Perceived by the nose.
SOARED, *pp.* Ascended.
SWORD, *n.* A weapon for cutting.
SWARD,† *n.* A grassy surface.
SOLE, *n.* The bottom of the foot.
SOUL, *n.* The spirit of man.
SOLD, *pp.* Disposed of for a price.
SOLED, *pp.* Furnished with soles.
SOULED, *a.* Having a mind.
SOLDER, *n.* Metallic cement.
SOLDIER,† *n.* A warrior.
SOME, *a.* More or less.
SUM, *n.* The whole.
SON, *n.* A male child.
SUN, *n.* The luminary that makes the day
SOOT, *n.* Condensed smoke.
SUIT, *n.* A set of things.
SUET, *n.* A hard fat.
SUITE, *n.* A train of followers.
SOOTH, *n.* Truth; reality.
SOOTHE, *v. t.* To allay.
STAID, *a.* Sober; grave.
STAYED, *pp.* Supported.
STAIR, *n.* One in a flight of steps.
STARE, *v. n.* To look with fixed eyes.
STAKE, *n.* A small post.
STEAK, *n.* A slice of beef.

STALK, n. The stem of a plant.
STORK, n. A bird.
STATIONARY, a. Motionless.
STATIONERY, n. Pens, ink, paper, &c.
STEEL, n. A refined kind of iron.
STEAL, v. t. To take by theft.
STRAIGHT, a. Not crooked.
STRAIT, n. A narrow pass.
SUCCOR, n. Aid; relief.
SUCKER, n. A shoot of a plant.
SWAP, n. A blow.
SWOP, v. t. To barter.
SWEAT, n. Perspiration.
SWEET, a. Pleasing to the taste.
TACKS, n. Small nails.
TAX, n. A tribute.
TACT, n. Skill.
TACK, n. A small nail.
TAIL, n. The last end.
TALE, n. A narrative.
TALENTS, n. Abilities.
TALONS, n. The claws of a bird.
TAPER, n. A wax candle.
TAPIR, n. An animal.
TARE, n. A weed.
TEAR, v. t. To pull in pieces.
TEAR,† n. Moisture from the eyes.
TAUGHT, pp. Instructed.
TAUT, a. Tight.
TEAM, n. Two or more horses.
TEEM, v. i. To be full.
TEAR, n. The water from the eyes.
TIER, n. A row; a rank.
TEAS, n. The different kinds of tea.
TEASE, v. t. To harass; to annoy.
TENOR, n. General course.
TENURE, n. Act of holding.
TENSE, a. Drawn tight.
TENTS, n. Movable lodgings.
THE. The definite article.
THEE, pro. The objective case of THOU.
THEIR, pro. Belonging to them.
THERE, adv. In that place.
THREW, pret. of THROW.
THROUGH, prep. From end to end.
THROE, n. Extreme pain.
THROW, v. t. To hurl.
THRONE, n. The seat of a king.
THROWN, pp. Cast; hurled.
THYME, n. An aromatic plant.
TIME, n. Duration.
TIDE, n. Stream.
TIED, pp. Bound.

TINY, a. Little; small.
TINNY, a. Like tin.
TO, prep. Noting motion toward.
TOO, adv. Noting excess.
TWO, a. One and one.
TOAD, n. An animal.
TOED, a. Having toes.
TOWED, pp. Drawn along.
TOE, n. A finger of the foot.
TOW, v. t. To draw along.
TOLD, pp. Mentioned; related.
TOLLED, pp. Sounded slowly.
TOLED, pp. Allured.
TOLE, v. t. To allure.
TOLL, n. A tax upon travelers.
TON, n. A weight; 20 cwt.
TUN, n. A large cask.
TOUR, n. A circuit.
TOWER, n. A building.
TRACKED, pp. Followed by marks.
TRACT, n. A region; a small pamphlet.
TRAVAIL, v. i. To labor with pain.
TRAVEL, v. i. To make journeys.
TRAY, n. A shallow vessel.
TREY, n. A three at cards.
TREATISE, n. A discourse.
TREATIES, n. Agreements between governments.
TOMB, n. A monument over a grave.
TOME, n. A volume; a book.
EWES, n. Female sheep.
YEWS, n. Evergreen trees.
USE,† n. Service.
VALE, n. Space between hills.
VAIL, n. Money given to servants.
VEIL, n. A thin cover over the face.
VALLEY, n. A hollow between hills.
VALUE,† v. t. To rate at a certain price.
VANE, n. A weather-cock.
VEIN, n. A blood vessel.
VAIN, a. Meanly proud.
VENAL, a. Mercenary; base.
VENIAL, a. That may be forgiven.
VENT, n. A hole for air to escape.
WENT, pret. of GO.
VENUS, n. One of the planets.
VENOUS, a. Relating to the veins.
VERACITY, n. Habitual truth.
VORACITY, n. Rapacity; greediness.
VIAL, n. A small bottle.
VIOL, n. A musical instrument.
VILE, a. Base; wicked.
PHIAL, n. A small bottle.

WORDS OF SIMILAR PRONUNCIATION.

VICAR, *n.* A substitute.
WICKER, *a.* Made of twigs.
VICE, *n.* A spot or defect.
VICE. Instead of.
  VIOLATE, *v. t.* To transgress.
  VIOLET, *n.* A delicate flower.
VIRTU, *n.* A love of the fine arts.
VIRTUE, *n.* Moral goodness.
  WADE, *v. n.* To walk through water.
  WEIGHED, *pp.* Balanced.
WAIL, *v. t.* To moan; to lament.
WALE, *n.* A mark left by a stripe.
WHALE, *n.* An animal shaped like a fish, and living in the sea, but having warm blood, and breathing the air.
WAIST, *n.* Part of the body.
WASTE, *n.* Wanton destruction.
WAIT, *v. i.* To stay for.
WEIGHT, *n.* Heaviness.
  WAIVE, *v. t.* To relinquish.
  WAVE, *n.* A moving swell of water.
WANT, *v. t.* To desire.
WONT, *n.* Custom; habit.
  WEAR, *v. t.* To impair by use.
  WARE, *n.* Commodity.
WHERE, *adv.* In which place.
WERE,† *pret. plu.* From the verb BE.
WART, *n.* A hard excrescence.
WORT, *n.* Unfermented beer.
  WHACKS, *n.* Heavy blows.
  WAX, *n.* The substance which forms the cells of bees.
WAY, *n.* A road; a passage.
WHEY, *n.* The thin part of milk.
WEIGH, *v. t.* To examine by balance.
  WEAK, *a.* Not strong.
  WEEK, *n.* Seven days.
WEAL, *n.* Happiness; welfare.
WHEAL, *n.* A pustule.
WHEEL, *n.* A circular body.
VEAL,† *n.* The flesh of a calf.
  WEASEL, *n.* A small animal.
  WEEZEL, *a.* Thin; weazen.
WETHER, *n.* A ram.
WHETHER, *adv.* Which of two.
WEATHER, *n.* The state of the atmosphere.
  WEN, *n.* A tumor.
  WHEN, *adv.* At what time.
WERT. The second person of the verb BE.
WORT, *n.* Unfermented beer.

WET, *n.* Water; moisture.
WHET, *v.* To sharpen.
WHAT, *pro.* That which.
WOT, *v. t.* To know.
WHICH, *pro.* A pronoun.
WITCH, *n.* A sorceress.
WHIG, *n.* The name of a party.
WIG, *n.* False hair worn on the head.
WHILE, *adv.* During the time that.
WILE, *n.* A deceit; a fraud.
WHINE, *n.* A plaintive noise.
WINE, *n.* The juice of the grape.
VINE,† *n.* Any plant that trails.
WHIR, *v. n.* To turn round with noise.
WERE, *pret. plu.* of the verb BE.
WHIST, *n.* A game at cards.
WIST, *pp.* Thought; knew.
WHITE, *n.* The color of snow.
WIGHT, *n.* A person; a being.
WITE, *n.* Blame; reproach.
WHIT, *n.* A very small part.
WIT, *n.* Quickness of fancy.
WHITHER, *adv.* To which place.
WITHER, *v. i.* To fade; to dry up.
WHY, *adv.* To what reason.
VIE, *v. i.* To strive.
WOOD, *n.* The substance of trees.
WOULD, *v.* Was willing.
WORSTED, *n.* Woolen yarn.
WORSTED, *pp.* Defeated.
WRAPPED, *pp.* Wound.
RAPPED, *pp.* Struck with a quick blow.
WREAK, *v. t.* To execute.
REEK, *v.* To emit vapor.
WREATH, *n.* Any thing curled.
WREATHE, *v. t.* To encircle; to curl.
WRECK, *n.* Dissolution by violence.
RECK, *v. t.* To heed; to care for.
WRETCH, *n.* A miserable person.
RETCH, *v. i.* To make an effort to vomit.
WRING, *v. t.* To turn with violence.
RING, *n.* A circle; sound.
  YOLK, *n.* The yellow part of an egg.
  YOKE, *n.* A wooden bandage placed on the neck of oxen.
YOUR, *pro.* Belonging to you.
EWER, *n.* A vessel for water.

DICTATION EXERCISES.

I'll go through the *aisle* of the church which is on the *Isle* of Wight. The shoemaker said his *awl* was *all* that procured him a living.

He commenced to *bawl*, because he had lost his *ball*. The *baroness* was surprised at the *barrenness* of the country. The captain, with the *assistance* of his *assistants*, sailed the *barque* laden with *bark*. They *barred* the door against the *bard*. He gave his *assent* to the proposition for their *ascent* of Mount Washington.

I have *been* to the *bin* to get some grain. *Beer* brought him to his *bier*. He *bored* a hole in the *board*. The *bow* of the boat was made of the *bough* of the *beech* which grew near the *beach*. The *bass* drum was taken by a *base* fellow. The *bee* must *be* busy in order to lay up his winter store.

Two weeks after the child was *born* it was *borne* to that *bourn* whence no traveler returns. The wind caused the *bough* to *bow*. The man was *bred* to his calling, but his calling was not *bread* to him.

After passing through the *cañon* the *canon* was read amid the roar of *cannon*. While one brother was *ceiling* the room the other was *sealing* a letter. The *seller* lives in a *cellar*. After taking the *census* he lost his *senses*. The servant was *sent* with a *cent* to get some *scent*.

The leader of the *choir* sent for a *quire* of music paper. His *choler* having risen he seized his opponent by the *collar*. From the *site* of the house a magnificent *sight* opened to our view.

The fit of *coughing* which caused the *colonel* to be laid in his *coffin* was produced by his eating a *kernel*. The artist made a sketch of the *crane* with a *crayon*. Notwithstanding he was his *cousin*, he wished to *cozen* him. The *color* of the *culler* was raised by the insult. His *counsel* was asked and obtained by the *council*.

The *Dane* did not *deign* to notice him. He said the *dey* was a *day* too late. Each one of the *crews* was provided with a *cruse* for the *cruise*. Upon his *signet* was engraved a *cygnet*. The *disease* caused his *decease*.

The *dyer dyes* daily, yet he *dies* not. Three scruples make a *drachm*, but many persons take a *dram* without a scruple. The *errant* knight, while on his *errand*, proved to be an *arrant* coward. He can *earn* the *urn* by *dyeing*, and yet keep from *dying*.

You must not frighten the *ewe* which is lying by that *yew* of beautiful *hue*. She made a *feint* to *faint*. The landlord gave us *fair fare*. My *father* said I should go no *farther*. He performed a great *feat* with his *feet* at the *fete*. Upon the smoke ascending, the swallow *flew* from the *flue*. He *fain* would *feign* to go to the *fane*.

The *fore* parts of the *four* animals were put aside *for* eating. The domestic *fowl* was killed by a *foul* domestic. He strode to the *gate* with a lofty *gait*. It is wicked to *gamble*, but not to *gambol*. At the *fort* his *forte* is gunnery. A majority of the *guild* wished to *gild* the sign.

The *guest guessed* that they would make a fire in the *great grate*. The *hair* of the *hare* is of a brown color.

I *heard* the lowing of the *herd*. When *our hour* shall come, we will sing a *hymn* to *Him* above. The *hussar* who was *in* the *inn* cried out *huzza*.

DICTATION EXERCISES.

The reason why bakers *knead* their bread is because they *need* it. I *know* no *knight* who will go there in the *night*. If the *gnu knew* that the hay was *new*, why did he not eat it? The *jester* by his *gesture* showed his *intense intents*.

The pupil endeavored to *lessen* the *lesson*. The body has *lain* in the *lane* for three days. Every *lier* is not a *liar*, though he can perform on the *lyre*. He bought some *liniment* for his bruised *lineament*.

The *martial marshal* received a valuable *mare* from the *mayor*. The *male* wore a coat of *mail*. He was in a *maze* amidst the *maize*. The *mead* was the *meed* which he required.

That *miner minds* the *minor mines*. The *mower* could mow no *more*, for he had *missed* the place in the *mist*. It is not *meet* to *mete* out such *meat*. You should not *meddle* with the *medal*. Does it require the *might* of a man to kill a *mite?*

The noise of the *oar* comes *o'er* the water. By an *ordinance* of parliament the *ordnance* was increased. *None* but a *nun* can enter a nunnery. Does the *neigh* of a horse mean *nay?*

Can you *pare* a *pear* with a *pair* of scissors? He placed his *palette* upon the *pallet*, and went to gratify his *palate*. Of the *patients* none had *patience*. The *piece* of *pane* in the wound caused great *pain*, therefore he had no *peace*.

He laid down to rest having a broken *pillar* for a *pillow*. As soon as he ceased running the perspiration began to *pour* from every *pore*.

The *principal principle* of a student should be uprightness. The *praise* which his rival received *preys* upon his spirits.

His *relict* kept the razor as a *relic*. The *residents* had changed their *residence*. The *rigor* of the climate caused the death of the *rigger*.

He said it was *right* to *write* to the *wright* about the *rite*. He *rode* home by the *road*, after he had *rowed* to the place of meeting. The *rows* in the street caused him to *rouse* from his stupor.

So you *sew* when you ought to *sow*. The pirate has determined to *seize* every vessel he *sees* upon the *seas*. The *serf sighs* at the *size* of the *surf* through which he is compelled to go. To bathe in the *surge* he had a dress made of *serge*. He *sighed* because of a pain in his *side*.

Without his *son* the *sun* had no light for him. *Your ewer* was broken at the fountain. *Why* do men *vie* with each other? We endeavored to *wreathe* a *wreath*.

The bread earned by the *sweat*† of thy brow is *sweet* to thee, O man. It requires *tact* to *tack* through the *straight strait*. *There their* horses stand. This is the spear which he *threw through* the fence.

He *told* his friend that he was *toled* to the church by hearing the bell *tolled*. He wrote a *treatise* on the principal *treaties* recorded in history. The only *use* he had for his *yews* was to shelter his *ewes*.

The *vile* man injured the *viol* by means of a *vial*. The *vicar* was walking down the lane with his *wicker* basket. A *wave* of his brother's hand caused him to *waive* his claim.

He asked him *whether* the *weather* was favorable to the young *wether*. He *wist* not whether it was *whist* or not. He did not know *whither* to carry the flower *which* the *witch* said was commencing to *wither*. He did not know *when* the *wen* would heal. She went over the *way* to *weigh* the *whey*.

WORDS SIMILARLY SPELLED,

BUT DIFFERENTLY PRONOUNCED AND APPLIED.

Ab′sent, *a.* Not present.
Absent′, *v.* To keep away.
Ab′stract, *n.* An abridgment.
Abstract′, *v.* To draw from.
Abuse (abuze), *v.* To ill use.
Abuse (abuce), *n.* Ill usage.
Ac′cent, *n.* Stress of the voice.
Accent′, *v.* To give the accent.
Af′fix, *n.* A syllable added.
Affix′, *v.* To add to the end.
At′tribute, *n.* A quality.
Attrib′ute, *v.* To assign as a cause.
Aug′ment, *n.* Increase.
Augment′, *v.* To make larger.
Au′gust, *n.* The eighth month.
August′, *a.* Grand, majestic.
Bow (bo), *n.* For shooting with.
Bow (bow), *n.* A bending of the head.
Buf′fet, *n.* A stroke of the fist.
Buffet′, *n.* A cupboard.
Char, *v.* To burn partly.
Char, *n.* A small job.
Col′league, *n.* A partner.
Colleague′, *v.* To unite with another.
Col′lect, *n.* A short prayer.
Collect′, *v.* To gather together.
Com′ment, *n.* An exposition.
Comment′, *v.* To make remarks upon.
Com′merce, *n.* Trade between nations.
Commerce′, *v.* To traffic; to trade.
Com′mune, *n.* A district in France.
Commune′, *v.* To converse.
Com′pact, *n.* An agreement.
Compact′, *a.* Solid.
Com′plot, *n.* A joint plot.
Complot′, *v.* To form a plot.
Com′port, *n.* Behavior.
Comport′, *v.* To suit.
Com′pound, *n.* A mixture.
Compound′, *v.* To mix.
Com′press, *n.* A pad used in surgery.
Compress′, *v.* To press together.
Con′cert, *n.* A musical entertainment.
Concert′, *v.* To plan together.
Con′crete, *n.* A mixture used by masons.
Concrete′, *v.* To bring into one mass.
Con′cord, *n.* Agreement.
Concord′, *v.* To agree with.
Con′duct, *n.* Behavior.
Conduct′, *v.* To lead.
Con′fine, *n.* A boundary.
Confine′, *v.* To restrain; to imprison.
Con′flict, *n.* A contest.
Conflict′, *v.* To dash.
Con′jure, *v.* To practise charms.
Conjure′, *v.* To entreat.
Con′serve, *n.* A sweetmeat.
Conserve′, *v.* To preserve with sugar.
Con′sole, *n.* A truss or bracket.
Console′, *v.* To comfort.
Con′sort, *n.* A companion.
Consort′, *v.* To associate with.
Con′test, *n.* A struggle.
Contest′, *v.* To dispute.
Con′text, *n.* The general series of a discourse.
Context′, *a.* Interwoven.
Con′tract, *n.* An agreement.
Contract′, *v.* To get smaller.
Con′trast, *n.* Opposition of things.
Contrast′, *v.* To set in opposition.
Con′vent, *n.* A nunnery.
Convent′, *v.* To call before a judge.
Con′verse, *n.* The opposite.
Converse′, *v.* To talk together.
Con′vert, *n.* One changed.
Convert′, *v.* To change.
Con′vict, *n.* A criminal found guilty.
Convict′, *v.* To find guilty.
Con′voy, *n.* A protecting force.
Convoy′, *v.* To accompany for protection.
Coun′termand, *n.* A contrary order.
Countermand′, *v.* To give a contrary order.
Cruise, *n.* A voyage.
Cruise, *n.* A small bottle.
Des′cant, *n.* A song; a discourse.
Descant′, *v.* To harangue.

WORDS SIMILARLY SPELLED.

DES'ERT, n. A sandy waste.
DESERT', v. To forsake.
DIFFUSE', a. Using many words.
DIFFUSE', v. To spread abroad.
DI'GEST, n. A collection of laws.
DIGEST', v. To dissolve food in the stomach.
DIS'COUNT, n. A sum deducted.
DISCOUNT', v. To deduct.
DOES (doze), n. The plural of DOE.
DOES (dus), v. Third person of DO.
EN'TRANCE, n. The place for entering.
ENTRANCE', v. To fill with delight.
ES'CORT, n. A body-guard.
ESCORT', v. To attend and guard.
ES'SAY, n. An attempt; a treatise.
ESSAY', v. To try.
EXCUSE' (excuce), n. An apology.
EXCUSE' (excuze), v. To make an apology.
EX'ILE, n. A person banished from his country.
EXILE', v. To send out of one's country. [try.
EX'PORT, n. A commodity sent out.
EXPORT', v. To send to a foreign country.
EX'TRACT, n. Something extracted.
EXTRACT', v. To draw out.
FORE'CAST, n. A forethought.
FORECAST', v. To foresee.
FORE'TASTE, n. Anticipation.
FORETASTE', v. To taste before.
FER'MENT, n. Internal motion.
FERMENT', v. To set in motion.
FRE'QUENT, a. Often done.
FREQUENT', v. To visit often.
GAL'LANT, a. Brave.
GALLANT', n. A man attentive to ladies.
GREASE (greace), n. Oily matter.
GREASE (greeze), v. To smear with oil or fat.
GOUT, n. A disease of blood.
GOUT (goo), n. Taste; relish.
GILL (g soft), n. A measure.
GILL (g hard), n. The lung of a fish.
HOUSE, n. A dwelling.
HOUSE (houze), v. To put in a house.
IM'PORT, n. Meaning; a commodity brought into a country.
IMPORT', v. To mean; to bring into a country.
IM'PRESS, n. An impression.
IMPRESS', v. To make an impression.

IM'PRINT, n. The name of a publisher.
IMPRINT', v. To make an impression.
IN'CENSE, n. Perfume exhaled by fire.
INCENSE', v. To excite to wrath.
IN'CREASE, n. A growing larger.
INCREASE', v. To grow larger.
IN'LAY, n. Something inserted.
INLAY', v. To insert.
IN'STINCT, n. Natural impulse.
INSTINCT', a. Animated.
IN'SULT, n. An affront.
INSULT', v. To disrespect.
IN'TERCHANGE, n. Mutual change.
INTERCHANGE', v. To exchange.
IN'TERDICT, n. A prohibition.
INTERDICT', v. To prohibit.
IN'TIMATE, a. Friendly; familiar.
IN'TIMATE, v. To hint.
INVAL'ID, a. Not legal.
INVALID' (-eed), n. A person in a sickly state.
LEAD (led), n. A metal.
LEAD (leed), v. To conduct.
LIVE (live), a. Alive.
LIVE (liv), v. To exist; to enjoy life.
LOWER, v. To let down.
LOWER (lou-er), v. To grow cloudy.
MIN'UTE, n. A short space of time.
MINUTE', a. Small; very little.
MISCON'DUCT, n. Bad conduct.
MISCONDUCT', v. To behave ill.
MOUSE, n. A small animal. [mice.
MOUSE (mouze), v. To hunt after
MOW, v. To cut grass with scythe.
MOW (mou), n. A heap of hay in a barn.
NO'TABLE, a. Remarkable.
NOT'ABLE, a. Thrifty; careful.
OB'JECT, n. Purpose or design.
OBJECT', v. To oppose by words.
OR'DINARY, a. Common; plain.
ORD'INARY, n. A house of entertainment.
OUT'GO, n. Expenses of living.
OUTGO', v. To surpass.
OUT'WORK, n. Work done outside.
OUTWORK', v. To surpass at working.
O'VERCHARGE, n. Too heavy a charge.
OVERCHARGE', v. To charge too much.
O'VERTHROW, n. Defeat.
OVERTHROW', v. To defeat.
PER'FUME, n. Fragrance.
PERFUME', v. To make odorous.

Per'mit, n. A written authority.
Permit', v. To allow.
Pol'ish, v. To brighten.
Po'lish, a. Pertaining to Poland.
Prec'edent, n. Example.
Prece'dent, a. Going before.
Pre'fix, n. A syllable placed at the beginning of a word.
Prefix', v. To place before.
Prel'ude, n. Any thing introductory.
Prelude', v. To begin with.
Prem'ise, n. A proposition in logic.
Premise', v. To explain beforehand.
Prem'ises, n. Lands, &c., attached to a house.
Premi'ses, v. Does premise.
Pres'age, n. Something that foreshows an event.
Presage', v. To foreshadow.
Pres'ent, n. A gift.
Present', v. To give formally.
Prod'uce, n. What is produced.
Produce', v. To yield; to bring forth.
Prog'ress, n. Onward movement.
Progress', v. To proceed onwards.
Proj'ect, n. A design, contrivance.
Project', v. To plan; to cast forward.
Pro'test, n. A declaration against.
Protest', v. To declare against.
Ra'rity, n. Something very scarce.
Rar'ity, n. State of thinness.
Read, v. To peruse.
Read, (red), p. Did read.
Rec'reate, v. To refresh after labor.
Re'-create, v. To form anew.
Reb'el, n. One who rebels.
Rebel', v. To rise against and resist the law.
Rec'ollect, v. To call back to memory.
Re'-collect, v. To gather again.
Rec'ord, n. A register.
Record', v. To place on record.
Ref'use, n. That which is left or rejected.
Refuse', v. To decline compliance with.
Rep'rimand, n. A censure.
Reprimand', v. To censure; to blame.
Re'pent, a. Creeping.
Repent', v. To regret; to be contrite.

Re'print, n. A *second* printing or edition.
Reprint', v. To print again.
Re'tail, n. Sale by small quantities.
Retail', v. To sell in small quantities.
Row (roe), n. A line; v. To propel with oars.
Row (rou), n. A scuffle; a brawl.
Sewer (sow-er), n. A person who sews.
Sewer (soo-er), n. A large drain.
Slough (slou), n. A miry ditch.
Slough (sluff), n. The cast skin of a serpent; foul matter from a sore.
Sow (sou), n. The feminine of boar.
Sow (so), v. To scatter seed.
Sub'ject, n. One who owes allegiance; the thing under consideration; a. Liable to.
Subject', v. To reduce to submission.
Su'pine, n. A participial noun.
Supine', n. Lying lazily on the back.
Sur'name, n. The family name.
Surname', v. To add another name.
Sur'vey, n. A view; a measurement.
Survey', v. To measure; to view.
Tar'ry, v. To stop; to delay.
Tar'ry, a. Full of tar.
Tear (tare), n. A rent; v. To rend.
Tear (teer), n. Drops of water from the eye.
Tor'ment, n. Torture; pain.
Torment', v. To torture.
Transfer', v. To make over to another.
Trans'fer, n. The act of transferring.
Trans'port, n. Unusual joy; rapture.
Transport', v. To exile; to enrapture.
Undress', v. To take off the clothes.
Un'dress, n. A state of partial clothing.
Un'derwork, n. Subordinate labor.
Underwork', v. To work at lower wages.
Use (uce), n. Occupation; utility.
Use (uze), v. To employ; to make use of.
Wind, n. Air put in motion.
Wind, v. To turn as on a reel.
Wound, n. A flesh-cut; a hurt.
Wound, v. Did wind.

WORDS SPELLED AND PRONOUNCED ALIKE,
BUT OF VARIOUS MEANINGS AND APPLICATIONS

ADDRESS', *v.* To accost.
ADDRESS', *n.* Deportment.
ADDRESS', *n.* Dexterity.
ADDRESS', *n.* Direction of a letter.
ADDRESS', *n.* A speech.
  AIR, *n.* A melody.
  AIR, *n.* The fluid we breathe.
  AIR, *n.* Manner; look.
AN'GLE, *n.* A corner.
AN'GLE, *v.* To fish with a hook.
  APPA'RENT, *a.* Plain; visible.
  APPA'RENT, *a.* Seeming; not real.
ARCH, *n.* A part of a curve.
ARCH, *a.* Sly; shrewd.
ARCH, *a.* Chief; superior.
ART, *n.* Skill.
ART, *v.* Part of the verb TO BE.
BACH'ELOR, *n.* An unmarried man.
BACH'ELOR, *n.* A junior graduate.
  BAIT, *n.* To put food upon.
  BAIT, *v.* To take refreshment.
  BAIT, *v.* To worry with dogs.
BALL, *n.* A globe.
BALL, *n.* An entertainment of dancing.
BANK, *n.* A heap of earth.
BANK, *n.* A place where money is kept.
BANK, *n.* A bench for rowers.
BAR, *n.* A rail to stop a passage.
BAR, *n.* A bank of sand in a river.
BAR, *n.* A railing; an enclosure.
  BARK, *n.* The rind of a tree.
  BARK, *n.* A kind of ship.
  BARK, *n.* The noise of a dog.
BASE, *n.* The lowest part.
BASE, *a.* Mean; worthless.
  BASTE, *v.* To beat with a stick.
  BASTE, *v.* To pour fat on roasting meat.
  BASTE, *v.* To sew slightly.
BAT, *n.* A club for striking a ball.
BAT, *n.* A small, winged animal.
BAT, *n.* A sheet of cotton for quilting.
  BAT'TER, *v.* To beat; to crush.
  BAT'TER, *n.* A mixture of eggs, &c.

BAY, *n.* A hollow in the coast.
BAY, *n.* A tree.
BAY, *n.* In an attitude of defence.
BAY, *n.* A color; a kind of brown.
BAY, *v.* To bark.
  BEAM, *n.* A heavy piece of timber.
  BEAM, *n.* A ray of light.
  BEAM, *n.* Part of a scales.
BEAR, *v.* To carry.
BEAR, *n.* A rough savage animal.
BEAR, *v.* To hold up.
BEAR, *v.* To produce.
BEAR, *v.* To press.
BEAR, *n.* A kind of barley.
  BEA'VER, *n.* An animal.
  BEA'VER, *n.* The fur of the beaver.
  BEA'VER, *n.* Part of a helmet.
BECOME', *v.* To be changed.
BECOME', *v.* To be suitable to.
  BEE'TLE, *n.* An insect.
  BEE'TLE, *n.* A heavy mallet.
  BEE'TLE, *v.* To overhang.
BEG, *v.* To ask for with humility.
BEG, *v.* To assume without proof.
BILL, *n.* The beak of a bird.
BILL, *n.* An account of money.
BILL, *n.* A kind of axe.
BILL, *n.* An act before a legislature.
BIL'LET, *n.* A note.
BIL'LET, *n.* A small log of wood.
BIL'LET, *v.* To quarter soldiers.
BIT, *n.* A small piece.
BIT, *n.* The mouth-piece of a bridle.
BIT, *n.* A boring tool.
BLADE, *n.* The cutting part of a tool.
BLADE, *n.* A leaf of grass.
BLADE, *n.* The shoulder bone.
BLADE, *n.* A sharp, lively man.
BLOW, *n.* A stroke.
BLOW, *v.* To puff.
BLOW, *v.* To blossom.
BLUFF, *n.* A high steep bank.
BLUFF, *a.* Coarse in manner.
BLUFF, *a.* Obtuse; blunt.
BLUFF, *n.* A game at cards.

BOARD, n. A thin plank.
BOARD, v. To live with for a price.
BOARD, n. A council.
BOARD, v. To enter a ship by force.
BOLT, n. The bar of a door.
BOLT, v. To sift.
BOLT, v. To leave or desert suddenly.
BOOT, n. Covering for the foot and leg.
BOOT, n. Part of a coach.
BOOT, n. Profit; advantage.
BOOT, n. The thing given in addition.
BORE, v. To make a round hole.
BORE, v. To vex or weary.
BORE, n. A round hole.
BORE, n. A thing that annoys.
BORE, n. An influx of the tide.
BORE, pp. Carried; sustained.
BOUND, n. A limit.
BOUND, n. A leap.
BOUND, v. Did bind.
BOWL, n. A hollow dish.
BOWL, n. A round mass or ball.
BOWL, v. To roll along.
BOX, n. A kind of tree.
BOX, n. A case or chest.
BOX, n. A slap on the ear.
BOX, v. To fight with the fists.
BRACE, v. To strengthen; to make firm.
BRACE, n. A pair; a couple.
BRACE, n. A tool.
BRAKE, n. A thicket.
BRAKE, n. An instrument for dressing flax.
BRAKE, n. The handle of a pump.
BRAKE, n. A machine to retard the motion of wheels. [brass.
BRA'ZIER, n. One who works in
BRA'ZIER, n. A pan to hold coals.
BROOK, n. A stream of water.
BROOK, v. To endure; to suffer.
BRUSH, n. An instrument for clean-
BRUSH, n. A rude assault. [ing.
BRUSH, n. A collection of twigs or bushes.
BRUSH, v. To rub with a brush.
BRUSH, v. To touch lightly on the surface.
BRUSH, v. To move with haste.
BUTT, n. A large cask.
BUTT, n. A kind of hinge.
BUTT, n. A person who is the object of jests.
BUTT, v. To strike with the head.

CALF, n. The young of a cow.
CALF, n. The thick part of the leg.
CAN, n. A metallic vessel.
CAN, v. To be able.
CAPE, n. A headland.
CAPE, n. An article of dress.
CA'PER, v. To skip and jump.
CA'PER, n. The bud of a plant.
CAP'ITAL, a. Affecting the head or life.
CAP'ITAL, a. First in importance.
CAP'ITAL, n. A chief city.
CAP'ITAL, n. Money invested in business.
CARD, n. A piece of stiff paper.
CARD, n. A kind of advertisement.
CARD, v. To comb wool.
CASE, n. A covering or sheath.
CASE, n. State of things.
CASE, n. Variation of nouns.
CASE, n. An action at law.
CASHIER', n. One who has charge of money.
CASHIER', v. To dismiss for malconduct.
CAST, v. To throw.
CAST, v. To form in a mould.
CAST, v. To compute; to reckon.
CAST, n. A moulded form.
CAT'ARACT, n. A waterfall.
CAT'ARACT, n. A disease of the eye.
CHARGE, n. A trust to defend.
CHARGE, n. Command.
CHARGE, n. An accusation.
CHARGE, n. Cost; expense.
CHARGE, v. To load; to burden.
CHARGE, v. To attack.
CHASE, v. To pursue.
CHASE, v. To adorn by raised work.
CHASE, n. A printer's type frame.
CHASE, n. Hunting; field sport.
CHECK, n. A stop; restraint.
CHECK, n. A reprimand.
CHECK, n. An order for money.
CHECK, n. A mark.
CHECK, n. A kind of cloth.
CHORD, n. The string of a musical instrument.
CHORD, n. Harmony of sounds.
CHORD, n. The line which joins the two ends of an arc.
CLEAVE, v. To adhere; to stick.
CLEAVE, v. To separate.
CLEAVE, v. To split off.

CLUB, n. A heavy stick.
CLUB, n. A society.
CLUB, n. The name of a card.
  COCK'LE, n. A shell fish.
  COCK'LE, n. A weed.
  COLLA'TION, n. Comparison.
  COLLA'TION, n. A slight repast.
    COMB, n. An instrument for the hair.
    COMB, n. The crest of a cock.
    COMB, n. The cells in which bees put their honey.
    COMB, v. To roll over as a wave.
    COMB, n. A valley.
    COMB, v. To adjust with a comb.
COMMIT', v. To intrust.
COMMIT', v. To do; to perpetrate.
COMMIT', v. To send to prison.
  CONCORD'ANCE, n. Agreement.
  CONCORD'ANCE, n. An index to words in the Bible.
CONFORM', v. To make like.
CONFORM', v. To comply with.
  CONSIST'ENCY, n. Agreement with one's self.
  CONSIST'ENCY, n. Thickness.
COP'Y, n. A model to be imitated.
COP'Y, n. An imitation.
  CORD, n. A small rope.
  CORD, n. A measure of wood.
CORD'IAL, a. Hearty; sincere.
CORD'IAL, n. Any thing that comforts.
  CORN, n. Grain.
  CORN, n. A hard substance on the foot.
  CORN, v. To salt.
  CORN, n. A single seed.
COUNT, v. To number.
COUNT, n. A foreign title.
COUNT, n. A point in an indictment.
  COUNT'ER, n. A table in a shop.
  COUNT'ER, a. Contrary to.
  COUNT'ER, n. One who counts.
  COUNT'ER, n. A substitute for money.
COURT, v. To woo; to solicit.
COURT, n. Seat of justice.
COURT, n. Space before a house.
COURT, n. Residence of a prince.
COURT, n. A little street.
  CRAB, n. A shell fish.
  CRAB, n. A wild apple.
  CRAB, n. An engine for launching ships.
  CRAB, n. A morose person.

CRAFT, n. Trade; manual art.
CRAFT, n. Cunning.
CRAFT, n. Sailing vessels.
  CRANE, n. A long legged bird.
  CRANE, n. A machine for lifting weights.
  CRANE, n. A crooked pipe.
CRIB, n. A rack or manger.
CRIB, n. A small house.
CRIB, n. A child's bed.
CRIB, v. To steal.
CRIB, v. To confine in a small space.
  CRICK'ET, n. An insect. [ball.
  CRICK'ET, n. A game with bat and
CRIT'ICAL, a. Inclined to find fault.
CRIT'ICAL, a. Discerning. [point.
CRIT'ICAL, a. Relating to turning
  CROP, n. The harvest.
  CROP, n. The craw of a bird.
  CROP, v. To cut short.
CROSS, n. A gibbet.
CROSS, n. Trial of patience.
CROSS, a. Opposite; contrary.
CROSS, a. Ill-tempered.
CROSS, prep. From side to side.
CROSS, v. To pass across.
CROSS, v. To cancel.
CROSS, v. To thwart.
  CROW, n. A bird.
  CROW, n. A bar of iron.
  CROW, v. To boast; to exult.
  CROW, v. To make a noise like a cock.
CRY, v. To proclaim loudly.
CRY, v. To lament aloud.
CRY, n. The call of an animal.
  CUE, n. A braid of hair.
  CUE, n. A suggestion; a hint.
  CUE, n. A turn of mind.
  CUE, n. A rod used in billiards.
DAM, n. The mother of an animal.
DAM, n. A bank to confine water.
  DATE, n. The time of an event.
  DATE, n. A fruit.
DEAL, n. Quantity.
DEAL, n. Fir timber.
DEAL, v. To traffic.
DEAL, v. To distribute.
  DEAR, a. Beloved; prized.
  DEAR, a. Expensive.
DECK, v. To ornament; to cover.
DECK, n. The floor of a ship.
DESERT', n. That which is deserved.
DESERT', v. To forsake.

Despatch', n. Hasty execution.
Despatch', v. To put to death.
  Die, v. To pass from life.
  Die, n. A stamp.
  Die, n. A little cube.
  Di'et, n. A course of food.
  Di'et, n. A German parliament.
  Di'vers, n. Those who plunge under water.
  Di'vers, a. Several.
  Divine', a. Godlike; heavenly.
  Divine', n. A theologian.
  Divine', v. To foretell; to predict.
  Divine', v. To guess; to conjecture.
  Dock, n. A plant; a weed.
  Dock, v. To cut off.
  Dock, n. A place in court.
  Dock, n. A place where ships lie.
Dom'ino, n. A kind of hood.
Dom'ino, n. A flat piece of ivory dotted like dice.
  Down, n. Soft feathers.
  Down, n. An open plain.
  Down, n. A sand bank in the sea.
  Down, adv. Not up.
Draw, v. To drag along.
Draw, v. To let out a liquid.
Draw, v. To delineate.
Draw, v. To attract toward.
  Drill, v. To bore holes.
  Drill, v. To exercise recruits.
Drone, n. The male honey bee.
Drone, n. A sluggard.
Drone, n. A humming noise.
Drone, v. To live in idleness.
Drone, v. To read in a dull tone.
  Drug, n. A medicinal substance.
  Drug, n. An unsaleable thing.
  Drug, v. To give drugs to.
Dun, a. Dark-colored.
Dun, v. To call for payment.
  Ear, n. The organ of hearing.
  Ear, n. A spike of corn.
Egg, n. A body laid by birds.
Egg, v. To incite.
  Eld'er, a. Older.
  Eld'er, n. The name of a shrub.
Ellip'sis, n. An omission of words.
Ellip'sis, n. An oval.
  Engross', v. To occupy the whole.
  Engross', v. To copy writings.
Entertain', v. To amuse.
Entertain', v. To hold in the mind.

E'ven, a. Level; equal.
E'ven, n. The evening.
E'ven, adv. Truly; likewise.
  Exact', a. Accurate.
  Exact', v. To demand; to extort.
Express', v. To utter; to declare.
Express', v. To squeeze out.
Express', n. A speedy conveyance.
Express', a. Plain; clear.
  Fair, a. Pleasing; handsome.
  Fair, a. Just; honest.
  Fair, a. Clear; pleasant.
  Fair, n. A large market.
Fare, n. Price of passage.
Fare, n. Food for the table.
  Fast, a. Firmly fixed.
  Fast, a. Swift.
  Fast, n. Abstinence from food.
Fawn, n. A young deer.
Fawn, v. To court servilely.
  Feed, v. To give food to.
  Feed, pp. Paid; rewarded.
Fell, v. Did fall.
Fell, v. To cut down.
Fell, a. Cruel; barbarous.
Fell, n. A barren hill.
  Fel'low, n. An associate.
  Fel'low, n. One of a pair.
  Fel'low, n. A mean wretch.
  Fel'low, n. A trustee of a college.
Fel'on, n. A criminal.
Fel'on, n. A painful tumor.
  Felt, v. Perceived by the touch.
  Felt, n. Cloth formed without weaving.
Fer'ret, n. A kind of weasel.
Fer'ret, n. A kind of narrow tape.
Fer'ret, v. To drive out of a lurking-place.
  Fig'ure, n. Form; shape.
  Fig'ure, n. A number.
  Fig'ure, n. A statue.
  Fig'ure, n. A form of speech.
File, n. A fine rasp. [put.
File, n. A wire on which papers are
File, n. A line of soldiers.
File, v. To place on a file.
  Fil'let, n. A small band on the hair.
  Fil'let, n. Part of a leg of veal.
Fine, a. Not coarse.
Fine, a. Splendid.
Fine, n. A forfeit.
  Firm, a. Strong; steady.
  Firm, n. The name of a partnership.

FIT, *a.* Proper; suitable.
FIT, *n.* A paroxysm.
FIT, *v.* To suit.
FIT, *n.* An interval.
FLAG, *n.* A water plant.
FLAG, *n.* A broad flat stone.
FLAG, *n.* An ensign or standard.
FLAG, *v.* To hang loose.
FLAG, *v.* To grow spiritless.
FLAT'TER, *a.* More flat.
FLAT'TER, *v.* To praise falsely.
FLEET, *n.* A company of ships.
FLEET, *a.* Moving rapidly.
FLUE, *n.* A passage for smoke.
FLUE, *n.* Soft fur or down.
FOIL, *n.* A blunt sword.
FOIL, *n.* A thin plate of metal.
FOIL, *v.* To baffle; to defeat.
FOLD, *n.* An enclosure for sheep.
FOLD, *n.* A double.
FOOT, *n.* The extremity of the leg.
FOOT, *n.* The base.
FOOT, *n.* A measure.
FORCE, *n.* Strength.
FORCE, *v.* To compel.
FORGE, *v.* To form by the hammer.
FORGE, *v.* To counterfeit.
FORGE, *n.* A furnace where iron is heated.
FORM'ER, *n.* Maker; author.
FOR'MER, *a.* Before in time.
FOR'TUNE, *n.* Chance; luck.
FOR'TUNE, *n.* Wealth; riches.
FOUND, *v.* Did find.
FOUND, *v.* To establish.
FOUND, *v.* To cast.
FOUND'ER, *n.* One who establishes.
FOUND'ER, *n.* One who moulds metals.
FOUND'ER, *v.* To fill with water and sink.
FRET, *n.* Raised work in architecture.
FRET, *v.* To be peevish.
FRET, *v.* To wear away by rubbing.
FRIEZE, *n.* A term in architecture.
FRIEZE, *n.* A coarse cloth.
FRY, *n.* A swarm of young fishes.
FRY, *v.* To cook in a pan.
FULL'ER, *a.* Nearer full.
FULL'ER, *n.* A cleanser of cloth.
FUSE, *v.* To liquefy by heat.
FUSE, *n.* A combustible tube.
GALL, *n.* An excrescence on the oak.
GALL, *n.* A secretion of the body.
GALL, *n.* Malignity.

GAL'LEY, *n.* A printer's frame.
GAL'LEY, *n.* A boat.
GAL'LEY, *n.* The kitchen in a ship.
GAME, *n.* An amusement.
GAME, *n.* A single match of play.
GAME, *n.* Animals taken by hunting.
GIN, *n.* A machine for clearing cotton seeds.
GIN, *n.* An alcoholic liquor.
GIN, *n.* A snare.
GLOSS, *n.* A smooth shining surface.
GLOSS, *n.* A comment.
GORE, *n.* Clotted blood.
GORE, *n.* A triangular piece.
GORE, *v.* To cut triangularly.
GORE, *v.* To pierce with a horn.
GRAIN, *n.* Corn.
GRAIN, *n.* A single seed.
GRAIN, *n.* Any minute particle.
GRAIN, *n.* A small weight.
GRAIN, *v.* To represent the veins of wood.
GRATE, *n.* A range of bars.
GRATE, *v.* To rub on a rough surface.
GRATE, *v.* To make a harsh noise.
GRATE'FUL, *a.* Thankful.
GRATE'FUL, *a.* Agreeable; pleasing.
GRAVE, *a.* Solemn; serious.
GRAVE, *n.* The place of burial.
GRAVE, *v.* To carve figures.
GRAZE, *v.* To feed on grass.
GRAZE, *v.* To touch lightly in passing.
GREEN, *a.* Colored like grass.
GREEN, *a.* Fresh; new.
GREEN, *a.* Unripe; immature.
GROSS, *a.* Large; coarse.
GROSS, *a.* Indelicate; rude.
GROSS, *n.* The weight of all parts together.
GROSS, *n.* Twelve dozen.
GROUND, *n.* The earth; the soil.
GROUND, *pp.* Reduced to powder.
GROUND, *v.* To run aground.
GROUND, *v.* To base; to establish.
GROUND, *pp.* Sharpened by grinding.
GULL, *n.* One easily cheated.
GULL, *n.* A sea-bird.
GULL, *v.* To trick; to cheat.
GUST, *n.* Sense of tasting; relish.
GUST, *n.* A sudden, violent blast.
HAB'IT, *n.* State of a thing.
HAB'IT, *n.* Custom.
HAB'IT, *n.* Dress.

HAIL, n. Frozen rain.
HAIL, v. To call to from a distance.
HAIL, v. To salute.
HALT'ER, n. One who limps.
HAL'TER, n. A rope to hang criminals.
HAM'PER, n. A large packing basket.
HAM'PER, v. To perplex.
HATCH, v. To produce young from [eggs.
HATCH, n. A half door.
HAWK, n. A bird.
HAWK, v. To force up phlegm.
HAWK, v. To offer for sale by outcry in the streets.
HEAV'EN, n. The sky.
HEAV'EN, n. The eternal abode of the good.
HELP, v. To assist; to aid.
HELP, v. To avoid; to prevent.
HEM, n. The sewed border of a garment.
HEM, n. A voluntary cough.
HIDE, n. The skin of an animal.
HIDE, v. To conceal.
HIND, a. Backward.
HIND, n. A female deer.
HIND, n. A peasant.
HOB'BY, n. A species of falcon.
HOB'BY, n. A pacing horse.
HOB'BY, n. A favorite pursuit.
HOP, v. To jump on one leg.
HOP, n. A climbing plant.
HOST, n. The master of a feast.
HOST, n. Landlord of an inn.
HOST, n. An army.
HOST, n. Any great number.
HUE, n. Color.
HUE, n. An outcry.
IN'STANT, a. Urgent; immediate.
IN'STANT, n. A moment.
I'RONY, a. Partaking of iron.
I'RONY, n. Mockery.
JAM, n. A conserve of fruits.
JAM, v. To wedge in.
JAR, n. An earthen vessel.
JAR, n. A rattling sound.
JAR, v. To clash; to shake.
JET, n. A black fossil.
JET, n. A spout of water.
JET, v. To project.
JOUR'NAL, n. A daily register.
JOUR'NAL, n. The part of a shaft which revolves upon a support.
JUST, a. Right.
JUST, adv. Exactly; nearly.

KEN'NEL, n. A dog house.
KEN'NEL, n. The gutter of a street.
KEY, n. An instrument to open a lock.
KEY, n. That which solves a difficulty.
KIND, n. Species; sort.
KIND, a. Ready to confer favors.
KITE, n. A bird of prey.
KITE, n. A paper toy to fly.
LACE, n. A string.
LACE, n. Fine net work.
LAKE, n. Water surrounded by land
LAKE, n. A color.
LAP, v. To lick up.
LAP, v. To fold over.
LAP, n. The part formed by the knees in a sitting posture.
LAST, a. Latest.
LAST, v. To endure.
LAST, n. The mould on which shoes are made. [woods.
LAWN, n. An open space between
LAWN, n. A linen fabric.
LAY, v. To place down.
LAY, v. To wager.
LAY, v. Did lie.
LAY, n. A song.
LAY, a. Not clerical.
LEAN, v. To incline.
LEAN, n. Muscular part of flesh
LEAN, a. Not fat; thin.
LEAVE, n. Permission.
LEAVE, n. Departure.
LEAVE, v. To forsake.
LEAVE, v. To suffer to remain.
LEAVE, v. To refer for decision.
LEFT, pp. Not taken.
LEFT, a. Pertaining to the left hand.
LET, v. To permit.
LET, v. To lease.
LET, n. Hindrance.
LET'TER, n. A mark used in writing
LET'TER, n. A written message.
LET'TER, n. One who lets.
LIE, v. To rest.
LIE, v. To utter falsehoods.
LIE, n. A fiction.
LIGHT, a. Not heavy.
LIGHT, a. Trivial; frivolous.
LIGHT, v. To settle on.
LIGHT, v. To set on fire.
LIGHT, n. That by which objects are rendered perceptible to the sight.

LIGHT'EN, v. To fill with light.
LIGHT'EN, v. To make less heavy.
LIGHT'EN, v. To flash as lightning.
LIGHT'ER, n. One who lights.
LIGHT'ER, n. A large open boat.
LIKE, a. Resembling.
LIKE, v. To approve.
LIKE, adv. As.
LIME, n. A calcareous earth.
LIME, n. The linden tree.
LIME, n. A species of lemon.
LINE, n. A string.
LINE, v. To cover inside.
LINE, n. That which has length without breadth.
LINK, n. A single ring of a chain.
LINK, v. To connect.
LINK, n. A torch.
LIST, n. A limit; a bound.
LIST, v. To wish; to choose.
LIST, n. A roll or catalogue.
LIST, v. To listen; to hearken.
LIST, n. A strip of cloth.
LIST, n. The inclination of a ship to one side.
LIT'TER, n. A portable bed.
LIT'TER, n. Straw laid under animals.
LIT'TER, n. A number of things in disorder.
LIT'TER, n. A brood of young animals.
LOCK, n. Any thing that fastens.
LOCK, n. A tuft of hair.
LOCK, n. An inclosure in a canal.
LONG, a. Protracted.
LONG, v. To desire earnestly.
LOT, v. To sort; to portion.
LOT, n. Fortune; chance.
LOT, n. A quantity of goods.
LOT, n. A field.
LOW, a. Not high; humble.
LOW, v. To bellow as a cow.
MACE, a. An ensign of authority.
MACE, n. A kind of spice.
MAGAZINE', n. A storehouse.
MAGAZINE', n. A pamphlet.
MAIL, n. Armor.
MAIL, n. A post bag.
MAIN, a. Chief.
MAIN, n. Strength.
MAIN, n. The ocean.
MAIN, n. The continent.
MALL, n. A heavy beetle.
MALL, n. A public walk.

MAN'GLE, v. To cut and tear.
MAN'GLE, v. To smooth linen.
MAN'IFEST, a. Plain; not concealed.
MAN'IFEST, n. A list of the cargo of a ship.
MAN'IFEST, v. To make appear; to show.
MARCH, n. The third month.
MARCH, v. To walk in procession.
MASH, n. A mixture.
MASH, v. To crush.
MAST, n. The fruit of forest trees.
MAST, n. The spar to which the sails of a ship are fixed.
MATCH, n. One that suits with another.
MATCH, n. A contest; a game.
MATCH, v. To equal; to suit.
MATCH, n. A thing that easily inflames.
MAT'TER, n. Material substance.
MAT'TER, n. Subject of discourse.
MAT'TER, n. Consequence.
MAY, n. The fifth month.
MAY, v. To be able.
MEAD, n. A meadow.
MEAD, n. Honeywine.
MEAL, n. A repast.
MEAL, n. The flour of corn.
MEAN, a. Low; base.
MEAN, a. Middle; moderate.
MEAN, n. A middle state.
MEAN, v. To intend; to signify.
MEET, v. To come together.
MEET, a. Proper; suitable.
MEW, n. A sea fowl.
MEW, v. To cry as a cat.
MEW, v. To shut up.
MINE, n. A cavern dug for minerals.
MINE, pro. Belonging to me.
MINT, n. A plant.
MINT, n. A place where money is coined.
MIN'UTE, n. Sixty seconds.
MIN'UTE, n. A short record.
MOLE, n. A little animal.
MOLE, n. A spot on the skin.
MOLE, n. A mound.
MOOD, n. The inflection of a verb.
MOOD, n. Temper.
MOOR, n. A marsh or fen.
MOOR, n. A native of Barbary.
MOOR, v. To anchor a vessel.

Mor'tar, n. Cement for bricks.
Mor'tar, n. A short wide cannon for bombs.
Mor'tar, n. A vessel in which substances are pulverized.
Mould, n. The ground in which plants grow.
Mould, n. A shape or model.
Mould, v. To form.
Mould, n. A substance which gathers on bodies in a damp place.
Mould'er, v. To turn into dust.
Mould'er, n. One who shapes.
Must, v. To be compelled.
Must, v. To mould.
Must, n. New wine.
Nail, n. A sharp spike of iron.
Nail, n. A measure of cloth.
Nail, n. The covering of the finger
Nap, n. A short sleep. [tip.
Nap, n. The down on cloth.
Neat, n. An ox or cow.
Neat, a. Elegant; cleanly.
Nerv'ous, a. Strong; vigorous.
Nerv'ous, a. Having weak nerves.
Net, n. A texture of twine.
Net, n. Clear after all deductions.
No, a. Not any.
No, adv. The word of denial.
Oblige', v. To compel.
Oblige', v. To please.
Or'der, n. Regularity.
Or'der, n. A command.
Or'der, n. A class. [sense.
Or'gan, n. A natural instrument of
Or'gan, n. A musical wind instrument.
Ounce, n. A small weight.
Ounce, n. An animal like a panther.
Pack'et, n. A small bundle.
Pack'et, n. A boat.
Pad, n. A road.
Pad, n. A soft saddle or cushion.
Paint'er, n. One who paints.
Paint'er, n. A rope used to fasten
Pale, a. Wanting color. [a boat.
Pale, n. A narrow board.
Pale, n. An inclosure.
Pall, n. A mantle of state.
Pall, n. A covering for the dead.
Pall, v. To become insipid.
Pal'let, n. A small or rude bed.
Pal'let, n. A board on which a painter holds his colors.

Palm, n. A tree.
Palm, n. Victory; triumph.
Palm, n. The inner part of the hand.
Palm, v. To impose upon by fraud.
Palm, n. A hand's breadth.
Pan'el, n. A list of jurors.
Pan'el, n. A small board set in a frame.
Pap, n. A nipple; a teat.
Pap, n. Soft food.
Pan'ic, n. Sudden fright.
Pan'ic, n. A plant.
Par'tial, a. Inclined to favor.
Par'tial, a. Affecting a part only.
Paste, n. A mixture of flour and water.
Paste, n. Imitations of precious stones.
Pat, a. Exactly suiting.
Pat, v. To strike lightly.
Pa'tient, a. Enduring calmly.
Pa'tient, n. A person under the care of a doctor.
Peck, n. A quarter of a bushel.
Peck, v. To pick up food with the beak.
Peck, v. To strike with a pointed instrument.
Peer, n. An equal.
Peer, n. A nobleman.
Peer, v. To look narrowly.
Pelt, n. A skin or hide.
Pelt, v. To strike with something thrown.
Pen, n. An instrument to write with.
Pen, n. A small enclosure.
Perch, n. A kind of fish.
Perch, n. A roosting place.
Perch, n. A measure.
Pet, n. A slight passion.
Pet, n. A favorite.
Pie, n. Types unsorted.
Pie, n. Fruit baked with paste.
Pike, n. A kind of fish.
Pike, n. A long lance.
Pike, n. The gate of a turnpike.
Pile, n. A beam driven.
Pile, n. A heap.
Pile, n. Nap; a hairy surface.
Pile, n. The head of an arrow.
Pine, n. A kind of tree.
Pine, v. To languish.
Pin'ion, n. A wing.
Pin'ion, n. Fetters for the arms.

WORDS SPELLED AND PRONOUNCED ALIKE. 31

Pin'ion, v. To confine by binding the arms.
Pin'ion, n. A small wheel working in the teeth of a larger wheel.
Pink, n. A flower.
Pink, n. A color.
Pink, n. The summit of excellence.
Pitch, n. Thickened tar.
Pitch, n. Degree of elevation.
Pitch, v. To throw headlong.
Pitch, v. To fix; to set up.
Pitch, v. To throw. [throws.
Pitch'er, n. One who pitches or
Pitch'er, n. An earthen vessel.
Plane, n. A level surface.
Plane, n. A carpenter's tool.
Plane, a. Level; even; flat.
Plant, n. A vegetable. [grow.
Plant, v. To put in the ground to
Plant, v. To set.
Plate, n. A shallow dish.
Plate, n. Wrought silver.
Plate, n. A flat piece of metal.
Poach, v. To boil slightly.
Poach, v. To steal game.
Poach, v. To tread soft ground.
Point, n. The sharp end.
Point, n. Place; station.
Point, v. To aim; to show.
Point, v. To sharpen.
Poke, n. A pouch; a pocket.
Poke, n. A lazy, dawdling person.
Poke, v. To push forward.
Poke, v. To grope, feel, or push one's way.
Pole, n. A long piece of timber.
Pole, n. A measure.
Pole, n. The extremity of an axis.
Pole, n. A native of Poland.
Pol'lard, n. A tree having its top cut off.
Pol'lard, n. A mixture of bran and meal.
Pore, n. A small opening.
Pore, v. To look earnestly.
Port, n. A harbor.
Port, n. A gate.
Port, n. The gun hole in a ship.
Port, n. A kind of wine.
Port, n. Carriage; demeanor.
Port, n. The left side of a ship.
Por'ter, n. A door keeper.
Por'ter, n. A carrier.
Por'ter, n. Strong beer.

Post, n. A piece of timber set upright.
Post, n. A messenger.
Post, n. Office; employment.
Post, n. A station.
Post, v. To travel quickly.
Post, v. To transcribe into a ledger.
Pounce, n. A fine powder.
Pounce, v. To fall on suddenly.
Pounce, n. Cloth with eyelet holes.
Pounce, n. The claw of a bird of prey.
Pound, n. Twenty shillings.
Pound, n. A prison for stray beasts.
Pound, n. A weight.
Pound, v. To beat heavily.
Precip'itate, v. To tumble headlong. [hasty.
Precip'itate, a. Headstrong;
Precip'itate, n. A sediment.
Prefer', v. To choose before another.
Prefer', v. To promote.
Pretend', v. To represent falsely.
Pretend', v. To lay claim.
Prime, a. First in time.
Prime, a. First-rate; highest.
Prime, n. The best part.
Prime, v. To put powder so as to fire a charge.
Prime, v. To apply a first coat of paint.
Pri'or, a. Preceding in time.
Pri'or, n. The chief monk of a convent.
Prune, v. To cut off branches.
Prune, n. A dried plum.
Pulse, n. The motion of an artery.
Pulse, n. Beans, peas, &c.
Pump, n. An engine to raise water.
Pump, n. A light shoe.
Punch, n. A mixed liquor.
Punch, v. To push with fist.
Punch, n. An instrument for cutting holes.
Pu'pil, n. The apple of the eye.
Pu'pil, n. A scholar.
Pu'pil, n. A ward.
Pur'chase, v. To buy.
Pur'chase, n. Convenience for using force.
Purl, v. To decorate with fringe.
Purl, v. To flow with a gentle noise.
Purl, n. A malt liquor.
Quail, n. A bird.
Quail, v. To quake; to tremble.

QUAR'TER, n. Fourth part.
QUAR'TER, n. Mercy shown by a conqueror.
QUAR'TER, n. Eight bushels.
QUAR'TER, v. To lodge soldiers.
QUAR'TER, n. A particular region.
  QUAR'TERED, pp. Divided into four equal parts.
  QUAR'TERED, pp. Stationed for lodging, &c.
QUAR'RY, n. Place from which stones are dug.
QUAR'RY, n. The game flown at by a hawk.
QUIV'ER, n. A case for arrows.
QUIV'ER, v. To shake or tremble.
RACE, n. A generation.
RACE, n. A contest in running.
RACK, n. A frame.
RACK, n. A liquor.
RACK, v. To torture.
RACK, v. To draw off from the lees.
RAIL, n. A bar.
RAIL, v. To use insolent language.
RAIL, n. A bird.
RAKE, n. A farming instrument.
RAKE, n. A vicious man.
RAL'LY, v. To come back to order.
RAL'LY, v. To banter; to jeer.
RAM, n. A male sheep.
RAM, v. To drive in violently.
RANK, a. Overgrown.
RANK, a. Rancid.
RANK, n. Dignity.
RANK, n. A row.
RAR'ITY, n. A scarce thing.
RAR'ITY, n. Thinness.
RASH, a. Acting without caution.
RASH, n. An eruption.
RAY, n. A fish.
RAY, n. A beam of light.
REAR, n. The hinder part.
REAR, v. To raise up.
REAR, v. To educate.
REEF, n. A portion of a sail.
REEF, n. A chain of rocks under water.
REFU'SAL, n. A denial.
REFU'SAL, n. The right of choice.
REND'ER, n. One who tears.
REN'DER, v. To restore.
REN'DER, v. To go or pass freely.
REN'DER, v. To translate; to construe.

RENT, n. A tear; a break.
RENT, n. Money paid for holding a thing.
REST, n. Repose.
REST, n. Remainder.
RID'DLE, n. A puzzling question.
RID'DLE, n. A sieve.
RID'DLE, v. To make many holes in.
RIG, v. To dress.
RIG, n. A trick.
RIGHT, a. Correct.
RIGHT, a. Straight.
RIGHT, a. Not left.
RIGHT, n. Justice.
RIGHT, n. Just claim.
RING, n. A circle.
RING, v. To sound.
RING, v. To fit with rings.
ROAD, n. A way.
ROAD, n. A place at sea where ships may anchor.
ROCK, n. A vast mass of stone.
ROCK, v. To move backward and forward.
ROCK'ET, n. A plant.
ROCK'ET, n. A species of firework.
ROE, n. A female deer.
ROE, n. The eggs of fish.
ROSE, n. A flower.
ROSE, v. Did rise.
ROUT, n. A clamorous multitude.
ROUT, v. To defeat and disperse.
ROW, v. To impel with oars.
ROW, n. Things in a line.
RUE, n. A plant.
RUE, v. To regret.
RUSH, n. A plant.
RUSH, v. To move forward with violence.
SA'BLE, n. A kind of weasel.
SA'BLE, a. Black; dark.
SACK, n. A large bag.
SACK, n. A kind of wine.
SACK, v. To plunder.
SACK, n. A kind of coat.
SAGE, n. A plant.
SAGE, a. Wise; prudent.
SAP, n. The juice of plants.
SAP, v. To undermine.
SASH, n. A belt.
SASH, n. A window frame.
SAW, n. A proverb.
SAW, v. Did see.
SAW, n. A toothed instrument for cutting.

SCALE, n. The dish of a balance.
SCALE, n. A little shell on a fish's skin.
SCALE, n. A regular gradation.
SCALE, v. To climb.
SCALE, v. To peel off in thin pieces.
SCREEN, n. Something that affords shelter or concealment.
SCREEN, n. A kind of sieve.
SCREEN, v. To protect; to hide.
SCREEN, v. To sift; to separate.
SCUT'TLE, n. A hole in a roof or deck. [haste.
SCUT'TLE, v. To run with affected
SCUT'TLE, n. A utensil for coal.
SCUT'TLE, v. To make holes in, in order to sink.
SEAL, n. The sea calf.
SEAL, n. A stamp.
SEA'SON, n. One of the four parts of the year.
SEA'SON, n. A fit time.
SEA'SON, v. To give a relish to.
SEA'SON, v. To prepare for use by time.
SEE, v. To perceive by the eye.
SEE, n. A diocese.
SEN'TENCE, n. To doom.
SEN'TENCE, n. An assemblage of words making complete sense.
SET, v. To place.
SET, v. To bring to a fine edge.
SET, v. To sink below the horizon.
SET, n. A number of things suited to each other.
SHAFT, n. An arrow. [pit.
SHAFT, n. A narrow perpendicular
SHAFT, n. The pole of a carriage.
SHED, n. A building.
SHED, v. To cause to flow.
SHEER, a. Unmingled; pure.
SHEER, v. To turn aside.
SHEER, a. Very thin.
SHEET, n. A broad piece of cloth.
SHEET, n. A rope.
SHOAL, n. A great multitude.
SHOAL, n. A sand bank under water.
SHOAL, a. Shallow.
SHORE, n. The coast.
SHORE, n. A prop under a building.
SHRUB, n. A bush.
SHRUB, n. An alcoholic mixture.
SIG'NAL, n. A sign to give a notice.
SIG'NAL, a. Eminent.

SIN'GULAR, a. Single.
SIN'GULAR, a. Remarkable.
SIN'GULAR, a. Unusual; odd.
SINK, n. A drain.
SINK, v. To go down.
SIZE, n. Bulk.
SIZE, n. A sticky substance.
SLEDGE, n. A heavy hammer.
SLEDGE, n. A vehicle with low wheels.
SLUG, n. A piece of metal.
SLUG, n. A slow, lazy fellow.
SMACK, n. A loud kiss.
SMACK, n. A quick, smart blow.
SMACK, n. A fishing vessel.
SMELT, n. A small sea fish.
SMELT, v. To melt ore.
SMELT, v. Did smell.
SNARL, v. To growl.
SNARL, n. Entanglement.
SOIL, n. The ground; land.
SOIL, v. To make dirty.
SOLE, n. The bottom of the foot.
SOLE, n. A small sea fish.
SOLE, a. Single; only.
SOUND, n. A noise.
SOUND, n. A shallow sea.
SOUND, n. A probe.
SOUND, a. Uninjured.
SOUSE, n. Pickle made of salt.
SOUSE, v. To plunge into water.
SPAR, n. A mast or boom.
SPAR, n. A mineral.
SPAR, v. To dispute.
SPELL, n. A charm.
SPELL, n. A short time.
SPELL, n. A turn of work.
SPELL, v. To indicate the proper letters of a word.
SPIR'IT, n. The soul of man.
SPIR'IT, n. Temper; courage.
SPIR'IT, n. A distilled liquor.
SPIT, n. A long iron prong.
SPIT, n. Saliva.
SPIT, v. To eject from the mouth.
SPIT, v. To turn up ground with a spade. [der.
SPOKE, n. A bar of a wheel or lad-
SPOKE. Pret. of SPEAK.
SPRING, n. One of the seasons.
SPRING, n. An elastic body.
SPRING, n. A leap.
SPRING, n. A fountain.
SPRING, v. To rise, or come forth.
SPRING, v. To leap; to jump.

SPRUCE, *a.* Neat without elegance.
SPRUCE, *n.* A tree.
STA'BLE, *a.* Fixed; firm.
STA'BLE, *n.* A house for beasts.
STAFF, *n.* A stick.
STAFF, *n.* A stanza.
STAFF, *n.* A number of officers.
STAKE, *n.* A stick.
STAKE, *n.* A thing at hazard.
STALK, *v.* To walk with lofty steps.
STALK, *n.* The stem of a plant.
STALL, *n.* A crib for an animal.
STALL, *n.* A bench on which any thing is exposed for sale.
STAND'ARD, *n.* A flag.
STAND'ARD, *n.* A rule of measure.
STA'PLE, *n.* A loop of metal.
STA'PLE, *n.* A principal commodity.
STA'PLE, *n.* The fibre of cotton, &c.
STA'PLE, *a.* Settled.
STATE, *n.* Condition.
STATE, *n.* Dignity; grandeur.
STATE, *n.* A civil community.
STATE, *n.* A district of country.
STATE, *v.* To make known.
STAVE, *n.* A narrow piece of wood.
STAVE, *v.* To break in pieces.
STAVE, *v.* To prevent; to delay.
STAY, *v.* To continue in a place.
STAY, *v.* To support.
STAY, *v.* To stand still.
STAY, *n.* A prop; a support.
STEEP, *a.* Precipitous.
STEEP, *v.* To soak.
STEER, *n.* A young bullock.
STEER, *v.* To direct a course.
STEM, *n.* A stalk.
STEM, *n.* The fore part of a ship.
STEM, *v.* To bear up against.
STERN, *a.* Severe.
STERN, *n.* The hind part of a ship.
STICK, *n.* A piece of wood.
STICK, *v.* To pierce; to stab.
STICK, *v.* To adhere.
STILL, *a.* Quiet.
STILL, *v.* To calm.
STILL, *n.* A vessel for distilling.
STILL, *adv.* This time.
STILL, *conj.* Notwithstanding.
STOCK, *n.* The stem of a tree.
STOCK, *n.* A family; a race.
STOCK, *n.* The capital of a merchant.
STOCK, *n.* The wooden part of a gun.
STOCK, *n.* Supply provided.
STOCK'ING, *ppr.* Filling.
STOCK'ING, *n.* A cover for the leg.
STOCKS, *n.* The public funds.
STOCKS, *n.* A place of punishment.
STOCKS, *n.* The frame on which ships are built.
STOOP, *v.* To bend forward.
STOOP, *n.* A drinking vessel.
STOOP, *n.* The steps to a door.
STO'RY, *a.* A narrative or history.
STO'RY, *n.* A falsehood.
STO'RY, *n.* A floor of a building.
STO'RY, *n.* An anecdote.
STRAIN, *v.* To filter.
STRAIN, *v.* To sprain.
STRAIN, *v.* To force.
STRAIN, *n.* Style.
STRAIN, *n.* A passage of music.
STRAND, *n.* A shore or beach.
STRAND, *n.* One of the parts of a [rope.
STROKE, *n.* A blow.
STROKE, *v.* To rub gently.
STUD, *n.* A piece of timber.
STUD, *n.* A kind of button.
STUD, *n.* A nail.
STUD, *n.* A collection of horses.
STY, *n.* A hog pen.
STY, *n.* A tumor on the eyelid.
SUCCEED', *v.* To follow.
SUCCEED', *v.* To prosper.
SUF'FER, *v.* To permit; to allow.
SUF'FER, *v.* To endure; to bear.
SUIT, *n.* A set.
SUIT, *n.* Courtship.
SUIT, *n.* Prosecution.
SUIT, *v.* To fit.
SWAL'LOW, *n.* A bird.
SWAL'LOW, *v.* To take down the throat.
TA'BLE, *n.* An article of furniture.
TA'BLE, *n.* An index; a list.
TACK, *v.* To join; to fasten.
TACK, *n.* A small nail.
TACK, *v.* To change the course of a ship.
TAP, *v.* To pierce a cask.
TAP, *v.* To strike a very gentle blow.
TA'PER, *n.* A small light.
TA'PER, *v.* To grow smaller towards [the end.
TARE, *n.* A weed.
TARE, *n.* An allowance.
TART, *a.* Sour; sharp of taste.
TART, *n.* A kind of pie.
TAR'TAR, *n.* An acid salt.
TAR'TAR, *n.* An ill-natured person.

TATTOO', *n*. A drum beat.
TATTOO', *v*. To mark the skin.
TEND, *v*. To go towards.
TEND, *v*. To watch; to guard.
TEND'ER, *n*. A attendant.
TEN'DER, *a*. Soft.
TEN'DER, *v*. To offer.
   TICK, *n*. Trust; credit.
   TICK, *n*. A little insect.
   TICK, *v*. To make a small noise.
   TICK, *n*. The case of a bed.
TILL, *v*. To cultivate.
TILL, *n*. A money box.
TILL, *conj*. To the time.
   TILL'ER, *n*. One who cultivates.
   TILL'ER, *n*. The handle of a rudder
TILT, *n*. An awning.
TILT, *v*. To set in a slanting position.
TILT, *v*. To thrust a weapon at.
TILT, *n*. A friendly encounter.
   TIRE, *n*. A head dress.
   TIRE, *n*. The iron band of a wheel.
   TIRE, *v*. To fatigue.
TOIL, *v*. To work hard.
TOIL, *n*. A net; a snare.
   TOLL, *v*. To sound with slow strokes.
   TOLL, *n*. A tax for some benefit conferred.
TONE, *n*. Sound.
TONE, *n*. Elasticity.
   TOP, *n*. The highest part of any thing.
   TOP, *n*. A toy.
TRAP, *n*. An instrument for catching.
TRAP, *v*. To adorn.
   TREAT, *v*. To negotiate.
   TREAT, *v*. To discourse on.
   TREAT, *v*. To behave towards.
   TREAT, *n*. A feast.
   TREAT, *v*. To entertain with food or drink without charge.
TRIP, *v*. To run or step lightly.
TRIP, *n*. An excursion.

TRIP, *v*. To strike the foot against.
TRIP, *n*. A stumble.
TROOP, *n*. A company.
TROOP, *n*. Horse soldiers.
TRUMP, *n*. A winning card.
TRUMP, *v*. To impose upon.
TRUMP, *n*. A musical instrument.
   TUM'BLER, *n*. A posture master.
   TUM'BLER, *n*. A drinking-glass.
TWINE, *v*. To twist.
TWINE, *n*. A small cord.
   USH'ER, *v*. To introduce.
   USH'ER, *n*. An underteacher.
VAULT, *n*. A cellar.
VAULT, *v*. To leap.
   VERGE, *n*. Brink; edge.
   VERGE, *v*. To tend towards.
   VERGE, *n*. The mace of a dean.
   VERGE, *n*. A shaft in a watch.
VICE, *n*. A machine for griping.
VICE, *n*. Wickedness.
VICE. In the place of.
   WA'GES, *n*. Pay for services.
   WA'GES, *v*. Carries on.
WAX, *v*. To smear with wax.
WAX, *v*. To grow; to increase.
WAX, *n*. The substance of which the honey comb is formed.
   WEAR, *n*. The act of wearing.
   WEAR, *n*. A kind of dam.
   WEAR, *v*. To impair by friction.
   WEAR, *v*. To carry upon the person.
WELL, *n*. A deep narrow pit of water.
WELL, *a*. Being in health.
WELL, *adjv*. Rightly; properly.
   WHIST, *intj*. Be silent; be still.
   WHIST, *n*. A game at cards.
WOUND, *v*. Did wind.
WOUND, *n*. A hurt.
   YARD, *n*. An enclosure of ground.
   YARD, *n*. A measure.
   YARD, *n*. A long piece of timber to extend the sails of a ship.

RULES FOR SPELLING.

Rule I.

Words of one syllable ending with *f, l,* or *s, preceded* by a single vowel, double the final letter; as,

doff	all	mass
cuff	ball	pass
sniff	call	miss
stiff	fall	class
bluff	hall	glass

Exceptions to Rule I.

as	of	us
gas	yes	pus
has	his	thus
was	is	clef
if	this	

Rule II.

Words of one syllable ending with any other consonant than *f, l,* or *s,* do not double the final letter; as,

drab	path	stoop
snub	gush	plump
twig	leak	malt
strong	weak	debt
slept	sleep	whip

Exceptions to Rule II.

abb	err	fizz
add	inn	fuzz
ebb	mitt	buzz
egg	lamm	shirr
odd	wapp	jagg

Rule III.

Words of one syllable and English verbs do not end with *c*, but take *ck* or double *c*; as,

hack	smack	knock
lack	stack	shock
pack	track	stock
rack	wreck	chuck
sack	quack	cluck

Note.—In general, words derived from the learned languages do not need the *k*, and common use discards it; as, Italic, stoic, music, maniac, public, &c.

Rule IV.

Words of one syllable, when they end with a single consonant preceded by a single vowel, double their final letter before a suffix that begins with a vowel; as,

Bag	bag'gage	Let	let'ting
Chap	chap'ping	Man	man'ned
Dig	dig'ging	Rob	rob'ber
Fib	fib'bing	Stab	stab'bing
Gab	gab'ble	Trod	trod'den

Rule V.

Words *accented* on the last syllable, when they end with a single consonant preceded by a single vowel, double their final letter before a suffix that begins with a vowel.

NOTE 1.—The accent of the derivative must continue on the same syllable as in the radical; thus, refer' with *ible* gives refer'rible (double *rr*), but in ref'erable the accent is changed, and we have single *r;* also, prefer', pref'erence; confer', con'ference; refer', ref'erence.

NOTE 2.—The final vowel is doubled after a vowel preceded by *qu*, the same as if it were a single vowel.

NOTE 3.—*X, y,* and *k* are never doubled in English words. Words derived from *gas* have only one *s*, as *gases*.

Abet'	abet'-tor	Inter'	inter'-ring
Beget'	beget'-ting	Prefer'	prefer'-ring
Beset'	beset'-ting	Refer'	refer'-ring
Compel'	compel'-ling	Concur'	concur'-ring
Excel'	excel'-ling	Demur'	demur'-ring

Rule VI.

The final consonant of a word, when not preceded by a single vowel, or when the accent is not on the last syllable, remains single on the addition of a suffix.

NOTE.—It has been the practice to double the *l* in all words ending in *l* preceded by a single vowel, though not accented on the last syllable, when a syllable was added commencing with a vowel; but it evidently accords with the analogy of the language, that all such words should conform to the rule.

Trav'-el	trav'-el-er	Ben'-e-fit	ben'-e-fit-ed
Trav'-el	trav'-el-ing	Buf'-fet	buf'-fet-ed
Du'-el	du'-el-ist	Clos'-et	clos'-et-ed
Wor'-ship	wor'-ship-er	De-vel'-op	de-vel'-op-ed
Wor'-ship	wor'-ship-ing	En-vel'-op	en-vel'-op-ed

Rule VII.

Words of more than one syllable that end in *l* (except those that are formed from monosyllables ending in double *ll*), terminate with one *l;* as,

ras'-cal	tran'-quil	con-trol'
ex-tol'	re-bel'	med'-al
na'-tal	scan'-dal	par'-cel
lo'-cal	fru'-gal	plu'-ral
grav'-el	shov'-el	bush'-el

Rule VIII.

Words ending with any double letter, preserve it double before any additional termination not beginning with the same letter; as,

Woo	woo'-er	Shrill	shrill'-ness
See	see'-ing	Small	small'-ness
Bliss	bliss'-ful	Droll	droll'-ness
Odd	odd'-ly	Free	free'-dom
Gruff	gruff'-ly	Grass	grass'-less

Exceptions to Rule VIII.

Certain irregular derivatives ending in *t*, from verbs ending in *ll* or *ss*,— as *dwelt* from *dwell;* *spelt* from *spell;* *shalt* from *shall;* *wilt* from *will;* *blest* from *bless;* *past* from *pass*,—are exceptions to the foregoing rule.

Rule IX.

Words ending with any double letter, preserve it double in all words formed from them by means of prefixes; as,

See	fore-see'	Sell	under-sell'
Spell	mis-spell'	Add	super-add'
Roll	un-roll'	Swell	over-swell'
Pass	re-pass'	Stall	fore-stall'
Press	de-press'	Call	mis-call'

Rule X.

Primitive words ending with a silent *e*, omit the *e* upon adding a syllable beginning with a vowel.

NOTE.—The added syllables are chiefly the following, viz.: *ed, ing, er, age, ous, ar, al, ish, able, ible, ance, ence, ure, en, est, ity, y*.

Re-move'	re-mov'-al	Im-pede'	im-ped'ing
Live	liv'-ing	A-muse'	a-mus'-ing
Force	for'-ci-ble	De-plore'	de-plo'-ra-ble
Eye	ey'-ing	Ex-cuse'	ex-cu'-sa-ble
Come	com'-ing	Con-ceive'	con-ceiv'a-ble

Exceptions to Rule X.

EXCEPTION 1.—Words ending in *ce* or *ge* retain the *e* before the suffixes *ible* and *ous*, to prevent change in the pronunciation; as,

Trace	trace'-a-ble	Cour'-age	cour-a'-geous
Change	change'-a-ble	Chal'-lenge	chal'-lenge-a-ble
Out'-rage	out-ra'-geous	Charge	charge'-a-ble
Peace	peace'-a-ble	Ser'-vice	ser'-vice-a-ble
Mar'-riage	mar'-riage-a-ble	Pierce	pierce' a-ble

EXCEPTION 2.—When the final *e* is preceded by *o*, the final *e* is retained before *ing;* as, *shoe, shoe'-ing; hoe, hoe'-ing*.

NOTE.—In some words it is necessary to retain the *e* before *ing* to prevent ambiguity; as, *singe, singe'-ing*, not *sing'-ing; tinge, tinge'-ing*, not *ting'-ing*.

Words ending in *ee* drop the final letter only when the addition begins with *e;* as, *see, seer*, not *see'-er; flee, fleest*, not *flee'-est; a-gree', a-greed'*, not *a-gree'-ed*.

Rule XI.

The following words, ending with *e* preceded by *c*, change the *e* into *i* before a suffix commencing with a vowel.

Space	spa'-cious	Jus'-tice	jus-ti'-cia-ry
Grace	gra'-cious	Com'-merce	com-mer'-cial
Vice	vi'-cious	Fi-nance'	fi-nan'-cial
Pal'-ace	pa-la'-cious	Face	fa'-cial
Sol'-ace	so-la'-cious	Dis-grace'	dis-gra'-cious
Of'fice	{ of-fi'-cial { of-fi'-cious	Sac'-ri-fice Prej'-u-dice	sac-ri-fi'-cial prej-u-di'-cial
Suf-fice'	suf-fi'-cient	Ben'-e-fice	ben-e-fi'-cial
Mal'-ice	ma-li'-cious	Art'-i-fice	art-i-fi'-cial
Aus'-pice	aus-pi'-cious	Av'-a-rice	av-a-ri'-cious
Ca-price'	ca-pri'-cious	Su'-per-fice	su-per-fi'-cial

Rule XII.

When a suffix beginning with a consonant is added to a word ending with *e*, the *e* is retained.

Judge	judge'-ment	A-bridge'	a-bridge'-ment
Judge	judge'-ship	Ac-knowl'-edge	ac-knowl'-edge-ment
Lodge	lodge'-ment	Ar-range'	ar-range'-ment
Rude	rude'-ness	A-base'	a-base'-ment
Rude	rude'-ly	De-range'	de-range'-ment

NOTE.—It has been the prevailing usage to spell the words *abridgement, acknowledgement*, and *judgement* without the final *e* of the primitive, but many respectable writers now adopt the more correct, though less usual spelling, by inserting the *e*. Webster omits the *e* in these words, as also in *lodgement*, but retains it in *judgeship*.

Exceptions to Rule XII.

When the *e* is preceded by a vowel, it is sometimes omitted; as *duly* from *due; truly* from *true; awful* from *awe; argument* from *argue;* but much more frequently retained; as, *dueness* from *due; trueness* from *true; blueness* and *bluely* from *blue; rueful* from *rue; shoeless* from *shoe; eyeless* from *eye*.

Wholly is also an exception, as nobody writes it *wholely*.

Rule XIII.

Words ending with *ate* drop the letters *te* in derivatives formed by adding the suffix *cy*.

Pri'-mate	pri'-ma-cy	E-pis'-co-pate	e-pis'-co-pa-cy
Pri'-vate	pri'-va-cy	Cel'-i-bate	cel'-i-ba-cy
Leg'-ate	leg'-a-cy	Con-fed'-er-ate	con-fed'-er-a-cy
Prel'-ate	prel'-a-cy	De-gen'-er-ate	de-gen'-er-a-cy
Pi'-rate	pi'-ra-cy	Il-lit'-er-ate	il-lit'-er-a-cy

Rule XIV.

Words ending with *ant* or *ent* drop the *t* in derivatives formed by adding the suffix *ce* or *cy*.

Va'-cant	va'-can-cy	De-pend'-ent	de-pend'-en-cy
In'-fant	in'-fan-cy	Ter'-ma-gant	ter'-ma-gan-cy
Pli'-ant	pli'-an-cy	El'-e-gant	el'-e-gance
Ten'-ant	ten'-an-cy	Ar'-ro-gant	ar'-ro-gance
Stag'-nant	stag'-nan-cy	Ra'-di-ant	ra'-di-ance

Rule XV.

When primitive words ending with *y* preceded by a consonant take an additional syllable, the *y* is changed into *i*.

NOTE.—This rule applies to derivatives, but not to compound words; as, *mercy seat, penny-worth, lady-ship, giddy-head*, &c.

Ra'-cy	ra'-ci-ness	Like'-ly	like'-li-hood
I'-cy	i'-ci-cle	An'-gry	an'-gri-ly
Spi'-cy	spi'-ci-ness	Hun'-gry	hun'-gri-ly
Jui'-cy	jui'-ci-ness	Air'-y	air'-i-ness
Fan'-cy	fan'-ci-ful	Lone'-ly	lone'-li-ness

Exceptions to Rule XV.

EXCEPTION 1.—The *y* is retained before the termination *ing* or *ish*, to prevent the doubling of *i*.

Ba'-by	ba'-by-ish	Cop'-y	cop'-y-ing
Pit'-y	pit'-y-ing	Fan'-cy	fan'-cy-ing
Com-ply'	com-ply'-ing	Stead'-y	stead'-y-ing

EXCEPTION 2.—Words ending in *ie* and dropping the *e*, by Rule X. change *i* into *y*, to prevent the doubling of *i*.

Die	dy'-ing	Tie	ty'-ing
Vie	vy'-ing	Un-tie'	un-ty'-ing
Lie	ly'-ing	Out-vie'	out-vy'-ing

EXCEPTION 3.—In a few instances, the final *y* is changed into *e* before *ous* and its compounds; as,

Beau'-ty	beau'-te-ous	Du'-ty	du'-te-ous
Plen'-ty	plen'-te-ous	Pit'-y	pit'-e-ous

NOTE.—Words ending with *y* form the plural of nouns, the persons of verbs, participles, comparatives, and superlatives by changing *y* into *i*, when the *y* is preceded by a consonant; as, *spy, spies; carry, carriest; happy, happier, happiest*. As the present or imperfect participle ends with *ing*, it retains the *y*, to prevent the doubling of *i*.

Rule XVI.

Primitive words ending with *y* preceded by a vowel, do not change *y* into *i* before an additional syllable.

Day	day'-ly	De-lay'	de-lay'-er
Key	key'-hole	Dis-play'	dis-play'-er
Coy	coy'-ly	Ar-ray'	ar-ray'-ed
Boy	boy'-ish	Be-tray'	be-tray'-er
Joy	joy'-ful	Por-tray'	por-tray'er
Gay	gay'-ly	Es'-say	es'-say-ist

Exceptions to Rule XVI.

From *lay, pay, say, stay* are formed *laid, paid, said*, and *staid;* but the regular words *layed, payed*, and *stayed* are sometimes used. *Raiment* from *arrayment*, is never written with the *y*. *Daily* is more common than the regular form, *dayly*.

NOTE.—In some instances, where the suffix begins with *i*, the final *y* is rejected; as, *eulogy, eulogist; sympathy, sympathize*.

Rule XVII.

The final *y* of a radical word, when preceded by *t*, is generally omitted before a suffix beginning with *a* or *o*.

Pu'-ri-ty	pu'-ri-tan	Eq'-ui-ty	eq'-ui-ta-ble
Fe-lic'-i-ty	fe-lic'-i-tous	In-iq'-ui-ty	in-iq'-ui-tous
Gra-tu'-i-ty	gra-tu'-i-tous	Ca-lam'-i-ty	ca-lam'-i-tous
Ne-ces'-si-ty	ne-ces'-si-tous	Fa-tu'-i-ty	fa-tu'-i-tous
U-biq'-ui-ty	u-biq'-ui-tous	Grav'-i-ty	grav'-i-tate

Rule XVIII.

Words ending with *le* preceded by a consonant, drop the *le* upon receiving the suffix *ly*.

Nim'-ble	nim'-bly	Peace'-a-ble	peace'-a-bly
Hum'-ble	hum'-bly	Mov'-a-ble	mov'-a-bly
No'-ble	no'-bly	Af'-fa-ble	af'-fa-bly
Doub'-le	doub'-ly	Laugh'-a-ble	laugh'-a-bly
Peb'ble	peb'-bly	Blam'-a-ble	blam'-a-bly

Rule XIX.

Words ending with *ble*, upon taking the suffix *ity* or *ities*, take *i* between the letters *b* and *l*.

A'-ble	a-bil'-i-ty	Mu'-ta-ble	mu-ta-bil'-i-ty
Sta'-ble	sta-bil'-i-ty	Prac'-ti-ca-ble	prac-ti-ca-bil'-i-ty
Li'-a-ble	li-a-bil'-i-ty	Sep'-a-ra-ble	sep-a-ra-bil'-i-ty
Ca'-pa-ble	ca-pa-bil'-i-ty	Ad'-mi-ra-ble	ad-mi-ra-bil'-i-ty
Du'-ra-ble	du-ra-bil'-i-ty	A'-mi-a-ble	a-mi-a-bil'-i-ty

Rule XX.

The plural number of nouns is regularly formed by adding *s* or *es* to the singular.

NOTE.—When the singular ends with a sound which will unite with that of *s*, the plural is generally formed by adding *s* only, and the number of syllables is not increased; but when the sound of *s* cannot be united with that of the primitive word, the regular plural adds *s* to final *e*, and *es* to other terminations, and forms a separate syllable.

Mob	mobs	Fan'-cy	fan'-cies
Pen	pens	Mon'-ey	mon'-eys
Bed	beds	Jour'-ney	jour'-neys
Lid	lids	Com'-pa-ny	com'-pa-nies
Babe	babes	Gal'-ler-y	gal'-ler-ies

Rule XXI.

The following words ending with *d*, change the *d* into *s* in the annexed derivatives, for euphony:

De-fend'	de-fense'	de-fen'-sive
Of-fend'	of-fense'	of-fens'-ive
Ex-pend'	ex-pense'	ex-pen'-sive
In-tend'	in-tense'	in-ten'-sive
Pre-tend'	pre-tense'	pre-ten'-sion
Dis-pend'	dis-pense'	dis-pens'-ing
Ex-pand'	ex-panse'	ex-pan'-sive

Pro-pend'	pro-pense'	pro-pen'-si-ty
Re-spond'	re-sponse'	re-spon'-sive
Sus-pend'	sus-pense'	sus-pen'-sion
Dis-tend'	dis-ten'-sion	dis-ten'-sive
Ex-tend'	ex-ten'-sion	ex-ten'-sive
De-scend'	de-scen'-sion	de-scen'-sive
As-cend'	as-cen'-sion	as-cen'-sive
Ab-scind'	ab-scis'-sa	ab-scis'-sion
Re-scind'	re-scis'-sion	re-scis'-so-ry
Rep-re-hend'		rep-re-hen'-sion
Com-pre-hend'		com-pre-hen'-sion
Ap-pre-hend'		ap-pre-hen'-sion
Con-de-scend'		con-de-scen'-sion
Cor-re-spond'		cor-re-spon'-sive

Rule XXII.

The following words ending with *t*, change the *t* into *s*, in the annexed derivatives for euphony:

Sub-mit'	sub-mis'-sion	sub-mis'-sive
De-mit'	de-mis'-sion	de-mis'-sive
Re-mit'	re-mis'-sion	re-mis'-sive
Ad-mit'	ad-mis'-sion	ad-mis'-si-ble
E-mit'	e-mis'-sion	em'-is-sa-ry
Com-mit'	com-mis'-sion	com-mis'-sion-er
O-mit'	o-mis'-sion	o-mis'-si-ble
Per-mit'	per-mis'-sion	per-mis'-si-ble
In-ter-mit'	in-ter-mis'-sion	in-ter-mis'-sive

The above words double the *s*, because the final consonant of the accented syllable is preceded by a *single vowel*.

A-vert'	a-ver'-sion	a-verse'-ly
Sub-vert'	sub-ver'-sion	sub-ver'-sive
Ad-vert'	ad-verse'	ad-vers'-i-ty
Re-vert'	re-ver'-sion	re-ver'-si-ble
Di-vert'	di-ver'-sion	di-ver'-si-ty
In-vert'	in-ver'-sion	in-verse'-ly
Con-vert'	con-ver'-sion	con-verse'-ly
Per-vert'	per-ver'-sion	per-ver'-si-ty
An-i-mad-vert'	an-i-mad-ver'-sion	

The above words have but single *s*, because the final consonant of the accented syllable of the radical is preceded by a *consonant*.

Rule XXIII.

The possessive case of nouns is formed in the singular number by adding *s*, preceded by an apostrophe; and in the plural, when the word ends with *s*, by adding an apostrophe only.

	Possessive Singular.	Possessive Plural.
Boy	boy's	boys'
Maid	maid's	maids'
Giant	gi'-ant's	gi'-ants'
Man	man's	men's
Child	child's	chil'-dren's
Ox	ox's	ox'-en's

Rule XXIV.

Words ending in *er* or *or*, often drop the *e* or *o* before a suffix commencing with a vowel.

Act'-or	act'-ress	Ad-ven'-tur-er	ad-ven'-tur-ess
Ar'-bi-ter	ar'-bi-tress	Am-bas'-sa-dor	am-bas'-sa-dress
Au'-di-tor	au'-di-tress	Ben-e-fac'-tor	ben-e-fac'-tress
Chant'-er	chant'-ress	Foun'-der	foun'-dress
Con-duct'-or	con-duct'-ress	En-chant'-er	en-chant'-ress

Rule XXV.

Mistakes are often made in spelling words commencing with prefixes, by inserting or omitting a letter. To avoid errors, consider whether the first letter of the primitive word is the same as the last letter of the prefix. If they be alike, that letter is doubled; if unlike, they remain single.

Com'-pa-ny	ac-com'-pa-ny	..........two c's
Cus'-tom	ac-cus'-tom	.... "
Join	ad-join'	................one d
Grieve	ag-grieve'	..............two g's
Mis'-sion	com-mis'-sion	.... " m's
Re-spond'	cor-re-spond'	.... " r's
Com-pose'	de-com-pose'	...........one c
Sat'-is-fy	dis-sat'-is-fy	............two s's
Solve	dis-solve'	.... "
No'-ble	en-no'-ble	..............two n's
Leg'-i-ble	il-leg'-i-ble	.... " l's
Lib'-er-al	il-lib'-er-al	.... "
Mor'-tal	im-mor'-tal	............two m's

Rule XXVI.

The following words ending in *f* or *fe*, change *f* into *v*, and add *es* in their plurals:

	Plurals.		Plurals.
Sheaf	sheaves	Leaf	leaves
Loaf	loaves	Beef	beeves
Thief	thieves	Calf	calves
Half	halves	Elf	elves
Shelf	shelves	Self	selves
Wolf	wolves	Life	lives
Knife	knives	Wife	wives

NOTE.—The verbs formed from the following words ending with *f* or *fe*, have the *f* changed into *v*:

Safe	save	Strife	strive
Grief	grieve	Proof	prove
Be-lief	be-lieve'	Re-lief'	re-lieve'

Rule XXVII.

The following words ending with *f* or *fe*, retain the *f*, and add *s* in their plurals:

Chief	chiefs	Brief	briefs	Fief	fiefs
Grief	griefs	Clef	clefs	Oaf	oafs
Waif	waifs	Coif	coifs	Gulf	gulfs
Hoof	hoofs	Roof	roofs	Proof	proofs
Woof	woofs	Turf	turfs	Scarf	scarfs
Dwarf	dwarfs	Fife	fifes	Strife	strifes
Safe	safes	Wharf	wharfs	Staff	staffs

Ker'-chief	ker'-chiefs	Mis'-chief	mis'-chiefs
Be-lief'	be-liefs'	Re-lief'	re-liefs'
Re-proof'	re-proofs'	Ca'-lif	ca'-lifs
Hand'-ker-chief	hand'-ker-chiefs	Mis'-be-lief	mis'-be-liefs

Rule XXVIII.

Compounds generally retain the orthography of the simple words which compose them; as, horse-man, up-hill, shell-fish, knee-deep, inn-keeper, &c.

PART SECOND.

PREFIXES
OF SAXON OR ENGLISH ORIGIN.

FORMULA.—ABOARD,—a-b-o-a-r-d,—aboard.—*Board* is a primitive word; the Saxon prefix *a* signifies *on, in, to, at;*—when combined they form the word *aboard*, which means *on board*.

A.
Signifies *on, in, to,* or *at.*

A-BOARD', *ad. on* board; in a ship.
A-FIRE', *ad. on* fire.
A-SLEEP', *ad. in* sleep; sleeping.
A-STERN', *ad. to* the stern.
A-HEAD', *ad. to* the head; further on.
A-FAR', *ad. at* a distance.

Be.
Signifies *to make.*

Be-CALM', *v. to make* calm.
Be-DAUB', *v. to* daub over.
Be-DECK', *v. to* deck; to adorn.
Be-DIM', *v. to make* dim.
Be-FOUL', *v. to make* foul.
Be-NUMB', *v. to make* numb.

En.
Signifies *in, into,* or *on; to make.*

En-CIR'CLE, *v.* to put *in* a circle.
En-DAN'GER, *v.* to put *in* danger.
En-ACT', *v.* to make *into* an act.
En-CAMP', *v.* to form *into* a camp.
En-DEAR', *v. to make* dear.
En-FEE'BLE, *v. to make* feeble.

Em, for En.
Signifies *to make, to give.*

Em-BEL'LISH, *v. (beau*), to make* beautiful.
Em-POW'ER, *v. to give* power to.
Em-BOD'Y, *v. to give* a body to.
Em-BOT'TLE, *v. to put* in a bottle.

---

* NOTE.—The words in parentheses are the roots from which the English words are derived. The pupil will find the meanings of the roots under their respective heads, though in general the meaning is indicated where the root is used.

Fore.
Signifies *before*.

Fore'-NOON, *n.* the part of the day *before* noon.
Fore-RUN'NER, *n.* one who runs *before*.
Fore-SEE', *v.* to see *before*hand.
Fore'-SIGHT, *n.* a seeing *before*hand.
Fore-TELL', *v.* to tell *before*hand.
Fore-DOOM', *v.* to doom *before*hand.

Im.
Signifies *to make*.

Im-BIT'TER, *v. to make* bitter.
Im-BROWN', *v. to make* brown.
Im-POV'ERISH, *v. to make* poor.
Im-PEARL', *v. to make* like pearls.

Mis.
Signifies *wrong*.

Mis-APPLY', *v.* to apply *wrong*.
Mis-BELIEF', *n. wrong* belief.
Mis-CAL'CULATE, *v.* to calculate *wrong*.
Mis'-CONDUCT, *n. wrong* conduct.
Mis-GUIDE', *v.* to guide *wrong*.
Mis-PLACE', *v.* to place *wrong*.

Out.
Signifies *beyond, more than*.

Out-BID', *v.* to bid *beyond* or *more than* another.
Out-LIVE', *v.* to live *beyond*.
Out-RUN', *v.* to run *beyond*.
Out-SHINE', *v.* to shine *more than*.

Over.
Signifies *above* or *over, too much, too great*.

Over-BUR'DEN, *v.* to burden *too much*.
Over-FLOW', *v.* to flow *over*.
Over-LOAD', *v.* to load *too much*.
Over-RUN', *v.* to run *over* or *above*.
Over-SPREAD', *v.* to spread *over* or *above*.
Over-VAL'UE, *v.* to value *too much*.

Un, before a Verb.
Signifies *to take off, to reverse the act of*.

Un-BAR', *v. to take off* the bar.
Un-CHAIN', *v. to take off* the chain.
Un-HINGE', *v. to take off* of the hinge.
Un-PIN', *v. to take out* the pin.
Un-SEAL', *v. to take off* the seal.
Un-YOKE', *v. to take off* the yoke.

Un, before an Adjective.
Signifies *not*.

Un-A'BLE, *a. not* able.
Un-AC'TIVE, *a. not* active.

Un-ARMED', *a. not* armed.
Un-BRO'KEN, *a. not* broken.
Un-CER'TAIN, *a. not* certain.
Un-JUST', *a. not* just.

Under.
Signifies *beneath, less than.*
Under-BID', *v.* to bid *less than* another.
Under-OF'FICER, *n.* an officer *under* another.
Under-SHER'IFF, *n.* one who is *under* the sheriff.
Under-VAL'UE, *v.* to rate *under* its value.

With.
Signifies *from* or *against.*
With-DRAW', *v.* to draw *from* or away.
With-STAND', *v.* to stand *against.*
With-HOLD', *v.* to hold *from.*

LATIN PREFIXES.

FORMULA.—AVERT,—a-v-e-r-t,—avert,—*vert* is derived from the Latin word *verto*, to turn;—the Latin prefix *a* signifies *from* or *away*;—when combined, they form the word *avert*, which means *to turn from or away.*

A.
Signifies *from* or *away.*
A-VERT', *v.* (*verto*), to turn *from.*
A-VOCA'TION, *n.* (*voco*), a calling *away.*
A-VUL'SION, *n.* (*vello*), a tearing *away.*

Ab.
Signifies *from* or *away.*
Ab-JECT', *v.* (*jacio*), to cast *away.*
Ab-LU'TION, *n.* (*luo*), a washing *away.*
Ab-RADE', *v.* (*rado*), to rub *away.*
Ab-RUPT', *a.* (*ruptum*), broken *from* or *off.*
Ab-SOLVE', *v.* (*solvo*), to loose *from.*
Ab-SORB', *v.* (*sorbeo*), to suck *from* or *up.*

Abs.
Signifies *from* or *away.*
Ab's-ENT, *a.* (*ens*), a being *away.*
Abs-TAIN', *v.* (*teneo*), to hold *from.*
Abs-TRACT', *v.* (*traho*), to draw *from.*

Ad.
Signifies *to.*
Ad-APT', *v.* (*aptus*), to fit *to.*
Ad-DUCE', *v.* (*duco*), to lead *to.*
Ad'-EQUATE, *a.* (*equus*), equal *to.*
Ad-HERE', *v.* (*hæreo*), to stick *to.*
Ad-JA'CENT, *a.* (*jaceo*), lying *to* or *near.*
Ad-JOIN', *v.* (*jungo*), to join *to.*

*A, for Ad.**
Signifies *to*.

A-SCEND', *v.* (*scando*), to climb *to*.
A-SCRIBE', *v.* (*scribo*), to write or impute *to*.
A-SPERSE', *v.* (*spargo*), to sprinkle *to* or *upon*.
A-SPIRE', *v.* (*spiro*), to breathe *to*.
A-V'ENUE, *n.* (*venio*), the way of coming *to* (a place).
A-VOW', *v.* (*votum*), to vow *to*.

Ac, for Ad.
Signifies *to*.

Ac-CEDE', *v.* (*cedo*), to yield *to*.
Ac-CEPT', *v.* (*capio*), to take *to*.
Ac-CESS', *n.* (*cedo*), approach *to*.

Af, for Ad.
Signifies *to*.

Af-FIX', *v.* (*fixus*), to fix *to*.
Af-FLICT', *v.* (*fligo*), to strike *to* or *at*.
Af'-FLUX, *n.* (*fluo*), a flowing *to*.

Ag, for Ad.
Signifies *to*.

Ag'-GRAVATE, *v.* (*gravis*), to make heavy *to*.
Ag'-GRANDIZE, *v.* (*grandis*), to make great *to*.
Ag-GRESS', *v.* (*gradior*), to go *to* or *against*.

Al, for Ad.
Signifies *to*.

Al-LE'VIATE, *v.* (*levis*), to make light *to*.
Al-LUDE', *v.* (*ludo*), to play or advert *to*.
Al-LU'VIAL, *a.* (*luo*), washing *to*.
Al-LY', *v.* (*ligo*), to bind *to*.

An, for Ad.
Signifies *to*.

An-NEX', *v.* (*necto*), to tie *to*.
An-NI'HILATE, *v.* (*nihil*), to make *to* nothing.
An-NOUNCE', *v.* (*nuncio*), to tell *to*.
An-NUL', *v.* (*nullus*), to reduce *to* nothing.

Ap, for Ad.
Signifies *to*.

Ap-PA'RENT, *a.* (*pareo*), becoming visible *to*.
Ap-PEND', *v.* (*pend*), to hang *to*.
Ap-PERTAIN', *v.* to pertain *to*.
Ap-PROX'IMATE, *v.* (*prope*), to come near *to*.

Ar, for Ad.
Signifies *to*.

Ar-RANGE', *v.* (*rang*), to put *to* or *in* order.
Ar'-ROGATE, *v.* (*rogo*), to ask or assume *to* (one's self).

---

* For the sake of euphony, (an agreeable sound in language,) the *form* of the prefix is frequently changed. Thus, we have ascend, for adscend; avenue, for advenue, &c.

LATIN PREFIXES.

As, for *Ad*.
Signifies *to*.

As-SAIL', *v.* (*salio*), to leap *upon* or *against*.
As-SIGN', *v.* (*signum*), to mark or allot *to*.
As-SIM'ILATE, *v.* (*similis*), to make like *to*.
As-SIST', *v.* (*sisto*), to stand *to* or *by*.
As-SO'CIATE, *v.* (*socio*), to join *to*.
As-SUME', *v.* (*sumo*), to take *to*.

At, for *Ad*.
Signifies *to*.

At-TAIN', *v.* (*tango*), to touch *to*.
At-TEND', *v.* (*tendo*), to stretch *to*.
At-TEST', *v.* (*testis*), to bear witness *to*.
At-TRACT', *v.* (*traho*), to draw *to*.
At-TRIB'UTE, *v.* (*tribuo*), to give or ascribe *to*.

Am.
Signifies *round* or *about*.

Am-BI'TION, *n.* (*eo*), a going *about*.
Am'-PUTATE, *v.* (*puto*), to cut *round* or *off*.

Ante.
Signifies *before*.

Ante-CE'DENT, *a.* (*cedo*), going *before*.
An'te-ROOM, *n.* a room *before* the main one.
Ante-DATE' *v.* (*datum*), to date *before*.
Ante-DILU'VIAN, *a.* (*diluvium*), *before* the flood.
Ante-MERID'IAN, *a.* (*meridies*), *before* midday.
Ante-MUN'DANE, *a.* (*mundus*), *before* the world.

Circum.
Signifies *round* or *about*.

Circum-JA'CENT, *a.* (*jaceo*), lying *round*.
Circum-NAV'IGATE, *v.* to navigate *round*.
Circum-SCRIBE', *v.* (*scribo*), to write *round*, to inclose.
Cir'cum-SPECT, *a.* (*specio*), looking *round*, cautious.

Cis.
Signifies *on this side*.

Cis-AL'PINE,* *a.* *on this side* of the Alps.
Cis-ATLAN'TIC, *a.* *on this side* of the Atlantic.

Con. (*Cum*.)
Signifies *together* or *with*.

Con-CUR', *v.* (*curro*), to run *together*.
Con-FLICT', *v.* (*fligo*), to strike *together*.
Con'-FLUENCE, *n.* (*fluo*), a flowing *together*.
Con-NECT', *v.* (*necto*), to tie *together*.
Con-SPIRE', *v.* (*spiro*), to breathe *together*.
Con-STRUCT', *v.* (*struo*), to build *together*.

---

* *Cisalpine*, on this side of the Alps, in regard to Rome, that is on the south side of the Alps. *Transalpine*, on the north side of the Alps.

Co, for Con.
Signifies *together* or *with*.

Co-E'QUAL, *a.* equal *with*.
Co-E'VAL, *a.* (*ævum*), of the same age *with*.
Co-EXIST', *v.* to exist *together*.
Co-HEIR', *n.* one who is heir *with* another.
Co-HERE', *v.* (*hæreo*), to stick *together*.
Co-OP'ERATE, *v.* (*opera*), to work *together*.

Cog, for Con.
Signifies *together* or *with*.

Cog'-NATE, *a.* (*nascor*), born *together* or *with*.

Col, for Con.
Signifies *together* or *with*.

Col-LAPSE', *n.* (*labor*), a falling *together*.
Col-LATE', *v.* (*latum*), to bring *together*.
Col-LECT', *v.* (*lego*), to gather *together*.
Col'-LOCATE, *v.* (*locus*), to place *together*.
Col'-LOQUY, *n.* (*loquor*), a speaking *together*.
Col-LU'SION, *n.* (*ludo*), a playing *together*.

Com, for Con.
Signifies *together* or *with*.

Com'-MERCE, *n.* (*mercor*), a trading *together*.
Com-MIX', *v.* to mix *together*.
Com-MO'TION, *n.* (*moveo*), a moving *together*.
Com-PEL', *v.* (*pello*), to drive *with*.
Com-POSE', *v.* (*pono*), to put *together*.
Com-PRESS', *v.* (*premo*), to press *together*.

Cor, for Con.
Signifies *together* or *with*.

Cor-REL'ATIVE, *a.* relative *with*.
Cor-ROB'ORATE, *v.* (*robur*), to make strong *together*.
Cor RODE', *v.* (*rodo*), to gnaw *together*.

Contra.
Signifies *against*.

Contra-DICT', *v.* to speak *against* or *contrary to*.
Con'tro-VERT, *v.* (*verto*), to turn *against*.

Counter, for Contra.
Signifies *against*.

Counter-BAL'ANCE, *v.* to balance *against*.
Counter-MARCH', *v.* to march in an opposite direction.

De.
Signifies *down* or *from*.

De-CLINE', *v.* (*clino*), to bend *down*.
De-DUCE', *v.* (*duco*), to lead *from*.
De-FEND', *v.* (*fendo*), to strike *down*.
De-JECT', *v.* (*jacio*), to cast *down*.
De-PEND', *v.* (*pendeo*), to hang *from*.
De-POSE', *v.* (*pono*), to put *down*.

Dis.

Signifies *to take from, away, off,* or *out; not.*

Dis-A'BLE, *v.* to render *not* able.
Dis-ARM', *v. to take away* arms.
Dis-BELIEVE', *v. not* to believe.
Dis-BUR'DEN, *v. to take off* a burden.
Dis-HON'EST, *a. not* honest.
Dis-LOY'AL, *a. not* loyal.

Dis.
Signifies *apart.*

Dis-PEL', *v.* (*pello*), to drive *apart.*
Dis-SECT', *v.* (*seco*), to cut *apart.*
Dis-SOLVE', *v.* (*solvo*), to loose *apart.*
Dis-TEND', *v.* (*tendo*), to stretch *apart.*
Dis-TORT', *v.* (*tortum*), to twist *apart.*
Dis-TRACT', *v.* (*traho*), to draw *apart.*

Di, for Dis.
Signifies *apart.*

Di-SPERSE', *v.* (*spargo*), to sprinkle *apart.*
Di-VERGE', *v.* (*vergo*), to tend *apart.*
Di-VERT', *v.* (*verto*), to turn *apart.*
Di-GRESS', *v.* (*gradior*), to go *apart.*
Di-LUTE', *v.* (*luo*), to wash *apart.*

Dif, for Dis.
Signifies *apart.*

Dif'-FER, *v.* (*fero*), to bear *apart.*
Dif-FUSE', *v.* (*fundo*), to pour *apart.*

Ex.
Signifies *out* or *out of.*

Ex-ACT', *v.* (*ago*), to take or force *out of.*
Ex-CEPT', *v.* (*capio*), to take *out.*
Ex-CITE', *v.* (*cito*), to call *out.*
Ex-CLAIM', *v.* (*clamo*), to cry *out.*
Ex-CLUDE', *v.* (*claudo*), to shut *out.*
Ex-PAND', *v.* (*pando*), to spread *out.*
Ex-PEL', *v.* (*pello*), to drive *out of.*
Ex-PORT', *v.* (*porto*), to carry *out.*

E, for Ex.
Signifies *out* or *out of.*

E'-DICT, *n.* (*dico*), what is spoken *out.*
E-DUCE', *v.* (*duco*), to lead *out.*
E'-GRESS, *n.* (*gradior*), a going *out.*
E-JECT', *v.* (*jacio*), to cast *out.*
E-LECT', *v.* (*lego*), to choose *out.*
E-RASE', *v.* (*rado*), to rub *out.*

• Ef, for Ex.
Signifies *out* or *out of.*

Ef-FACE', *v.* (*facies*), to take *out* the face.
Ef'-FLUX, *n.* (*fluo*), a flowing *out.*

Extra.
Signifies *beyond*.

Extra-MUN′DANE, a. (*mundus*), *beyond* the world.
Extra-OR′DINARY, a. *beyond* ordinary.

In, *before a Verb*.
Signifies *in* or *into*, *on* or *upon*.

In-CLINE′, v. (*clino*), to lean *into*.
In-CLUDE′, v. (*claudo*), to shut *in*.
In-CUR′, v. (*curro*), to run *upon*.
In-FLICT′, v. (*fligo*), to strike *upon*.
In′-FLUX, n. (*fluo*), a flowing *into*.
In-HALE′, v. (*halo*), to breathe *in*.

Il, *for In*.
Signifies *in* or *into*, *on* or *upon*.

Il-LU′MINATE, v. (*lumen*), to put light *into*.
Il-LU′SION, n. (*ludo*), a playing *upon*.

Im, *for In*.
Signifies *in* or *into*, *on* or *upon*.

Im-MERSE′, v. (*mergo*), to plunge *into*.
Im-PEL′, v. (*pello*), to drive *on*.
Im-PEND′, v. (*pendeo*), to hang *upon* or *over*.
Im-PORT′, v. (*porto*), to carry *into*.
Im-POSE′, v. (*pono*), to put *upon*.
Im-PRIS′ON, v. to put *in* prison.

Ir, *for In*.
Signifies *in* or *into*, *on* or *upon*.

Ir′-RITATE, v. (*ira*), to put *in* anger.
Ir-RUP′TION, n. (*ruptum*), a breaking *into*.

In, *before an Adjective*.
Signifies *not*.

In-AC′TIVE, a. *not* active.
In-AN′IMATE, a. (*anima*), *not* having life.
In-CAU′TIOUS, a. *not* cautious.
In-COM′PETENT, a. *not* competent.

Ig, *for In*.
Signifies *not*.

Ig-NO′BLE, a. *not* noble.
Ig-NOMIN′IOUS, a. (*nomen*), *not* having a name.

Il, *for In*.
Signifies *not*.

Il-LE′GAL, a. *not* legal.
Il-LEG′IBLE, a. (*lego*), that can *not* be read.
Il-LIB′ERAL, a. *not* liberal.
Il-LIC′IT, a. *not* permitted

Im, for In.
Signifies *not*.

Im-MOR′AL, *a. not* moral.
Im-MOR′TAL, *a. not* mortal.
Im-PAR′TIAL, *a. not* partial.
Im-PA′TIENT, *a. not* patient.
Im-PER′FECT, *a. not* perfect.

Ir, for In.
Signifies *not*.

Ir-RA′TIONAL, *a. not* rational.
Ir-REFUT′ABLE, *a. not* to be refuted.
Ir-REG′ULAR, *a. not* regular.
Ir-RESIST′IBLE, *a. not* to be resisted.

Inter.
Signifies *between* or *among*.

Inter-FERE′, *v.* (*ferio*), to strike *between*.
In′ter-LUDE, *n.* (*ludo*), a part *between* plays.
Inter-POSE′, *v.* (*pono*), to place *between*.
Inter′-ROGATE, *v.* (*rogo*), to ask *between*.
Inter-RUPT′, *v.* (*ruptum*), to break *between*.
Inter-SECT′, *v.* (*seco*), to cut *between*.

Intro.
Signifies *within*.

Intro-DUCE′, *v.* (*duco*), to lead *within*.
Intro-VERT′, *v.* (*verto*), to turn *within*.

Ob.
Signifies *in the way, against, out*.

Ob′-LOQUY, *n.* (*loquor*), something spoken *against*.
Ob′-STACLE, *n.* (*sto*), something standing *in the way*.
Ob-TRUDE′, *v.* (*trudo*), to thrust *against*.
Ob′-VIATE, *v.* (*via*), to put *out of* the way.

Oc, for Ob.
Signifies *in the way, up, down*.

Oc-CA′SION, *n.* (*cado*), a falling *in the way*.
Oc′-CUPY, *v.* (*capio*), to take *up*.
Oc-CUR′, *v.* (*curro*), to run *in the way*.

Of, for Ob.
Signifies *in the way, against*.

Of-FEND′, *v.* (*fendo*), to strike *against*.
Of′-FER, *v.* (*fero*), to bear *in the way*.

Op, for Ob.
Signifies *in the way, against*.

Op-POSE′, *v.* (*pono*), to put *in the way*.
Op-PRESS′, *v.* (*premo*), to press *against*.
Op-PUGN′, *v.* (*pugna*), to fight *against*.

Per.
Signifies *through* or *thoroughly*.

Per'-FECT, *a.* (*facio*), made *thoroughly*.
Per-SPIRE', *v.* (*spiro*), to breathe *through*.
Per-VADE' *v.* (*vado*), to go *through*.
Pe-RUSE', *v.* (*usum*), to read *through*.

Post.
Signifies *after*.

Post-PONE', *v.* (*pono*), to put *after* or *off*.
Post'-SCRIPT, *n.* (*scribo*), something written *after*.

Pre.
Signifies *before*.

Pre-CEDE', *v.* (*cedo*), to go *before*.
Pre-DICT', *v.* (*dico*), to *fore*tell.
Pre-FER', *v.* (*fero*), to bear or esteem *before*.
Pre'-FIX, *n.* (*fixus*), something fixed *before*.
Pre-SIDE', *v.* (*sedeo*), to sit *before*.
Pre-VENT', *v.* (*venio*), to come *before*.

Preter.
Signifies *beyond* or *past*.

Pre'ter-IT, *a.* (*eo*), gone *past*.
Preter-NAT'URAL, *a. beyond* natural.

Pro.
Signifies *for, forward, forth* or *out*.

Pro-CEED', *v.* (*cedo*), to go *forward*.
Pro-MOTE', *v.* (*moveo*), to move *forward*.
Pro-PEL', *v.* (*pello*), to drive *forward*.
Pro-DUCE', *v.* (*duco*), to lead *forth*.
Pro-CLAIM', *v.* (*clamo*), to cry *out*.
Pro-TRACT', *v.* (*traho*), to draw *out*.
Pro-VOKE', *v.* (*voco*), to call *out*.

Re.
Signifies *back* or *again, anew*.

Re-CEDE', *v.* (*cedo*), to go *back*.
Re-CLAIM', *v.* (*clamo*), to call *back*.
Re-CLINE', *v.* (*clino*), to lean *back*.
Re'-FLUX, *n.* (*fluo*), a flowing *back*.
Re-FUSE', *v.* (*fundo*), to pour *back*.
Re-VOKE', *v.* (*voco*), to call *back*.

Retro.
Signifies *back* or *backwards*.

Retro-CES'SION, *n.* (*cessum*), the act of going *back*.
Ret'ro-GRADE, *v.* (*gradior*), going *backward*.
Ret'ro-SPECT, *n.* (*specio*), a looking *backwards*.

LATIN PREFIXES.

Se.
Signifies *aside* or *apart*.

Se-CEDE', *v.* (*cedo*), to go *apart*.
Se-CLUDE', *v.* (*claudo*), to shut up *apart*.
Se-DUCE', *v.* (*duco*), to lead *aside*.
Se-DI'TION, *n.* (*itum*), a going *aside*.

Sine.
Signifies *without*.

Sim'-PLE, *a.* (*plico*), *without* fold.
Sin-CERE', *a.* (*cera*), *without* wax.
Si'ne-CURE, *n.* (*cura*), a situation *without care.*

Sub.
Signifies *under*.

Sub-JA'CENT, *a.* (*jaceo*), lying *under*.
Sub-MARINE', *a.* (*mare*), *under* the sea.
Sub-SCRIBE', *v.* (*scribo*), to write *under*.
Sub-TRACT', *v.* (*traho*), to draw *under* or *from*.

Suc, for Sub.
Signifies *under, up*.

Suc-CEED', *v.* (*cedo*), to go *under* or *after*.
Suc-COR', *v.* (*curro*), to run *under*.
Suc-CUMB', *v.* (*cubo*), to lean *under*.

Suf, for Sub.
Signifies *under*.

Suf'-FER, *v.* (*fero*), to bear *under*.
Suf-FUSE', *v.* (*fundo*), to pour *under*.

Sup, for Sub.
Signifies *under, up*.

Sup-PORT', *v.* (*porto*), to bear *up*.
Sup-POSE', *v.* (*pono*), to put *under*.
Sup-PRESS', *v.* (*premo*), to press *under*.

Super.
Signifies *above* or *over, upon*.

Super-ABOUND', *v.* to *over*abound.
Super-ADD', *v.* to add *over* and *above*.
Super-FINE', *a. over*fine.
Super-SEDE', *v.* (*sedeo*), to sit *above*.
Super-VI'SOR, *n.* (*video*), an *over*seer.
Super-SCRIBE', *v.* (*scribo*), to write *upon*.

Sur, (Fr. for Super.)
Signifies *above, over, upon*.

Sur-MOUNT', *v.* to mount *above*.
Sur-VIVE', *v.* (*vivo*), to live *over* or *after*.
Sur'-FACE, *n.* (*facies*), *upon* the face.
Sur-VEY', *v.* (*video*), to look *upon*.

Sus, for Sub.
Signifies *under, up, upwards.*

Sus-PECT', *v. (specio),* to look *under.*
Sus-PEND', *v. (pendeo),* to hang *up.*
Sus-TAIN', *v. (teneo),* to hold *up.*

Trans.
Signifies *across, over* or *beyond, through.*

Tra-DUCE', *v. (duco),* to lead *across.*
Trans-FER', *v. (fero),* to carry *over.*
Trans-LATE', *v. (latum),* to carry *over.*
Trans-MIT', *v. (mitto),* to send *over.*

Ultra.
Signifies *beyond.*

Ul'tra-IST, *n.* one who is *beyond.*
Ultra-MON'TANE, *a. (mons), beyond* the mountains.
Ultra-MUN'DANE, *a. (mundus), beyond* the world.

SUFFIXES.

FORMULA.—MANUAL,—m-a-n-u-a-l,—manual,—*manu* is derived from the Latin word *manus,* the hand;—the suffix *al* signifies *of, relating* or *pertaining to; befitting* or *becoming;*—when combined, they form the word *manual,* which means *relating or pertaining to the hand.*

Ac.
Signifies *of,* or *belonging to.*

CAR'DIac, *a. (cardia,* Gr.), *belonging to* the heart.
ELEGI'ac, *a. (elegia,* Gr.), *belonging to* elegy.
DEMO'NIac, *a. belonging to* a demon.

Aceous.
Signifies *of* or *consisting of, like* or *resembling.*

ARENA'ceous, *a. (arena), consisting of* sand.
ARGILLA'ceous, *a. (argilla), consisting of* clay.
FARINA'ceous, *a. (farina), consisting of* meal.
HERBA'ceous, *a. (herba), consisting of* herbs.

Acy.
Signifies *being,* or *state of being; office of.*

AC'CURacy, *n. a being* accurate.
DEL'ICacy, *n. a being* delicate.
OB'STINacy, *n. a being* obstinate.
CU'Racy, *n. the office of* a curate.

Age.
Signifies *collection of; state of being; an allowance for.*

BAG'Gage, *n. a collection of* bags.
CORD'age, *n. a collection of* cords.
HERB'age, *n. a collection of* herbs.
BOND'age, *n. state of being* in bonds.

Al.

Signifies *of, relating* or *pertaining to ; befitting* or *becoming.*

Fil'ial, *a. (filius), relating to* or *becoming* a son.
Flo'ral, *a. (flos), relating to* flowers.
Man'ual, *a. (manus), relating to* the hand.
Ment'al, *a. (mens), relating to* the mind.

An, Ian, Ean.

Signifies *belonging, relating* or *pertaining to.*

Agra'rian, *a. (ager), relating to* the fields.
Chris'tian, *a. relating to* Christ.
Plebe'ian, *a. relating to* the people.
Europe'an, *a. relating to* Europe.

An, Ian.

Signifies *one who,* or *the person that.*

Art'isan, *n. one who* is skilled in an art.
Chris'tian, *n. one who* believes in Christ.
Europ-e'an, *n. one who* lives in Europe.
Histo'rian, *n. one who* writes history.

Ance, Ancy.

Signifies *being* or *state of being; ing.**

Con'stancy, *n. state of being* constant.
Ig'norance, *n. state of being* ignorant.
Vig'ilance, *n. state of being* vigilant.
Assist'ance, *n. (sisto),* a standi*ng* to.

Ant.

Signifies *one who,* or *the person that.*

Assail'ant, *n. one who* assails.
Assist'ant, *n. one who* assists.
Claim'ant, *n. one who* claims.
Com'batant, *n. one who* combats.
Attend'ant, *n. one who* attends.
Depend'ant, *n. one who* depends on another.

Ant.

Signifies *ing.*

Brill'iant, *a. (briller),* shini*ng.*
Attend'ant, *a.* attendi*ng;* accompanyi*ng.*
Depend'ant, *a. (pendeo),* hangi*ng* down.
Con'sonant, *a. (sonus),* soundi*ng* together.
Observ'ant, *a.* observi*ng.*
Pleas'ant, *a.* pleasi*ng.*

Ar.

Signifies *in the form of; like; relating to; having.*

Cir'cular, *a. (circulus), in the form of* a circle.
Glob'ular, *a. (globus), in the form of* a globe.

---

* *Ing* has a participial meaning, and is defined by the expression *continuing to;* because it denotes primarily, *continuance of action,* or *condition.*

IN'SULAr, a. (insula), *relating to* an island.
JU'GULar, a. (jugulum), *relating to* the throat.
OC'ULar, a. (oculus), *relating to* the eyes.
CEL'LULar, a. (cella), *having* cells.

Ar.
`Signifies *one who*.

BEG'Gar, n. *one who* begs.
LI'ar, n. *one who* tells lies.
SCHOL'ar, n. *one who* goes to school.

Ard.
Signifies *one who*.

DRUNK'ard, n. *one who* gets drunk.
SLUG'Gard, n. *one who* is sluggish.
DO'Tard, n. *one whose* mind is impaired.
NIG'Gard, n. *one who* is a miser.

Ary.
Signifies *one who* or *the person that*.

AD'VERSary, n. *one who* is adverse.
EM'ISSary, n. *one who* is sent out.
MIS'SIONary, n. (mitto), *one who* is sent.
TRIB'UTary, n. *one who* pays tribute.

Ary.
Signifies *the place where*, or *the thing that*.

A'PIary, n. (apis), *the place where* bees are kept.
GRAN'ary, n. (granum), *the place where* grain is stored.
LI'BRary, n. (liber), *the place where* books are kept.
LU'MINary, n. (lumen), *the thing that* gives light.

Ary.
Signifies *belonging, relating*, or *pertaining to*.

HON'ORary, a. *pertaining* or *relating to* honor.
LIT'ERary, a. (litera), *pertaining* or *relating to* letters.
MIL'ITary, a. (miles), *pertaining* or *relating to* soldiers.
PUL'MONary, a. (pulmo), *pertaining* or *relating to* the lungs.

Ate.
Signifies *having, being*.

COR'PORate, a. (corpus), *having* a body.
INAN'IMate, a. (anima), *not having* life.
INTES'Tate, a. (testis), *not having* a will.
DES'PERate, a. (spero), *being* out of hope.

Ate.
Signifies *one who* or *the person that*.

CU'Rate, n. (cura), *one who* has the care.
DEL'EGate, n. (lego), *one who* is sent from.
GRAD'Uate, n. (gradior), *one who* takes a degree.
PO'TENTate, n. (posse), *one who* has power.

Ate.

Signifies *to make, to give, to put,* or *to take.*

DEBIL'ITate, *v.* (*debilis*), *to make* feeble.
FACIL'ITate, *v.* (*facilis*), *to make* easy.
FRUS'TRate, *v.* (*frustra*), *to make* vain.
REN'Ovate, *v.* (*novus*), *to make* new again.
DEC'ORate, *v.* (*decor*), *to give* ornament.
REG'ULate, *v.* (*rego*), *to give* rules.

Ble, Able, Ible.

Signifies *may be* or *can be; worthy of.*

BLAM'*able*, *a.* that *may be* blamed.
DISCERN'*ible*, *a.* that *can be* discerned.
INHAB'IT*able*, *a.* that *can be* inhabited.
CONTEMPT'*ible*, *a. worthy of* contempt.

Cle.

Signifies *little* or *small.*

CAN'TIcle, *n.* (*cano*), a *little* song.
I'CIcle, *n.* a *small* stick of ice.
PED'Icle, *n.* (*pes*), a *little* flower stem.

Dom.

Signifies *the place where; state of being.*

DUKE'*dom*, *n. the place where* a duke reigns.
KING'*dom*, *n. the place where* a king reigns.
FREE'*dom*, *n. the state of being* free.
WIS'*dom*, *n. the state of being* wise.

Ee.

Signifies *one who,* or *one to whom.*

ABSENT*ee'*, *n. one who* is absent.
REFUG*ee'*, *n.* (*fugio*), *one who* flies.
ASSIGN*ee'*, *n. one to whom* anything is assigned.
TRUST*ee'*, *n. one to whom* a trust is given.

Eer.

Signifies *one who* or *the person that.*

AUCTION*eer'*, *n. one who* sells at an auction.
ENGIN*eer'*, *n. one who* has charge of an engine.
MOUNTAIN*eer'*, *n. one who* lives on a mountain.
MUTIN*eer'*, *n. one who* is guilty of mutiny.

En.

Signifies *made of.*

BRA'*zen*, *a. made of* brass.
HEMP'*en*, *a. made of* hemp.
WOOD'*en*, *a. made of* wood.
WOOL'*en*, *a. made of* wool.

En.

Signifies *to make.*

DEEP'*en*, *v. to make* deep.
FAST'*en*, *v. to make* fast.
GLAD'*den*, *v. to make* glad.
HARD'*en*, *v. to make* hard.

Ence, Ency.
Signifies *being* or *state of being; ing.*

IM'PUDence, *n.* (*pudeo*), *state of being* without shame.
CONCUR'Rence, *n.* (*curro*), a runn*ing* together.
CON'FLUence, *n.* (*fluo*), a flow*ing* together.
EL'OQUence, *n.* (*loquor*), a speak*ing* out.

Ent.
Signifies *one who,* or *the person that.*

ADHE'Rent, *n.* (*hæreo*), *one who* sticks to.
A'Gent, *n.* (*ago*), *one who* acts.
PA'TIent, *n.* (*patior*), *one who* suffers.
PRES'IDent, *n. one who* presides.

Ent.
Signifies *ing* or *being.*

COHE'Rent, *a.* (*hæreo*), stick*ing* together.
EFFUL'Gent, *a.* (*fulgeo*), shin*ing* forth.
PEND'ent, *a.* (*pendeo*), hang*ing.*
PO'Tent, *a.* (*potens*), *being* powerful.

Er.
Signifies *one who* or *the person that.*

BUILD'er, *n. one who* builds.
BUY'er, *n. one who* buys.
FISH'er, *n. one who* fishes.
INQUIR'er, *n. one who* inquires.

Escence.
Signifies *state of growing* or *becoming.*

CONVALES'cence, *n.* (*valeo*), *state of growing* well.
PUTRES'cence, *n.* (*putris*), *state of becoming* rotten.

Escent.
Signifies *growing* or *becoming.*

CONVALES'cent, *a. growing* well.
QUIES'cent, *a.* (*quies*), *becoming* quiet.

Ful.
Signifies *full of.*

CARE'ful, *a. full of* care.
DOUBT'ful, *a. full of* doubt.
FEAR'ful, *a. full of* fear.
HOPE'ful, *a. full of* hope.

Fy.
Signifies *to make.*

FOR'TIfy, *v.* (*fortis*), *to make* strong.
MAG'NIfy, *v.* (*magnus*), *to make* great.
PU'RIfy, *v.* (*purus*), *to make* pure.
REC'TIfy, *v.* (*rego*), *to make* right.

Hood.
Signifies *the state of.*

Boy'hood, n. *the state of* a boy.
Child'hood, n. *the state of* a child.
Knight'hood, n. *the state of* a knight.
Girl'hood, n. *the state of* a girl.

Ic, Ical.
Signifies *of, pertaining to, like.*

Academ'ical, a. *pertaining to* an academy.
Angel'ical, a. *of* or *pertaining to* an angel.
Hero'ic, a. *like* a hero.
Ocean'ic, a. *of* or *pertaining to* the ocean.

Ice.
Signifies *a being,* or *thing that.*

Just'ice, n. *a being* just.
Mal'ice, n. (*male*), *a being* evil.
Serv'ice, n. *the thing that* is served.
No'tice, n. (*nosco*), *the thing that* makes known.

Ics.
Signifies *the science* or *art of.*

Eth'ics, n. *the science of* manners or morals.
Op'tics, n. *the science of* seeing.

Id.
Signifies *being* or *ing.*

Frig'id, a. (*frigus*), *being* cold.
Splen'did, a. (*splendo*), *shining.*
Tor'rid, a. (*torreo*), *parching.*
Viv'id, a. (*vivo*), *living.*

Ile.
Signifies *belonging to; may* or *can be; easily.*

Fe'brile, a. (*febris*), *belonging to* a fever.
Hos'tile, a. (*hostis*), *belonging to* an enemy.
Juv'enile, a. (*juvenis*), *belonging to* youth.
Frag'ile, a. (*frango*), *easily* broken.

Ine.
Signifies *of* or *belonging.*

Divine', a. (*divus*), *belonging* to God.
Ca'nine, a. (*canis*), *belonging* to dogs.
Fem'inine, a. (*femina*), *belonging* to woman.
In'fantine, a. *belonging* to an infant.

Ion.
Signifies *the act of; state of being; ing.*

Expul'sion, n. (*pello*), *the act of* driving out.
Inspec'tion, n. (*specio*), *the act of* looking into.
Anima'tion, n. *the state of being* animate.
Corrup'tion, n. *the state of being* corrupt.
Precis'ion, n. *the state of being* precise.
Expan'sion, n. (*pando*), a spreading out.

Ise, Ize.
Signifies *to make, to give.*

Civ'ilize, *v. to make* civil.
Fer'tilize, *v. to make* fertile.
Le'galize, *v. to make* legal.
Mod'ernize, *v. to make* modern.

Ish.
Signifies *somewhat; belonging to; like.*

Black'ish, *a. somewhat* black.
Green'ish, *a. somewhat* green.
Scot'tish, *a. belonging to* Scotland.
Span'ish, *a. belonging to* Spain.
Fool'ish, *a. like* a fool.
Fop'pish, *a. like* a fop.

Ish.
Signifies *to make.*

Cher'ish, *v. (carus), to make* dear.
Embel'lish, *v. (beau), to make* beautiful.
Fin'ish, *v. (finis), to make* an end.
Pub'lish, *v. (vulgus), to make* public.

Ism.
Signifies *state of being; an idiom; doctrine of.*

Bar'barism, *n. state of being* barbarous.
Fanat'icism, *n. state of being* a fanatic.
Her'oism, *n. state of being* a hero.
Id'iotism, *n. state of being* an idiot.

Ist.
Signifies *one who,* or *the person that.*

Art'ist, *n. one who* practises an art.
Bot'anist, *n. one who* studies botany.
Flor'ist, *n. (flos), one who* cultivates flowers.
Hu'morist, *n. one who* is fond of humor.

Ite.
Signifies *one who,* or *the person that.*

Ca'naanite, *n. one who* dwells in Canaan.
Fa'vorite, *n. one who* is favored.
Le'vite, *n. one who* is descended from **Levi**.

Ity, or Ty.
Signifies *being* or *state of being.*

Abil'ity, *n. state of being* able.
Captiv'ity, *n. state of being* a captive.
Docil'ity, *n. state of being* docile.
Fertil'ity, *n. state of being* fertile.

Ive.
Signifies *one who,* or *the person that.*

Cap'tive, *n. (capio), one who* is taken.
Fu'gitive, *n. (fugio), one who* flies.
Op'erative, *n. (opera), one who* works.
Na'tive, *n. (nascor), one who* is born.

SUFFIXES.

Ive.
Signifies *having power*, or *ing*.

CORRECT'*ive*, a. *having power* to correct.
INVENT'*ive*, a. *having power* to invent.
ADHE'*sive*, a. (*hæreo*), stick*ing* to.
ATTRACT'*ive*, a. attract*ing*.

Less.
Signifies *without*.

ART'*less*, a. *without* art.
CHILD'*less*, a. *without* a child.
FRUIT'*less*, a. *without* fruit.
POW'ER*less*, a. *without* power.

Like.
Signifies *like* or *resembling*.

GOD'*like*, a. *like* or *resembling* God.
MAN'*like*, a. *like* or *resembling* man.
WAR'*like*, a. *like* or *resembling* war.

Ling.
Signifies *little*, *young*.

DAR'*ling*, n. a *little* dear.
DUCK'*ling*, n. a *little* or *young* duck.
GOS'*ling*, n. a *little* or *young* goose.
LORD'*ling*, n. a *little* or *young* lord.

Ly, for Like.
Signifies *like* or *resembling*.

COW'ARD*ly*, a. *like* or *resembling* a coward.
FA'THER*ly*, a. *like* or *resembling* a father.
PRINCE'*ly*, a. *like* or *resembling* a prince.
WORLD'*ly*, a. *like* or *resembling* the world.

Ment.
Signifies *being* or *state of being*; *act of*; *the thing that*.

EXCITE'*ment*, n. *state of being* excited.
RETIRE'*ment*, n. *state of being* retired.
CHASTISE'*ment*, n. *act of* chastising.
ACQUIRE'*ment*, n. *the thing* acquired.

Mony.
Signifies *state of being*; *thing that*.

AC'RI*mony*, n. (*acris*), the *state of being* sharp.
MAT'RI*mony*, n. (*mater*), the *state of being* a mother.
PAT'RI*mony*, n. (*pater*), the *thing* inherited from a father.
TES'TI*mony*, n. (*testis*), the *thing that* is affirmed by a witness.

Ness.
Signifies *a being* or *state of being*.

BASE'*ness*, n. the *state of being* base.
BOLD'*ness*, n. the *state of being* bold.
COOL'*ness*, n. the *state of being* cool.
FOND'*ness*, n. the *state of being* fond.
GLAD'*ness*, n. the *state of being* glad.

Or.

Signifies *one who,* or *the person that.*

COLLECT'or, *n. one who* collects.
CREA'TOR, *n. one who* creates.
DIRECT'or, *n. one who* directs.
IM'ITATor, *n. one who* imitates.
INSPECT'or, *n. one who* inspects.
PREDICT'or, *n. one who* predicts.

Ory.

Signifies *the place where; thing that.*

DEPOS'ITory, *n. the place where* things are deposited.
DOR'MITory, *n. (dormio), a place where* persons sleep.
FAC'TORY, *n. (facio), a place where* articles are made.
MEM'ory, *n. the thing* or faculty *that* remembers.

Ory.

Signifies *of; belonging* or *relating to; ing.*

PREF'ATORY, *a. belonging* or *relating to* a preface.
VALEDIC'TORY, *n. (vale, dico), relating to* a farewell.
EXPLAN'ATORY, *a.* explain*ing.*
SATISFAC'TORY, *a.* satisfy*ing.*

Ose.

Signifies *full of.*

JOCOSE', *a. (jocus), full of* jokes.
VERBOSE', *a. (verbum), full of* words.

Ous.

Signifies *full of; consisting of; ing.*

DAN'GERous, *a. full of* danger.
GLO'RIous, *a. full of* glory.
GRIEV'ous, *a. full of* grief.
LABO'RIous, *a. full of* labor.
MUR'DERous, *a.* murder*ing.*

Ry.

Signifies *a being; the art of; the place where.*

BRA'VEry, *n. a being* brave.
SLA'VEry, *n. a being* a slave.
COOK'Ery, *n. the art of* a cook.
SUR'GEry, *n. the art of* a surgeon.

Ship.

Signifies *office of; state of.*

CLERK'ship, *n. the office of* a clerk.
HORSE'MANship, *n. the office of* a horseman.
FRIEND'ship, *n. the state of* a friend.
RI'VALship, *n. the state of* a rival.

Some.

Signifies *somewhat; full of.*

DARK'some, *a. somewhat* dark.
GLAD'some, *a. somewhat* glad.
WEA'RIsome, *a. somewhat* weary.
FROL'ICsome, *a. full of* frolic.

SUFFIXES.

Ster.
Signifies *one who*.

GAME'ster, *n. one who* games or gambles.
SONG'ster, *n. one who* sings.
YOUNG'ster, *n. one who* is young.

Tude, Ude.
Signifies *being* or *state of being*.

AL'TItude, *n. (altus),* the *state of being* high.
FOR'TItude, *n. (fortis),* the *state of being* brave.
REC'TItude, *n. (rectus),* the *state of being* right.
SER'VItude, *n. (servio), n.* the *state of being* a slave.

Ule.
Signifies *little* or *small*.

ANIMAL'cule, *n.* a *little* animal.
GLOB'ule, *n.* a *little* globe.
GRAN'ule, *n. (granum),* a *little* grain.
RET'Icule, *n.* a *little* net or bag.

Ure.
Signifies *the thing; state of being; act of*.

CREA'Ture, *n. the thing* created.
ENCLO'sure, *n. the thing* that is enclosed.
SCRIP'Ture, *n. (scribo), the thing* written.
COMPO'sure, *n.* the *state of being* composed.
EXPO'sure, *n.* the *state of being* exposed.
DEPART'ure, *n.* the *act of* departing.

Ward.
Signifies *in the direction of*, or *looking toward*.

EAST'ward, *ad. in the direction of* the east.
HEAV'ENward, *ad. in the direction of* heaven.
HOME'ward, *ad. looking towards* home.
WIND'ward, *ad. looking towards* the wind.

Y.
Signifies *the being; the state of being; ing*.

HON'ESTy, *n. state of being* honest.
MAS'TERy, *n. state of being* master.
MOD'ESTy, *n. state of being* modest.
COL'LOQUy, *n. (loquor),* a talk*ing* together.

Y.
Signifies *full of; consisting* or *made of*.

BLOOD'y, *a. full of* blood.
BRI'Ny, *a. full of* brine.
DEW'y, *a. full of* dew.
CLAY'ey, *a. consisting of* clay.
FLESH'y, *a. consisting of* flesh.
ROCK'y, *a. consisting of* rock.

GREEK PREFIXES.

A, An, (a Privative.*)
Signifies *want of, not,* or *without.*

*A*BYSS', *n.* (*byssos*), *without* a bottom.
An'ARCHY, *n.* (*arche*), *want of* government.
*A*NOM'ALY, *n.* (*omalos*), *not* or *none* like.
*A*P'ATHY, *n.* (*pathos*), *want of* feeling.
A'THEIST, *n.* (*theos*), one *without* a God.

Amphi, Ambi, (ἀμφι, and *ambo,* Lat. *both.*)
Signifies *both* or *double.*

*Amphi*B'IOUS, *a.* (*bios*), living *both* on land and in water.
*Ambi*DEX'TROUS, *a.* (*dexter*), using *both* hands.

Ana, (ἀνα.)
Signifies *through, up, back,* or *again.*

*Ana*L'YSIS, *n.* (*lysis*), a loosing *back* or *again.*
*Ana*T'OMY, *n.* (*tomos*), a cutting *through* or *up.*

Anti, Ant, (ἀντι.)
Signifies *against, opposite* or *opposed to.*

*Ant*ARC'TIC, *n.* (*arctos*), *opposite to* the north.
*Anti*BIL'IOUS, *a.* (*bilis*), *against* bile.
*Anti*P'ATHY, *n.* (*pathos*), feeling *against.*

Apo, Aph, (ἀπο.)
Signifies *from* or *away.*

*Apo*C'RYPHA, *n.* (*crypto*), writings concealed *from.*
Apos'TATE, *n.* (*sto*), one who stands *from* or *away.*
Apos'TLE, *n.* (*stello*), one sent *from.*
Aphe'LION, *n.* the point farthest *from* the sun.

Cata, Cat, (κατα.)
Signifies *down, from side to side.*

Cat'ALOGUE, *n.* (*logos*), words or names written *down.*
*Cat*ARRH', *n.* (*rheo*), a flowing *down.*
Cat'ECHISE, *v.* (*echeo*), to make sounds *from side to side.*

Dia, Di, (δια.)
Signifies *through, asunder.*

*Di*ÆR'ESIS, *n.* (*æresis*), a taking *asunder* or separately.
*Dia*G'ONAL, *a.* (*gonia*), *through* the angles.
*Dia*M'ETER, *n.* (*metrum*), the measure *through.*
*Dia*PH'ANOUS, *a.* (*phano*), appearing *through.*

---

* *Privative, n.* a letter or syllable prefixed to a word, which changes it from an affirmative to a negative sense.

GREEK PREFIXES.

En, Em.
Signifies *in* or *on*.

*En*DEM'IC, *a.* (*demos*), arising *in* or *among* the people.
*En*THU'SIAST, *n.* (*theos*), one who believes that God is *in* him.
Em'PHASIS, *n.* (*phano*), a stress of voice *on*.

Epi, (επι.)
Signifies *upon*.

*Ep*iDEM'IC, *a.* (*demos*), *upon* the people.
Ep'iGRAM, *n.* (*grapho*), something written *upon*.
Ep'iLOGUE, *n.* (*logos*), what is spoken *upon* or *after*.
Ep'iTAPH, *n.* (*taphos*), *upon* one who is buried.

Hyper, (ὑπερ.)
Signifies *above, over,* or *beyond*.

*Hyper*BO'REAN, *a.* (*boreas*), *beyond* the north.
*Hyper*CRIT'ICAL, *a. over*critical.
Hyper'BOLE, *n.* (*bole*), a shooting *beyond* the mark.

Eu, or Ev, (ευ.).
Signifies *good*.

*Eu*LO'GIUM, *n.* (*logos*), a *good* word.
Eu'PHONY, *n.* (*phone*), a *good* sound.
*Ev*AN'GEL, *n.* (*angelos*), *good* tidings; the gospel.

Hypo, (ὑπο.)
Signifies *under*.

*Hypo*TH'ESIS, *n.* (*thesis*), what is placed *under*.

Meta, (μετα.)
Signifies *beyond, according to*.

Met'APHOR, *n.* (*phero*), a word carried *beyond* its ordinary meaning
*Meta*PHYS'ICS, *n.* (*physis*), the science of things *beyond* nature.
Meth'OD, *n.* (*odos*), *according to* a way or plan.

Para, Par, (παρα.)
Signifies *beside, like* or *similar*.

Par'ALLEL, *a.* (*allelon*), *beside* one another.
Par'αPHRASE, *n.* (*phrasis*), a phrase *beside* or *like* another.
Par'ODY, *n.* (*ode*), a song or poem *like* or *imitative* of another.

Peri, (περι.)
Signifies *round, about*.

*Peri*CRA'NIUM, *n.* (*cranium*), *round* the cranium.
*Peri*M'ETER, *n.* (*metrum*), the measure *round*.

Syn, (συν.)
Signifies *together, with*.

Syn'OD, *n.* (*odos*), a way or coming *together*.
Synon'YMOUS, *a.* (*onoma*), named *together* or *like*.
Synop'SIS, *n.* (*opto*), a looking *together*.
Syn'TAX, *n.* (*tactos*), a pulling *together*.

***Sy*, for *Syn*.**
Signifies *together, with*.

*Sys'*TEM, *n.* (*stasis*), a standing *together*.
*Sys'*TOLE, *n.* (*stello*), a sending *together*.

***Syl*, for *Syn*.**
Signifies *together, with*.

*Syl'*LABLE, *n.* (*labo*), a taking *together*.

***Sym*, for *Syn*.**
Signifies *together, with*.

*Sym'*METRY, *n.* (*metrum*), a measuring *together*.
*Sym'*PATHY, *n.* (*pathos*), a feeling *with*.

GREEK ALPHABET.

Letter.		Sound.	Name.
Α	α	a	Alpha.
Β	β ϐ	b	Beta.
Γ	γ	g	Gamma.
Δ	δ	d	Delta.
Ε	ε	e as in *met*	Epsilon.
Ζ	ζ	z	Zeta.
Η	η	e as in *me*	Eta.
Θ	θ ϑ	th	Theta.
Ι	ι	i	Iota.
Κ	κ	k	Kappa.
Λ	λ	l	Lambda.
Μ	μ	m	Mu.
Ν	ν	n	Nu.
Ξ	ξ	x	Xi.
Ο	ο	o as in *not*	Omicron.
Π	π	p	Pi.
Ρ	ρ	r	Rho.
Σ	σ, ς final	s	Sigma.
Τ	τ	t	Tau.
Υ	υ	u or y	Upsilon.
Φ	φ	ph	Phi.
Χ	χ	ch	Chi.
Ψ	ψ	ps	Psi.
Ω	ω	o as in *no*	Omega.

ANGLO-SAXON ROOTS AND DERIVATIVES.

Æft—Behind.   Bæftan—Behind.

Aft, *ad.* behind; astern.
Aft'er, *prep.* following in place or time.
Abaft', *ad.* behind; towards the stern of a ship.
Behind, *ad.* at the back of.
Behind'hand, *a.* in arrears; backward.

Beatan—to Beat; Bate.

Abate', *v.* to lessen; to diminish.
Beat, *v.* to strike; to bruise.
Bate, *v.* to lessen; to grow less.
Beat'en, *p. a.* made smooth by treading.
Unabat'ed, *a.* not abated.
Unbat'ed, *a.* not lessened.
Unbeat'en, *a.* not beaten.
Abate'ment, *n.* diminution; decrease.

Betan—to Push Forward; to Promote.

Abet', *v.* to encourage; to aid. | Abet'ter, *n.* one who abets.

Abidan—to Stay in a Place; to Dwell.

Abide', *v.* to stay in a place; to wait
Bide, *v.* to dwell; to wait for. [for.
Abid'ing, *n.* continuance; stay.
Abode', *n.* a dwelling-place.

Aboard', *ad.* *a-board,* within a ship.

Bodian—to Command; to Announce; to Foretell.

Bode, *v.* to foreshow.
Abode', *v.* to foretoken.
Forebode', *v.* to foretell.
Unforbod'ing, *a.* giving no omens.
Abod'ing, *n.* presentiment.
Bode'ment, *n.* an omen.
Bod'ing, *n.* an omen.
Forebod'er, *n.* one who forebodes.
Forebod'ing, *n.* perception beforehand.

Abutan—About; Around.

About', *prep.* round; near to. | About', *ad.* here and there.

Abufan. Be—By, and ufan—Aloft.

Above', *prep.* in a higher place; more than.
Above'all, *ad.* in the first place.
Above'board, *ad.* in open sight.
Above'ground, *a.* alive.

Abreast', *ad.* *a, breast,* side by side.

Abroad', *ad.* *brad,* from home; in another country.

Cursian—to Curse; to Doom.

Accurse', *v.* to doom to misery.
Accursed', *a.* doomed; execrable.
Curse, *v.* to wish evil to; to afflict.
Cursed, *a.* deserving a curse.

Æce—Pain.

Ache, n. a continued pain. | Unach′ing, a. not feeling pain.

Ac, aac—an Oak.

Oak, n. a forest tree.
A′corn, n. (corn, grain), the seed of the oak.

Bar′nacle, n. (bearn, a child), a shell-fish.
Oak′en, n. made of oak.
Ac′ton, n. oaktown.

Æcer—a Field.

A′cre, n. 4840 square yards of land. | A′cred, a. possessing acres.

Adl—Diseased; Corrupted.

Ad′dlepate, n. a person of weak intellect. | Ad′dle, a. barren; unfruitful.

Ado′, n. a, do, trouble; bustle; unnecessary turmoil.

Afraid′, a. (afered, aferan, to frighten), struck with fear.

Foran—Before; Fore.

Afore′, prep. before; sooner than.
Afore′hand, ad. previous provision.
Afore′named, a. named before.
Afore′said, a. said before.

Before′, prep. in front of.
Fore, a. coming or going first.
Forearm′, v. to prepare for attack.
Before′hand, ad. previously.

Gan—to Go. Agan—Gone; Past.
Gang—a Going; a Journey; a Path.

Age, n. any period of time.
Aged, a. old.
Go, v. to walk; to move; to proceed.
Went, pret. of Go.
Gone, pp. of Go; advanced.
Non′age, n. minority; under age.
Go′er, n. one who goes.
Go′by, n. a passing by; evasion.
Gait, n. manner and air of walking.
Go-to, int. come, come.

Ago, ad. in time past.
Ago′ing, ppr. a. in motion.
Agone′, ad. in time past.
Forego′, v. to quit; to give up.
Gad, v. to ramble about.
Gad′der, n. one who goes about idly.
Outgo′, v. to surpass; to go beyond.
Overgo′, v. to surpass.
Undergo′, v. to suffer; to endure.
Gang, n. a troop; a band.

Gang′way, n. a passage.

Gast—the Breath; a Spirit.

Gast, v. to frighten; to terrify.
Aghast′, a. struck with horror.
Gas, n. an æriform fluid.
Gas′eous, a. having the form of gas.

Ghast′ly, ad. like a ghost.
Ghast′liness, n. paleness; frightful aspect.
Ghost, n. the soul; the spirit.
Ghost′ly, a. relating to the soul.

Note.—Gastric, (comes from the Greek gaster,) belonging to the stomach.

Æge, ege—Fear.

A′gue, n. an intermitting fever with cold fits. | A′gued, a. shivering.

Eglan—to PAIN; to TROUBLE.

AIL, *v.* to pain; to trouble.
AIL'ING, *ppr. a.* sickly.
AIL'MENT, *n.* disease.

ALBE'IT, *ad. all, be, it,* although, notwithstanding.

Eld—AGE; TIME. *Eald*—OLD.

OLD, *a.* advanced in years.
ELD, *n.* old age; old people.
AL'DERMAN, *n.* a magistrate.
OLDEN, *a.* old; ancient.
EL'DER, *n.* one more advanced in years; a church officer.
CO-EL'DER, *n.* an officer with.
EL'DERLY, *a.* bordering upon old age.
EL'DEST, *a.* oldest.

Acerran—to TURN.

AJAR', *ad.* half or partly open.

Ealé, from Ælan—to KINDLE; to INFLAME.

ALE'HOUSE, *n.* a house where ale is sold.
ALE, *n.* fermented malt liquor.

Eal—ALL.

AL'SO, *ad. swa,* in the same manner; likewise.
ALL, *a.* the whole; every one.

Lecgan—to LAY.

LAY, *v.* to place; to put; to calm.
ALLAY', *v.* to quiet; to soothe.
LAY'ER, *n.* a stratum; one that lays.
FORELAY', *v.* to lay beforehand.
INLAY', *v.* to insert other substances.
MISLAY', *v.* to lay in a wrong place.
OUT'LAY, *n.* expenditure.
OVERLAY', *v.* to cover; to smother.
UNLAID', *a.* not placed.
UPLAY', *v.* to lay up.
LEDGE, *n.* a layer; a stratum.
LED'GER, *n.* an account book.
LEG'ER, *n.* a resident.
ALLAY'MENT, *n.* the act of allaying.
BELAY', *v.* to block up; to fasten a rope.

Hlot—LOT.

LOT, *n.* fortune; chance; portion.
LOT'TERY, *n.* a game of chance.
ALLOT', *v.* to give by chance.
ALLOT'MENT, *n.* that which is allotted.

Lyfan—to PERMIT.

ALLOW', *v.* to admit; to permit.
DISALLOW', *v.* to refuse permission.
ALLOW'ABLE, *a.* that may be allowed.
ALLOW'ANCE, *n.* permission; sanction.

Belæwan—to BETRAY.

ALLURE', *v.* to entice; to decoy.
ALLUR'ING, *p. a.* enticing.

Almes—ALMS.

ALMS, *n.* what is given to the poor.
AL'MONER, *n.* one who gives alms.
ALMS'GIVER, *n.* one who gives alms.
ALMS'HOUSE, *n.* a house for the poor.

***Lyft*—the Air; the Heavens.**

Loft, n. the highest floor.	Lof'ty, a. high; proud.
Aloft', ad. on high; in the air.	Lof'tiness, n. elevation; pride.

Alone', a. *all, one,* single; solitary.

***Lang*—Long. *Leng*—Length. *Hlanc*—Lank.**

Length, n. extent from end to end.	Lin'gering, a. slow.
Length'en, v. to make longer.	Long, a. extended.
Length'wise, ad. in the direction of the length.	Along', ad. at length.
	Along'side, ad. side by side.
Length'y, a. long.	Lank, a. thin; slender; spare.
Lin'ger, v. to delay; to loiter.	Lank'y, a. tall and thin.

Lank'ness, n. slimness; leanness.

***Hlowan, hlewan*—to Low; to Bellow. *Hlud*—Loud.**

Loud, a. noisy; so as to be heard far.	Loud'ness, n. force of sound.
Loud'ly, ad. noisily.	Aloud', ad. with a great noise.

***Hraed*—Prompt.**

Read'y, a. prepared; willing.	Read'ily, ad. promptly; quickly.
Read'iness, n. promptitude.	Alread'y, ad. now; at this time.

Altogeth'er, ad. *all, to, gather,* completely; without exception.

Al'ways, ad. *all, way,* perpetually; constantly.

Am—the first person singular of the verb to Be.

***Mœgen*—Power; Strength; Main.**

Main, a. principal; chief; mighty: force.	Main'mast, n. the principal mast.
	Main'land, n. the principal land; the continent.
Main'ly, ad. principally; chiefly.	
Main'sail, n. the principal sail.	Amain', ad. with force; violently.

***Mase*—a Whirlpool.**

Maze', n. a labyrinth; perplexity; uncertainty.	Unamazed', a. not perplexed.
	Ma'zy, a. winding; perplexed.
Amaze', v. to astonish; to perplex.	Ama'zing, p. a. astonishing; wonderful.
Amazed', a. perplexed.	

Bemaze', v. to bewilder.

***Ambeht*—a Servant; a Message.**

Ambas'sador, n. a person sent from one power to another.	Em'bassy, n. the message of an ambassador.

***Middel*—Equally Distant.**

Mid'dle, a. equally distant from the extremes.	Midst, n. the middle.
	Mid'dleaged, a. middle of life.
Mid'dling, a. middle rank or size.	Mid'heaven, n. middle of the sky.

ANGLO-SAXON ROOTS AND DERIVATIVES. 73

MID'NIGHT, n. middle of the night.
MID'STREAM, n. middle of the stream.
MID'SUMMER, n. middle of the summer.
MID'WAY, n. the middle of the way.

MID'WINTER, n. the middle of the winter.
MID'RIFF, n. the diaphragm.
AMIDST', prep. in the middle.
AMID', prep. in the middle.

Missian—to MISS.

MISS, v. to fail in aim; not to succeed. | AMISS', a. faulty; wrong; improper.

Amang, from mengan—to MIX.

AMONG', AMONGST', prep. mingled with.

Angel—a HOOK.

AN'GLE, v. to fish with a rod and hook. | AN'GLER, n. one who angles.
AN'GLING, n. fishing with a rod and line.

NOTE.—ANGLE, a corner, comes from the Greek ἀγκύλη, any thing bent.

Æl—OIL. *Ælan*—to OIL; to SMEAR.

OIL, n. an unctuous animal matter.
OIL'Y, a. like oil; greasy.

ANNEAL', v. to heat and cool slowly in oil.
NEAL, v. to temper by heat and oil.

A'NON, ad. *on, an,* in one; quickly; soon; in a short time.

ANOTH'ER, a. *an, other,* not the same; some other; one more.

Answarian. And—AGAINST, and *Swaran*—to SWEAR.

AN'SWER, v. to speak in return; to reply to.

AN'SWER, n. a reply.
AN'SWERABLE, a. admitting a reply.

Ænig—ANY.

AN'Y, a. every; whoever. | AN'YWHERE, ad. in any place.

APACE', ad. *a, pace,* quickly, hastily.

Apa—APE.

APE, n. a kind of monkey.
APE, v. to imitate, to mimic.

A'PISH, a. like an ape; silly.
A'PISHNESS, n. mimicry.

Æpl—APPLE.

AP'PLE, n. the fruit of the apple tree. | AP'PLE-JACK, n. cider brandy.

NOTE.—APPLE OF THE EYE, the pupil of the eye. APPLE OF DISCORD, cause of general contention. APPLE-PIE ORDER, perfect order.

Arisan—to ARISE.

ARISE', v. to mount upward; to get up.

RISE, v. to get up; to grow.
ROUSE, v. to wake from repose.
AROUSE', v. to wake from sleep; to excite.

Earm—an ARM.

ARM, *n.* the limb from the hand to the shoulder.
ARM'FUL, *n.* what the arm can hold.
ARM'LET, *n.* a bracelet.
ARM'PIT, *n.* the cavity under the shoulder.

NOTE.—ARMS, weapons of defence, is from the Latin (*armo*).

Arewe—ARROW.

AR'ROW, *n.* the pointed weapon shot from a bow.
AR'ROWY, *a.* like an arrow; swift; straight.

Æse—ASH.

ASH, *n.* a tree or its wood.
ASH'EN, *a.* made of ash.

Asca—DUST.

ASH'ES, *n.* the remains of any thing burnt.
ASH'Y, *a.* like ashes; pale.

Acsian—to ASK.

ASK, *v.* to beg; to demand; to question; to inquire.
ASK'ER, *n.* a petitioner; an inquirer.
UNASKED', *a.* not asked.

Æsp—ASP; ASPEN.

ASP, AS'PEN, *n.* a tree with trembling leaves.
AS'PEN, *a.* trembling.

NOTE.—ASP, a serpent, comes from the Latin (*aspis*).

Nafegar—a NAVE BORER.

AU'GER-HOLE, *n.* a hole made by an auger.
AU'GER, *n.* a tool for boring holes.

NOTE.—AUGUR, to predict, is from the Latin (*augur*).

Awacian—AWAKE.

AWAKE', *v.* to rouse from sleep.
AWAKE', *a.* not asleep.
AWA'KEN, *v.* to rouse from sleep.

Ege—FEAR; DREAD.

AWE, *n.* reverential fear; dread.
AW'FUL, *a.* that strikes with awe.
AWE'STRUCK, *a.* impressed with awe.

Awk and ward.

AWK'WARD, *a.* clumsy; inelegant.
AWK'WARDNESS, *n.* clumsiness.

NOTE.—AWK, wrong, left-handed, ungainly; WARD, a suffix signifying direction or tendency to or from.

Writhan—WRITHE.

WRITHE, *v.* to twist; to distort.
AWRY', *ad.* obliquely; asquint.

Bæc—the BACK.

BACK, n. the hinder part; behind.
BACK, v. to place on the back; to maintain; to move back.
BACK'BITE, v. to speak ill of the absent.
BACK'BONE. n. the bone of the back.
BACK'GROUND, n. the ground behind.
BACK'SLIDE, v. to apostatize.
BACK'WARD, ad. with the back forwards; unwilling.

Bacan—to BAKE.

BAKE, v. to dry and harden by heat.
BAK'ER, n. one who bakes.
BAK'ERY, n. a baker's workplace.
BA'CON, n. hog's flesh dried in smoke
BATCH, n. the quantity baked at once.
BASK, v. to warm by laying in the sun.

Beag—a CROWN; a GARLAND.

BADGE, n. a mark or token of distinction.

Baelg—a BAG.

BAG, n. a sack; a pouch.
BAG'GAGE, n. the trunks, &c., of a traveler.
BAG'PIPE, n. a musical instrument.
BEL'LOWS, n. an instrument for blowing a fire.
BEL'LY, n. the part of anything which swells out.
BILGE, n. the part of a ship's bottom which swells out.
BIL'LOW, n. a swollen wave.
BULGE, v. to swell out.

Batan—to LURE FISH WITH FOOD ON A HOOK.

BAIT, v. to put meat on a trap as a lure; to give refreshment on a journey.

Balc—a BEAM; a RIDGE.

BAL'CONY, n. a gallery before a window.
BALK, n. a great beam; a ridge of land.
BALK, v. to disappoint; to frustrate.

Behlæstan—to LOAD A SHIP. From bat, a boat, and hlæst, a load.

BAL'LAST, n. heavy matter put at the bottom of a ship to keep it steady.

Bannan—to PROCLAIM.

BAN, n. a public notice.
BANS, n. proclamation of marriage.
BAN'DIT, n. an outlaw.

Bindan—to BIND.

BIND, v. to confine with bonds; to gird.
BOUND, pp. made fast by a band; confined.
BAND, n. anything which binds.
BAND'AGE, n. that which binds.
BOND, n. anything that binds.
BOND'AGE, n. slavery.
BAN'NER, n. a flag; a standard.
BOUND, n. a limit; that which restrains.
BOUND'ARY, n. a limit.
BOUND'EN, a. obliged.
BOUND'LESS, a. without bound.

NOTE.—A banner is a band, bond, or sign of union.—BOUND, to jump, to leap, is from the French (bondir).

Bana—Destruction.

Bane, *n.* poison. | Bane'ful, *a.* poisonous.

Banc—a Bench; a Hillock; a Bank.

Bank, *n.* a mound or ridge; a place for money.
Imbank', *v.* to inclose with a bank.
Bank'rupt, *n.* one who cannot pay his debts.
Bench, *n.* a long seat.

Bar—Naked. *Abarian*—to Strip Off.

Bare, *a.* naked; without clothes.
Bare'ly, *ad.* nakedly; merely.
Bare'ness, *n.* nakedness.
Bare'faced, *a.* shameless; impudent.
Bare'headed, *a.* with the head bare.
Bar'ren, *a.* unfruitful.
Bar'renness, *n.* sterility.

Beorcan—to Bark.

Bark, *v.* to make the noise of a dog.

Note.—Bark, the rind of a tree, comes from the Danish (*bark*), and Bark, a vessel, comes from the French (*barque*).

Bere—Barley.

Bar'ley, *n.* a species of grain.
Bere, *n.* a species of barley.
Beer, *n.* a liquor made of malt and hops.
Barn, *n.* (*ern*, a place), a house for farm produce.

Note.—Barn, from *bere*, barley, and *ern*, a place: a place for barley.

Beorma—Barm.

Barm, *n.* yeast. | Barm'y, *a.* containing barm.

Bat, beatan—to Beat.

Bat, *n.* a heavy stick. | Bat'on, *n.* a staff, a club.
Bat, *n.* a mass of cotton for quilts.

Note.—Bat, an animal, comes from the Danish (*bakke*).

Bæth—a Bath.

Bath, *n.* a place to bathe in. | Bathe, *v.* to wash in a bath.
Ba'ther, *n.* one who bathes.

Bellan—to Bawl.

Bawl, *v.* to cry aloud. | Bel'low, *v.* to make a noise like a bull.
Bel'lowing, *n.* a loud noise.

Bugan—to Bend.

Bay, *n.* an arm of the sea bending in.
Bay-win'dow, *n.* a window bending outward.
Bight, *n.* a bend of a rope.
Bow, *v.* to bend towards; an act of re-
Bu'gle, *n.* a hunting-horn. [spect.
Embay', *v.* to inclose in a bay.
Embow', *v.* to bend; to arch.

Note.—Bay, a brown color, comes from the Latin (*badius*); Bay, the laurel, comes from the Greek (*baion*), and Bay, to bark, comes from the French (*aboyer*).

Beon—to Be.

BE, *v.* to exist; to become. | BE'ING, *n.* existence.

NOTE.—BE, as a prefix, is the same word as *by*, and signifies *about, before.*

Beacen—a Sign.

BEA'CON, *n.* something to give notice or to direct. | BECK, *v.* to make a sign with the head.
BECK'ON, *v.* to make a sign to.

Bead—a Prayer. Biddan—to Pray, because one was dropped down a string every time a prayer was said.

BEA'DLE, *n.* (*bydel*, from *biddan*, to bid), a petty officer in a parish. | BEAD, *n.* a little ball.

Beam—a Tree.

BEAM, *n.* a ray of light; *v.* to shine forth. | BEAM, *n.* a piece of timber.

Beran—to Bear.

BEAR, *v.* to carry; to support; to endure.
BEAR'ING, *n.* gesture; mien.
FORBEAR', *v.* to cease from; to abstain.
FORBEAR'ANCE, *n.* command of temper; patience.
MISBORN', *a.* (*mis*), born to evil.
OVERBEAR', *v.* (*ofer*), to bear down; to repress.
UNBEAR'ABLE, *a.* not to be borne.
BORN, *pp.* brought forth.
| BORNE, *pp.* carried.
UNDERBEAR', *v.* to support; to endure.
UPBEAR', *v.* to raise aloft.
BAR'ROW, *n.* a small hand carriage.
BIRTH, *n.* the act of coming into life.
BIRTH'DAY, *n.* the day of one's birth.
BIRTH'PLACE, *n.* the place of one's birth.
BIRTH'RIGHT, *n.* the rights to which one is born.
BERTH, *n.* a room in a ship; a place

Bera—Bear.

BEAR, *n.* an animal. | BEAR'LIKE, *a.* resembling a bear.
BEAR'ISH, *a.* having the quality of a bear.

BEARD, *n.* *beard,* the hair on the lips and chin; *v.* to oppose to the face.

BEA'VER, *n.* *beofer,* an animal.

Becuman—to Happen; to Befall.

BECOME', *v.* to suit; to befit.
BECOM'ING, *a.* graceful; seemly.
MISBECOME', *v.* not to become.
| UNBECOME', *v.* not to become; not to be suitable to.
UNBECOM'ING, *a.* unsuitable; improper.

Bed—to Lay or Spread.

BED, *n.* something to sleep on.
BED'DING, *n.* the materials of a bed.
BED'CLOTHES, *n.* the coverlets on a bed.
| BED'RIDDEN, *a.* confined to bed by age or sickness.
BED'STEAD, *n.* the frame of a bed.
BED TIME, *n.* the time to go to bed.

Beo—Bee.

Bee, *n.* an insect that makes honey and wax.

Bee'hive, *n.* a box for holding bees.

Bece or boc—Beech; Book.

Note.—Boc, a book; from *boc*, a beech tree, the wood of this tree or its bark having been used to write upon.

Beech, *n.* a forest tree.
Beech'en, *a.* made of beech.

Book, *n.* a volume in which we read or write

Bytl—a Mallet.

Bee'tle, *n.* a heavy wooden mallet; an insect.
Bee'tle, *v.* to jut out; to hang over.

Bee'tle-browed, *a.* having prominent brows.
Bee'tle-headed, *a.* dull; stupid.

Beginnan—to Begin.

Begin', *v.* to commence.

Begin'ning, *n.* the first part.

Begone', *int.* be, gone, go away; hence.

Behefe—Gain.

Behalf', *n.* favor; cause; sake.

Be habban—to Restrain.

Behave', *v.* to conduct; to act.

Behav'ior, *n.* conduct; demeanor.

Behaes—a Self-command.

Behest', *n.* promise; a command.

Healdan—to Hold.   Helma—a Helve or Handle.

Hold, *v.* to grasp; to keep; to retain.
Hold'er, *n.* one that holds.
Helve, *n.* the handle of an axe.
Helm, *n.* the stick by which a rudder is turned.
Helms'man, *n.* one who controls a helm.
Hilt, *n.* a handle of a sword.
Hold'back, *n.* hinderance; restraint.
Hold'fast, *n.* that which holds.

Behold', *v.* to view; to see.
Behold'en, *p. a.* bound in gratitude.
Behold'er, *n.* one who beholds.
Forehold'ing, *n.* prediction.
Unbeheld', *a.* unseen.
Uphold', *v.* to support; to sustain.
Uphol'sterer, *n.* one who furnishes houses.
Uphol'stery, *n.* furniture for houses.
Withhold', *v.* to hold back; to refuse.

Behoflan—to Want; to Be Necessary.

Behoove', *v.* to be necessary; to want. | Behoof', *n.* profit; advantage.

Bealcan—to Swell or Heave.

Belch, *v.* to eject wind from the stomach.

Geliefan—to Trust; to Believe.

Believe', v. to credit; to put confidence in.
Belief', n. opinion; faith.
Believ'er, n. one who believes.
Disbelieve', v. not to believe.

Misbelieve', v. to believe erroneously.
Misbelief', n. erroneous belief.
Unbelieve', v. not to believe or trust.
Unbelief', n. incredulity; infidelity.
Unbeliev'er, n. an infidel.

Bell—Bell.

Bell, n. a hollow sounding vessel of metal.
Bel'fry, n. the place where a bell is hung.

Bell'founder, n. one who makes bells.
Bell'metal, n. a mixture of copper and tin.

Bell'wether, n. a sheep which carries a bell.

Below', prep. *be, low,* under, in place, time, or dignity.

Belt, n. *belt,* a girdle; a band.

Bendan—to Bend.

Bend, v. to make crooked; to incline.
Bend, n. a curve; a crook.

Bent, n. state of being curved; fixed purpose.

Becwæthan—to Say; to Give by Will.

Bequeath', v. to leave by will to another.

Bequest', n. something left by will.

Bereave', v. *bereafan,* to deprive of; to take away from.

Ber'ry, n. *beria,* any small fruit containing seeds.

Secan—to Seek.

Seek, v. to look for; to search for.
Sought, p. looked for; searched for.
Beseech', v. to entreat; to beg; to implore.
Besought', p. entreated; implored.

Forsake', v. to leave; to desert.
Forsook', p. quitted; deserted.
Forsak'en, a. deserted; left.
Unsought', a. not sought; without seeking.

Beside', Besides, ad. *be, side,* at the side of; over and above.

Be'som, n. *besm,* a broom.

Best, a. *best,* good in the highest degree.

Stow—a Place; to Stow.

Stow, v. to place; to lay up.
Stow'age, n. room for laying up.

Bestow', v. to give; to confer.
Bestow'al, n. the act of bestowing.

Bestow'er, n. one who bestows.

Streowian—to Strew.

Strew, v. to scatter; to spread.
Bestrew', v. to sprinkle over.

Strew'ed, p. scattered.

Stridan, strædan—to SPREAD.

STRIDE, *v.* to walk with long steps; *n.* a long step.

BESTRIDE′, *v.* to place a leg on each side.

Bad—BET.

BET, *n.* a wager; to wager.

BET′TOR, *n.* one who bets.

BET′TER, *v. betrian,* to improve; to advance; *a.* superior.

BETWEEN′, *prep. be, twegen,* in the intermediate space.

Wicce—WITCH.

WITCH, *n.* a woman given to unlawful arts.
WITCH′ERY, *n.* enchantment; sorcery.
WITCH′CRAFT, *n.* the practices of witches.

BEWITCH′, *v.* to charm; to enchant.
BEWITCH′ERY, *n.* fascination; charm.
BEWITCH′ING, *a.* fascinating; enchanting.

BEYOND′, *prep. be, geond,* on the farther side of.

Biddan—to ASK; to PRAY; to COMMAND.

BID, *v.* to command; to offer.
BID′DER, *n.* one who bids.
BID′DING, *n.* command; offer of a price.
FORBID′, *v.* to prohibit; to oppose.
FORBID′DEN, *p. a.* prohibited.

FORBID′DING, *a.* repulsive.
OUTBID′, *v.* to offer a higher price.
OVERBID′, *v.* to bid more.   [ed.
UNBID′, *v.* not invited; not commanded.
UNFORBID′DEN, *a.* permitted; allowed.

BIER, *n. baer,* a carriage for the dead.

Byggan—to BUILD.

BIG, *a.* great; large; huge.

BIG′NESS, *n.* bulk; size.

Byl—BILE.

BILE, *n.* a sore, painful tumor terminating in a pustule.

NOTE.—This word is now more commonly spelt *boil*, although the orthography of bile is more in accordance with its etymology.
BILE, an animal fluid, comes from the Latin (*bilis*).

Bile—BILL.

BILL, *n.* the beak of a fowl.

BILL, *v.* to caress; to fondle.

Bil—STEEL.

BILL, *n.* a hatchet with a point, like the beak of a bird.

BIL′LET, *n.* a small log of wood.

NOTE.—BILL, a written paper, comes from the French (*billet*).

BIN, *n. bin,* a manger; a cell or chest for grain, wine, &c.

Bird—BIRD.

BIRD, *n.* a general name for the feathered kind.
BIRD'CAGE, *n.* an inclosure to keep birds in.
BIRD'CATCHER, *n.* one who catches birds.
BIRD'LIME, *n.* a glue to catch birds.
BIRD'S'-EYE, *a.* seen from above.

Bitan—to BITE.

BITE, *v.* to crush with the teeth.
BITE, *n.* the wound made by the teeth.
BIT, *n.* a small piece; the part of a bridle to put into a horse's mouth.
BI'TING, *n.* the act of biting; *a.* sharp; severe.

Biter—BITTER.

BIT'TER, *a.* biting to the taste; sharp.
BIT'TERLY, *ad.* in a bitter manner.
BIT'TERNESS, *n.* a bitter taste; malice; sorrow.

Blæc or *blac*—BLACK; BLEAK.

BLACK, *a.* of the color of night.
BLACK'EN, *v.* to make black.
BLACK'GUARD, *n.* a mean, wicked fellow.
BLACK'SMITH, *n.* a smith that works in iron.
BLEAK, *a.* pale; cold; dreary.
BLEAK'LY, *ad.* in a cold situation.
BLEAK'NESS, *n.* dreariness; coldness.

BLADE, *n. blaed,* a spire of grass; the cutting part of an instrument.

Blegen—a BLISTER; a BLAIN.

BLAIN, *n.* a pustule; a blotch.
CHIL'BLAIN, *n.* a sore caused by frost.

Blæst, blæstan—to PUFF; to BLOW.

BLAST, *n.* a gust or puff of wind; an explosion of gunpowder in rocks.
BLAST, *v.* to wither; to injure; to split rocks.
BLAST'ING, *n.* destruction; explosion.
BLUS'TER, *v.* to roar as a storm.
BLUS'TERING, *n.* noise; tumult.
BLIS'TER, *n.* a thin bladder on the skin.
BLOW, *v.* to make a current of air.
BLOW'ING, *n.* the motion of the wind.
BLOAT, *v.* to swell; to puff up.

NOTE.—BLOW, a stroke, a sudden calamity, comes from the Dutch (*blouwer*).

Blætan—BLEAT.

BLEAT, *v.* to cry as a sheep.
BLA'TANT, *a.* bellowing as a calf.
BLEAT'ING, *n.* the cry of lambs or sheep.

Blæse—a BLAZE.

BLAZE, *n.* a flame; a stream of light; a white spot.
BLAZE, *v.* to make public; to make a white mark on a tree.
BLA'ZONRY, *n.* the art of blazoning.
BLA'ZON, *v.* to adorn; to display; to make public.
EMBLA'ZON, *v.* to deck in glaring colors.
EMBLA'ZONRY, *n.* pictures on shields.

Blæcan—to FADE; to WHITEN.

BLEACH, *v.* to make white.
BLEACH'ERY, *n.* a place for bleaching

Bledan—to BLEED.

BLEED, *v.* to lose or draw blood. | BLEED'ING, *n.* a running of blood.

BLEND, *v. blendan,* to mingle together.

Blessian—to CONSECRATE; to BLESS.

BLESS, *v.* to make happy; to wish happiness to. | BLESS'ED, *p. a.* happy; holy.
BLESS'ING, *n.* a prayer for happiness.

Belieth, 3d *per. sing.* of *belicgan*—to DESTROY.

BLIGHT, *n.* a pestilence among plants; mildew. | BLIGHT, *v.* to cause to wither or decay.

Blind—BLIND.

BLIND, *a.* wanting sight; *v.* to make blind. | BLIND'NESS, *n.* want of sight; ignorance.
BLIND'LY, *ad.* without sight. | BLIND'FOLD, *v.* to hinder from seeing.

Blican—to SHINE; to DAZZLE.

BLINK, *v.* to wink; to look with frequent winking. | BLINK, *v.* to purposely evade.

Blis—JOY; GLADNESS.

BLISS, *n.* the highest happiness. | BLISS'FUL, *a.* happy in the highest degree.
BLISS'FULLY, *ad.* in a blissful manner. |

Blithe—JOYFUL; MERRY.

BLITHE, *a.* gay; joyous. | BLITHE'SOME, *a.* gay; cheerful; merry.
BLITHE'LY, *ad.* in a blithe manner. |

Blod—BLOOD.

BLOOD, *n.* the red fluid that circulates in the bodies of animals. | BLOOD'SHOT, *a.* filled with blood; red.
BLOOD'Y, *a.* stained with blood; cruel. | BLOOD'THIRSTY, *a.* desirous to shed blood.
BLOOD'INESS, *n.* the state of being bloody. | BLOOD'VESSEL, *n.* a vein or artery.

Blosma—a FLOWER. *Blowan*—to BLOOM.

BLOS'SOM, *n.* the flower of a plant. | BLOW, *v.* to flower; to bloom; *n.* a blossom.
BLOOM, *n.* blossom.
BLOOM'ING, *a.* thriving in health, beauty, and vigor. | BLOWTH, *n.* bloom; blossom.

NOTE.—BLOW, a stroke, comes from the Dutch (*blowe*).

Bleo—BLUE.

BLUE, *n.* one of the primary colors. | BLU'ISH, *a.* blue in a small degree.
BLUE'NESS, *n.* the quality of being blue. | BLUE'-EYED, *a.* having blue eyes.

Blinnan—to Stop.

Blunt, *a.* dull on the edge or point; rough; rude.
Blunt'ness, *n.* want of edge; abruptness.
Blunt'ly, *ad.* in a blunt manner.

Ablisian—to Blush.

Blush, *v.* to redden with shame or confusion. [face.
Blush'ing, *n.* the reddening of the
Blush'less, *a.* without a blush; impudent.
Outblush', *v.* to exceed in rosy color
Unblush'ing, *a.* not blushing; destitute of shame.

Bar—Boar.

Boar, *n.* the male swine.
Boar'ish, *a.* swinish; brutal; cruel.
Brawn, *n.* the flesh of a boar; the muscular part of the body.
Brawn'y, *a.* muscular; fleshy; hard.
Brawn'iness, *n.* strength; hardness.

Bord—an Edge; a Side.

Board, *n.* a flat piece of wood; a table; food.
Board, *v.* to lay with boards; to live at for a price.
Board'er, *n.* one who boards.
Bor'der, *n.* the outer part or edge.
Imbor'der, *v.* to bound.

Note.—The Anglo-Saxon table was formed merely by placing a *board* upon trestles at the time of eating, and it was designated simply by the name of *board*.

Bat—a Boat or Ship.

Boat, *n.* a small, open vessel.
Boat'man, *n.* one who manages a boat.
Boat'swain, *n.* an officer in a ship.

Bodig—Body.

Bod'y, *n.* the material part of an animal.
Bod'ily, *a.* relating to the body; entirely.
Bod'ied, *a.* having a body.
Bod'ice, *n.* short stays for women.
Bod'yguard, *n.* a guard to protect the person.

Byl—Bile or Boil.

Bile, Boil, *n.* a sore, painful tumor.

Note.—Boil, to be agitated by heat, comes from the Latin (*bullio*).

Bald—Bold; Audacious.

Bold, *a.* daring; brave; impudent.
Bold'ly, *ad.* in a bold manner.
Bold'ness, *n.* courage; impudence.
Bold'faced, *a.* impudent.

Bolla—Any Round Vessel.

Boll, *n.* a round pod or capsule.
Bowl, *n.* a vessel to hold liquids.

Note.—Bowl, to roll, comes from the French (*boule*).

Bolster—a Pillow.

Bol'ster, *n.* a long pillow; *v.* to support; to hold up.

Bolt—a House; an Arrow.

Bolt, *n.* an arrow; the bar of a door.
Bolt, *v.* to leave or desert suddenly.
Bolt, *v.* to fasten with a bolt; to spring out suddenly.

Note.—Bolt, to sift, to separate from bran, comes from the Ger. (*beuteln*).

Ban—Bone.

Bone, *n.* the firm, hard substance in an animal body.
Bo′ny, *a.* full of bones.
Bone′ache, *n.* pain in the bones.

Beom—a Beam.

Boom, *n.* a pole used to extend a sail; a bar across a harbor, &c.

Note.—Boom, a deep hollow sound, comes from the Dutch *bommen*, to sound hollow.

Bene—a Prayer; a Petition.

Boon, *n.* a gift; a favor.

Note.—Boon, gay, merry, kind, comes from the Latin (*bonus*).

Gebur—a Countryman or Farmer. *Buan*—to Till.

Boor, *n.* a cultivator of the soil; a rude peasant.
Boor′ish, *a.* clownish; rude.
Bur′liness, *n.* bulk; bluster.
Boor′ishly, *ad.* in a boorish manner.
Bur′ly, *a.* (*boor-like*), big; tumid; boisterous.

Bote—Compensation; Satisfaction.

Boot, *v.* to profit; to advantage.
Boot′less, *a.* useless; unprofitable.
Boot′y, *n.* spoil; plunder.
To Boot, *ad.* over and above; besides.

Note.—Boot, a covering for the foot, comes from the French (′*otte*).

Borian—to Bore.

Bore, *v.* to make a hole by turning. | Bore, *v.* to vex or weary.

Burh—a City. *Beorg*—a Hill; a Citadel; a Refuge.

Bor′ough, *n.* a corporate town.
Burgh, *n.* a corporate town.
Bur′gess, *n.* a freeman of a burgh.
Bur′gher, *n.* a freeman of a burgh.
Bur′gomaster, *n.* a magistrate of a city.
Burg′lar, *n.* a thief who breaks into a house.
Burg′lary, *n.* housebreaking.
Burg′larious, *a.* relating to housebreaking.
Bur′row, *n.* a hole in the ground for [rabbits, &c.

Borgian—to Borrow; and *Bohr*—a Pledge.

Bor′row, *v.* to take the use of for a time.
Bor′rowing, *n.* the act of taking a loan.
Bor′rower, *n.* one who borrows.

Bosum—Bosom.

Bo′som, *n.* the breast; the heart. | Bo′som, *a.* confidential; intimate.

Both, a. *ba, twa,* the two; the one and the other.

Botm—BOTTOM.

BOT'TOM, *n.* the lowest part.
BOT'TOMED, *a.* having a bottom.
BOT'TOMLESS, *a.* without a bottom.
BOT'TOMRY, *n.* borrowing money on a ship.

Boga—ANYTHING CURVED; a BRANCH. *Bugan*—to BOW; to BEND.

BOUGH, *n.* a branch of a tree.
BOW, *n.* an instrument for shooting arrows; any thing in the form of a curve.
BOW'WINDOW, *n.* a projecting window.
BOW'LEGGED, *a.* having crooked legs.
BOW'STRING, *n.* the string of a bow.
BOW'SPRIT, *n.* the spar projecting from the head of a ship.

Bur—a DWELLING; a COTTAGE.

BOW'ER, *n.* a retired chamber; a shady recess.
BOW'ERY, *a.* having bowers; shady.
NEIGH'BOR, *n.* (*neah,* nigh), one who lives near.
NEIGH'BORHOOD, *n.* a place near.
NEIGH'BORLY, *a.* becoming a neighbor; kind; civil.
UNNEIGH'BORLY, *a.* not becoming a neighbor; not kind.

Box—BOX.

BOX, *n.* a case made of wood; a chest.

NOTE.—BOX, a blow with the fist, comes from the Welsh (*bock*), and BOX, a tree or shrub, from the Latin (*buxus*).

Boye—BOY.

BOY, *n.* a male child.
BOY'ISH, *a.* like a boy; childish.
BOY'HOOD, *n.* the state of a boy.

Bredan—to BRAID.

BRAID, *v.* to weave together.
BRAID, *n.* a texture; a knot.

Brægen—BRAIN.

BRAIN, *n.* the soft whitish mass inclosed in the skull.
BRAIN'LESS, *a.* silly; thoughtless.
BRAIN'SICK, *a.* disordered in the brain.

Brembel—BRAMBLE.

BRAM'BLED, *a.* overgrown with brambles.
BRAM'BLE, *n.* the blackberry bush.

Braes—BRASS.

BRASS, *n.* a yellow metal composed of copper and zinc.
BRA'ZIER, *n.* one who works in brass.
BRA'ZEN, *a.* made of brass; impudent.
BRAZE, *v.* to solder with brass.
BRA'ZENFACED, *a.* impudent; shameless.

Bread or *breod*—BREAD.

BREAD, *n.* food made of ground corn; support of life.

Bræd—BREADTH.

BREADTH, *n.* measure from side to side.

Brecan or *bracan*—to BREAK; to BRUISE.

BREAK, *v.* to part by violence.
BROACH, *v.* to tap; to let out liquor.
BRACK, *n.* a breach; a crack.
BRAKE, *n.* an instrument for retarding motion.
CRAKE, *n.* a thicket.
BRAY, *v.* to grind small.

BREACH, *n.* a gap; a quarrel; an infraction.
BREECH, *n.* the hinder part of anything.
OUT'BREAK, *n.* a bursting forth.
BREAK'ER, *n.* a wave broken by a rock.

BREAK'FAST, *n.* the first meal of the day.

NOTE.—BRAY, the noise of an ass, comes from the French (*braire*).

Breost—BREAST.

BREAST, *n.* the fore part of the body.
BREAST'BONE, *n.* the bone of the breast.
BREAST'KNOT, *n.* a knot worn on the breast.

BREAST'PIN, *n.* an ornament for the breast.
BREAST'WORK, *n.* a work as high as the breast.

Brœth—BREATH.

BREATH, *n.* the air drawn in and expelled by the lungs.
BREATH'ING, *n.* respiration.

BREATHE, *v.* to draw in and expel the air.
BREATH'FUL, *a.* full of breath.

BREATH'LESS, *a.* out of breath.

Bredan—to NOURISH.   *Brod*—a BROOD.

BREED, *v.* to give birth to; to bring up.
BREED, *n.* a race; a kind.
BREED'ING, *n.* education; manners; nurture.

BROOD, *n.* the number hatched at once.
BROOD, *v.* to sit as on eggs; to think long and anxiously about.
BRED, *pp.* brought up; nourished.

Briwan—to BREW; to MIX.

BREW, *v.* to make malt liquor; to mingle.
BREW'AGE, *n.* a mixture.

BREW'ER, *n.* one who brews.
BROTH, *n.* liquor in which flesh has been boiled.

BREW'ERY, *n.* a place for brewing.

Bryd—BRIDE.

BRIDE, *n.* a woman about to be married, or newly married.
BRI'DAL, *a.* a wedding; belonging to a wedding.

BRIDE'GROOM, *n.* a man about to be married, or newly married.
BRIDE'MAID, *n.* she who attends on the bride.

BRIDE'MAN, *n.* he who attends on the bridegroom.

Brycg—BRIDGE.

BRIDGE, *n.* a building raised over water for convenience of passage.

Bridl—BRIDLE.

BRI'DLE, *n.* the reins by which a horse is governed; a restraint.

BRI'DLE, *v.* to hold up the head in pride or resentment.

BRI'DLE, *v.* to restrain; to control.

Brær—BRIER; a PRICKLE.

BRI'ER, n. a prickly shrub. | BRI'ERY, a. full of briers.

Beorht or bryht—BRIGHT.

BRIGHT, a. clear; shining.
BRIGHT'EN, v. to make bright.
BRIGHT'LY, a. with lustre.
BRIGHT'NESS, n. lustre; glitter.
BERT, a. bright; a suffix used in forming names.

Brymme—BRIM.

BRIM, n. the upper edge of a vessel.
BRIM'FUL, a. full to the brim.
BRIM'LESS, a. without a brim.
BRIM'MING, a. full to the top.

Byrnan—to BURN. Brun—BROWN.

BURN, v. to consume with fire; to wound with fire.
BURN, n. a wound caused by fire.
BURNT, p. a. consumed; scorched.
BURN'ING, n. fire; flame.
OUTBURN', v. to exceed in burning.
UNBURNED', a. not burnt.
BRIN'DED, a. streaked, as if burnt.
BRIN'DLED, a. streaked; spotted.
BRUNT, n. the heat or violence of an onset; shock.

BROWN, n. the name of a color.
BROWN'ISH, a. somewhat brown.
BROWNSTUD'Y, n. deep thoughtfulness.
AU'BURN, a. brown; of a dark tan color.
BRAND, n. a burning piece of wood; a mark of infamy.
BRAND, v. to mark with a hot iron.
BRAND'ISH, v. to wave; to flourish.
BRIM'STONE, n. sulphur.

NOTE.—BURN, a brook, used in Scotland, comes from the Gothic (*brunna*).

Bryne—SALT LIQUOR.

BRINE, n. water impregnated with salt.
BRIN'ISH, a. saltish; like brine.
BRI'NY, a. salt; like brine.

Bringan—to BRING.

BRING, v. to fetch from; to attract.

Bristl, byrst—BRISTLE.

BRIS'TLE, n. the hair of a swine; stiff hair.
BRIS'TLE, v. to stand erect.
BRIST'LY, a. thick set with bristles.

Bryttian—to BREAK.

BRIT'TLE, a. easily broken. | BRIT'TLENESS, n. aptness to break.

Brad, bræd—BROAD.

BROAD, a. wide; extended from side to side.
BROAD'EN, v. to make broad.
BROAD'LY, ad. in a broad manner.
BROAD'CLOTH, n. a fine woolen cloth.
BROAD'SIDE, n. the side of a ship.

Brucan—to USE; to EMPLOY; to BEAR.

BROKE, v. to transact business for others.
BRO'KAGE, n. profit gained by promoting bargains.
BRO'KER, n. an agent or negotiator.
BRO'KERAGE, n. the pay or reward of a broker.
BROOK, v. to bear; to endure.

Broc—BROOK.

BROOK, *n.* a stream; a rivulet.

Brom—BROOM.

BROOM, *n.* a shrub; a brush with a long handle for sweeping.

BROOM'STICK, *n.* the handle of a broom.

Brother—BROTHER.

BROTH'ER, *n.* one born of the same parents.

BROTH'ERLY, *a.* like a brother; affectionate.

BROTH'ERLESS, *a.* without a brother.

Brœw—BROW.

BROW, *n.* the ridge over the eye; the forehead.

BROW'BEAT, *v.* to depress by stern looks.

Brysan—to BRUISE.

BRUISE, *v.* to crush or mangle by blows.

Bucca—BUCK.

BUCK, *n.* the male of certain animals.

BUCK'SKIN, *n.* leather made from a buck's skin.

BUCK'ET, *n. buc,* a vessel for drawing water.

Byldan—to CONFIRM; to ESTABLISH.

BUILD, *v.* to raise an edifice; to construct.

BUILD'ER, *n.* one who builds.
BUILD'ING, *n.* a fabric; an edifice.

Byndel—BUNDLE.

BUN'DLE, *n.* a number of things bound together.

Byrthen—BURDEN.

BUR'DEN, *n.* what is borne; a load.

BUR'DENSOME, *a.* heavy; grievous.

BURST, *v. berstan,* to break or fly asunder by internal force.

Birgan or *birian*—to BURY.

BUR'Y, *v.* to cover with earth; to put into a grave.

BUR'IAL, *n.* interment.
BUR'YING, *n.* burial.

Brastlian—to BRUSTLE; to BUSTLE.

BUS'TLE, *v.* to be busy with quick motion.

BRUS'TLE, *v.* to rustle; to crackle.

Biseg—BUSY.

BUS'Y, *a.* employed with earnestness; active.

BUS'ILY, *ad.* in a busy manner.
BUS'INESS, *n.* employment; trade.

BUS'Y-BOD'Y, *n.* a meddling person.

BUT, *con. butan,* except; except that.

***Bocsum*—FLEXIBLE;** *boga*—a BOUGH, and *sum*—SOME.

BUX'OM, *a.* gay; lively; brisk. | BUX'OMLY, *ad.* wantonly.

***Bycgan*—to BUY;** *boht*—BOUGHT.

BUY, *v.* to obtain for money; to purchase. | BUY'ER, *n.* one who buys.
BOUGHT, *pp.* purchased.

***Be* or *bi*—BY.**

BY, *prep.* denotes the way or means. | BY, *ad.* in presence or passing near.

***Cealf*—CALF.**

CALF, *n.* the young of a cow; a stupid fellow. | CALVES, *n.* the plural of calf.
CALF'SKIN, *n.* the skin of a calf.

***Caeggian*—to LOCK.**

CAGE, *n.* an enclosure for birds or beasts. | CAGE, *v.* to shut up.

***Cunnan*—to KNOW; to HAVE POWER.**

CAN, *v.* to be able; to have power. | CUN'NING, *a.* artfully deceitful.
KEN, *v.* to see at a distance; to know. | CUN'NING, *n.* fraudulent dexterity.

***Canna*—CAN.**

CAN, *n.* a vessel for liquor. | CAN'NED, *a.* preserved in cans.

***Car*—CARE.**

CARE, *n.* anxiety; caution; charge. | CARE'FULLY, *ad.* heedfully.
CARE'FUL, *a.* anxious; watchful. | CARE'LESSLY, *ad.* without care.
CARE'LESS, *a.* having no care; heedless.

***Carl*—a MALE. *Ceorl*—a CHURL.**

CARLE, *n.* a strong, rude man. | CHURL, *n.* a surly man; a miser.
CHURL'ISH, *a.* rude; harsh.

***Ceorfan*—to CARVE.**

CARVE, *v.* to cut meat at table; to cut into elegant forms. | CARV'ING, *n.* the act of carving; sculpture.

***Castel*—CASTLE.**

CAS'TLE, *n.* a fortified house. | CAS'TELLAN, *n.* the governor of a castle.

***Ceaf*—CHAFF.**

CHAFF, *n.* the husks of grain. | CHAF'FY, *a.* full of chaff.
CHAF'FINCH, *n.* a bird said to like chaff.

Ceap, ceapian—to BARGAIN; to TRADE; to BUY.

CHEAP, a. having a low price.
CHEAP'EN, v. to lessen value.
CHEAP'LY, ad. at a small price.
CHEAP'NESS, n. lowness of price.

CHAF'FER, v. to treat about a bargain; to haggle.
CHAP'MAN, n. a dealer.
CHAP, v. to barter; to exchange.

CHAP, n. a boy; an inferior person.

NOTE.—CHAP, to break into small clefts or gapings by heat or cold, to become sore by clefts, &c., is from A.-S. *geypped*, opened.

Cerran—to BURN.

CHAR'COAL, n. coal made by charring wood.

CHAR, v. to burn to a cinder.

Cearig, cearian—to TAKE CARE; to BE ANXIOUS.

CHA'RY, a. careful; cautious.
CHA'RINESS, n. caution; nicety.

CHA'RILY, ad. warily; frugally.

Ceat—CIRCUMVENTION.

CHEAT, v. to defraud; to impose upon. | CHEAT'ER, n. one who practises fraud.

Ceac, ceowan—to CHEW.

CHEEK, n. the side of the face.
CHEW, v. to crush with the teeth.

CHEEK'BONE, n. the bone of the cheek.
CHEW'ING, n. mastication.

NOTE.—CHECK BY JOWL, an old expression signifying *closeness*, or *face to face*.

Cyse—CHEESE.

CHEES'Y, a. having the nature of cheese.

CHEESE, n. the pressed curd of milk.

Cyst—CHEST.

CHEST, n. a large box; the thorax.

Cicen—CHICKEN.

CHICK'EN, n. the young of a hen. | CHICK'ENHEARTED, a. cowardly.

Cidan—to CHIDE.

CHIDE, v. to scold; to find fault.
CHID'INGLY, ad. in a reproving manner.

CHID'ING, n. scolding; rebuke.

Cild—CHILD.

CHILD, n. an infant; a very young person.

CHILD'HOOD, n. the state of children.
CHILD'ISH, a. like a child.

CHILD'LESS, a. without children.

Cele—CHILL.

CHILL, a. cold; dull.
CHIL'LINESS, n. coldness; shivering.

CHILL'Y, a. somewhat cold.

Cyn—Chin.

Chin, n. the lower part of the face. | Chin'cough, n. the whooping cough.

Cina—a Fissure.

Chink, n. a crack; a gap. | Chink, v. to jingle.
Chink'y, a. opening in narrow clefts.

Aceocan—to Suffocate.

Choke, v. to suffocate; to stop up. | Choke'full, a. as full as possible.

Ceosan—to Choose.

Choose, v. to take by preference; to pick out. | Choos'ing, n. selection; choice.
Choice, n. the power of choosing.
Choice'ness, n. nicety; particular value.

Ciern, cyrran—to Turn.

Churn, n. a vessel used in making butter. | Churn'ing, n. the act of making butter.

Clæmian—to Glue; to Smear.

Clam, v. to clog with glutinous matter. | Clam, n. the name of a shell fish.
Clam'my, a. glutinous; sticky.

Clappan—to Move with Beats Like the Heart.

Clap, v. to strike together with quick motion. | Clap'perclaw, v. to scold; to revile.

Claw—Claw.

Claw, n. the foot of a beast or bird having hooked nails. | Claw, v. to scratch, pull, or tear with the nails.

Clæg—Sticky; Viscous.

Clay, n. a tenacious kind of earth.
Clay'ey, a. like clay. | Clay'pit, n. a pit where clay is dug
Clay'marl, n. a whitish, chalky clay

Clæn—Clean.

Clean, a. free from dirt.
Clean'ly, a. free from dirt; neat; pure.
Clean'liness, n. freedom from dirt; neatness. | Cleanse, v. to free from dirt; to purify.
Cleans'ing, n. the act of purifying.
Unclean', a. not clean; dirty.

Cleafan—to Cleave.

Cleave, v. to split; to divide.
Cleav'er, n. a butcher's axe.
Cleft, n. an opening made by splitting. | Clove, pret. divided.
Clo'ven, a. divided; parted.
Clo'ven-footed, a. having the foot divided into two parts.

Cifian—to CLEAVE.

CLEAVE, *v.* to adhere; to hold to.

Gleaw—SKILLFUL; CLEVER.

CLEV'ER, *a.* skillful; dexterous; ingenious.
CLEV'ERNESS, *n.* dexterity; skill; ingenuity.
CLEV'ERLY, *ad.* dexterously; ingeniously.

Cliwe—a BALL OF THREAD.

CLEW, *n.* a ball of thread; a guide. | CLEW, *v.* to guide as by a thread.

NOTE.—The thread unwound from a clew used to guide one in a labyrinth.

Clif—CLIFF.

CLIFF, *n.* a steep bank. | CLIFF'Y, *a.* broken; craggy.

Climan—to CLIMB.

CLIMB, *v.* to ascend with labor; to mount.
CLIMB'ER, *n.* one who climbs.
CLIMB'ING, *n.* the act of ascending.

Clingan—to SHRINK UP.

CLING, *v.* to hang upon; to adhere. | CLING'STONE, *n.* a kind of peach.

Clyppan—to EMBRACE.

CLIP, *v.* to cut with shears; to cut short.
CLIP'PER, *n.* one who clips; a fast sailing vessel.
CLASP, *n.* a hook to hold anything close.
CLASP'KNIFE, *n.* a knife which folds into the handle.

Lach—a GARMENT.

CLOAK, *n.* a loose outer garment. | CLOAK, *v.* to hide; to mask.

Clucga—a BELL; CLOCK.

CLOCK, *n.* an instrument to measure time.
CLOCK'WORK, *n.* the machinery of a clock; well adjusted work.

Clud—a STONE; a HILLOCK.

CLOD, *n.* a lump of earth.
CLOD'DY, *a.* consisting of clods.
CLOD'POLL, *n.* a dolt; a blockhead.
CLOT, *n.* a concretion of soft or fluid matter.
CLOT'TY, *a.* full of clots.

Clath—CLOTH.

CLOTH, *n.* any thing woven.
CLOTHE, *v.* to cover; to dress.
CLOTH'IER, *n.* a maker or seller of cloth.
CLOTHES, *n.* garments; dress.
CLOTH'ING, *n.* dress; garments; vesture.

ANGLO-SAXON ROOTS AND DERIVATIVES.

Ge-hlod—Covered; Cloud.

Cloud, *n.* a collection of visible vapor in the air.
Cloud'y, *a.* covered with clouds.
Cloud'capt, *a.* topped with clouds.
Cloud'iness, *n.* the state of being cloudy.
Cloud'less, *a.* without clouds; clear; bright.

Note.—This word is of doubtful etymology.

Clæfer-wyrt—Small Clover.

Clo'ver, *n.* a species of trefoil. | Clov'ered, *a.* covered with clover.

Cleofan—to Divide.

Club, *n.* an association of persons each contributing his share.
Club, *n.* a room in which a club meets.

Note.—Club, a heavy stick, a bludgeon, comes from the Danish (*klub*).

Clauster—a Cloister; a Bunch.

Clus'ter, *n.* a bunch; a collection. | Clus'ter, *v.* to collect in bunches.

Ge-læccan—to Seize; to Catch.

Clutch, *v.* to seize; to grasp. | Clutch, *n.* gripe; grasp.

Col—Coal.

Coal, *n.* a common fossil fuel.
Coal'ery, *n.* a place where coals are dug.
Coal'black, *a.* black in the highest degree.
Coal'mine, *n.* a mine in which coals are dug.
Coal'miner, *n.* one who works in a coal mine.
Coal'pit, *n.* a pit in which coals are dug.
Coll'ier, *n.* a digger of coals; a coal merchant. [dug.
Coll'iery, *n.* a place where coals are

Cocc—Cock.

Cock, *n.* the male of birds; a small heap of hay; to set erect; to strut.
Cock'ade, *n.* a ribbon worn on the hat.
Cock'atrice, *n.* a serpent. [hat.
Cock'atoo, *n.* a bird of the parrot kind.
Cock'crowing, *n.* the dawn; early morning.
Cock'loft, *n.* the room over the garret.
Cock'pit, *n.* the lower deck of a ship of war.

Ceald—Cold.

Cold, *a.* not hot; frigid; chill.
Cold'ly, *ad.* without heat; without concern.
Cold'ness, *n.* want of heat; unconcern.
Cold'hearted, *a.* indifferent; wanting passion.
Cold'blooded, *a.* without feeling.
Cool, *a.* somewhat cold.
Cool'ish, *a.* rather cool.
Cool'ly, *ad.* without heat or passion
Cool'ness, *n.* gentle cold; indifference.
Cool'headed, *a.* without passion.

Colt—COLT.

COLT, n. a young horse. | COLT'ISH, a. like a colt; frisky; wanton.

Camb—a VALLEY.

COMB, n. the dry part of a valley.
COMB, n. the cells in which bees deposit honey.

COMB, n. an instrument for the hair.
COMB, v. to divide, clean, and adjust the hair.

NOTE.—Hence the names of places situated in valleys end in *comb;* as Alcomb, Bascomb, Chelcomb. Sometimes the name of the owner is annexed; as, *Comb*-Bassett, *Comb*-Raleigh. Sometimes *b* is changed into *p*, as *Comp*ton.—BOSWORTH.

Cuman—to COME.

COME, v. to draw near; to advance towards.
COM'ING, n. approach; arrival; advancing near.

OVERCOME', v. *ofer,* to conquer; to subdue.

Civeman—COMELY.

COME'LINESS, n. grace; beauty; dignity. | COME'LY, a. graceful: decent.

Cop—the TOP, or the HEAD.

COP, n. the head; the top.
COPE, n. a cover for the head or top.
CO'PING, n. the top or cover of a wall.
COP'PED, a. rising to a top or head.

COB, n. the head; anything round; a strong pony.
COB'BLE, n. a roundish stone.
COB'-IRONS, n. irons with a knob at the end.

NOTE.—COPE, to contend, to struggle, comes from the Greek.—COBBLE, to mend coarsely, to do clumsily, comes from the Danish (*kobler*).

Corn—CORN.

CORN, n. seeds which grow in ears; grain.
CORN'CHANDLER, n. one who retails corn.

CORN, v. to sprinkle with salt.
CORN'FIELD, n. a field where corn is growing.
CORN'HEAP, n. a store of corn.

NOTE.—CORN, an excrescence on the foot, is from the Latin *cornu*, a horn.

Cota—COT.

COT, n. a small house; a hut.
COTE, n. a cottage; a sheep fold.
COT'TAGE, n. a small house; a hut.

COT'TAGER, n. one who lives in a cottage.
COT'TER, n. one who lives in a cot.

Cof—a CAVE; a REPOSITORY.

COVE, n. a small creek or bay; a shelter.
COF'FER, n. a chest, generally for keeping money.

COF'FER-DAM, n. a water-tight case fixed in the bottom of a river, in order to keep a space dry to build upon.

Crabba—CRAB.

CRAB, n. a shell fish; a peevish person. | CRAB'BED, a. peevish; morose.

Cu—Cow.

Cow, n. the female of the bull.
Cow'LIKE, a. resembling a cow.
Cow'HOUSE, n. a house in which cows are kept.
Cow'POX, n. the vaccine disease.
Cow'SLIP, n. a species of primrose.
Cow, v. to depress with fear.
Cow'HERD, n. (*hyrde,* a keeper), one who tends cows.
Cow'LICK, n. a tuft of hair turned up as if licked by a cow.
Cow'ARD, n. (from *cowherd*), one destitute of courage.
Cow'ARDICE, n. want of courage.
Cow'ARDLY, a. fearful; mean.

Cradel—CRADLE.

CRA'DLE, n. a bed in which infants are rocked.
CRA'DLE, n. a scythe for grain.

Cræft—ART; SKILL; TRADE.

CRAFT, n. trade; fraud; cunning.
CRAFT'Y, a. cunning; artful; sly.
CRAFT'ILY, ad. cunningly; artfully.
CRAFT'INESS, n. cunning; stratagem.
CRAFTS'MAN, n. an artificer; a mechanic.

Crammian—to CRAM.

CRAM, v. to stuff completely full; to thrust in by force.

Cran—a kind of HERON.

CRANE, n. a bird; a machine for raising heavy goods.

Crafian—to CRAVE; to ASK; to IMPLORE.

CRAVE, v. to ask earnestly; to long for.
CRA'VEN, n. a coward; one who implores for his life when vanquished.
CRA'VING, n. unreasonable desire.

CREEK, n. *crecca,* a small inlet; a cove.

Creopan—to CREEP.

CREEP, v. to move as a worm; to move slowly or feebly.
CREEP'INGLY, ad. slowly; like a reptile.

Cread or cruth—a CROWD.

CREW, n. a ship's company; a company.
CROWD, n. a confused multitude; v. to press close.

Cryb—CRIB.

CRIB, n. a manger; a child's bed; v. to confine.

Cricc—a STICK.

CRICK, n. a painful stiffness in the neck.
CRICK'ET, n. a play with bats and ball.
CRUTCH, n. a support used by the lame.

Ge-crympt—CURLED.

CRIMP, *v.* to pinch up in ridges. | CRIMP'ING, *n.* the act of crimping.

Crocca—a POT; a PITCHER.

CROCK, *n.* an earthen vessel. | CROCK'ERY, *n.* earthen ware.

Cropp—the TOP; an EAR OF CORN.

CROP, *n.* the stomach of a bird. | CROP, *n.* the harvest; produce.

NOTE.—CROP, to cut off, comes from the Dutch *krappen*, to cut off.

Hreopan—CROUP.

CROUP, *n.* a disease in the throat.

NOTE.—CROUP, the rump of an animal, comes from the Italian (*groppa*).

Craw—CROW.

CROW, *n.* a bird; the cry of a cock. | CROW'-FOOT, *n.* a flower.
CROW'S'-FEET, *n.* the wrinkles under the eyes.

Cruma—CRUMB; to GNAW or BREAK.

CRUMB, *n.* a small particle; a fragment. | CRUM'BLE, *v.* to break or fall into small pieces.

Cunnan—to KNOW; CUNNING.

CUN'NING, *a.* skilful; artful; sly. | CUN'NINGLY, *ad.* skilfully; artfully.

Cupp—CUP.

CUP, *n.* a drinking vessel. | CUP'BOARD, *n.* a case with shelves for cups, &c.
CUP'BEARER, *n.* an attendant at a feast. |

DAM, *v. demman,* to confine water.

NOTE.—DAM, a female parent, is from DAME, which comes from the Latin *domina*, the mistress of a family.

Dearran—to DARE.

DARE, *v.* to have courage. | DAR'ING, *a.* bold; fearless.
DARE, *v.* to challenge; to defy. | DAR'INGLY, *ad.* boldly; courageously.

Deorc—DARK.

DARK, *a.* wanting light; gloomy. | DARK'LY, *ad.* obscurely.
DARK'EN, *v.* to make dark. | DARK'NESS, *n.* absence of light.
DARK'ISH, *a.* approaching to dark. | DARK'SOME, *a.* gloomy; obscure.

Deor or *dyre*—PRECIOUS; BELOVED.

DEAR, *a.* beloved; precious; costly. | DEARTH, *n.* scarcity; famine.
DEAR'LY, *ad.* with fondness; at a high price. | DEAR'-BOUGHT, *a.* purchased at a high price.
DEAR'NESS, *n.* fondness; costliness. | DAR'LING, *a.* beloved; favorite.
ENDEAR', *v.* to make dear; to make beloved.

Adastrigan—to FRIGHTEN; to DISMAY.

DAS'TARD, *n.* a coward.
DAS'TARDLY, *ad.* cowardly; mean.
DAS'TARDY, *n.* cowardliness.

NOTE.—COWARD, DASTARD, POLTROON, and CRAVEN signify one wanting courage, and they are all used as terms of reproach; but, of the four words, *coward* is the least reproachful.

Dohtor—DAUGHTER.

DAUGH'TER, *n.* a female child. | DAUGH'TERLY, *a.* like a daughter.

Dæg—DAY. *Dagian*—DAWN.

DAY, *n.* the time from sunrise to sunset.
DAI'LY, *a.* happening every day.
DAY'BREAK, *n.* the first appearance of light; dawn.
DAY'DREAM, *n.* a vision to the waking senses.
DAY'LIGHT, *n.* the light of day.
DAY'TIME, *n.* the time in which there is light.
DAWN, *n.* the break of day; to begin to grow light.
DAWN'ING, *n.* break of day; morning.
DAI'SY, *n.* (*day's-eye*), a flower.
DAI'SIED, *a.* full of daisies.

Dead—DEAD.

DEAD, *a.* deprived of life; dull; still.
DEAD'EN, *v.* to deprive of sensation.
DEAD'LY, *a.* destructive; mortal.
DEAD'NESS, *n.* loss of life.
DEATH, *n.* extinction of life.
DEAD'DRUNK, *a.* so drunk as to be helpless.
DEAD'LIFT, *n.* the lifting of a thing at the utmost disadvantage.
DEATH'LIKE, *a.* resembling death.

Deaf—DEAF.

DEAF, *a.* wanting the sense of hearing. | DEAF'EN, *v.* to make deaf.
DEAF'NESS, *n.* want of power to hear.

Dæl—a PART. *Dælan*—to DIVIDE.

DEAL, *n.* a part; a thin plank.
DEAL, *v.* to divide; to distribute.
DEAL'ER, *n.* one who deals; a trader.
DEAL'ING, *n.* action; intercourse; traffic.
DOLE, *v.* to deal; to distribute.
IN'TERDEAL, *n.* mutual dealing; traffic.

NOTE.—DOLE, grief, sorrow, comes from the Latin (*doleo*).

Decan—to COVER.

DECK, *v.* to cover; to adorn.
DECK, *n.* the floor or cover of a ship.
DECK'ER, *n.* one who adorns.
FORE'DECK, *n.* the fore part of the deck.
UNDECKED', *a.* not decked.

Dæd—DEED.

DEED'LESS, *a.* without action; without exploits. | DEED, *n.* an action; an exploit.

Deman—DEEM.

DEEM, *v.* to think; to judge.

Deop—Deep.

Deep, *a.* extending far below the surface; profound.
Deep'en, *v.* to make deep.
Deep'ly, *ad.* to a great depth.
Depth, *n.* measure from the surface downwards.

Delfan—to Dig.

Delf, *n.* a mine; a pit; earthenware.
Delve, *v.* to dig.
Del'ver, *n.* one who digs.

Denu—Den; a Dale; a Plain.

Den, *n.* a cavern; the cave of a wild beast.

Note.—Den, a termination in the names of places, signifies *a valley* or *woody plain*.

Disc—a Plate; a Table; Dish.

Desk, *n.* an inclined table for writing or reading.
Dish, *n.* a vessel for serving up food; a plate.
Dish'water, *n.* water in which dishes are washed.

Deofol—Devil.

Dev'il, *n.* a fallen angel; an evil spirit.
Dev'ilish, *a.* like a devil; wicked.

Deaw—Dew.

Dew, *n.* moisture from the atmosphere.
Dew'y, *a.* like dew.
Dew'drop, *n.* a drop of dew.
Dew'lap, *n.* the flesh which hangs from the throat of an ox.
Bedew', *v.* to moisten gently.

Dic—a Dike.

Dig, *v.* to turn up the earth; to excavate.
Dig'ger, *n.* one who digs.
Dike, *n.* a bank; a mound.
Ditch, *n.* a trench dug in the ground.

Dim—Dim.

Dim, *a.* not seeing clear; obscure; *v.* to cloud.
Dim'ly, *ad.* not clearly; obscurely.
Dim'ness, *n.* dulness of sight.
Dim'sighted, *a.* having weak eyes.

Dynt—a Stroke; a Blow. *Dint*—a Hole.

Dim'ple, *n.* a small hollow in the cheek or chin.
Dim'pled, *a.* set with dimples.
Dim'ply, *a.* full of dimples.
Dint, *n.* a mark; force.
Dint, *v.* to mark by a blow.

Dyne—Noise. *Dynan*—to Make a Noise; to Dine.

Din, *n.* a loud noise; *v.* to stun with noise.
Dine, *v.* to eat or give a dinner.
Din'ner, *n.* the chief meal of the day.
Di'ningroom, *n.* the room for dining.
Din'nertime, *n.* the time for dinner.
Dun, *v.* to claim a debt importunately.

Dyppan—to Dip.

Dip, *v.* to put into any liquor; to enter slightly.
Dive, *v.* to plunge under the water.

Dysi—Dizzy.

Diz'zy, *a.* giddy; whirling.
Diz'ziness, *n.* giddiness; vertigo.

Don—to Do.

Do, *v.* to practise; to perform.
Did, *v.* executed; performed.
Done, *v.* executed; performed.
Doings, *n.* things done; transactions

Dol—a Dolt.

Dolt, *n.* a heavy, stupid fellow.
Dolt'ish, *a.* stupid; dull.
Dull, *a.* stupid; sluggish; blunt.
Dul'ness, *n.* stupidity; heaviness.
Dull'head, *n.* a blockhead; a dolt.

Deman—to Think; to Judge.

Dooms'day, *n.* the day of final judgment.
Doom, *v.* to judge; to condemn.

Duru—Door.

Door, *n.* the entrance into a house or apartment.
Door'case, *n.* the frame of a door.

Dah, the past participle of *deawian*—to Moisten; to Wet.

Dough, *n.* wet flour; unbaked paste. | Dough'y, *a.* like dough; soft.

Dohtig—Brave; Noble; Good.

Dough'ty, *a.* brave; valiant; noble. | Dough'tiness, *n.* valor; bravery.

Duva—Dove.

Dove, *n.* a species of pigeon.
Dove'cot, *n.* (*cota*), a house for doves.
Dove'tail, *n.* a joint in the form of an expanded dove's tail.
Dove'like, *a.* resembling a dove.

Note.—The dove is the emblem of love, simplicity, purity, and innocence.

Dun—Down.

Down, *n.* a bank of sand thrown up by the sea; a tract of poor, hilly land.

Adune, the past participle of *duflan*—to Sink.

Down, *prep.* from a higher to a lower place.
Down, *ad.* on the ground, or any flat surface.
Down'ward, *ad.* in a descending course.
Down'cast, *a.* dejected.
Down'fall, *n.* ruin; calamity
Down'right, *a.* plain; open; direct.

Note.—Down, the soft feathers of a bird, comes from the Danish (*duun*).

Dwæs—DULL; STUPID.   *Dwæscan*—to EXTINGUISH.

DOZE, *v.* to sleep lightly.
DO'ZY, *a.* sleepy; drowsy; sluggish.
DO'ZINESS, *n.* sleepiness.
DO'ZING, *ppr.* sleeping lightly.
DAZE, *v.* to blind by too strong a light.

DAZ'ZLE, *v.* to overpower with light.
DAZ'ZLING, *p. a.* striking with splendor.
BEDAZ'ZLE, *v.* to make the sight dim by lustre.

Drehnigean—to DRAIN; to STRAIN.   *Drygan*—to DRY.

DRAIN, *v.* to draw off gradually; to exhaust.

DRAIN, *n.* a channel for water to flow off.

Dragan—to DRAG.

DRAG, *v.* to pull along by force.
DRAG, *n.* whatever serves to retard.
DRAUGHT, *n.* the act of drawing; the quantity drunk at once.
DRAW, *v.* to pull along; to attract.
DRAW'ABLE, *a.* that may be drawn.
DRAW'ER, *n.* a sliding box in a case or table.
DRAW'ING, *n.* delineation.
DRAWN, *a.* having equal advantage.
DRAW'BACK, *n.* any loss of advantage.

DRAW'BRIDGE, *n.* a bridge which may be opened.
DRAY, *n.* a low cart.
DRAY'HORSE, *n.* a horse which draws a dray.
DRAY'MAN, *n.* a man who attends a dray.
DRAWL, *v.* to speak in a slow, tedious manner.
DREDGE, *n.* a drag for taking oysters.
DREDGE, *v.* to gather with a dredge.

Dræd—DREAD.

DREAD, *n.* great fear; terror.
DREAD'FUL, *a.* terrible; awful.

DREAD'FULLY, *ad.* terribly.
DREAD'LESS, *a.* fearless; intrepid.

Dreorig—DREAR.

DREAR, *a.* dismal; gloomy.   [ful.
DREAR'Y, *a.* dismal; gloomy; mourn-

DREAR'ILY, *ad.* dismally; gloomily.
DREAR'INESS, *n.* dismalness.

Drencan—to GIVE TO DRINK.

Adrencan—to DROWN; to PLUNGE or OVERWHELM.

DRENCH, *v.* to wet thoroughly; to soak.
DRINK, *v. drinc,* to swallow liquors.
DRINK, *n.* liquor to be swallowed.

DRINK'ABLE, *a.* that may be drunk.
DROWN, *v.* to overwhelm in water.
DRUNK, *a.* intoxicated with liquor.
DRUNK'ARD, *n.* one habitually drunk.

DRUNK'EN, *a.* intoxicated with liquor.

Driopan—to DRIP.   *Dropian*—to DROP.

DRIP, *v.* to fall in drops.
DRIB'BLE, *v.* to fall in drops.
DRIB'BLING, *n.* a falling in drops.
DRIB'LET, *n.* a small quantity or sum.
DRIV'ELER, *n.* an idiot; a dotard.

DRIV'EL, *v.* to let the spittle fall like a child.
DROOP, *v.* to sink or hang down.
DROP, *n.* a globule of liquid.
DROP, *v.* to let fall.

Drugoth, drygan or *doigan*—to DRY.

DROUGHT, *n.* a long continuance of dry weather.

DROUTH, *n.* want of rain.

Drifan—to DRIVE.

DRIVE, *v.* to force along; to urge forward.
DRIVE, *n.* a passage in a carriage.
DRIFT, *n.* anything driven at random.
DRIFT, *v.* to be driven along by a current of water.
DROVE, *n. draf,* a number of cattle driven.
ADRIFT', *a.* or *ad.* impelled or moving without direction.

Thirlian—to TURN, WIND or TWIST.

DRILL, *n.* an instrument; a row of grain.
THRILL, *v.* to pierce; to feel a sharp, shivering sensation.
DRILL, *v.* to bore and make a hole by turning an instrument; to teach and train by frequent exercise.

Dreosan—to FALL; to PRECIPITATE; to DROP or DROOP.

DRIZ'ZLE, *v.* to fall in small drops.
DRIZ'ZLING, *ppr.* falling in small drops.
DRIZ'ZLY, *a.* shedding small rain.
DROSS'Y, *a.* worthless; foul.
DROSS, *n.* the scum of metals; any worthless matter.
DROWSE, *v.* to make heavy with sleep.
DROW'SY, *a.* sleepy; heavy; dull.
DROW'SILY, *ad.* sleepily; lazily.
DROW'SINESS, *n.* sleepiness.

Dran—DRONE.

DRONE, *n.* the male of the honey bee; one who produces nothing; a low humming sound.
DRONE, *v.* to live in idleness.
DRON'ISH, *a.* idle; indolent.

Druge, from *dreogan*—to ACT; to SUFFER.

DRUDGE, *n.* one employed in mean labor.
DRUDGE, *v.* to labor in mean offices.
DRUD'GERY, *n.* mean labor; hard work.

Dri, drig or *dryg*—DRY.

DRY, *a.* free from moisture; not wet.
DRY'LY, *ad.* without moisture; coldly.
DRY'NESS, *n.* want of moisture.
DRY'SHOD, *a.* without wet feet.
DRUG, *n. (drigan,* to dry), any substance used in medicine.
DRUG'GIST, *n.* one who deals in drugs.

Gedufian—to DUCK.

DUCK, *v.* to put suddenly under water.
DUCK, *n.* a water fowl.
DUCK'LING, *n.* a young duck.
DUCK'LEGGED, *a.* short-legged.

Thystre—DARK; OBSCURE.

DUSK, *a.* tending to darkness.
DUSK, *n.* twilight
DUSK'ISH, *a.* moderately dark.
DUSK'Y, *a.* somewhat dark; obscure.

Dumb—DUMB.

DUMB, *a.* mute; not able to speak.
DUMB'NESS, *n.* incapacity to speak; silence.
DUM'FOUND, *v.* to make dumb; to confuse.

Dust—Dust.

Dust, *n.* earth or other matter reduced to powder.
Dust'y, *a.* filled or covered with dust.
Dust'iness, *n.* the state of being covered with dust.

Dweorg—Dwarf.

Dwarf, *n.* a person below the usual size.
Dwarf'ish, *a.* below the natural size.
Dwarf'ishness, *n.* littleness of stature.

Dwinan—to Fade; to Vanish.

Dwin'dle, *v.* to shrink; to grow less. | Dwine, *v.* to pine away; to decline.

Deagan—to Dye.

Dye, *v.* to tinge; to color; to stain. | Dye'ing, *n.* the art of coloring cloth.

Ælc—Each; Every.

Each, *a.* every one of any number.

Eare—Ear.

Ear, *n.* the organ of hearing.
Ear'ring, *n.* an ornament for the ear.
Ear'shot, *n.* reach of the ear.
Ear'wig, *n.* an insect; a whisperer.
Ear, *n.* that part of corn which contains the seeds.

Eorl—Chief; Leader.

Earl, *n.* a title of nobility. | Earl'dom, *n.* the dignity of an earl.

Ær—Before.   Ærest—First.

Ere, *ad.* before; sooner than.
Ere-long', *ad.* before long.
Ere-now', *ad.* before this time.
Ere-while', *ad.* some time ago.
Ear'ly, *a.* soon; being in good time.
Erst, *ad.* first; at first; formerly.

Earnian—to Deserve.

Earn, *v.* to gain by labor. | Earn'ing, *n.* that which is earned.

Eornest—Earnest.

Ear'nest, *a.* ardent; zealous; eager. | Ear'nestly, *ad.* warmly; eagerly.

Eorthe—Earth.

Earth, *n.* the matter which composes the globe.
Earth'en, *a.* made of earth or clay.
Earth'ly, *a.* belonging to the earth.
Earth'y, *a.* consisting of earth.
Earth'quake, *n.* a convulsion of the earth.
Earth'worm, *n.* a mean, sordid wretch.

Eath—Easy; Ready; Gentle.

Ease, *n.* quiet; rest; facility.
Ea'sy, *a.* not difficult; quiet.
Ea'sily, *ad.* without difficulty.
Ea'siness, *n.* the quality of being easy.

East—East.

East, n. the quarter where the sun rises.
East'erly, a. coming from the east.
East'ern, a. being in the east.
East'ward, ad. towards the east.

Etan—to Eat.

Eat, v. to chew and swallow; to take food.
Eat'able, a. that may be eaten.
Eat'er, n. one that eats.
Eat'ing, n. the act of chewing and swallowing.

Efese—a Brim.

Eaves, n. the edges of the roof of a house.
Eaves'dropper, n. one who listens under the windows.

Ebbe—Ebb.

Ebb, n. the going out of the tide; decline.
Eb'bing, n. flowing out.

Ed—Again; Back.   Ea—Running Water.

Ed'dy, n. water running back or contrary to the current; a whirlpool.
Ed'dy, v. to move circularly.
Ed'dying, p. a. moving circularly; whirling.

Ecg—Edge.

Edge, n. the cutting part of a blade; the brink.
Edged, a. sharp; keen.
Edge'less, a. blunt; obtuse.
Edge'wise, ad. with the edge forward.

Æg—Egg.   Eggian—to Egg.

Egg, n. that from which the young of some animals is produced.
Egg, v. to incite.
Ey'ry, n. a place where birds of prey build their nests.

Aehta—Eight.

Eight, a. n. twice four.
Eighth, a. the ordinal of eight.
Eight'een, a. eight and ten.
Eight'fold, a. eight times the quantity.
Eight'score, a. n. eight times twenty.

Eke, v. *ecan,* to lengthen; to prolong.

Elboga—Elbow.

El'bow, n. the joint of the arm below the shoulder.
El'bow, n. a sudden or abrupt turn.
El'bow, v. to push one's way.
El'bow-room, n. room or space for exertion.

Elf—Elf.

Elf, n. a fairy; v. to entangle the hair.
Elf'in, a. relating to fairies.
Elf'lock, n. a knot of hair twisted.

Ellm—Elm.

Elm, *n.* a forest tree. | El'my, *a.* abounding with elm-trees.

Hleapan—to Leap; to Jump; to Run.

Leap, *v.* to jump; to spring.
Leap'frog, *n.* a play of children.
Leap'year, *n.* every fourth year.
Outleap', *v.* to leap beyond.

Overleap', *v.* to leap over.
Elope', *v.* to run away privately.
Elope'ment, *n.* a running away secretly.

Elles—Else.

Else, *pron.* other; one besides. | Else'where, *ad.* in another place.

Æmti—Empty.

Emp'ty, *a.* containing nothing. | Emp'tiness, *n.* state of being empty.

Ende—End.

End, *n.* conclusion; termination.
End'ing, *n.* conclusion.

End'less, *a.* without end.
End'wise, *ad.* on end; erectly.

Genoh—Plenty; Sufficiency.

Enough', *a.* sufficient; that satisfies desire. | Enough', *ad.* in a sufficient degree.

Ærend—Message; Business; Care.

Er'rand, *n.* that which is intrusted to a messenger. | Er'rand-boy, *n.* a boy to deliver messages.

Æfen—Even.

Eve, E'ven, *n.* the close of the day. | E'vening, *n.* the close of the day.
E'ventide, *n.* the time of the evening.

Efen—Even.

E'ven, *a.* level; smooth; equal. | E'venly, *ad.* equally.
E'venness, *n.* the state of being even.

Æfer—Ever.

Ev'er, *ad.* at any time; always.
Ev'ergreen, *n.* always green.
Everlast'ing, *a.* lasting without end.

Evermore', *ad.* always; eternally.
Ev'ery, *a. ælc,* each one.
Ev'erywhere, *ad.* in every place.

Forev'er, *ad.* at all times; without end.

Efel or *Yfel*—Evil.

E'vil, *a.* not good; bad; wicked.
E'villy, *ad.* not well.

E'vilness, *n.* badness; wickedness.
E'vildoer, *n.* one who does evil.

Eowu—Ewe.

Ewe, *n.* a female sheep.

Eage—Eye.

Eye, *n.* the organ of vision; *v.* to watch.
Eye'less, *a.* without eyes.
Eye'let, *n.* a small hole for a cord.
Eye'ball, *n.* the apple of the eye.
Eye'beam, *n.* a glance from the eye.
Eye'brow, *n.* the hairy arch over the eye.
Eye'lash, *n.* the hair that edges the eye.
Eye'lid, *n.* the membrane that shuts over the eye.
Eye'-service, *n.* service performed only under inspection.
Eye'sight, *n.* the sight of the eye.
Dai'sy, *n.* (*day's-eye*), a flower.
Ineye', *v.* to put an eye in; to inoculate.
Overeye', *v.* to superintend; to observe.

Fægen—Glad; Joyful.

Fain, *a.* glad; pleased; delighted. | Fain, *ad.* gladly; very desirously.

Fynigean—to Become Musty; to Decay.

Faint, *v.* to pass away quickly.
Faint'ing, *n.* a swoon.
Faint'ly, *ad.* feebly.
Faint'-hearted, *a.* timorous.

Fæger—Fair.

Fair, *a.* beautiful; white; clear. | Fair'ly, *ad.* openly; justly.
Fair'ness, *n.* beauty; honesty.

Note.—Fair, a stated market, comes from the Latin (*forum*).

Fyllan—to Cut Down; to Fall. Feallan—to Fall.

Fall, *v.* to drop down; to sink.
Fall, *n.* the act of falling; autumn.
Befall', *v.* to happen to.
Fell, *v.* to cause to fall; to cut down.
Fell, *v.* to sew or hem.

Fealo—Fallow.

Fal'low, *a.* ploughed but not sown; pale red or yellow; left to rest after tillage.

Fann—a Fan.

Fan, *n.* an instrument for agitating the air. | Fan, *v.* to affect by air put in motion.

Fengan—to Take; to Seize.

Fang, *v.* to seize; to catch.
Fang, *n.* the tusk of an animal.
Fan'gle, *n.* a silly attempt.
Fan'gled, *a.* gaudy; ridiculously showy.
Newfan'gled, *a.* formed with affectation of novelty.
Fin'ger, *n.* one of the extreme parts of the hand.

Feor—Far. Fyrst—Superlative of Feor.

Far, *a.* distant; remote.
Far'most, *a.* most distant.
Afar', *ad.* at or to a distance.
First, *a.* earliest in time.
First'born, *n.* the eldest child.
First'fruits, *n.* earliest produce.
Far'ther, *a.* more remote.
Far'thest, *a.* most distant or remote.
Far'fetched, *a.* forced; strained.

Fær—a JOURNEY. *Faran*—to GO; to TRAVEL.

FARE, *v.* to go; to travel; to happen well or ill.
FARE, *n. faru,* food; price of conveyance.
FAREWELL', *ad.* adieu; the parting compliment.
FAREWELL', *n.* leave; departure.
FER'RY, *v.* to carry over water in a boat.
FER'RY, *n.* the place where a boat passes over.
FER'RY-BOAT, *n.* a boat to pass over in.
WHER'RY, *n.* a light, sharp rowboat.
MISFARE', *v.* to be in a bad state.
WEL'FARE, *n.* happiness; prosperity.
FORD, *n.* a shallow place in a river.
FORD, *v.* to pass a river by walking on the bottom.
FORD'ABLE, *a.* passable on foot.

Feorm—PROVISIONS. *Feormian*—to SUPPLY WITH FOOD.

FARM, *n.* land under cultivation; *v.* to lease or let.
FARM'ER, *n.* one who cultivates a farm.
FARM'ING, *n.* cultivation of land.

Fœstan—to HOLD; to STOP.

FAST, *v.* to abstain from food. | FAST'DAY, *n.* a day of religious fasting.

Fœst—STOPPED; FIXED.
Fyst, from *fœstnian*—to SEIZE; to FASTEN UPON.

FAST, *a.* firm; strong; fixed.
FAST'EN, *v.* to make fast; to make firm.
FASTEN'ING, *n.* that which fastens.
FAST'NESS, *n.* strength; a strong place.
FIST, *n.* the clenched hand.
FIS'TICUFFS, *n.* blows with the fist.

NOTE.—FAST, speedy, quick, is from the Welsh (*fest*).

Fætt, fedan—to NOURISH.

FAT, *a.* plump; fleshy; full fed.
FAT, *n.* the unctuous part of animal flesh.
FAT'NESS, *n.* the quality of being fat.
FAT'TEN, *v.* to make or grow fat.
FAT'TY, *a.* having the qualities of fat.
VAT, *n.* a large cistern.

Fœder—BEGETTER.

FA'THER, *n.* the male parent. | FA'THERLESS, *a.* without a father.
FA'THERLY, *a.* like a father; tender.

Fœthem—the SPACE OF BOTH ARMS EXTENDED.

FATH'OMLESS, *a.* that cannot be fathomed.
FATH'OM, *n.* a measure of six feet.

NOTE.—Fathoms are marked on lines and used in measuring the depth of water.

Fœhth, past part. of the verb *fian*—to HATE.

FAUGH, *int.* an expression of abhorrence.

Fægnian—to REJOICE; to FLATTER.

FAWN, *v.* to court servilely; to cringe. | FAWN'ER, *n.* one who fawns.
FAWN'ING, *n.* gross or low flattery.

NOTE.—FAWN, a young deer, comes from the French (*faon*).

ANGLO-SAXON ROOTS AND DERIVATIVES. 107

Fær, færan—to TERRIFY.

FEAR, *n.* dread; terror; awe. | FEAR'FUL, *a.* timorous; afraid.
FEAR'LESS, *a.* free from fear.

Fyther—FEATHER.

FEATH'ER, *n.* the plume of birds. | FEATH'ERLESS, *a.* having no feathers.
FEATH'ERED, *a.* clothed with feathers. | FEATH'ERY, *a.* resembling a feather.

Feoh—CATTLE; MONEY; a STIPEND or REWARD.

FEE, *n.* reward; recompense. | FEE'-SIMPLE, *n.* a tenure to property;
FEE, *v.* to bribe; to hire. | an absolute estate of inheritance.

NOTE.—"This word *feoh* is one of the oldest in all the European languages. Cattle was the first kind of property; and by bartering, this word came to signify money in general."—BOSWORTH.

FEE, in American law, an estate of inheritance of which the holder has the entire disposal without condition, and which is transmissible to his heirs. FEE-SIMPLE, called *simple* (*i. e.* pure), because clear of any condition, limitation, or restriction to particular heirs.

Foda, foster—FOOD. *Fedan*—to FEED.

FEED, *v.* to supply with food. | FOS'TER, *v.* to feed; to cherish.
FEED'ER, *n.* one that feeds. | FOS'TERING, *n.* the act of nursing.
FEED'ING, *n.* the act of feeding. | FOS'TERCHILD, *n.* a child nursed by
FOOD, *n.* any thing that nourishes. | one who is not its parent.
FOOD'LESS, *a.* not affording food. | FOS'TERBROTHER, *n.* one nursed at
FOD'DER, *n.* (from *fedan*,) food for | the same breast.
cattle. |

Felan—to FEEL.

FEEL, *v.* to perceive by the touch. | FEEL'ING, *n.* the sense of touch.
FEEL'INGLY, *ad.* tenderly.

Fælga. Fæla—MUCH, and *gan*—to Go.

FEL'LY, or FEL'LOE, *n.* the outward wooden rim of a wheel.

Felag. Fe—FAITH, and *lag*—BOUND.

FEL'LOW, *n.* a companion; an equal. | FEL'LOWSHIP, *n.* companionship.
FELLOW-FEEL'ING, *n.* sympathy.

Fælian, fællan—to OFFEND.

FEL'ON, *n.* one guilty of felony. | FEL'ONY, *n.* a crime which incurs the
FELO'NIOUS, *a.* cruel. | forfeiture of life or property.

Felt—FELT.

FELT, *n.* a hide or skin; cloth made | FILTRA'TION, *n.* the act of filtering.
without weaving. | FIL'TER, *n.* a piece of felt, &c., through
FELT'MAKER, *n.* one who makes felt. | which liquids are passed to clear
FIL'TRATE, *v.* to strain. | them.

Feawa—FEW.

FEW, *a.* not many; small in number. | FEW'NESS, *n.* smallness of number.

Ficol—FICKLE; CRAFTY.

FICK'LE, *a.* changeable; inconstant. | FICK'LENESS, *n.* changeableness.

Fithele—FIDDLE.

FID'DLE, *n.* a violin. | FID'DLER, *n.* one who plays on a fiddle.

Feld, the past part. of the verb *fellan*—to FELL.

FIELD, *n.* a piece of land; battle-ground.
FIELD'-MARSHAL, *n.* the commander of an army.
FIELD'-PIECE, *n.* a small cannon.
FIELD'SPORTS, *n.* shooting and hunting.
FELL, *n.* a hill.
FELL, *v.* to hew or cut down; to sew or hem.

NOTE.—The word *field* properly means a clearing, where the trees have been *felled* or cut down.

Feond, flan, or *feon*—to HATE.

FIEND, *n.* a deadly enemy.
FIEND'LIKE, *a.* resembling a fiend.
FIEND'ISH, *n.* having the qualities of a fiend.
FEUD, *n.* a deadly quarrel.

NOTE.—FEUD, a right to land on condition of military service, comes from the Latin (*feudum*).

FIGHT, *v. feohtan,* to contend in battle; *n.* a contest.

Film—a THIN, LIGHT COAT.

FILM, *n.* a thin skin; *v.* to cover with a thin skin. | FILM'Y, *a.* composed of films.

Fylth, afylan—to DEFILE.

FILTH, *n.* dirt; nastiness.
FILTH'Y, *a.* nasty; foul.
FILTH'ILY, *ad.* nastily; foully.
FILTH'INESS, *n.* nastiness; foulness.

Findan—to FIND.

FIND, *v.* to obtain by searching.
FIND'ER, *n.* a discoverer.
FIND'ING, *n.* discovery; verdict of a jury.
FIND'INGS, *n.* the tools and materials used by shoemakers.

Fyr—FIRE.

FIRE, *n.* the igneous element.
FIR'ING, *n.* fuel; discharge of fire-arms.
FIRE'ARMS, *n.* guns, muskets, &c
FIRE'BRAND, *n.* a piece of wood kindled.
FIRE'SIDE, *n.* the hearth; home.
FIRE'WOOD, *n.* wood for fuel.

Fisc—FISH.

FISH, *n.* an animal that inhabits water.
FISH'ING, *n.* the art of catching fish.
FISH'ERY, *n.* the place of fishing.
FISH, *v.* to try to take by artifice.

ANGLO-SAXON ROOTS AND DERIVATIVES.

Floh, fleogan—to FLY or CAUSE TO FLY.

FLY, *v.* to move with wings; to pass swiftly.
FLY'ING FISH, *n.* a small fish which flies.
FLAG, *n.* an ensign; a water plant.
FLAG, *v.* to hang loose; to grow weak.
FLAG'GY, *a.* weak; lax.
FLAG'STAFF, *n.* the staff upon which the flag is elevated.
FLEDGED, *a.* feathered; able to fly.
UN'FLEDGED, *a.* not fledged; young.
UNFLAG'GING, *a.* not drooping; untiring.
FLEE, *v.* to run from danger.
FLINCH, *v.* to withdraw from.

FLING, *v.* to cast from the hand.
FLEET, *v.* to fly swiftly; to haste away.
FLEET, *a.* rapid; swift; quick.
FLEET'ING, *p. a.* passing away rapidly.
FLEET'LY, *ad.* swiftly; nimbly.
FLEET'NESS, *n.* swiftness.
FLICK'ER, *v.* to flap or move the wings without flying; to waver; to fluctuate.
FLAW, *n.* a crack; a defect; a sudden gust.
FLEA, *n.* a small insect.
FLIGHT, *n.* the act of flying or fleeing.
FLIGHT'Y, *a.* flecting; wild.
FLIT, *v.* to fly rapidly.

NOTE.—FLAG, a broad, flat stone, comes from the A.-S. *flean*, to flay.

Flaxe—a FLASK.

FLAG'ON, *n.* a drinking vessel. | FLASK, *n.* a kind of bottle.

Fleax—FLAX.

FLAX, *n.* a fibrous plant. | FLAX'EN, *a.* made of flax.
FLAX'SEED, *n.* the seed of flax; linseed.

Fleos or *flys*, from *flean*—to FLAY.

FLAY, *v.* to strip off the skin.
FLEEC'Y, *a.* like a fleece.
FLEECE, *n.* the wool shorn from one sheep.
FLAG, *n.* a broad flat stone for paving.

Flota or *fliet*—a SHIP.

FLEET, *n.* a company of ships.

NOTE—FLEET, swift of pace, comes from the A.-S. *fleogan*, to fly.

Flæsc—FLESH.

FLESH, *n.* the muscular part of the body.
FLESH'Y, *a.* full of flesh; plump.
FLESH'INESS, *n.* plumpness; fatness.
FLESH'LESS, *a.* without flesh.

Flint—FLINT.

FLINT'Y, *a.* consisting of flint; hard; cruel. | FLINT, *n.* a hard stone.

Fleardian—to TRIFLE.

FLIRT, *v.* to throw with a jerk; to coquet.
FLIRTA'TION, *n.* act of flirting; coquetry.
FLIRT, *n.* a sudden jerk; a coquette.

Fleotan, from *flowan*—to FLOW.

FLOAT, *v.* to swim on the surface.
FLOOD, *n. flod,* a great flow of water.
FLOE, *n.* a mass of floating ice.
FLOW, *v.* to run as water.
OVERFLOW', *v. ofer,* to run over.

Flocc—FLOCK.

FLOCK, *n.* a company of birds or small beasts.
FLOCK, *v.* to come together in numbers.

NOTE.—*Flock* is often limited to a collection of sheep, to distinguish them from a *herd* or *drove* of larger cattle.

Flor—FLOOR.

FLOOR, *n.* the part of a room on which we walk.
FLOOR, *v.* to cover with a floor; to knock down.

Flitan—to DISPUTE.

FLOUT, *v.* to mock; to sneer.
FLOUT, *v.* to show contempt.
FLOUT'INGLY, *ad.* in an insulting manner.

Foh, flan—to HATE.

FOE, *n.* an enemy.
FOE'MAN, *n.* an enemy in war.

Fegan—to COLLECT. *Fog*—COLLECTION.

FOG, *n.* a thick mist.
FOG'GY, *a.* misty; dull.

Fealdan—to FOLD.

FOLD, *v.* to double one part over another.
FOLD'ING, *n.* a doubling.

FOLKS, *n. folc,* people; multitude.

Folgian—to FOLLOW.

FOL'LOW, *v.* to go or come after.
FOL'LOWER, *n.* one who follows.

Fonne—a FOOL.

FOND, *a.* foolishly tender and loving.
FOND, *a.* loving ardently.
FOND'LE, *v.* to treat with tenderness.
FOND'LY, *ad.* with great tenderness.
FOND'NESS, *n.* foolish tenderness.

Fot—a FOOT. *Fet*—FEET.

FOOT, *n.* that by which anything is supported.
FOOT'ING, *n.* ground for the foot.
FOOT'BALL, *n.* a ball driven by the foot.
FOOT'BRIDGE, *n.* a bridge for foot passengers.
FOOT'STEP, *n.* trace; track; mark.
FOOT'STOOL, *n.* a stool for the feet.
FET'TER, *n.* a chain for the feet.
FET'TER, *v.* to bind; to chain.

Getan—to Get.

Get, v. to procure; to obtain.
Beget', v. to produce.
Forget', v. to lose memory of.
Forget'ful, a. apt to forget.
Forget'fulness, n. loss of memory; neglect.

Forc—Fork.

Fork, n. an instrument divided at the end into two or more points or prongs.
Fork'ed, a. opening into two or more parts.

Forma. Fore and mær—More.

For'mer, a. before another in time; past.
For'merly, ad. in time past; of old.

Weard—Motion Towards.

For'ward, ad. toward a place in front.
For'wardness, n. eagerness; boldness.
For'wards, ad. straight before.
In'ward, internal.
In'wardly, internally.

Ful, foul—Dirty; Impure.

Foul, a. dirty; filthy; hindered from motion.
Foul'ly, ad. filthily; not fairly.
Foul'ness, n. filthiness.
Foul'mouthed, a. using scurrilous language.
Foul'spoken, a. slanderous.
Befoul', v. to make foul.
Ful'some, a. nauseous; offensive.
Defile', v. *gefylan,* to make foul; to pollute.

Note.—Defile', a narrow pass, an army movement, comes from the Latin *de*, from, off, and *filum*, a thread.

Feower—Four.

Four, a. twice two.
Fourth, a. the ordinal of four.
Four'fold, a. four times as much.
Four'score, a. four times twenty.
For'ty, a. four times ten.
Four'square, a. having four equal sides.
Fir'kin, n. the fourth part of a barrel.
Far'thing, n. the fourth part of a penny.

Fugel—a Bird; Fowl.

Fowl, n. a winged animal; a bird.
Fowl'er, n. a sportsman who pursues birds.
Fowl'ing, n. the act of shooting birds.
Fowl'ingpiece, n. a gun for shooting birds.

Fox—Fox.

Fox, n. a cunning animal.
Fox'y, a. cunning; artful.

Fremman—to Frame or Form.

Frame, v. to fit one thing to another.
Frame'work, n. that which supports anything else.

Freo—Free. Freond, from freon—to Free; to Love.

Free, *a.* having liberty.
Free'dom, *n.* liberty; independence.
Free'ly, *ad.* with freedom.
Free'ness, *n.* openness; liberality.
Freed'man, *n.* a slave manumitted.
Free'hold, *n.* property held in perpetual right.
Free'stone, *n.* a kind of stone easily worked.

Frol'ic, *n.* a wild prank; a scene of gayety and mirth.
Frol'icsome, *a.* full of wild gayety.
Friend, *n. freond,* an intimate acquaintance.
Friend'less, *a.* without friends.
Friend'ly, *a.* kind; favorable.
Friend'ship, *n.* personal kindness.
Befriend', *v.* to favor; to assist.

Fersc—Fresh; Pure; Sweet.

Fresh, *a.* cool; new; not salt.
Fresh'en, *v.* to make fresh.
Fresh'et, *n.* an inundation.
Fresh'ness, *n.* newness; vigor; spirit.

Refresh', *v.* to cool; to relieve after fatigue.
Refresh'ing, *p.* or *a.* reviving.
Refresh'ment, *n.* food; rest.

Fretan—to Eat or Gnaw.

Fret, *v.* to wear away; to vex; to rut. | Fret'ful, *a.* disposed to fret; peevish.
Fret'ting, *ppr.* wearing away; vexing.

Frig-dæg. Friga—the Goddess of Love; dæg—a Day.

Fri'day, *n.* the sixth day of the week.

Frihtan—to Alarm; to Terrify.

Fright, *v.* to terrify; *n.* sudden terror.
Fright'en, *v.* to terrify.
Fright'ful, *a.* terrible; dreadful.

Affright', *v.* to impress with sudden fear.
Affright'ful, *a.* terrible; dreadful.

Fra—Fro. Fram—From.

Fro, *ad.* backward.
From, *prep.* noting privation, distance, or absence.

Fro'ward, *a. weard,* perverse; peevish.
Fro'wardness, *n.* perverseness.

Freosan—to Freeze. Frost—Frost.

Freeze, *v.* to harden into ice.
Frost, *n.* the power of freezing.
Fro'zen, *p. a.* congealed by cold.
Frost'ed, *a.* as if covered with hoar frost.

Frost'y, *a.* producing frost.
Frost'bitten, *a.* nipped by the frost.
Frost'work, *n.* work resembling hoar frost.
Hoar-frost, *n.* frozen dew.

Fyllan—to Fill.

Fill, *v.* to make full; to satisfy; to occupy.
Full, *a.* having no empty space.
Ful'ly, *ad.* completely.

Full'ness, *n.* the state of being full.
Fulfill', *v.* to accomplish; to perform.
Fulfill'ment, *n.* completion.

Fullian—to Whiten.

Full, *v.* to cleanse and thicken cloth in a mill.

Full'er, *n.* one who fulls cloth.
Fuller's-earth', *n.* a kind of clay.

Faegen—GLAD.

FUN, n. sport; merriment. | FUN'NY, a. droll; comical.

Furlang. Fur—a FURROW, and lang—LONG.

FUR'LONG, n. the eighth part of a mile. | FUR'ROW, n. a trench made by a plough.

Feor—FAR. Faran—to GO; to ADVANCE.

FUR'THER, a. at a greater distance.
FUR'THEST, a. at the greatest distance.
FUR'THERMORE, ad. moreover; besides.

FORTH, ad. forward; abroad.
FORTH'COMING, a. ready to appear.
FORTH'WITH, ad. immediately; without delay.

Fus—READY; QUICK. Fysan—to HASTEN.

FUSS, n. a tumult; a bustle.

Gabban—to MOCK; to JEST.

GAB, v. to talk idly; n. loquacity; the mouth.
GAB'BLE, v. to talk without meaning.
GIB'BER, v. to speak rapidly and inarticulately.

GIB'BERISH, n. talk without meaning.
GIBE, v. to sneer; to taunt; to deride.
GIB'INGLY, ad. scornfully.
JAB'BER, v. to talk idly.

Ga or Gan—to GO.

GO, v. to be in motion.
GAD, n. a heavy whip.
GAD'FLY, n. a fly that stings cattle.

GOAD, n. a pointed stick to drive oxen; to incite.
GAD, v. to rove about idly.

NOTE.—WENT, now used as the preterit of GO, is a part of the verb WEND.

Gynan—to GAIN. Gewinnan—to WIN.

GAIN, v. to obtain; to win; to attain.
GAIN'ER, n. one who gains.

GAIN'FULLY, ad. profitably.
GAIN'LESS, a. unprofitable.

Gealla—the GALL.

GALL, n. the bile; anything very bitter.

NOTE.—GALL, to fret by rubbing the skin, to vex, comes from the French (*galer*), and GALL, an excrescence on the oak tree, comes from the Latin (*galla*).

Gamen—a JEST; SPORT; GAME.

GAME, n. sport; jest; a match at play.
GAME, n. animals pursued in the field.
GAM'BLE, v. to play for money.

GAM'BLER, n. one who plays for money.
GAME'STER, n. one addicted to play.

NOTE.—GAMBOL, to dance, to skip, to frisk, comes from the Italian (*gamba*).

Geapan—to OPEN; to GAPE.

GAPE, v. to open the mouth wide; to yawn.
GAP, n. an opening; a hole.

AGAPE', ad. staring with open mouth.
GASP, v. to open the mouth to catch breath.

Gearwian—to PREPARE.

GAR'ISH, *a.* gaudy; showy. | GAR'ISHNESS, *n.* showy finery.
GEAR, *n.* furniture; ornaments.

Gyrdan—to GIRD or ENCLOSE.

GAR'DEN, *n.* a piece of ground enclosed for flowers, fruit, &c. | GAR'DENER, *n.* one who cultivates a garden.

Geat—GATE.

GATE, *n.* a frame which opens or closes a passage. | GATE'WAY, *n.* the way through a gate.

Gaderian—to GATHER.

GATH'ERING, *n.* an assembly; a collection. | GATH'ER, *v.* to collect; to assemble.

Gæc—a CUCKOO.

GAWK, *n.* a cuckoo; a fool. | GAWK'Y, *a.* awkward; ungainly.

Gesean—to SEE.

GAZE, *v.* to look intently. | GAZE'FUL, *a.* looking intently.

Gidig—GIDDY.

GID'DY, *a.* having a sensation of whirling in the head. | GID'DINESS, *n.* the state of being giddy.
GID'DILY, *ad.* carelessly.

Gold—YELLOW; GOLD.   *Geldan*—GOLDEN.

GOLD, *n.* a precious metal of a bright yellow color. | GILD'ING, *n.* the art of overlaying with gold.
GOLD'EN, *a.* made of gold. | GILT, *n.* gold laid on the surface.
GILD, *v.* to overlay with gold. | ENGILD', *v.* to brighten.

Gyrd—a TWIG; a BRANCH.   *Gyrdan*—to GIRD; to SURROUND.

GIRD, *n.* a twitch; a pang. | GIR'DLE, *n.* a band; a belt.
GIRD, *v.* to bind round. | GIRT, *n.* a circular bandage.
GIRD'ER, *n.* the principal timber in a floor. | GIRTH, *n.* a circular bandage.
 | BEGIRD', *v.* to surround.

Gifan—to GIVE.

GIVE, *v.* to bestow; to confer; to yield. | FORGIVE', *v.* to pardon; to remit.
GIFT, *n.* the thing given. | FORGIVE'NESS, *n.* pardon.
GIFT'ED, *a.* endowed with powers. | FORGIV'ING, *a.* disposed to forgive.
GIV'ER, *n.* one who gives; a donor. | MISGIVE', *v.* to fill with doubt.

Glæd—GLAD.

GLAD, *a.* cheerful; pleased. | GLAD'LY, *ad.* with gladness.
GLAD'DEN, *v.* to make glad; to delight. | GLAD'NESS, *n.* joy; cheerfulness.
 | GLAD'SOME, *a.* pleased; gay.

Glæs—Glass.

Note.—The old Germans called Amber *gles*.

Glass, *n.* a hard, brittle, transparent substance.
Glass'y, *a.* like glass.
Glaze, *v.* to cover with glass.
Gla'zier, *n.* one who glazes windows.

Gloss, *n.* a smooth, shining surface.
Gloss, *v.* to palliate by specious representation.
Gloss'y, *a.* smooth and shining.
Gloss'iness, *n.* polish.

Gleam—Gleam.

Gleam, *n.* a shoot of light; *v.* to shine suddenly.
Gleam'ing, *n.* shooting as rays of light.

Glie—Sport; Music.

Glee, *n.* joy; merriment; a sort of song.
Glee'ful, *a.* merry; cheerful.
Glee'some, *a.* full of merriment.

Glomung—Twilight.

Gloom, *n.* partial darkness; melancholy.
Gloom'y, *a.* obscure; dismal.
Gloom'ily, *ad.* dimly; dismally.
Gloom'iness, *n.* obscurity; melancholy.
Glum, *v.* to look sullen.

Glof—Glove. Cleofen—Cloven; Split.

Glove, *n.* a cover for the hand, with a sheath for each finger.

Glowan—to Glow.

Glow, *v.* to be red with heat; to feel passion.
Glow'ingly, *ad.* brightly; with passion.

Gnorne—Sorrowful; Complaining.

Gnarl, *v.* to growl; to snarl.
Gnar'ly, *a.* having knots; knotty.
Gnarl'ed, *a.* full of knots.
Knurl, *v.* to gnarl.

Gnagan—to Scrape; to Gnaw.

Gnaw, *v.* to bite or scrape off with the teeth.
Gnaw'er, *n.* one that gnaws.

Gat—Goat.

Goat, *n.* an animal.
Goat'herd, *n.* one who tends goats.
Go'thamite, one who lives in Gotham.
Goth'am, *n.* (*goats' home*), a name sportively applied to the city of New York.

Gor—Mud; Gore.

Gore, *n.* clotted blood; *v.* to wound with a horn.
Go'ry, *a.* bloody.

Note.—Gore, a triangular piece of cloth, comes from the W. (*gor*, an opening).

God—God. *God*—Good.

God, *n.* the Supreme Being.
God'dess, *n.* a female divinity.
God'head, *n.* the divine nature.
God'less, *a.* impious; wicked.
God'ly, *a.* pious; religious.
God'liness, *n.* piety.
God'child, *n.* one for whom a person becomes sponsor at baptism.
God'father, *n.* a male sponsor at baptism.
God'mother, *n.* a female sponsor at baptism.
Gos'pel, *n.* (*god-spell; god,* good, and *spell,* history or tidings), the evangelical history of our Saviour; the word of God.

God'like, *a.* divine.
Dem'igod, *n.* half a god.
Gos'sip, *n.* (*god,* good, and *sib,* relation), a sponsor; an idle tattler.
Gos'siping, *n.* a running about to tattle.
Good, *a.* not bad; proper; wholesome; useful; happy; kind.
Goods, *n.* property; merchandise.
Good'ly, *a.* beautiful; graceful.
Good'liness, *n.* beauty; grace.
Good'ness, *n.* excellence; kindness.
Goodbreed'ing, *n.* elegance of manners.
Goodhu'mor, *n.* cheerfulness of mind.
Goodna'tured, *a.* mild; kind.

Note.—"In Anglo-Saxon God signifies both *God* and *good;* but Man is used to denote *man* and *wickedness.* The Saxons call him *God,* which is literally, *the Good;* the same word thus signifying the Deity and his most endearing quality."—Bosworth.

Gos—Goose.

Goose, *n.* a water-fowl.
Gos'ling, *n.* a young goose.

Geese, *n.* the plural of goose.

Grafan—to Carve; to Dig.

Graft, *v.* to insert a shoot of one tree into the stock of another.
Grave, *v.* to write on hard substances.
Groove, *n.* a channel cut with a tool.

Grave, *n.* (*graef,* a ditch, a trench), a pit for a dead body.
Grove, *n. graef,* an avenue of trees.

Note.—Grave, solemn, serious, comes from the Latin *gravis,* heavy.
Grove is cut out, hollowed out of a thicket of trees; it is not the thicket itself.

Grenian—to Grow; Grain.

Grain, *n.* the direction of the fibers; temper.

Note.—Grain, a seed, a corn, comes from the Latin (*granum*).

Gripan—to Seize. *Grapian*—to Touch with the Hands.

Gripe, *v.* to hold hard; to grasp.
Grap'ple, *v.* to lay fast hold of.

Grap'nel, *n.* a small anchor.
Grope, *v.* to search by feeling.

Græs—to Shoot Forth; to Sprout; Grass.

Grass, *n.* the common herbage of the fields.

Græg—Gray.

Gray, *a.* white with a mixture of black.

Gray'beard, *n.* an old man.

Grasian—to Graze.

Graze, *v.* to eat grass.

Graz'ier, *n.* one who raises cattle.

Great—GREAT.

GREAT, *a.* large; vast; important. | GREAT'LY, *ad.* in a great degree.
GREAT'NESS, *n.* the state of being great.

Grœdig—GREEDY; COVETOUS.

GREED'Y, *a.* ravenous; eager to obtain. | GREED'INESS, *n.* ardent desire.

Grene—GREEN; FLOURISHING.

GREEN, *a.* of the color of growing plants; fresh. | GREEN'NESS, *n.* the state of being green.

Gretan—to GO TO MEET; WISHING PEACE.

GREET'ING, *n.* addressing with kind wishes. | GREET, *v.* to salute; to welcome.

Grim—FIERCE; FEROCIOUS.

GRIM, *a.* frightful; hideous. | GRIM'LY, *ad.* horribly; sourly.
GRIM'ACE, *n.* distortion of the face.

Grindan—to BRUISE; to GNASH.

GRIND, *v.* to reduce to powder; to rub; to oppress. | GRIND'STONE, *n.* a stone on which tools are sharpened.
GRIST, *n.* corn or grain to be ground at one time.

Greot—SAND; DUST.

GRIT, *n.* the coarse part of meal; sand or gravel. | GRIT'TY, *a.* containing grit.

Granan—to LAMENT; MOURN; WEEP.

GROAN, *v.* to breathe or sigh as in pain. | GROAN'ING, *n.* a deep sigh.
GRUNT, *v.* to murmur as a hog.

Grund—GROUND; EARTH; BOTTOM.

GROUND, *n.* the surface of land.
GROUND, *v.* to place or fix; to run aground. | GROUND'LESS, *a.* void of reason.
GROUND'LESSLY, *ad.* without reason or cause.
AGROUND', *ad.* stranded.

Growan—to GROW.

GROW, *v.* to increase in size. | GROW'ING, *ppr.* increasing.
GROWTH, *n.* increase; product.

Geomrian—to GRIEVE.

GRUM'BLE, *v.* to murmur with discontent. | GRUM'BLER, *n.* one who grumbles.

Weard—a GUARD; WATCH.

GUARD, *v.* to protect; to defend. | GUARD'ED, *a.* cautious; circumspect.
GUAR'DIAN, *n.* a protector.

Ge and *wiglian*—to DECEIVE.   *Wile*—GUILE.

GUILE, *n.* craft; cunning.
GUILE'FUL, *a.* wily; artful.
WILE, *n.* a deceit; a trick.
WI'LY, *a.* cunning; sly; insidious.

GUILE'LESS, *a.* free from guile.
BEGUILE', *v.* to deceive; to amuse.
WI'LILY, *ad.* fraudulently.
WI'LINESS, *n.* cunning; guile.

Gylt—a CRIME; a DEBT.

GUILT. *n.* the state of having committed a crime.
GUILT'Y, *a.* justly chargeable with a crime.

GUILT'LESS, *a.* free from crime.
GUILT'INESS, *n.* the state of being guilty.

Goma—the PALATE; the JAW; GUM.

GUM, *n.* the concrete juice of certain trees; a tree.

GUM'MY, *a.* consisting of gum.

Haccan—to HACK.

HACK, *v.* to chop; to cut clumsily. | HACK, *n.* a small cut.

NOTE.—HACK, a horse let out for hire, is from the French (*haquenée*).

Hægl—HAIL.

HAIL, *n.* drops of rain frozen while falling.

HAIL'STONE, *n.* a single ball of hail.

Hær—HAIR.

HAIR, *n.* a small filament issuing from the skin.
HAIR'Y, *a.* covered with hair.

HAIR'BREADTH, *n.* a very small distance.
HAIR'CLOTH, *n.* cloth made of hair.

Healf—HALF.

HALF, *n.* one part of a thing which is divided into two equal parts.
HALVES, *n.* two equal parts of a thing.

HALVE, *v.* to divide into two equal parts.

Halig—HOLY: HALLOW.

HAL'LOW, *v.* to make holy.
HO'LY, *a.* good; religious; pure.
HO'LINESS, *n.* sanctity: piety.
HO'LYDAY, *n.* a religious festival.

HOL'IDAY, *n.* a festival day.
HAL'IDOM, *n.* an adjuration by what is holy.

Healtian—to HOLD AND TO STOP.

HALT, *v.* to limp; to stop. | HALT, *a.* lame; crippled.
HALT, *n.* a stop in a march.

Hælfter—a HOLDER; HALTER.

HAL'TER, *n.* a rope for confining an animal.

HAL'TER, *n.* a rope to hang criminals.

Hamer—HAMMER.

HAM'MER, n. an instrument for driving or beating.

HAM'MER, v. to beat with a hammer.

HAM'MERCLOTH, n. the cloth which covers a coach-box

NOTE.—The coach box was formerly used to carry a *hammer*, pincers, a few nails, &c.

Hand—HAND.

HAND, n. the palm with the fingers.
HAND, v. to give; to lead.
HAND'FUL, n. as much as the hand can hold.
HAN'DLE, v. to touch; to manage.
HAN'DLE, n. that part of a thing which is held in the hand.
HAND'Y, a. ready; convenient.
HAND'ILY, ad. with skill; with dexterity.
HAND'IWORK, n. work done by the hand

HAND'CUFF, n. a fetter for the wrist.
HAND'SEL, n. (*syllan,* to give), the first act of using any thing; a gift.
HAND'SOME, a. dextrous; ready.
HAND'SOME, a. beautiful; graceful; elegant.
HAND'SOMELY, ad. dextrously; with skill.
UNHAND', v. to let go.
UNHAN'DLED, a. not handled; not touched.

Hangian—to HANG.

HANG, v. to suspend; to fasten to something above so as to leave without support below.
HANG'ING, n. death by a halter.
HINGE, n. a joint on which a door turns.

OVERHANG', v. to jut over; to impend.
UNHANGED', a. not punished by hanging.
UNHINGE', v. to take from the hinges; to displace.

Here—an ARMY, and beorg—a REFUGE. Here-beorg—HARBOR.

HAR'BOR, n. a place of refuge, or safety.

HAR'BORER, n. one who shelters another.

HAR'BINGER, n. a forerunner; a precursor.

NOTE.—HARBINGER is properly a person who goes before to provide *harbor* of lodgings for those that follow.

Heard—HARD; the primary sense is PRESSED.

HARD, a. firm; not soft; difficult.
HARD'EN, v. to make hard.
HARD'LY, a. with difficulty; scarcely.

HARD'NESS, n. the quality of being hard.
HARD'SHIP, n. toil; fatigue.

Hara—HARE.

HARE, n. a small quadruped.
HARE'BRAINED, a. giddy; wild.

HARE'LIP, n. a divided upper lip, like that of a hare.

Hearm—GRIEF; OFFENCE; HURT.

HARM, n. injury; crime.

HARM'FUL, a. hurtful.

HARM'LESS, a. not hurtful; unhurt.

Hearpe—HARP.

HARP, n. a musical instrument.

HARP, v. to dwell on.

HARP'ING, n. a continual dwelling on.

Hærefæst—HARVEST; AUTUMN.

HAR'VEST, *n.* the season of gathering the crops.
HAR'VEST, *v.* to gather in.
HAR'VEST-HOME, *n.* the time of gathering the harvest.

Hæt—a COVER; HAT.

HAT, *n.* a cover for the head.
HAT'TER, *n.* one who makes hats.

Hæca—a RAILING; GATE; HATCH.

HATCH, *n.* a half door; the openings in a ship's deck.
HATCH'WAY, *n.* the way through the hatches.

NOTE.—HATCH, to produce young from eggs, comes from the German (*hecken*).

Hatian—to HATE.

HATE, *v.* to dislike greatly.
HATE'FUL, *a.* odious.
HATE'FULLY, *ad.* odiously.
HA'TRED, *n.* great dislike; enmity.

Habban—to HAVE; HOLD; DETAIN; COUNT.

HAVE, *v.* to possess; to hold; to enjoy.
HAV'ING, *n.* possessions; goods.
BEHAVE', *v.* to conduct; to act.
BEHAV'IOR, *n.* conduct.

Haga, hæg—a HEDGE; an INCLOSURE; HAW.

HAW, *n.* the berry of the hedge-thorn.
HAW'THORN, *n.* a thorn which bears the haw.

Hafoc—a HAWK.

HAWK, *n.* a bird of prey.
HAV'OC, *n.* waste; devastation.

NOTE.—HAWK, to force up phlegm, comes from the German (*hauch*), and HAWK, to sell by crying out in the streets, from the German (*hocken*).

Hæsl—a HAT or CAP; HAZEL.

HA'ZEL, *n.* a shrub; a light brown color.
HA'ZELNUT, *n.* the fruit of the hazel; a cap nut.

Heafod—HEAD.

HEAD, *n.* the part of an animal which contains the brain; the chief.
HEAD'LESS, *a.* having no head.
HEAD'ACHE, *n.* a pain in the head.
HEAD'LONG, *a.* rashly; hastily.
BEHEAD', *v.* to deprive of the head.
FORE'HEAD, *n.* the part of face which is above the eyes.

Hyran, heran—to HEAR; HEARKEN.

HEAR, *v.* to perceive by the ear.
HEAR'ING, *n.* perceiving by the ear.
HEAR'SAY, *n.* report; rumor.
REHEAR', *v.* to hear again.
REHEARSE', *v.* to repeat; to recite.
REHEARS'AL, *n.* repetition.
HEARK'EN, *v.* to listen; to attend.

Hǽl, or hǽlu—HEALTH. Hal—HEALTHY; SOUND; WHOLE.

HEAL, v. to grow well.
HEAL'ING, ppr. curing.
HEALTH, n. freedom from sickness.
HEALTH'FUL, a. free from sickness.
HEALTH'Y, a. enjoying health.
HEALTH'INESS, n. the state of health.
HALE, a. healthy; sound; hearty.
WHOLE, a. all; total; complete.

WHOLE'SALE, n. sale in large quantities.
WHOLE'SOME, a. contributing to health.
WHOLE'SOMELY, ad. in a wholesome manner.
WHOLE'SOMENESS, n. the quality of being wholesome.

WHOL'LY, ad. totally; completely.

Heorte—HEART.

HEART, n. the muscle which is the seat of life.
HEART'LESS, a. void of affection; without courage.

HEART'Y, a. cordial; sincere.
HEART'ILY, ad. from the heart.
HEART'INESS, n. sincerity; eagerness.
HEART'ACHE, n. sorrow; anguish.

Hebban—to RAISE. Heofon—RAISED; ELEVATED. Hefig—LIFTED WITH LABOR.

HEAVE, v. to lift; to raise; to throw.
HEAV'ING, n. a rising; a swell.
HEAV'EN, n. heofon, the regions above.
HEAV'ENLY, a. supremely excellent.

HEAV'ENWARD, ad. towards heaven.
HEAV'Y, a. weighty; dejected.
HEAV'ILY, ad. with great weight.
HEAV'INESS, n. weight; depression.
HEFT, n. weight; heaviness.

HEFT, v. to try the weight by lifting.

Hege—PROTECTION; HEDGE.

HEDGE, n. a fence made of thorns.
HEDGE, v. to encircle for defence.

HEDGE'HOG, n. an animal set with prickles.

HUG, v. to embrace closely.

Hedan—HEED.

HEED, v. to mind; to regard.
HEED'FUL, a. watchful; cautious; attentive.

HEED'LESS, a. negligent; careless.
HEED'LESSNESS, n. carelessness.

Hihtho—HEIGHT.

HEIGHT, n. space measured upwards.
HEIGHT'EN, v. to make higher.
HIGH, a. elevated; exalted; lofty.

HIGH'LY, ad. in a great degree.
HIGH'NESS, n. elevation; loftiness.
HIGH'WAY,* n. a public road.

* So called because the ground was raised to form a dry path.

Helpan—to HELP.

HELP, v. to assist; to aid.
HELP'ER, n. one who helps.

HELP'FUL, a. giving help.
HELP'LESS, a. without help.

Hem—a BORDER.

HEM, n. the edge of a garment doubled and sewed.

HEM, v. to border; to edge.

NOTE.—To HEM in, about, or around, signifies, to enclose; to environ; to confine.
HEM, a sort of voluntary cough, is from the Dutch (hemmen).

Hen—Hen.

Hen, n. the female of birds.
Hen'bane, n. (bane, poison), a poisonous plant.

Hen'pecked, a. governed by a wife.
Hen'roost, n. a place where poultry roost.

Heona—Hence.

Hence, ad. from this place; from this time.

Henceforth', ad. from this time forward.

Hyre—Her.

Herself', pro. a female which is the subject of discourse.

Her, pro. belonging to a female.

Heord—a Collection; an Assemblage.

Herd, n. a number of beasts together.
Horde, n. a clan of wandering people.

Herds'man, n. one who tends herds.

Her—Here.

Here, ad. in this place.
Hereaf'ter, ad. in time to come.

Here'abouts, ad. about this place.

Hill—Hill.

Hill, n. an elevation of ground.
Hill'y, a. full of hills.

Hill'ock, n. a little hill.

Him—Him.

Himself', pro. the emphatic form of He and Him.

Him, pro. the objective case of He.

Hyre—a Reward.

Hire, v. to engage for pay.
Hire, n. wages paid for service.

Hire'ling, n. one who serves for pay; a mercenary.

Hider—Hither.

Hith'er, ad. to this place; nearer.

Hith'erto, ad. to this time.

Har—Gray.

Hoar, a. white or gray with age.
Hoar'y, ad. white or gray with age.
Hoar'hound,* n. a plant.

Hoar'frost, n. dew frozen, or white frost.

* So called from its appearance.

Hord—Hoard.

Hoard, n. a quantity laid up in secret.

Hoard, v. to store secretly.

Has—Hoarse.

Hoarse, a. having the voice rough.

Hoarse'ness, n. roughness of voice.

Hucx—Irony.

Hoax, *n.* a trick played off in sport. | Hoax, *v.* to deceive in joke.

Hoppan—to Hop.

Hop, *v.* to leap on one leg; to dance.
Hop, *n.* a leap; a meeting for dancing.
Hop'per,* *n.* one who hops; a box into which corn is put to be ground.
Hob'ble, *v.* to walk lamely.

* So named from its shaking.

Note.—Hop, a plant used in brewing, comes from the Dutch.

Hul—Hole.

Hole, *n.* a cavity; a cell.
Hol'low, *n.* containing an empty space.
Hol'ster, *n.* (*heolster,* a hiding-place), a case for a horseman's pistol.
Hol'lowness, *n.* state of being hollow.

Ham—a House; a Village.

Home, *n.* one's own house, or country.
Home'less, *a.* without a home.
Home'ly, *a.* plain; not elegant.
Home'liness, *n.* plainness.
Home'made, *a.* made at home.
Home'spun, *a.* spun at home.
Ham'let, *n.* a small village.

Hunig—Honey.

Hon'ey, *n.* a sweet juice collected by bees.
Hon'eycomb, *n.* cells of wax for honey.
Hon'eymoon, *n.* the first month after marriage.
Hon'ied, *a.* covered with honey.

Hod—Hood.

Hood'wink, *v.* to blind by covering the eyes; to deceive. | Hood, *n.* a covering for the head.

Hopa—Hope.

Note.—The primary sense is, to reach forward.

Hope, *n.* expectation of good.
Hope'ful, *a.* full of hope.
Hope'fulness, *n.* promise of good.
Hope'less, *a.* wanting hope.

Horn—Horn.

Horn, *n.* a hard, pointed substance growing on the heads of some animals.
Horn'y, *a.* like horn.
Horn'pipe, *n.* a lively tune.

Hors—Horse.

Horse, *n.* a well-known quadruped. | Horse'manship, *n.* the art of riding.

Hos—Hose.

Hose, *n.* stockings. | Hos'ier, *n.* one who sells stockings.

Hat—Hot.

Hot, *a.* having heat; fiery.
Hot'ly, *ad.* with heat; violently.
Hot'ness, *n.* heat; fury.
Hot'spur, *n.* a violent, precipitate man.

Hu—How.

How, *ad.* in what manner.
Howbe'it, *ad.* nevertheless; yet.
Howev'er, *ad.* at all events.
Howsoev'er, *ad.* in whatsoever manner.

Yiellan—to Howl.

Howl'ing, *n.* uttering the cry of a wolf or dog.
Howl, *v.* to cry as a wolf or dog.

Hiw—Color; Form.

Hue, *n.* color; tint; dye.

Note.—Hue, a shouting, an alarm, comes from the French (*huer*, to hoot).

Hunger—Hunger.

Hun'ger, *n.* desire of food; pain felt from fasting.
Hun'gered, *a.* famished; starved.
Hun'gry, *a.* feeling pain from want of food.
Hun'grily, *ad.* with a keen appetite.

Huntian—to Hunt.

Hunt, *v.* to chase; to search for.
Hunt'er, *n.* one that hunts.
Hunts'man, *n.* one who practises hunting.
Hunt'ing, *n.* the diversion of the chase.

Hyrt—Wounded; Hurt.

Hurt, *v.* to harm; to injure.
Hurt, *n.* harm; wound.
Hurt'ful, *a.* injurious.
Hurt'less, *a.* harmless.

Hus—a House; a Covered Place.   Bonda—a Master.

House, *n.* a place of human abode.
House'less, *a.* without a house.
House'hold, *n.* a family living together.
House'wife, *n.* the mistress of a family.
Hus'band, *n.* a man joined to a woman by marriage.
Hus'bandry, *n.* tillage.
Hus'bandman, *n.* one who tills the ground.
Hus'tings, *n.* a council; a place where an election is held.
Out'house, *n.* a house separate from a dwelling-house.
Pent'house, *n.* a shed hanging aslope from the main wall.
Hov'el, *n.* a shed; a mean habitation.

Is—Ice.

Ice, *n.* water or other liquid made solid by cold.
Ice'berg, *n.* a mountain of ice.
I'cicle, *n.* a hanging shoot of ice.
I'cy, *a.* full of ice; made of ice.

Idel—VAIN; EMPTY.

I'DLE, *a.* doing nothing.
I'DLENESS, *n.* the state of being idle.
I'DLER, *n.* a lazy person.
I'DLY, *ad.* lazily; carelessly.

NOTE.—IDOL, an image, comes from the Greek (*eidos*).

IF, *con. gif,* supposing that; allowing that.

Yfel—EVIL; ILL.

ILL, *a.* bad; not good; sick.
ILL'NESS, *n.* sickness.
ILL'NATURE, *n.* bad temper.
ILL'WILL, *n.* enmity.

Waerc—ACHE; PAIN; IRK.

IRK, *v.* to weary.
IRK'SOME, *a.* wearisome; tedious.

Iren—IRON.

I'RON, *n.* the most common and useful of the metals.
I'RONY, *a.* made of iron; like iron.

NOTE.—IRONY, a mode of speech in which the meaning is contrary to the words, comes from the Greek (*eiron*).

Yrre—ANGRY.

JAR, *n.* a rattling vibration of sound; discord.
JAR, *v.* to clash; to quarrel.

NOTE.—JAR, an earthen vessel, comes from the French (*jarre*).

Cene—WAR'LIKE; EAGER.

KEEN, *a.* sharp; piercing; eager.
KEEN'NESS, *n.* sharpness; eagerness.
KEEN'LY, *ad.* sharply; eagerly.

Cepan—to KEEP.

KEEP, *v.* to hold; to retain.
KEEP'SAKE, *n.* a gift in token of regard.

Cwellan—to KILL.

KILL, *v.* to deprive of life.
QUELL, *v.* to crush; to subdue.
QUAIL, *v.* to fail in spirits; to quake; to tremble.

NOTE.—QUAIL, a bird, comes from the French (*caille*).

Cyln—a FURNACE or KITCHEN.

KILN, *n.* a large stove or oven.
KILN'DRY, *v.* to dry in a kiln.

Cyn—KIN; KIND; RELATION.

KIN, *n.* relation by blood.
KIND, *n.* race; sort; nature.
KIND'LY, *a.* natural; congenial.
KIN'DRED, *n.* relations by birth.
KIND'NESS, *n.* good will; favor.
KINS'MAN, *n.* a man of the same family.
UNKIND', *a.* not kind; not obliging.
KIND, *a.* disposed to do good to others.
KIND'LY, *ad.* with good will.

Cyning—a Chief; a Leader.

King, n. a monarch; a sovereign.
King'dom, n. the dominion of a king.
King'ly, a. belonging to a king.
King's-e'vil, a. scrofula.

Cyssan—to Kiss.

Kiss, v. to salute with the lips.
Kiss'er, n. one who kisses.

Cnapa—a Boy; a Servant; a Knave.

Note.—Originally a boy or young man, then a servant, and lastly a rogue.

Knave, n. a false, deceitful fellow.
Kna'vish, a. dishonest.
Kna'very, n. dishonesty.

Cneow—Knee.

Knee, n. a joint of the leg.
Kneel, v. to rest on the knees.
Kneel'ing, n. act of resting on the bent knees.

Cniht—a Boy; a Servant.

Knight, n. a title of honor.
Knight'hood, n. the dignity of a knight.

Cnytan—to Tie; to Knit.

Knit, v. to weave without a loom.
Knit'ting, ppr. uniting by needles.

Cnæp—a Top; a Button.

Knap, n. a protuberance.
Knob, n. a round ball at the end of a thing; a bunch.
Knob'by, a. full of knobs.
Knop, n. a knot; a tufted top.
Nape, n. the joint of the neck behind.

Cnott—Knot.

Knot, n. a complication made by knitting or tying.
Knot'ted, a. full of knots.
Knot'ty, a. full of knots; difficult.
Knot'tiness, n. difficulty.

Cunnan—to Know; to Be Able.

Know, v. to understand clearly.
Knowl'edge, n. learning; skill.
Acknowl'edge, v. to own; to confess.
Foreknow', v. to know before.
Unforeknown', a. not previously known.
Cun'ning, n. artifice; deceit.
Unknown', a. not known.
Unacknowl'edged, a. not owned.
Acknowl'edgement, n. recognition; confession.
Know'ing, a. skillful; intelligent.
Cun'ning, a. artfully deceitful; crafty.

Note.—Cunning, which was formerly much used in the sense of *knowing* or *skillful*, is now commonly used in an ill sense, implying art or craft.

Cnucl—a Joint.

Knuc'kle, n. a joint of the finger.
Knuc'kle, v. to yield; to submit.

Note.—Knuckle formerly signified any joint of the body.

Leode—a NATION; a PEOPLE.

LAD, *n.* a youth; a young man. | LASS, *n.* a girl; a young woman.

Hlad—a LOAD.   *Hladan*—to LOAD.

LADE, *v.* to load; to freight.
LOAD, *n.* a burden; a freight.
OVERLOAD', *v.* to burden too much. | UNLADE', *v.* to remove a cargo from a vessel.
UNLOAD', *v.* to take a load from.

Hladan—to DRAW OUT; to EMPTY.

LA'DLE, *n.* a large spoon with a long handle. | LADE, *v.* to throw out by dipping.

Hlæfdie—LADY.

NOTE.—From *hliftan*, to lift, *i. e.* one raised to the rank of her husband or lord.

LA'DY, *n.* a woman of high rank. | LA'DYLIKE, *a.* becoming a lady; elegant.

Lang—LONG.

LAG, *a.* coming behind; sluggish. | LAG'GARD, *n.* one who lags.

Lamb—LAMB.

LAMB, *n.* the young of a sheep. | LAMB'LIKE, *a.* like a lamb, mild.
LAMB'KIN, *n.* a little lamb.

Lam—LAME.

LAME, *a.* wanting the natural power or strength. | LAME'LY, *ad.* in a lame manner.
LAME'NESS, *n.* the state of being lame.

Land—LAND.

LAND, *n.* the solid matter of the earth.
LAND, *v.* to set or come on shore.
LAND'MARK, *n.* a mark to designate boundaries. | LAND'ING, *n.* a place to land at.
LAND'SCAPE, *n.* a picture of a portion of country.

Latost—LAST; contracted from LATEST.

LAST, *a.* latest; hindmost.
LAST, *v.* to remain; to continue. | LAST'ING, *p. a.* continuing; durable.
LAST'LY, *ad.* in the last place.

Laste—a FOOTSTEP.

LAST, *n.* the mold on which shoes are formed.

Læccan—to CATCH; to SEIZE.

LATCH, *n.* a fastening for a door.
LATCH'ET, *n.* the string that fastens a shoe. | LACE, *n.* a string or cord for tying.
LACE, *v.* to fasten with a string passed through opposite holes.

Lethrian—to ANOINT; to LATHER.

LATH'ER, *v.* to form a foam. | LATH'ER, *n.* froth or foam.

Læt, latian—to DELAY or RETARD.

LATE, *a.* not early; slow; recent.
LATE, *ad.* after the proper season.
LATE'LY, *ad.* not long ago.
LATE'NESS, *n.* the state of being out of time.

Hlihan—LAUGH.

NOTE.—Generally supposed to be formed from the sound,

LAUGH, *v.* to make that noise which sudden merriment excites.
LAUGH'INGLY, *ad.* in a merry way.
LAUGH'ABLE, *a.* exciting laughter.
LAUGH'TER, *n.* convulsive merriment.

Lagu—LAW; from *lecgan, lege*—to LAY.

LAW, *n.* a rule of action; a rule of justice.
LAW'FUL, *a.* agreeable to law.
LAW'FULLY, *ad.* agreeably to law.
LAW'LESS, *a.* not restrained by law.
LAW'YER, *n.* a professor of law.
LAW'GIVER, *n.* one who makes laws.
LAW'MAKER, *n.* one who makes laws.
LAW'SUIT, *n.* a process in law.
OUT'LAW, *n. ut,* one excluded from the benefit of the law.

Lead, læd—LEAD.

LEAD, *n.* a metal.
LEAD'EN, *a.* made of lead; heavy.

Lædan—LEAD.

LEAD, *v.* to guide; to conduct.
LEAD'ING, *a.* principal; chief.
LEAD'ER, *n.* one who leads.

Leafe—LEAF.

NOTE.—The original signification seems to be *broad, flat.*

LEAF, *n.* the thin, extended part of a tree, &c.
LEAF'Y, *a.* full of leaves.
LEAF'LESS, *a.* destitute of leaves.
LEAF'LET, *n.* a little leaf.

Læran—to TEACH.   *Leornian*—to LEARN.

LEARN, *v.* to gain knowledge of.
LEARN'ED, *a.* having learning.
LEARN'EDLY, *ad.* with knowledge.
LEARN'ING, *n.* skill in languages or science.
LORE, *n.* learning.

Lesan—to LET GO; to LOOSE.

LEASE, *v.* to let for a limited time.
LEASE'HOLD, *n.* held by lease.
LESSEE', *n.* one to whom a lease is given.

Lether—LEATHER.

LEATH'ER, *n.* dressed hides of animals.
LEATH'ERN, *a.* made of leather.
LEATH'ERY, *a.* resembling leather.

Leaf—LEAVE.   *Læfan*—to LEAVE; to PERMIT.

LEAVE, *n.* a grant of liberty; permission.
LEAV'INGS, *n.* things left behind; remnants.
LEAVE, *v.* to quit; to desist; to bequeath.

Hleo—a SHELTER.

LEE, *n.* a place sheltered from the wind.
LEE'WARD, *ad.* towards the lee; from the wind.

Læce—a PHYSICIAN; a LEECH.

LEECH, *n.* an aquatic worm which sucks blood.
LEECH'CRAFT, *n.* the art of healing.

Hleor—a FACE; LEER.

LEER, *v.* to turn the eye and cast a look from the corner of it.
LEER'INGLY, *ad.* with an oblique look

Lænan—to LEND. *Læn*—a LOAN.

LEND, *v.* to supply on condition of repayment.
LEND'ING, *v.* the act of making a loan.
LOAN, *n.* the act of lending.

Lengian—to LENGTHEN; so called from the lengthening of the day.

LENT, *n.* a fast of forty days before Easter.
LENT'EN, *a.* relating to Lent.

Lætan—to LET.

LET, *v.* to allow; to permit; to put out to hire.
OUT'LET, *v. ut*, a passage outwards.

Læfel—SMOOTH; EVEN; LEVEL.

LEV'EL, *a.* even; flat.
LEV'ELER, *n.* one who levels.

Læwd, past participle of *læwen*—to DELUDE; to MISLEAD.

LEWD, *a.* wicked.
LEWD'NESS, *n.* wickedness.

Lig, ligan—to LIE.

LIE, *v.* to utter a criminal falsehood.
LI'AR, *n.* one who utters lies.
BELIE', *v.* to slander.

Licgan—to LIE DOWN.

NOTE.—LIE (A.-S. *licgan*) differs from LAY (A.-S. *lecgan*, to lay, put, or set down,) only by grammatical use.

LIE, *v.* to rest horizontally.
RELI'ANCE, *n.* trust; confidence.
RELY', *v.* to lean or rest with confidence.

Leof—LIEF.

LIEF, *ad.* gladly; willingly.

NOTE.—*Lieve* for *lief* is vulgar.

Hlifian—to ARISE; to SOAR.

LIFT, *v.* to raise; to elevate.
LIFT'ING, *n.* the act of raising.

Leoht—LIGHT.   Gelihtan—to GLITTER.

LIGHT, *n.* the agent which produces vision.
LIGHT'EN, *v.* to illuminate; to shine.
LIGHT'ER, *n.* one who lights.
LIGHT'LESS, *a.* wanting light.
LIGHT'NING, *n.* the flash which precedes thunder.
LIGHT'SOME, *a.* luminous; gay; airy.
GLIT'TER, *v.* to shine; to sparkle.
GLIT'TERING, *a.* shining; brilliant.
GLIS'TEN, *v.* to sparkle with light.

Leoht, leohtan—to LIGHTEN.

LIGHT,* *a.* not heavy; active; nimble.
LIGHT'EN, *v.* to make less heavy.
LIGHT'ER, *n.* a large open boat.
LIGHT'NESS, *n.* want of weight; levity.
LIGHTS, *n.* the lungs of an animal.
LIGHT'HEADED, *a.* thoughtless; giddy.
LIGHT'HEARTED, *a.* gay; merry; cheerful.

* This word accords with LIGHT, the fluid in orthography, and may be from the the same radix.

Lihtan—to ALIGHT.

LIGHT, *v.* to fall or come by chance; to settle from flight.
ALIGHT', *v.* to come down; to dismount.

Lic—RESEMBLANCE.

LIKE, *a.* resembling; similar.
LIKE'LY, *a.* probable.
LIKE'LIHOOD, *n.* probability.
LIKE'NESS, *n.* resemblance; form.
LIK'EN, *v.* to represent as like; to compare.
DISLIKE', *v.* to regard with some aversion.
LIKE'WISE, *ad.* in like manner.

Lician, from lic, lac—a GIFT; WHAT PLEASES.

LIKE, *v.* to be pleased with.
LIK'ING, *n.* desire; pleasure.
LIKE'LY, *a.* that may be liked; pleasing.

Lim—LIMB; a MEMBER.

LIMB, *n.* a branch; a member.
LIMB'LESS, *a.* wanting limbs.
LIMP, *v.* to walk lamely.

NOTE.—LIMB, a border, comes from the Latin (*limbus*).

Lime—LIME.

LIME, *n.* a calcareous earth; the linden tree.
LIME'BURNER, *n.* one who burns stones to lime.
LIME'KILN, *n.* a furnace for lime.
LIME'STONE, *n.* the stone of which lime is made.

NOTE.—LIME, a species of lemon, comes from the French (*lime*)

List, from lesan, lysan—to COLLECT or ASSEMBLE.

LIST, *n.* a roll; a catalogue; a limit; a strip of cloth.

Hlystan—to LISTEN.

LIS'TEN, *v.* to hearken.
LIS'TENER, *n.* one who listens.

Lif—LIFE.   *Lifian*—to LIVE.

LIVE, *v.* to be in life; to exist.
LIVE, *a.* not dead; active.
LIVE'LY, *a.* brisk; vigorous.
LIVE'LIHOOD, *n.* means of living.
LIVE'LINESS, *n.* vivacity.

LIVE'LONG, *a.* long in passing.
LIFE, *n.* vitality; existence.
LIFE'LESS, *a.* void of life.
LIFE'LIKE, *a.* like a living person.
LIFE'TIME, *n.* continuance of life.

Lathian—to HATE; to DETEST.

LOATHE, *v.* to feel disgust at.
LOATH, *a.* unwilling.
LOATH'FUL, *a.* abhorring.

LOATH'SOME, *a.* disgusting.
LOATH'SOMENESS, *n.* quality of raising disgust.

LOATH'ING, *n.* disgust.

Loc—an ENCLOSURE; LOCK.

LOCK, *n.* an instrument to fasten a door; a tuft of hair.

LOCK'ET, *n.* a small lock.

Logian—to PLACE; to PUT; to LODGE.

LODGE, *v.* to place; to reside.
LODGE, *n.* a small house at a gate.

LODGE'MENT, *n.* the act of lodging.
DISLODGE', *v.* to remove from a place.

Liggan—to LIE; because it lies unmoved or inert.

LOG, *n.* a bulky piece of wood.

LOG'GERHEAD, *n.* a blockhead.

Locian—to LOOK.

LOOK, *v.* to direct the eye.

LOOK, *n.* air of the face; aspect.

Loma—UTENSILS; LOOM.

LOOM, *n.* a weaver's machine.

LUM'BER, *n.* anything useless; timber.

Leoman—to SHINE; to LOOM.

LOOM, *v.* to appear larger than the real dimensions.

LOOM'ING, *p. a.* appearing indistinctly large.

Leasan, lysan—to LOOSE; to PUT or TAKE AWAY.

LOOSE, *v.* to free from any fastening.
LOOSE'LY, *ad.* not firmly.
LOOS'EN, *v.* to relax; to free.

LOOSE'NESS, *n.* state of being loose.
LESS, *a.* smaller; not so large.
LESS'EN, *v.* to make or grow less.

LEST, *con.* that not; for fear that.

NOTE.—LESSON, a task, an exercise, is from the Greek (λέγω, to gather, to read).

Hlaford—LORD.   *Hlaf*—a LOAF; and *ford*—to SUPPLY.

LORD, *n.* a ruler; a nobleman.
LAIRD, *n.* the lord of a manor.
LORD'LIKE, *a.* befitting a lord.

LORD'LY, *a.* proud; haughty.
LORD'SHIP, *n.* the address of a lord.
LORD'LINESS, *n.* dignity; pride.

LOAF, *n.* a mass of bread, as baked.

Losian—to RUN AWAY; to BE LOST.

LOSE, *v.* to forfeit; not to win; to mislay.
LOST, *pp.* mislaid; destroyed.
LOSS, *n.* damage; waste.
LOS'ING, *a.* that incurs loss.
LORN, *a.* lost; forsaken.
FORLORN', *a.* forsaken; helpless.

Lufian—to LOVE.

LOVE, *v.* to regard with affection.
LOV'ABLE, *a.* worthy of love.
LOVE'LY, *a.* exciting love.
LOVE'LINESS, *n.* amiableness.
LOV'ER, *n.* one who is in love.
LOV'ING, *p. a.* kind; affectionate.
LOVE'LORN, *a.* forsaken by one's love.
LOVE'LOCK, *n.* a lock of hair.

Hlowan—to LOW; a HUMMING NOISE.

LOW, *v.* to bellow as a cow.
LOW'ING, *n.* the cry of cattle.

NOTE.—Low, not high, humble, is from the Dutch (*laag*).

Geluggian—to DRAG BY THE HAIR.

LUG, *v.* to drag; to pull.
LUG'GAGE, *n.* anything cumbrous to be carried.

Lust—DESIRE; WILL; POWER.

LUST, *n.* eagerness to possess or enjoy.
LUST'FUL, *a.* having evil desires.
LUS'TY, *a.* stout; vigorous.
LUS'TILY, *ad.* stoutly; with vigor.
LUS'TINESS, *n.* stoutness; vigor of body.
LIST, *v.* to desire; to wish; to choose.
LIST'LESS, *a.* indifferent; heedless.

Gemæd—TROUBLED IN MIND; MAD.

MAD, *a.* disordered in the mind; enraged.
MAD'DEN, *v.* to make or become mad.
MAD'DISH, *a.* somewhat mad.
MAD'NESS, *n.* distraction; fury.
MAD'CAP, *n.* a rash, hot-headed person.
MAD'MAN, *n.* a man void of reason.

Mæden—MAID.

MAID, *n.* an unmarried woman.
MAID'ENLY, *a.* like a maid.
MAID'EN, *n.* a young woman.

Macian—to MAKE.

NOTE.—The primary sense is, to cause, to act or do, to press, drive, strain or compel.

MAKE, *v.* to create; to form.
MAKE, *n.* form; structure.
MAK'ER, *n.* one who makes.
MAK'ING, *ppr.* forming; causing.

Man or *mon*—MAN.

MAN, *n.* a human being; a male.
MAN, *v.* to furnish with men.
MAN'FUL, *a.* bold; courageous.
MAN'HOOD, *n.* the state of a man.
MAN'IKIN, *n.* a little man.
MANKIND', *n.* the race of human beings.
MAN'LIKE, *a.* like a man.
MAN'LY, *a.* like a man.
MAN'LINESS, *n.* dignity; bravery.

Mentel—MANTLE; CLOAK.

MAN'TLE, *n.* a kind of cloak; work before a chimney.
MANTELET', *n.* a small cloak.

MAN'TLE, *v.* to cover; to spread; to rush to the face.
DISMAN'TLE, *v.* to strip; to divest.

Manig—MANY; MUCH.

MAN'Y, *a.* numerous; a great number.
MAN'YTIMES, *ad.* often.

MAN'IFOLD, *a. (feald,* fold, double), many in number.

Mearc—a BOUNDARY; a MARK; a SIGN; MARCH.

MARCH, *v.* to border; to join.
MARCH'ES, *n.* borders, limits, or frontiers of a country.
DEMARCA'TION, *n.* separation of territory.

MARK, *n.* a token by which any thing is known.
MARK, *v.* to impress; to brand.
MARKED, *p. a.* noted; prominent; conspicuous.

MARKS'MAN, *n.* one skillful to hit a mark.

NOTE.—MARCH, the name of a month, comes from the Latin (*Mars*), and MARCH, to move by steps, from the French (*marcher*).

Market—MARKET.

MAR'KET, *n.* a public place for buying and selling.

MAR'KETABLE, *a.* that may be sold.
MART, *n.* a place of public traffic.

Mearh—MARROW.

MAR'ROW, *n.* a soft, oily substance in bones; the best part of a thing.

MAR'ROWY, *a.* full of marrow; pithy.
MAR'ROWFAT, *n.* a kind of pea.

Mersc—MARSH.

MARSH, *n.* a watery tract of land.
MORASS', *n.* a marsh; a bog.

MARSH'Y, *a.* swampy; boggy.

Maca—an EQUAL; FELLOW or COMPANION.

MATE, *n.* one of a pair.
MATCH, *n.* an equal; a contest.
MATCH'LESS, *a.* having no equal.
COMATE', *n.* a companion.
IMMATCH'ABLE, *a.* that cannot be matched.
MISMATCH', *v.* to match unsuitably.

IN'MATE, *n.* one who dwells in the same house.
OVERMATCH', *v.* to conquer.
UNMATCHED', *a.* having no match or equal.
UNMATCH'ABLE, *a.* that cannot be matched.

NOTE.—MATCH, a combustible substance for lighting fires, comes from the French (*méche*), and MATE, a term in chess, from the Spanish (*mate—mater*, to kill).

Magan—to BE STRONG or ABLE; MAY.

MAY, *v.* to be able; to be possible.
MIGHT, *pret.* had power or liberty.
DISMAY', *n.* terror; fear.

DISMAY', *v.* to deprive of strength of mind.
UNDISMAYED', *a.* not discouraged.

TER'MAGANT, *n.* a brawling woman.

NOTE.—MAY, the fifth month, comes from the Latin (*Maius*).

Mædewe—a MEADOW.   *Mæd*—WHAT IS MOWN; *ewe*—WATER.

MEAD'OW, *n.* moist grass land.
MEAD, *n.* moist land covered with grass.
MEAD'OWY, *a.* resembling meadows.
MEAD'OWLARK, *n.* a bird.

Mæger—MEAGER.

MEA'GER, *a.* lean; thin.
MEA'GERLY, *ad.* thinly; poorly.
MEA'GERNESS, *n.* leanness; scantiness.

Mæl—a PART or PORTION.

MEAL, *n.* a portion of food taken at one time.
MEAL'TIME, *n.* the time for eating a meal.
PIECE'MEAL, *ad.* in or by pieces or fragments.

Melu, melo—MEAL; FLOUR.

NOTE.—The primary sense seems to be, soft, smooth.

MEAL, *n.* the edible part of grain.
MEAL'Y, *a.* of the softness of meal.
MEAL'Y-MOUTHED, *a.* using soft words.
MEL'LOW, *a.* soft with ripeness.
MEL'LOWNESS, *n.* softness; ripeness.

Mæne—FALSE; BAD.

MEAN, *a.* of low rank; base; coarse.
MEAN'LY, *ad.* basely; poorly.
MEAN'NESS, *n.* want of excellence; rudeness.

Mænan, manian—to HAVE IN THE MIND.

MEAN, *v.* to intend; to purpose.
MEAN'ING, *n.* intention; signification.

NOTE.—MEAN, the middle, comes from the Latin (*medius*).

Metan—to MEET; to FIND; to MEASURE; to COMPARE.

MEET, *v.* to come together.
MEET'ING, *n.* a coming together.
MEET, *a.* fit; proper; suitable.
MEET'NESS, *n.* fitness; propriety.
METE, *v.* to measure; to reduce to measure.
ME'TER, *n.* a measurer.

Meltan—to MELT; to DISSOLVE; to COOK.

MELT, *v.* to make or become liquid.
MELT'ING, *n.* the act of softening.
MOLT'EN, *a.* made of melted metal.
SMELT, *v.* to melt or fuse ore.

Mere—the SEA, and *mæden*—MAID;—MERMAID.

MER'MAID, *n.* a fabulous sea woman.
MER'MAN, *n.* the male of the mermaid.

Mirig—MERRY; PLEASANT.

MER'RY, *a.* gay of heart; jovial.
MER'RILY, *ad.* gaily; with mirth.
MER'RIMENT, *n.* mirth; gaiety.
MER'RYTHOUGHT, *n.* a forked bone in the breast of a fowl.
MIRTH, *n.* merriment; hilarity.
MIRTH'FUL, *a.* merry; gay.
MIRTH'FULLY, *ad.* in a merry manner.
MIRTH'LESS, *a.* joyless; cheerless.

Mœw—MEW.

MEW, *n.* a sea fowl.

NOTE.—MEW, to confine, to cage, comes from the French (*mue*), and MEW, to cry as a cat, from the Icelandic (*miaua*).

Miht—MIGHT.

MIGHT, *n.* strength; power.
MIGHT'Y, *a.* strong; powerful.
MIGHT'ILY, *ad.* powerfully; strongly.
MIGHT'INESS, *n.* power; greatness.

NOTE.—MIGHT, had power or liberty, is the preterit of the verb *may*.

Meolc—MILK.

MILK, *n.* a white fluid with which animals feed their young from the breast.
MILK'Y, *a.* like milk.
MILK'INESS, *n.* resemblance of milk.
MILK'SOP, *n.* a soft, effeminate person.
MILK'Y-WAY, *n.* the galaxy; a luminous zone in the sky.
MILCH, *a.* giving milk.

Mild—MILD.

MILD, *a.* kind; tender; soft.
MILD'LY, *ad.* kindly; gently.
MILD'NESS, *n.* gentleness; softness.

Mylen—MILL.

NOTE.—From the ancient Gaelic word *meil*, dust.

MILL, *n.* a machine for grinding.
MILL'ER, *n.* one who attends a mill.
MILL'DAM, *n.* a dam by which water is collected for turning a mill.
MILLED, *p. a.* stamped on the edge.
MILL'RACE, *n.* the channel in which the water of a mill-pond is conveyed to the wheel.
MILL'STONE, *n.* a stone for grinding corn.

NOTE.—MILL, the tenth part of a cent, or thousandth part of a dollar, comes from the Latin (*mille*, a thousand).

Minsian—to DIMINISH; to LESSEN.

MINCE, *v.* to chop into very small pieces.
MINCE, *v.* to half pronounce; to act with affected delicacy.
MINCE'-PIE, *n.* a pie made of minced meat.

Gemynd, gemunan—to REMEMBER.

MIND, *n.* the intelligent power in man.
MIND'FUL, *a.* attentive; heedful.
REMIND', *v.* to put in mind.

Mengan—to MINGLE.

MIN'GLE, *v.* to mix; to blend.
MIN'GLER, *n.* one who mingles.
COMMIN'GLE, *v.* to mix into one mass.
UNMIN'GLED, *a.* not mixed; pure.
IMMIN'GLE, *v.* to unite with numbers.
INTERMIN'GLE, *v.* to mingle together.
MON'GREL, *a.* of a mixed breed.

Mistœcan—to MISTEACH; to MISINFORM.

MISTAKE', *v.* to take wrong; to err.
MISTAKE', *n.* an error.

Mist—Mist.

Mist, *n.* a thick vapor.
Mist'y, *a.* overspread with mist.
Mist'ily, *ad.* not plainly.
Mist'iness, *n.* the state of being misty.

Mænan—to Lament; to Complain.

Moan, *v.* to deplore audibly. | Moan'ful, *a.* expressing sorrow.

Mal—a Spot, Mark, or Blot.

Mole, *n.* a natural spot on the skin.

Note.—Mole, a mound, a dyke, comes from the Latin (*moles*), and Mole, a small animal, from the Dutch (*mol*).

Mod—Mind; Disposition; Passion.

Mood, *n.* temper of mind; humor. | Mood'y, *a.* angry; out of humor.
Mood'iness, *n.* peevishness.

Note.—Mood, the variation of a verb to express manner of action or being, comes from the Latin (*modus*).

Mona—Moon.

Moon, *n.* the heavenly body which revolves round the earth.
Moon'less, *a.* not enlightened by the moon.
Moon'beam, *n.* a ray of light from the moon.
Moon'light, *n.* the light given by the moon.

Moon'shine, *n.* the light of the moon.
Moon'struck, *a.* lunatic.
Mon'day, *n.* the second day of the week.
Month, *n.* one of the twelve divisions of the year.
Month'ly, *a.* happening every month.

Mor—Waste Land.

Moor, *n.* a tract of poor land overrun with heath. | Moor'land, *n.* watery ground.

Note.—Moor, to secure by two anchors, comes from the Spanish (*amarrar*), and Moor, a native of northern Africa, from the Latin (*Maurus*).

Motian—to Meet for Conversation; to Discuss.

Moot, *v.* to argue or plead on a supposed cause. | Moot'ing, *n.* the exercise of disputing.

Morgen—Dispersed.

Morn, *n.* the first part of the day. | Morn'ing, *n.* the first part of the day
Mor'row, *n.* morning; the day after the present day.

Note.—Morrow and Morn have the same meaning, viz.: dissipated, dispersed, as clouds or darkness, whose dispersion, or the time when they are dispersed, these words express.

Mæst, super of mycel—Greatest.

Most, *a.* greatest in quantity or number.
Most'ly, *ad.* for the greatest part; chiefly.
Much, *a.* large in quantity.
More, *a.* greater in quantity.
Moreo'ver, *ad.* besides; over and above.

Modor—MOTHER.

MOTH'ER, *n.* a female parent.
MOTH'ERLESS, *a.* having lost a mother.
MOTH'ERLY, *a.* in the manner of a mother; tenderly.

MOTH'ER-TONGUE, *n.* a language to which another language owes its origin; one's native language.

NOTE.—MOTHER, a thick, slimy substance in liquors, comes from the German (*moder*, mud).

Molde—EARTH; POWDER; DUST.

MOULD, *n.* fine, soft earth; a substance like down on damp bodies.
MOULD'ER, *v.* to turn into dust.

MOULD'Y, *a.* overgrown with mould.
MOULD'INESS, *n.* the state of being mouldy.

NOTE.—MOULD, that in which anything is cast or receives its shape, and MOULDER, one who casts or shapes, comes from the Spanish (*molde*, a matrix).

Murnan—to MOURN

MOURN, *v.* to grieve; to be sorrowful.
MOURN'ER, *n.* one who mourns.
MOURN'ING, *n.* sorrow; the dress of sorrow.

MOURN'FUL, *a.* causing sorrow.
MOURN'FULLY, *ad.* sorrowfully.

Mus, plural *mys*—MOUSE.

MOUSE, *n.* a small animal.

MICE, *n.* the plural of mouse.

Muth—MOUTH.

MOUTH, *n.* the cavity between the jaws; an opening by which anything can be filled or emptied.
MOUTH, *v.* to utter with a loud, affected voice.

MOUTH'FUL, *a.* as much as the mouth can hold.
MOUTH'PIECE, *n.* one who speaks for others.

Mawan—to CUT DOWN; Mow; *n.* a LITTLE HEAP.

Mow, *v. mo,* to cut with a scythe.
Mow, *n. mow,* a loft in a barn.

MOWN, *p. a.* cut with a scythe.
MOW'ING, *n.* cutting with a scythe.

Milescian—to BECOME SOFT; MULCH.

MULCH, *v.* to cover with half-rotten straw.

MULCH, *n.* half-rotten straw.

Morther, morth—DEATH.

MUR'DER, *n.* the act of killing a human being unlawfully.

MUR'DEROUS, *a.* guilty of murder.

MUST, *v. mot,* to be obliged.

NOTE.—MUST, new wine, comes from the Latin (*mustum*), and MUST, to make mouldy, from the French (*moisir*).

Nægel—NAIL.

NAIL, *n.* a horny substance on the human fingers and toes; a piece of metal for fastening.

NAIL'ER, *n.* one who makes nails.
NAIL'ERY, *n.* a manufactory of nails.

Nacod—NAKED.

NA′KED, *a.* not covered. | NA′KEDNESS, *n.* want of covering.

Nama—NAME.

NAME, *n.* that by which a person or thing is called.
NAME′LESS, *a.* without a name. | NAME′LY, *ad.* by name; particularly.
NAME′SAKE, *n.* one who has the same name.

NICK′NAME, *n.* a name given in contempt.

Hnoppa—NAP.

NAP, *n.* the down on cloth. | NAP′LESS, *a.* threadbare.

Nearow, nearwian—to MAKE NARROW.

NAR′ROW, *a.* not broad or wide. | NAR′ROWLY, *ad.* closely; nearly.

NAR′ROWNESS, *n.* want of breadth.

Naht—NAUGHT. Ne—NOT; and wuht—a WHIT; ANYTHING.

NAUGHT, NOUGHT, *n.* nothing.
NAUGHT, *a.* worthless; bad. | NAUGHT′Y, *a.* wicked; sinful.
NAUGHT′ILY, *ad.* wickedly.

NAUGHT′INESS, *n.* wickedness.

Nafu—the MIDDLE; CENTRE; NAVE.

NAVE, *n.* the piece of timber in the centre of a wheel. | NAVE, *n.* the middle or body of a church.

NA′VEL, *n. nafel*, the point in the middle of the abdomen.

NOTE.—NAVAL, of or pertaining to ships, comes from the L. *navis* (Gr. ναῦς), a ship.

Neah—NEAR.

NEAR, *a.* not far distant; nigh.
NEAR′LY, *ad.* at no great distance.
NEAR′NESS, *n.* closeness.
NIGH, *a.* near; not distant. | NIGH′LY, *ad.* nearly.
NIGH′NESS, *n.* nearness.
NEXT, *a.* nearest in place, time, &c.
WELL-NIGH′, *ad.* almost.

NEIGH′BOR, *n. neahbur*, one who lives near.

Neat, nyten—CATTLE.

NEAT, *n.* cattle; oxen.
NEAT′HERD, *n.* one who takes care of cattle. | NEAT′S-FOOT, *n.* the foot of an ox, cow, &c.

NEAT, very clean, pure, elegant, comes from the Latin (*niteo*).

Neb—NEB.

NEB, *n.* the nose; the beak.
NIB, *n.* the bill of a bird; the point of anything. | NIB′BLE, *v.* to bite by little at a time.
NIB′BLER, *n.* one that nibbles.

Hnecca—NECK.

NECK, *n.* the part between the head and the body. | NECK′LACE, *n.* an ornament for the neck.

Nead—NEED; from ne—NOT, and ead—HAPPINESS; PROSPERITY.

NEED, n. want; necessity.
NEED'FUL, a. necessary.
NEED'LESS, a. unnecessary.
NEEDS, ad. necessarily.
NEED'Y, a. poor; necessitous.
NEED'ILY, ad. in want.
NEED'INESS, n. want; poverty.

Nœdl—NEEDLE.

NEE'DLE, n. a small, pointed instrument for sewing.
NEE'DLE-WORK, n. work executed with a needle.

Hnægan—NEIGH.

NEIGH, n. the voice of a horse.
NEIGH'ING, n. the voice of a horse.

Nest—NEST.

NEST, n. the place in which birds hatch and rear their young.
NES'TLE, v. to lie close.
NEST'LING, n. a young bird in the nest.
NEST'EGG, n. an egg left in the nest.

Net—NET.

NET, n. a texture of twine with meshes.
NET'WORK, n. work in the form of a net.

NOTE.—NET, clear after all deductions, comes from the French (*net*, entirely).

Neother, neothan—BENEATH; DOWNWARDS.

NETH'ER, a. lower; being in a lower place.
BENEATH', prep. under; lower in place, rank, or dignity.

Næfre—NEVER. Ne—NOT; and æfre—EVER.

NEV'ER, ad. not ever; at no time.
NEVERTHELESS', ad. notwithstanding that.

Niwe—NEW.

NEW, a. lately made, produced or discovered.
NEW'LY, ad. freshly.
NEW'NESS, n. freshness.
NEWS, n. recent account.
RENEW', v. to make anew or again.
RENEW'AL, n. the act of renewing.
ANEW', ad. over again.

Hnesc—SOFT; TENDER.

NICE, a. delicate; fine.
NICE'LY, ad. delicately; exactly.
NICE'NESS, n. delicacy.
NI'CETY, n. minute accuracy; pl. dainties.

Niht—NIGHT.

NIGHT, n. the time of darkness.
NIGHT'LY, ad. done every night.
NIGHT'INGALE, n. a bird which sings at night.
NIGHT'FALL, n. the close of the day.
NIGHT'MARE, n. a sensation of distressing weight on the chest during sleep.
FORT'NIGHT, n. (*fourteen*), the space of two weeks.
BENIGHT'ED, v. involved in darkness.

Na—No; Not.

No, *ad.* a word of denial or refusal.
Nay, *ad.* not only so, but more.
None, *a.* (*nan; ne,* not, and *an,* one), not one; not any.

Not, *ad.* (*naht; ne,* not, and *auht,* ought), a particle of denial.
Noth'ing, *n.* (*na,* no, and *thing*), not any thing.

Non—Noon.

Noon, *n.* mid-day.
Noon'ing, *n.* repose at noon.

Noon'day, *n.* mid-day.
Noon'tide, *n.* mid-day.

Fore'noon, *n.* the time from morning to mid-day.

North—North.

North, *n.* one of the cardinal points.
Nor'therly, *a.* towards the north.

Nor'thern, *a.* being in the north.
North'ward, *a.* towards the north.

North'-wind, *n.* the wind which blows from the north.

Næse—Nose.

Nose, *n.* the organ of smell.
Nos'tril, *n.* a cavity of the nose.

Noz'zle, *n.* the nose; the snout; the end.

Nose'gay, *n.* a bunch of flowers.

Note—Nose is of the same origin with A.-S. *næs,* a naze, or ness; the latter so common a termination to the names of projecting headlands, as Dungeness, Sheerness.

Numan—to Take Away; Numb.

Numb, *a.* deprived of sensation.
Numb'ness, *n.* torpor.

Num'skull, *n.* a dunce.
Benumb', *v.* to make torpid.

Hnut—Nut.

Nut, *n.* a fruit consisting of a kernel covered by a hard shell.
Nut'brown, *a.* brown like a nut long kept.

Nut'gall, *n.* an excrescence of the oak.
Nut'meg, *n.* a kind of aromatic nut.

Ata—Oat.

Oat, Oats, *n.* a grain.
Oat'meal, *n.* meal made of oats.

Oat'en, *a.* made of oats.

Of—Of.

Of, *prep.* from, or out of.
Off, *prep.* not on; from.
Off'ing, *n.* a considerable distance from the shore.

Off'scouring, *n.* refuse.
Off'set, *n.* a sprout.
Off'spring, *n.* children.
Aloof', *ad.* (*all, off*), at a distance.

On—On.

On, *prep.* being in contact with the upper part of any thing.

On'ward, *ad.* forward.
On'set, *n.* an attack.

On'slaught, *n.* an attack.

An, ane—ONE.

ONE, *n.* a single person or thing. | ONCE, *ad.* one time; formerly.
ON'LY, *a.* singly; one alone.

Was, wæs—WETNESS; OOZE.

OOZE, *n.* earth so wet as to flow gently. | OO'ZY, *a.* miry; muddy.

Openian—to OPEN; to BE MANIFEST.

O'PEN, *v.* to unclose; to unlock.
O'PENING, *n.* an aperture.
O'PENLY, *ad.* publicly; plainly.
O'PENNESS, *n.* plainness; clearness.
O'PEN-MOUTHED, *a.* ravenous; clamorous.
O'PEN-HEARTED, *a.* generous; candid.

Ort-geard. Ort—an HERB; *geard*—GARDEN.

OR'CHARD, *n.* an assemblage of fruit trees.
OR'CHARDIST, *n.* one who cultivates orchards.

NOTE.—Apples, pears, peaches, and cherries are the fruits principally cultivated in orchards.

Ordael. From *or*—GREAT, and *dael*—JUDGMENT.

OR'DEAL, *n.* any severe trial; test; experiment.

Ut—OUT. *Utærre*—OUTWARD; UTTER.

OUT, *ad.* on the outside; not within; *v.* to eject; to expel.
OUT'ER, *a.* being on the outside.
OUT'WARD, *a.* external; visible.
OUT'WARDLY, *ad.* externally.
UT'TER, *v.* to speak; to pronounce.
UT'TER, *a.* the greatest degree; complete.
UT'MOST, *a.* extreme.
UT'TERLY, *ad.* fully; completely.
UT'TERANCE, *n.* the act of speaking.
UT'TERMOST, *n.* the most that can be.

Agan—OWN.

NOTE.—OWE is formed from the A.-S. *agan*, by softening the guttural *g* into *w*, *aw*—*owe*.

OWE, *v.* to be indebted.
OW'ING, *ppr.* due; imputable to.
OUGHT, *v.* to be bound in duty.
OWN, *v.* to possess; to avow.
OWN'ER, *n.* one to whom a thing belongs.
OWN'ERSHIP, *n.* the right of possession.
DISOWN', *v.* to deny; to renounce.

Pæth. Pæthian—to GO; to TREAD FLAT; to FLATTEN.

PAD, *n.* a road; an easy-paced horse.
PAD, *v.* to travel gently.
PAD'LOCK,* *n.* a lock hung on a staple.
FOOT'PAD, *n.* a highwayman who robs on foot.
PAD, *n.* a soft saddle or cushion.
PATH, *n.* a way; a road.
PATH'LESS, *a.* having no path.
PATH'WAY, *n.* a narrow way.
FOOT'PATH, *n.* a path for foot passengers.

* A lock for a *pad*-gate, or a gate opening to a path.

Panne—a PAN.

PAN, *n.* a broad, shallow vessel. | PAN'CAKE, *n.* a thin cake fried in a pan,

Pearroc—a PARK.

PAD′DOCK, *n.* a small inclosure in a pasture for a sick animal.

PARK, *n.* a piece of inclosed ground.

NOTE.—PADDOCK, originally an inclosure in a park, for hounds to run matches in.

Pin—PUNISHMENT; TORTURE. *Pinan*—to PAIN.

PAIN, *n.* an uneasy sensation.
PAIN, *v.* to make uneasy.
PAIN′FUL, *a.* full of pain.
PAIN′FULLY, *ad.* with pain.
PAIN′LESS, *a.* free from pain.
PAINS, *n.* careful toil; trouble.

PAINS′TAKER, *n.* a laborious person.
PINE, *v.* to waste away with pain or distress of mind.
PIN′ING, *n.* a wasting away.
REPINE′, *v.* to fret; to be discontented.
REPIN′ING, *n.* the act of murmuring.

PANG, *n.* a sharp and sudden pain.

Pæccan—to DECEIVE BY FALSE APPEARANCE.

NOTE.—They who put *patches* on a little breach, to hide it, are careful that the color shall nearly as possible resemble that upon which they put it.

PATCH, *n.* a piece sewed on to cover a hole.

PATCH′WORK, *n.* work composed of pieces.

Pærl—PEARL.

PEARL, *n.* a white body found in oysters.

PEARL′Y, *a.* like pearls.

Pabob—PEBBLE.

PEB′BLE, *n.* a small, roundish stone. | PEB′BLY, *a.* full of pebbles.

Pocca—a BAG; POKE.

POKE, *n.* a bag; a sack.
POCK′ET, *n.* a small bag in a garment.
POCK′ETBOOK, *n.* a small book for the pocket.

PECK, *n.* the fourth part of a bushel.
POACH, *v.* to steal game.
PUCK′ER, *v.* to gather into plaits or folds.

POUCH, *n.* a small bag.

NOTE.—POKE, to thrust, comes from the Swedish (*poka*), and POACH, to boil slightly, from the French (*pocher*).

Pyndan—to SHUT IN; to PEN.

PEN, *n.* an inclosure for cattle; *v.* to inclose.
POUND, *n.* an inclosure for cattle which have been taken in trespassing.

PIN, *v.* to inclose; to confine.
PIN′FOLD, *n.* an inclosure for cattle.
POND, *n.* a small lake.
IMPOUND′, *v.* to put in a pound.

NOTE.—PEN, an instrument for writing, comes from the Latin (*penna*), and PIN, an instrument for fastening, from the Welsh (*pin*).

Penig—PENNY.

PEN′NY, *n.* a coin. | PEN′NILESS, *a.* wanting money.

NOTE.—The penny was formerly a silver coin, first struck in England by the Saxons. It was struck with a cross so deeply sunk in it, that it might be easily parted into halves, thence called *half-pennies*, or into four parts, thence called *fourthings* or farthings.

Pycan—to PICK; to PECK.

PICK, *v.* to strike with a pointed instrument.
PICK, *v.* to pull of with the fingers; to choose. [point.
PICK'AXE, *n.* an axe with a sharp
PICK'POCKET, *n.* one who steals from another's pocket.

PEAK, *n.* (*peac,* a point), the top of a hill.
PECK, *v.* to pick up food; to strike with the beak.
WOOD'PECKER, *n.* a bird.
BEAK, *n.* the bill of a bird; anything ending in a point.

Pyle—a PILLOW; a CUSHION.

PIL'LOW, *n.* a cushion to support the head in bed.

PILL'ION, *n.* a cushion for a woman to ride on.

Pinntreow—PIN-TREE.*

PINE, *n.* a forest tree.
PI'NY, *a.* abounding with pines.

PINE'APPLE, *n.* a fruit resembling the cone of the pine tree.

* From the leaves of the pine which resemble *pins.*

Pyt—PIT.

PIT, *n.* a hole in the earth.
PIT'FALL, *n.* a pit dug and covered over.

PIT'COAL, *n.* coal dug from the earth.
PIT'SAW, *n.* a large saw used by two men.

Pitha—KERNEL; PITH.

PITH, *n.* the soft spongy substance in the centre of plants and trees; strength; force.

PITH'LESS, *a.* without pith.
PITH'Y, *a.* containing pith; forcible.
PITH'ILY, *ad.* with force.

PITH'INESS, *n.* strength; force.

Plegan—to JOKE; to PLAY.

PLAY, *v.* to sport; to toy.
PLAY, *n.* sport; game.
PLAY'FUL, *a.* sportive.

PLAY'FULLY, *ad.* in a sportive manner.
PLAY'MATE, *n.* a companion in amusement.

PLAY'THING, *n.* a toy.

Plihtan—to EXPOSE TO DANGER; to PLEDGE; PLIGHT.

PLIGHT, *v.* to pledge; to give as security.
PLIGHT, *n.* condition; state.
PLOT, *n.* a conspiracy; a scheme.

COM'PLOT, *n.* a confederacy in crime.
COUN'TERPLOT, *n.* a plot opposed to a plot.
UN'DERPLOT, *n.* a clandestine scheme.

NOTE.—PLIGHT, to pledge, is never applied to property or goods.

Pluccian—to PLUCK; to PULL OFF.

PLUCK, *v.* to pull with quick motion.
PLUCK, *n.* courage; spirit.

PLUCK'ED, *a.* stripped off.

Pol—a POOL.

POOL, *n.* a small collection of water.

PUD'DLE, *n.* a small pool of dirty water.

NOTE.—POOL, the stakes played for in certain games, comes from the French (*poule,* a chicken).

Gepose—HEAVINESS; STUFFING OF THE HEAD; POSE.

POSE, v. to puzzle or put to a stand by asking difficult questions.

POS'ER, n. something that puzzles or silences.

NOTE.—POSE' (*po-zá*), posture, attitude, comes from the French (*posé*).

Prœte—PRETTY.

PRET'TY, a. neat; beautiful without dignity.

PRET'TINESS, n. beauty without dignity.

PRET'TILY, ad. neatly; pleasingly.

Priccian—to PRICK.

PRICK, v. to pierce with a small puncture.

PRICK'LE, n. a small, sharp point.
PRICK'LY, a. full of sharp points.

Pryt—PRIDE.

PRIDE, n. unreasonable self-esteem.
PRIDE'FUL, a. full of pride; insolent.
PRIDE'LESS, a. without pride.

PRID'INGLY, ad. with pride.
PROUD, a. having inordinate self-esteem.

PROUD'LY, ad. arrogantly; haughtily.

Preost—PRIEST.

PRIEST, n. one who officiates in sacred offices.

PRIEST'ESS, n. a female priest.
PRIEST'HOOD, n. the office of a priest.

PRIEST'LIKE, a. resembling a priest.

Preon—a BODKIN; PRONG.

PRONG, n. a pointed projection; the tine of a fork.

Profian—to PROVE; to TRY; to JUDGE.

PROVE, v. to show by testimony or argument.

PROOF, n. evidence; test; trial.
PROOF'LESS, a. wanting evidence.

Pullian—to PULL.

PULL, v. to draw forcibly; to pluck. | PULL'BACK, n. that which keeps back.

Cwacian—to QUAKE.

QUAKE, v. to shake; to tremble.
QUAK'ING, n. shaking.

QUAG'MIRE, n. (*quake, mire*), a shaking bog or marsh.

Cwealm—CONTAGION; PESTILENCE; QUALM.

QUALM, n. a sudden fit of sickness. | QUALM'ISH, a. sick at the stomach.

SQUEAM'ISH, a. having a taste difficult to please.

Cwen—a WOMAN; QUEEN.

QUEEN, n. the wife of a king. | QUEAN, n. a worthless woman.

Cwic—Alive; Living; Quick.

QUICK, *a.* living; swift; speedy.
QUICK'EN, *v.* to make alive; to hasten.
QUICK'LY, *ad.* soon; speedily.
QUICK'NESS, *n.* speed.

QUICK'LIME, *n.* lime unslacked.
QUICK'SAND, *n.* moving sand.
QUICK'SILVER, *n.* a fluid metal.
QUICK'WITTED, *a.* having ready wit.

Reaf—a Robe; a Garment.   Reaflan—to Reeve or Sew.

RAFT, *n.* a float made by fastening pieces of timber together.
RAFTS'MAN, *n.* one who manages a raft.
RAF'TER, *n.* *rafter*, a roof-timber.

NOTE.—A raft is made by lashing logs together by withes.

Hracod—Naked; Ragged.

RAG, *n.* a torn piece of cloth.
RAG'AMUFFIN, *n.* a paltry, mean fellow.
RAG'GED, *a.* rent in tatters; uneven.

Rægel, from wrigan—to Put On or Cover; to Clothe.

RAIL, *n.* a bar of wood or iron extending from one support to another.
RAIL, *n.* a woman's upper garment.

RAIL'ING, *n.* a fence or barrier.
RIG, *v.* to dress; to fit out.
RIG'GING, *n.* the sails and tackling of a ship.

NOTE.—RAIL, to use insolent language, comes from the Dutch (*rallen*, to chatter), and RAIL, a bird, from the French (*râle*).

Rinan—to Rain.

RAIN, *v.* to fall in drops from the clouds.
RAIN'BOW, *n.* a bow formed by the reflection of light by the clouds.

RAIN'WATER, *n.* water fallen from the clouds.
RAIN'Y, *a.* abounding in rain.

Ranc—Proud; Haughty; Rebellious.

RANK, *a.* luxuriant; gross; coarse.
RANK'LY, *ad.* luxuriantly; coarsely.
RAN'KLE, *v.* to fester; to be inflamed.

RANK'NESS, *n.* exuberance; strong scent.

NOTE.—RANK, a line, a row, class, comes from the French (*rang*).

Rendan—to Rend; to Tear.

RANT, *v.* to rave in violent language.
RANT'ER, *n.* one who rants.
RENT, *n.* a break; a breach; a tear.

REND, *v.* to tear with violence.
REND'ER, *n.* one who rends.

NOTE.—RENDER, to give up, to give back, comes from the Latin (*re, do*). RENT, a certain profit in money issuing out of lands, &c., in return for use, comes from the French (*rente*).

Hrepan—to Touch; to Rap.

RAP, *v.* to strike with a quick blow. | RAP'PER, *n.* one that raps.

NOTE.—RAP, to affect with ecstasy, comes from the Latin (*rapio*).

Rascal—a LEAN, WORTHLESS DEER.

RAS'CAL, *n.* a mean fellow; a scoundrel.
RASCAL'ITY, *n.* mean dishonesty; base fraud
RAS'CALLY, *a.* mean; vile; base.

Hrethian—to FIND FAULT; to SCOLD; to RATE.

RATE, *v.* to chide vehemently.
RAT'ING, *n.* a chiding; a scolding.

NOTE.—RATE, price, value, degree, comes from the Latin (*ratus*, to reckon).

Ræthe—QUICK; HASTY; RATH.

RATH, *a.* early; quick.
RATH'ER, *ad.* more willingly; in preference.

Hrefen, from *reaflan*—to PLUNDER; to DESTROY.

RAV'EN, *v.* to seize by violence; to devour.
RA'VEN, *n.* a bird.
RAV'ENOUS, *a.* furiously voracious.
RAV'IN, *n.* prey; plunder.
RAV'ENING, *a.* preying with rapacity.

Hreow, hrere—RAW; REAR; CRUEL; FIERCE.

RAW, *a.* not cooked; not covered with skin.
RAW'ISH, *a.* somewhat raw; cold and damp.
RAW'NESS, *n.* the state of being raw.
RAW'BONED, *a.* having little flesh.
RARE, *a.* nearly raw; imperfectly cooked.

NOTE.—RARE, thin, not dense, uncommon, comes from the Latin (*rarus*).

Ræcan—to REACH; to EXTEND.

REACH, *v.* to extend; to reach.
REACH'ER, *n.* one who reaches.
RETCH, *v.* to make an effort to vomit.

Rædan—to APPOINT; to ADVISE; to READ; to GUESS.

READ, *v.* to peruse; to understand by characters.
READ, *p.* or *a.* learned.
READ'ABLE, *a.* that may be read.
READ'ING, *n.* perusal of books.
RID'DLE, *n. rædelse*, something to be solved by conjecture.
UNRID'DLE, *v.* to solve.

Recan—to SAY; to NUMBER; to REGARD.

RECK, *v.* to care; to heed.
RECK'LESS, *a.* careless; heedless.
RECK'LESSNESS, *n.* carelessness.
RACK, *v.* to stretch or torture; to draw off.
RECK'ON, *v.* to number; to calculate.
RECK'ONING, *n.* calculation.
RACK, *n.* an engine of torture; a frame.

Read, reod, rud—RED.

RED, *n.* a color resembling blood.
RED'DEN, *v.* to make or grow red.
RED'DISH, *a.* somewhat red.
RED'NESS, *n.* the quality of being red.
RED'HOT, *a.* heated to redness.
RED'LEAD, *n.* lead calcined.
RUD'DY, *a.* of a red color.
RUD'DINESS, *n.* state of being ruddy

Reocan—to SMOKE; to FUME.

REEK, *n.* smoke; steam; vapor.
REEK, *v.* to smoke; to steam.

Rest—a QUIET, or a LYING DOWN; REPOSE.

REST, *n.* cessation of motion or labor; quiet.
REST, *v.* to cease from motion or labor.
REST'FUL, *a.* quiet.
REST'LESS, *a.* unsettled.
REST'LESSNESS, *n.* want of rest or quiet.
REST'ING-PLACE, *n.* a place of rest.

NOTE.—REST, that which is left, the remainder, comes from the Latin (*re, sto*).

Rim, gerim—a NUMBER; RECKONING.

RHYME, *n.* correspondence of sounds at the ends of verses.
RHYME'LESS, *a.* destitute of rhymes.

Ric—GREAT; NOBLE; POWERFUL; RICH.

RICH, *a.* wealthy; opulent.
RICH'ES, *n.* wealth.
RICH'LY, *ad.* abundantly.
RICH'NESS, *n.* wealth; abundance.
ENRICH', *v.* to make rich.

NOTE.—RIC as a termination denotes jurisdiction; as, *bishopric*; as a termination of names, *rich* or powerful, as *Alfric, Frederick*.

Hriddel, hreddan—to RID; to DELIVER.

RID, *v.* to free; to deliver.
RID'DANCE, *n.* deliverance.
RID'DLE, *v.* to separate by a sieve; to make many holes in.
RID'DLE, *n.* a coarse sieve.

NOTE.—RIDDLE, something to be solved by guessing, comes from the A.-S. (*rædan*, to read, to guess).

Ridan—to SIT or REST UPON.

RIDE, *v.* to travel on horseback or in a vehicle; to be carried.
RIDE, *n.* an excursion on horseback or in a vehicle.

Hreac—a RICK. Hric—the BACK; a RIDGE.

RIDGE, *n.* the top of the back; the top of a roof or slope.
RID'GY, *a.* having ridges.
RICK, *n.* a pile of corn or hay.

Ryf—RIFE.

RIFE, *a.* prevalent; abounding.
RIFE'LY, *ad.* prevalently; frequently.
RIFE'NESS, *n.* prevalence; abundance.

Reafian—to SEIZE or TAKE AWAY.

RIFF'RAFF, *n.* refuse; sweepings; the rabble.
RI'FLE, *v.* to rob; to plunder.
RIVE, *v.* to split; to cleanse; to rend.
RIFT, *n.* a cleft; a fissure.
ROB, *v.* to take by force without right.
ROB'BER, *n.* a thief.
ROB'BERY, *n.* theft by force.
ROVE, *v.* to wander.
ROV'ER, *n.* a wanderer; a robber.

NOTE.—RIFLE, a kind of gun, comes from the German (*reifeln*, to groove).

Hrympelle—a RUMPLE; a FOLD.

RIM'PLE; *n.* a wrinkle; a fold.
RIM'PLING, *n.* uneven motion.
RIP'PLE, *v.* the surface of water slightly agitated.
RIP'PLING, *n.* the noise of ripples.

Riht—Right.

Right, *a.* just; proper; straight.
Right'eous, *a.* just; virtuous.
Right'ful, *a.* just; lawful.
Right'fully, *ad.* according to right.
Right'ly, *ad.* just; properly.
Right'ness, *n.* correctness; straightness.
Up'right, *a.* straight up; honest; just.
Up'rightly, *ad.* honestly.
Up'rightness, *n.* honesty; integrity.

Hring—Ring.

Ring, *n.* a circle; a round line or course.
Ring'let, *n.* a curl.
Ring'leader, *n.* the leader of a riotous body.
Ring'worm, *n.* a disease.

Hringan—to Ring.

Ring, *v.* to cause to sound.
Ring, *n.* the sound of metals.
Rung, *pp.* did ring.
Ring'ing, *ppr.* causing to sound.

Note.—Rung, a step of a ladder, a heavy staff, comes from the Gaelic (*rong*, a spar).

Rip—a Harvest. Rippan—to Take what is Ripe.

Ripe, *a.* brought to perfection in growth; mature.
Ripe'ly, *ad.* maturely.
Ri'pen, *v.* to grow ripe.
Reap'er, *n.* one who reaps.
Ripe'ness, *n.* state of being ripe.
Rip, *v.* to tear; to separate.
Reap, *v.* to cut grain with a sickle; to gather; to obtain.

Note.—Ripe is related to the A.-S. *rippan*, to reap, and the English *rip*, to separate, to tear; for the fruits, at the time of their maturity, split, and are torn or plucked from the place where they were brought to perfection.—Bosworth.

Rad—a Riding; a Way; a Road.

Road, *n.* an open way; a public passage.
Road'stead, *n.* a place where ships can anchor.

Hrof—Roof: the Top; a Raised Part; to Wrinkle.

Roof, *n.* the cover of a building.
Roof'less, *a.* wanting a roof.
Ruff, *n.* a plaited ornament worn about the neck.
Ruff, *v.* to ruffle; to disorder.
Ruf'fle, *v.* to put out of form; to disorder.
Ruf'fle, *n.* plaited linen, &c., for ornament.

Hroc—Rook; Crow.

Rook, *n.* a species of crow.
Rook'ery, *n.* a nursery of rooks.

Note.—Rook, a castle in the game of chess, is from the Italian (*rocco*).

Rum—Room; Space. Ryman—to Make Way; to Enlarge.

Room, *n.* space; extent.
Roam, *v.* to wander about; to stroll.
Room'y, *a.* spacious; wide; large.

Rap—Rope.

Rope, *n.* a large cord.
Ro'py, *a.* tenacious; glutinous.

Rotian—to Rot.

Rot, *v.* to putrefy; to decay. | Rot'ten, *a.* putrid; unsound.

Hreof—Rough; Scabby.

Rough, *a.* having inequalities on the surface.
Rough'en, *v.* to make rough.
Rough'ly, *ad.* harshly.
Rough'ness, *n.* unevenness; harshness.
Rough'cast, *v.* to form rudely.
Rough'draught, *n.* a sketch.
Rough'hewn, *p. a.* unpolished; rude.
Rough'work, *v.* to work coarsely.
Rug'ged, *a.* rough; uneven.
Rug'gedness, *n.* state of being rugged.
Rug, *n.* a coarse coverlet for a bed.

Rother—an Oar; Rudder.

Rud'der, *n.* the instrument for steering a vessel. | Rud'der, *n.* anything that guides or governs.

Hreowan—to Repent; to Lament.

Rue, *v.* to be sorry for; to regret.
Rue'ful, *a.* sorrowful.
Rue'fully, *ad.* mournfully.
Rue'fulness, *n.* mournfulness.
Ruth, *n.* mercy; pity; sorrow.
Ruth'ful, *a.* merciful.
Ruth'fully, *ad.* sadly; sorrowfully.
Ruth'less, *a.* cruel; pitiless.
Ruth'lessness, *n.* want of pity.

Note.—Rue, a bitter herb, comes from the Greek (ῥυνή).

Rennan—to Run; to Flow.

Run, *v.* to move swiftly; to flee.
Run'ner, *n.* one who runs. [ly.
Run'ning, *n.* the act of moving swift-
Run'away, *n.* one who deserts.
Forerun'ner, *n.* a messenger sent before.
Overrun', *v.* to run or spread over.

Rics—Rush.

Rush, *n.* a plant.
Rush'y, *a.* abounding with rushes.
Rush'candle, *n.* a taper made of rush.
Rush'like, *a.* like a rush; weak.

Hreosan—to Rush; Shake; Waver, or Fall.

Rush, *v.* to move forward with violence.
Rush'ing, *n.* a violent course.
Rash, *a.* acting without caution.
Rash'ly, *ad.* hastily.
Rash'ness, *n.* inconsiderate haste.
Rash'er,* *n.* a thin slice of bacon for frying.

* Probably from the rashness or haste with which the cookery is despatched.

Note.—Rash, to slice, comes from the Italian (*raschiare*); Rash, an eruption, from the Italian (*rascia*, the itch).

Rust—Rust.

Rust, *n.* a crust which forms on the surface of metals.
Rust'y, *a.* covered with rust.
Rust'iness, *n.* the state of being rusty.
Rust, *v.* to gather rust; to become dull from want of action or exertion.

Note.—Rustic, *a.* relating to the country; *n.* an inhabitant of the country, comes from the Latin (*rusticus, rus*, the country).

Hristlan—to Rustle.

Rustle, v. to make a noise like the rubbing of dry leaves. | Rust'ling, n. the noise of that which rustles.

Rige—Rye.

Rye, n. a kind of grain. | Rye'grass, n. a kind of strong grass.
Rye'bread, n. bread made of rye.

Sacc—Sack.

Sack, n. a large bag. | Satch'el, n. a small sack or bag.
Sack'ful, n. as much as a sack can contain.

Note.—Sack, to plunder a town, comes from the Spanish (*sacar*), and Sack, a kind of wine, from the French (*sec*), the kind of wine now called *sherry*.

Sadel—Saddle.

Sad'dle, n. a seat placed on a horse's back. | Sad'dler, n. one who makes saddles.

Sigan—to Fall; to Sink.

Sag, v. to sink in the middle when supported at both ends.

Segel—Sail.

Sail, n. the sheet by which the wind impels a ship.
Sail, v. to be carried along by pressure of wind upon sails.
| Sail'er, n. a vessel which sails.
Sail'or, n. a seaman.
Sail'-loft, n. a place where sails are made.

Syllan—to Sell.

Sell, v. to give for a price.
Sale, n. the act of selling.
| Sale'able, a. fit for sale.
Sales'man, n. one that sells.

Salowig, salwig—Swarthy; Dark.

Sal'low, a. yellow; pale. | Sal'lowness, n. sickly paleness.

Sealt—Salt.

Salt, n. a substance used for seasoning and for preserving from corruption.
Salt'er, n. one who salts.
Salt'ish, a. somewhat salt.
Salt'less, a. not tasting of salt.
| Salt'ness, n. the state of being salt.
Salt'cellar, n. a vessel for holding salt.
Saltpe'ter, n. a mineral salt; niter.
Salt'work, n. a place where salt is made.

Note.—Salt, a leap, a jump, comes from the Latin (*saltum*).

Sand—Earth; the Shore.

Sand, n. small particles of stone.
Sand'ed, a. covered with sand.
Sand'y, a. full of sand.
| Sand'iness, n. the state of being sandy.
Sand'stone, n. a loose, friable kind of stone.

Same—ALIKE; AS WELL.

SAME, *a.* not different. | SAME'NESS, *n.* the state being the same.

Sæp—SAP; JUICE.

SAP, *n.* the vital juice of plants. | SAP'LING, *n.* a young plant or tree.
SAP'LESS, *a.* wanting sap; dry; old. | SAP'PY, *a.* abounding with sap.

NOTE.—SAP, to undermine, comes from the French (*saper*).

Sæter-dæg—SATURN'S DAY.

SAT'URDAY, *n.* the last day of the week.

Saga—SAW.

SAW, *n.* a cutting instrument with a | SAW'YER, *n.* one who saws.
toothed edge. | SAW'DUST, *n.* dust made by sawing.
SAW'PIT, *n.* a pit where wood is sawed.

Secgan, segan—to SAY.

SAY, *v.* to speak; to utter in words. | SAY'ING, *n.* an expression; a maxim.
SAW, *n.* a saying; a maxim.

NOTE.—SAW, the preterit of the verb *see*, is from the A.-S. *seon*, to see, to behold.
SAW, a cutting instrument, comes from the A.-S. *saga*, a saw.

Sceabb—SCAB.

SCAB, *n.* a crust formed over a sore. | SHAB'BINESS, *n.* meanness; ragged-
SCAB'BY, *a.* diseased with scabs. | ness.
SHAB'BY, *a.* mean; paltry. | SHAB'BILY, *ad.* meanly.

Scale—a SHELL; a HUSK.

SCALE, *n.* the dish of a balance. | SCA'LY, *a.* covered with scales.
SCALE, *n.* a small shell or crust. | SHELL, *n.* the hard covering of any-
SCALE'LESS, *a.* destitute of scales. | thing.
SHEL'LY, *a.* abounding with shells.

NOTE.—SCALE, to climb as by a ladder, comes from the Latin (*scala*, a ladder).

Scearfe—a FRAGMENT.

SCARF, *n.* a piece of dress that hangs | SCARF'SKIN, *n.* the outer skin of the
loose upon the shoulders. | body.

Scathian—to INJURE; to DAMAGE.

SCATH, *v.* to damage; to waste; to | SCATHE, *v.* to damage; to destroy.
destroy. | SCATH'FUL, *a.* injurious; destructive.
SCATH'LESS, *a.* without harm or damage.

Scateran—to POUR OUT; to DISPERSE.

SCAT'TER, *v.* to throw loosely about. | SHAT'TER, *v.* to break at once into
SCAT'TEREDLY, *ad.* loosely; separately. | many pieces.
SCAT'TERING, *n.* the act of dispersing.

Sceol—SHOAL; CROWD; SCHOOL.

SCHOOL, *n.* a shoal or multitude of fish.
SHOAL, *n.* a great multitude assembled; a crowd.
SHOAL, *n.* a place where the water is of little depth.
SHAL'LOW, *a.* not deep.

NOTE.—SCHOOL, a place where instruction is given, comes from the Latin (*schola*).

Scor, from *sceran*—to SHEAR; to CUT; SCORE.

SCORE, *n.* a notch, or mark cut on a stick; twenty; reason or motive.

NOTE.—SCORE, when used for twenty, has been well and rationally accounted for by supposing that our unlearned ancestors, to avoid the embarrassments of large numbers, when they had made twice ten notches, cut off the piece or tally containing them, and afterwards counted the scores or pieces cut off, and reckoned by the number of separated pieces, or by *scores*.—HORNE TOOKE.

Scur—a SCOURING; SCOUR.

SCOUR, *v.* to rub hard with something rough.
SCOUR'ING, *n.* the act of cleaning by rubbing.

Scul, in SCUL-EDGED, SCOWL-EYED—SCOWL.

SCOWL, *v.* to contract the brows; to look angry or sullen.
SCOWL, *n.* a frowning look of anger.

Screopan—to SCRAPE.

SCRAPE, *v.* to rub off the surface by an edge.
SCRAPE, *n.* difficulty or trouble.
SCRAP, *n.* a small piece.
SCRAP'ER, *n.* an instrument for scraping.

Hræman—to CRY ALOUD.

SCREAM, *n.* a shrill, quick, loud cry of pain.
SCREAM, *v.* to cry out shrilly.

Sceotan—to SHOOT, DART or RUSH.

SCUD, *v.* to flee; to pass over quickly.
SCUD'DING, *n.* a driving before a gale with no sail.
SCUD, *n.* loose, vapory clouds driven swiftly by the wind.
SCUT'TLE, *n.* scud, to run with affected haste.
SHOOT, *v.* to make fly with speed or violence.
SHOT, *n.* the act of shooting.
SHOUT, *v.* to utter a loud cry.
SHUT'TLE, *n.* a weaver's instrument.
SHUT'TLECOCK, *n.* *cork,* a cork stuck with feathers.
UP'SHOT, *n.* conclusion; end.

NOTE.—SCUTTLE, a hole in the deck or side of a ship, comes from the French (*écoutille*), and SCUTTLE, a utensil for holding coals, from the Latin (*scutilla*).

Sceorfa—SCURF.

SCURF, *n.* a dry, mealy crust.
SCURF'Y, *a.* like scurf.
SCUR'VY, *a.* vile; mean; *n.* a disease.
SCUR'VILY, *ad.* vilely; basely.

Seam—SEAM.

SEAM, *n.* the joining of two edges.
SEAM'LESS, *a.* having no seam.
SEAM'STRESS, *n.* a woman who sews.
SEAM'Y, *a.* showing the seam.

Sæ, se, siew—SEA.

SEA, *n.* a large body of salt water.
SEA'COAST, *n.* the edge of the sea.
SEA'WORTHY, *a.* fit to go to sea.
SEA'WARD, *a.* towards the sea.
SEA'BREEZE, *n.* wind blowing from the sea.
SEA'BOARD, *n.* the sea coast.
SEA'FARER, *n.* a seaman; a sailor.
SEA'GIRT, *a.* encircled by the sea.
SEAL, *n. seol,* a marine quadruped found in cold latitudes.

NOTE.—SEAL, a stamp for making impressions, comes from the Latin (*sigillum,* a little image or figure).

Seon—to SEE. Gesiht—SIGHT.

SEE, *v.* to perceive by the eye.
SEE'ING, *n.* sight; vision.
SEEN, *pp.* beheld; observed.
SEER, *n.* a prophet.
SAW, *v. sawon,* did see.
SIGHT, *n.* the sense of seeing.
SIGHT'LESS, *a.* wanting sight.
SIGHT'LY, *a.* pleasing to the eye.

NOTE.—The preterit perfect of *see* was anciently written *sigh,* whence *sighed, sighd, sight.* SEE, a diocese, comes from the Latin *sedes,* a seat, (from *sedeo,* to sit).

Sæd—SEED; SOWING.

SEED, *n.* the substance from which new plants spring.
SEED'LING, *n.* a plant just sprung from the seed.
SEED'Y, *a.* full of seed; poor and miserable looking.
SEED'TIME, *n.* the season of sowing.

Seothan—to SEETHE; BOIL, or COOK.

SEETHE, *v.* to boil; to decoct in hot liquor.
SOD'DEN, *p.* soaked and softened in water.

Sylf, seolf—SELF.

SELF, *n.* one's own person.
SELF'ISH, *a.* regarding only one's own interest.
SELF'ISHLY, *ad.* in a selfish manner.
SELF'ISHNESS, *n.* the quality of being selfish.
SELF'SAME, *a.* exactly the same.

Settan—to SET.

SET, *v.* to place; to plant; to regulate.
SET, *p. a.* regular; fixed; firm.
SET, *n.* a number of things suited to each other.
SET'TEE, *n.* a large seat with a back.
SET'TLE, *v.* to fix in any place or way of life
SET'TLEMENT, *n.* adjustment; a colony.
SET'TER, *n.* a kind of dog.
BESET', *v.* to surround.
BESET'TING, *p. a.* habitually attending.
OUT'SET, *n.* opening; beginning.

Sceacan—to SHAKE.

SHAKE, *v.* to agitate; to make to totter or tremble.
SHAK'ING, *n.* a vibratory motion.
SHOCK, *n.* a violent collision.
SHOCK'ING, *a.* that shocks; offensive.

Sceal—I AM OBLIGED; I OUGHT.

SHALL, *v.* an auxiliary verb denoting duty or obligation.
SHOULD, *v.* the preterit of SHALL.

Scead—Shade.   *Sceadan*—to Divide; to Shade; to Cover.
Sced—a Shade.   *Scedan*—to Pour Out; to Shed.

Shade, *n.* interception of light.
Shade, *v.* to shelter or screen from light or the rays of the sun.
Sha'dy, *a.* sheltered from light and heat.
Shad'ow, *n.* a figure formed by the interception of light.
Overshade', *v.* to cover so as to cause darkness.

Shad'owy, *a.* full of shade.
Overshad'ow, *v.* to throw a shadow over.
Sheath, *n.* the case or cover of any thing.
Sheathe, *v.* to put into a sheath.
Sheath'less, *a.* having no sheath.
Shed, *v.* to let fall; to pour out.
Shed'ding, *ppr.* flowing out; casting.

Shed, *n.* a slight covering to shade.

Note.—Shed is used in composition in the sense of *effusion;* as blood-*shed*.

Scama—Shame.

Shame, *n.* the emotion excited by the consciousness of guilt, or by the exposure of what ought to be concealed.

Shame'ful, *a.* disgraceful.
Shame'less, *a.* destitute of shame.
Shame'faced, *a.* modest; bashful.
Ashamed', *p. a.* touched with shame.

Sham, *n.* a false pretence; a fraud.

Note.—Sham, contracted from *ashamed*.

Scyppan—to Form; to Create; to Shape.

Shape, *v.* to form; to mould; to make.
Shape, *n.* form or figure.

Shape'less, *a.* destitute of regular form.

Shape'ly, *a.* well-formed.

Sceran—to Shear; to Shave; to Divide; from *scer*—a Share; a Shire.

Note.—Also the superintendence of a share.

Shear, *v.* to clip or cut from the surface.
Shear'er, *n.* one who shears.
Shears, *n.* large scissors.
Share, *v.* to part among two or more.
Share, *n.* the part allotted.
Shore, *n.* land bordering on water.

Sheer, *a.* pure and unmixed; very thin.
Sheer, *v.* to deviate or turn aside.
Shire, *n.* a county.
Sher'iff, *n.* (*scir-gerefa*, shire-reeve), the chief civil officer of a county.

Shirt, *n.* the under-garment worn by men.

Note.—Shore, a piece of timber to prop with, comes from the Dutch (*schoor*).
Shirt comes from *scirtan*, to shorten, (from *sceran*, to shear).

Scearp—Sharp.

Sharp, *a.* having a keen edge or fine point.
Sharp'en, *v.* to make sharp.
Sharp'er, *n.* a tricky fellow.

Sharp'ly, *ad.* keenly; acutely.
Sharp'ness, *n.* keenness of edge or point.
Sharp'set, *a.* hungry; eager.

Scafan—to Scrape; to Make Smooth.

Shave, *v.* to make smooth; to cut or pare close to the surface.

Scav'enger, *n.* a person employed to clean the streets.

Shav'ing, *n.* a thin slice pared off.

ANGLO-SAXON ROOTS AND DERIVATIVES. 155

Sceaf—a SHEAF; a BUNDLE OF CORN.

SHEAF, *n.* a bundle of stalks. | SHEAF, *v.* to make sheaves.

NOTE.—SHEAF (sometimes called SHEAVE), the wheel in the block of a pulley, comes from the Dutch (*schij*).

Scep—SHEEP.

SHEEP, *n.* an animal.
SHEEP'ISH, *a.* like a sheep; bashful.
SHEEPS' EYE, *n.* a modest, diffident look.
SHEP'HERD, *n. hyrde,* one who tends sheep.

SHEEP'ISHLY, *ad.* bashfully.
SHEP'HERDESS, *n.* a female who tends sheep.
SHEP'HERD'S-CROOK, *n.* an implement to secure a sheep by the legs without disturbing the flock.

Scyte—SHEET.

SHEET, *n.* a broad piece of linen or cotton cloth. | SHEET'ING, *n.* cloth for making sheets.

NOTE.—SHEET, a rope fastened to the lower corners of a sail, comes from the French (*écoute*).

Scylfe—SHELF.

SHELF, *n.* a board fixed on supporters for holding anything.
SHELV'ING, *p. a.* sloping; inclining.

SHELVE, *v.* to place on shelves; to slope.

Scyld—SHIELD. *Scyldan*—to COVER; to PROTECT.

SHIELD, *n.* defence; shelter; protection.
SHEL'TERLESS, *a.* destitute of shelter.

SHEL'TER, *n.* a cover; a protection.
SHEL'TER, *v.* to cover; to protect.

NOTE.—SHELTER is formed from *to shield*, A.-S. *scyldan*, to cover, to protect, preterit and past participle *shielt*, like *feel, felt; build, built.*—BARCLAY.

Scyftan—to DIVIDE; to VERGE; to DECLINE.

SHIFT, *v.* to change place; to move. | SHIFT'ING, *n.* act of changing.
SHIFT'LESS, *a.* destitute of energy.

Scinan—to SHINE. *Sceone*—BEAUTIFUL.

SHINE, *v.* to be bright; to glitter.
SHIN'ING, *p. a.* bright; splendid.
SHEEN, *n.* brightness; splendor.

SHI'NY, *a.* bright; splendid.
SHEEN, *a.* bright; glittering.

Scip—SHIP.

SHIP, *n.* a large vessel for sailing.
SHIP'PING, *n.* ships collectively.
SHIP'WRECK, *n.* the destruction of a ship.

SHIP'MENT, *n.* the act of loading a ship.

NOTE.—SHIP, as a termination, denotes state, office, or dignity; as, friend*ship*.

Sceoppa—a TREASURY; a STOREHOUSE; (*Dut. schap*, a shelf.)

SHOP, *n.* a place where things are sold. | SHOP'PING, *ppr.* visiting shops to buy.

Sceo—Shoe.

Shoe, *n.* a covering for the foot.
Shoe'less, *a.* destitute of shoes.
Shoe'maker, *n.* one who makes shoes.
Shod, *pp.* having the feet covered with shoes.

Scort—Short.

Short, *a.* not long in time or space.
Short'en, *v.* to make short.
Short'ly, *ad.* quickly; soon.
Short'ness, *n.* the quality of being short.

Scufan, sceofan—to Shove; Thrust; Cast; Put.

Shove, *v.* to push or press along.
Shov'el, *n.* an instrument with a handle and broad scoop.
Shuf'fle, *v.* to throw into disorder.
Shaft, *n.* anything straight.

Sceawian—to Look or See; to View.

Show, *v.* to present to view.
Show, *n.* a spectacle.
Show'y, *a.* splendid; gay.
Show'ily, *ad.* in a showy manner.

Scur—Shower of Rain; a Storm.

Show'er, *n.* a fall of rain of short duration.
Show'ery, *a.* raining in showers.

Screadian—to Cut Off.

Shred, *v.* to cut into pieces narrow and long.
Shred, *n.* a fragment; a strip.

Syrwan—to Ensnare; to Entrap.

Shrew, *n.* a peevish, brawling woman.
Shrewd, *a.* sly; cunning; artful.
Shrewd'ness, *n.* sly cunning.
Shrewd'ly, *ad.* cunningly; mischievously.
Shrew'ish, *a.* peevish; petulant.
Shrew'ishness, *n.* petulance.

Scrin—Casket; Chest.

Shrine, *n.* a case in which something sacred is deposited.
Enshrine', *v.* to preserve as sacred.

Scrincan—Shrink; to Wither; to Contract.

Shrink, *v.* to contract itself.
Shrink'age, *n.* contraction into a less compass.
Shrimp, *n.* a small crustaceous animal.
Shrimp'net, *n.* a net for catching shrimps.

Note.—Shrimps, when boiled, contract or draw together in a roundish shape.

Scrud—Clothing; Shroud.

Shroud, *n.* a cover; the dress of the dead.
Shrouds, *n.* ropes extending from the masts to the sides of a ship.

Scrob—Shrub.

Shrub, n. a bush; a small tree. | Shrub'bery, n. a plantation of shrubs.

Note.—Shrub, a liquor composed of spirits, acid, and sugar, comes from the Arabic (*sharab*).

Seoc—Sick.

Sick, a. afflicted with disease. | Sick'ly, a. not healthy.
Sick'en, v. to make, or become sick. | Sick'liness, n. the state of being sickly.
Sick'ish, a. somewhat sick. |
Sick'ness, n. disease.

Side—Side.

Side, n. the broad and long part of a thing. | Si'dle, v. to go side foremost.
 | Side'long, ad. on the side.
Side'ways, ad. on one side.

Sife, Siftan—to Sift.

Sieve, n. a vessel with a bottom of net work. | Sift, v. to separate by a sieve.

Siccet—a Sigh; a Groan. Sican—to Sigh.

Sigh, v. to inhale and expire a long breath audibly. | Sigh'ing, n. audible emission of breath.

Seolc—Silk.

Silk, n. a fine, soft thread spun by the silk-worm. | Silk'en, a. made of silk.
 | Silk'y, a. soft; tender.
Silk'iness, n. softness; smoothness.

Sælig—Happy.

Sil'ly, a. weak in intellect; foolish. | Sil'liness, n. weakness; harmless folly.

Seolfer, sylfor—Silver.

Sil'ver, n. a precious metal. | Sil'very, a. like silver.

Syn—Sin.

Sin, n. a violation of the Divine law. | Sin'less, a. free from sin.
Sin'ful, a. guilty of sin; wicked. | Sin'ner, n. one guilty of sin.

Siththan. Sith—After; and thænne—Then.

Since, conj. because that. | Since, ad. from the time that.

Sinu—Sinew.

Sin'ew, n. a tendon; strength. | Sin'ewy, a. strong; powerful.

Singan—to SING.

SING, *v.* to modulate the voice to melody.
SING'ING, *n.* the utterance of melodious sounds.
SING'ER, *n.* one who sings.
SING'SONG, *a.* bad intonation.
SONG, *n.* that which is sung.
SONG'STER, *n.* one that sings.
SONG'STRESS, *n.* a female singer.

Sincan—to SINK.

SINK, *v.* to fall down through any substance.
SINK, *n.* a drain.
SINK'ING, *ppr. a.* falling; declining.

Sipan—to SIP.

SIP, *v.* to drink in small quantities. | SIP'PET, *n.* a small sop.

Swuster—SISTER.

SIS'TER, *n.* a female born of the same parents.
SIS'TERHOOD, *n.* a society of females.
SIS'TERLY, *a.* like a sister.

Sittan—to SIT.

SIT, *v.* to rest on the lower part of the body.
SIT'TING, *n.* the act of resting on a seat.

SKATE, *n. sceadda*, a flat fish.

NOTE.—SKATE, a shoe for sliding on the ice, comes from the Dutch (*schaats*.)

Scylan—to DISTINGUISH; to SEPARATE; to SCALE.

SKILL, *n.* familiar knowledge of any art or science.
SKILL'FUL, *a.* knowing; dexterous.
SKILL'FULLY, *ad.* with skill.
SKILLED, *a.* knowing; dexterous.
SLATE, *n.* a kind of stone which readily splits into plates.
SLATY, *a.* resembling slate

Scin—SKIN.

SKIN, *n.* the natural covering of the flesh.
SKIN'NER, *n.* one who skins.
SKIN'NY, *a.* wanting flesh.
SKIN'DEEP, *a.* slight; superficial.

Scitan—to THROW OUT; SKITTISH.

SKIT'TISH, *a.* easily frightened; timid. | SKIT'TISHLY, *ad.* shyly.

Sleac, slaw—SLOW; IDLE; LAZY; REMISS.

SLACK, *a.* loose; not hard drawn.
SLACK'EN, *v.* to loosen; to relax.
SLACK'LY, *ad.* loosely; remissly.
SLACK'NESS, *n.* looseness.
SLOUCH, *n.* a lazy, idle fellow.
SLOUCH, *v.* to have a downcast clownish look.
SLOW, *a.* not swift; not ready.
SLOW'LY, *ad.* not speedily.
SLOW'NESS, *n.* want of speed.
SLOTH, *n.* slowness; laziness.
SLOTH'FUL, *a.* lazy; sluggish.
SLUG, *n.* a piece of metal shot from a gun.
SLUG, *n.* a slow, lazy, sleepy fellow.
SLUG'GARD, *n.* a slow, lazy person.
SLUG'GISH, *a.* lazy; dull; slow.
SLUG'GISHLY, *ad.* lazily; slowly.

Slaughter, from ***slaught,*** past part. of ***slean***—to SLAY; to BEAT.

SLAUGH'TER, *n.* destruction of life by violence.
SLAUGH'TEROUS, *a.* destructive; murderous.
SLAY, *v.* to put to death; to kill.
SLAY'ER, *n.* one who slays.
SLEDGE, *n.* a large, heavy hammer.
SLEET, *n. sliht,* a fall of hail or snow with rain.
SLEET'Y, *a.* consisting of sleet.

NOTE.—SLEDGE, a vehicle with low wheels for conveying loads, is from the Dutch (*slede.*) SLIHT, past participle of A.-S. *slean.*

Slith—SMOOTH; SLIPPERY.

SLEEK, *a.* smooth; glassy.
SLEEK'LY, *ad.* smoothly; softly.
SLEEK'NESS, *n.* smoothness.
SLICK, *a.* smooth; slippery; glossy.
SLEIGHT, *n.* an artful or adroit trick.
SLY, *a.* meanly; artful; crafty.
SLY'LY, *ad.* with secret artifice.
SLY'NESS, *n.* artful secrecy.

Slapan—to SLEEP.

SLEEP, *v.* to take rest by the suspension of the bodily and mental powers.
SLEEP'ER, *n.* one who sleeps.
SLEEP'INESS, *n.* inclination to sleep.
SLEEP'ING, *n.* the state of being at rest.
SLEEP'LESS, *a.* having no sleep.
SLEEP'Y, *a.* disposed to sleep.
SLEEP'ILY, *ad.* drowsily; lazily.

Slyf—a SLEEVE. *Slefan*—to CLOTHE; to COVER.

SLEEVE, *n.* the part of a garment which covers the arm.
SLEEVE'LESS, *a.* having no sleeves.

Slitan—to SLIT; to SLICE.

SLICE, *v.* to cut into broad, thin pieces.
SLIC'ER, *n.* one who slices.
SLIT, *v.* to cut lengthwise.

Slidan—to SLIDE.

SLED, *n.* a carriage with runners used on snow.
SLEIGH, *n.* a carriage with runners used on snow.
SLIDE, *v.* to move along without stepping.
SLID'ING, *p. a.* gliding.

Slim—SLIME.

SLIME, *n.* moist, adhesive earth.
SLIM'Y, *a.* consisting of slime.

Slingan—to SLING.

SLING, *n.* an instrument for throwing stones.
SLING, *v.* to throw; to hurl.

Slipan—to SLIP.

SLIP, *v.* to slide; to glide.
SLIP'PER, *n.* a loose kind of shoe.
SLIP'PERY, *a.* smooth, like ice.
SLIP'KNOT, *n.* a knot easily untied.
SLAB, *n.* a plane or table of stone.

Slumerian—to SLUMBER.

SLUM'BER, *v.* to sleep lightly.
SLUM'BERING, *n.* state of repose.

Slog—Slough.

Slough, n. a place of deep mud.
Slough'y, a. miry; muddy.

Sludge, n. mire; mud.
Sludg'y, a. miry.

Smæccan—to Taste.

Smack, v. to kiss with a sharp noise; to have a taste.
Smack, n. a loud kiss; a quick, smart blow.

Smat'ter, v. to talk with but little knowledge of the subject.
Smat'tering, n. superficial knowledge.

Note.—Smack, a fishing-vessel, comes from the Dutch (*smak schip*.)

Smæl—Small; Thin; Slender.

Small, a. little; minute; petty.
Small'ness, n. state of being small.

Small'ish, a. somewhat small.

Smeortan—to Smart.

Smart, v. to feel sharp pain.
Smart'ness, n. quickness; briskness.

Smart'ly, ad. sharply; briskly.

Smyrian, smere—Fat; Grease.

Smear, v. to overspread with anything unctuous.

Besmear', v. to bedaub; to soil.

Smitan—to Strike; to Smite; to Dash.

Smite, v. to give a blow to.
Smi'ter, n. one who smites.
Smith'craft, n. (*cræft*,) the art of a smith.

Smith, n. any one who strikes or smites with a hammer.

Smeoc—Smoke.

Smoke, n. the visible matter which is emitted by burning substances.
Smok'y, a. emitting smoke.

Smok'er, n. one who smokes.
Smoke'less, a. having no smoke.

Smethe—Smooth.

Smooth, a. even on the surface.
Smooth'er, n. one who smooths.

Smooth'ly, ad. not roughly.
Smooth'ness, n. evenness of surface.

Smoran—to Suffocate.

Smoth'er, v. to suffocate by excluding air.
Smoul'dering, a. burning and smoking without vent.

Smoul'der. v. to burn and smoke without flame or vent.

Smugan—to Creep.

Smug'gle, v. to import or export unlawfully.

Smug'gler, n. one who smuggles.

Snægel—Snail.

Snail, n. a slimy, slow creeping reptile. | Snail'like, ad. as a snail; very slow.

Smitta—SMUT.

SMUT, *n.* a spot made with soot or coal.
SMUT, *n.* obscene language.
SMUTCH, *v.* to blacken with smoke.
SMUT'TY, *a.* black with smoke; obscene.
BESMUT, *v.* to soil with soot or smoke.

Snican—to MOVE SOFTLY; to SNEAK; to CREEP.

SNEAK, *v.* to creep or steal away privately.
SNEAK'ING, *a.* servile; mean.
SNUG'NESS, *n.* state of being snug.
SNUG, *v.* to lie close, as in bed.
SNUG'GLE, *v.* to lie close and warm.
SNUG'LY, *ad.* closely.
SNAKE, *n.* a kind of serpent.
SNAK'Y, *a.* like a snake; sly.

Snora—a SNORING.

SNORE, *v.* to breathe audibly through the nose in sleep.
SNORT'ING, *n.* the act of blowing through the nose.
SNORT, *v.* to blow through the nose so as to utter a strong sound.

NOTE.—SNORE, a string or cord with which a boy spins a top comes from the Dutch (*snoer*, a string or cord.)

Snaw—SNOW.

SNOW, *n.* frozen vapor which falls in white flakes.
SNOW'DROP, *n.* an early flower.
SNOW'Y, *a.* white like snow.
SNOW'BALL, *n.* a round lump of snow.

Seobgend—COMPLAINING.

SOB, *v.* to sigh with convulsion.
SOB'BING, *p. a.* sighing with a heaving of the breast.

Seft—SOFT; MILD; QUIET.

SOFT, *a.* easily yielding to pressure.
SOFT'EN, *v.* to make or grow soft.
SOFT'LY, *ad.* gently; mildly.
SOFT'NESS, *n.* the quality of being soft; mildness.

Selan—to SOIL; SMEAR or STAIN.

SOIL, *v.* to make dirty; to stain.
SOIL'ING, *n.* the act of one who soils.

NOTE.—SOIL, the ground, earth, land, comes from the Latin (*solum.*)

Sol—a SOLE or SANDAL.

SOLE, *n.* the bottom of the foot.
SOLE, *n.* a flat fish.

NOTE.—SOLE, single; only; comes from the Latin (*solus.*)

Sum—SOME.

SOME, *a.* noting a quantity of a thing but indeterminate.
SOME'BODY, *n.* a person unknown.
SOME'HOW, *ad.* in some way not yet known.
SOME'THING, *n.* a portion more or less.
SOME'TIME, *ad.* at one time or other.
SOME'WHAT, *ad.* more or less.
SOME'WHERE, *ad.* in some place or other.

Soth—Sooth; Truth.

Sooth, n. truth; reality.
Sooth'sayer, n. a foreteller.
Sooth'say, v. to foretell.

Gesothian—to Flatter; to Assert; to Soothe.

Soothe, v. to calm; to mollify; to flatter.
Sooth'ingly, ad. with flattery.

Sar, sorg—Pain; Care.

Sore, n. a tender and painful place.
Sore'ly, ad. with great pain.
Sore'ness, n. the state of being sore.
Sor'row, n. pain of mind; grief.
Sor'rowful, a. mournful; sad.
Sor'ry, a. grieved for the loss of some good; mean; worthless.
Sor'rily, ad. meanly; wretchedly.

Sot—Sot.

Sot, n. a habitual drunkard.
Sot'tish, a. drunken; stupid; dull.

Sawl—Life; Soul.

Soul, n. the immortal spirit of man.
Soul'less, a. without soul; mean.

Sund—Healthy.

Sound, a. whole; healthy.
Sound'ness, n. health; truth.
Sound'ly, ad. heartily; rightly.

Sund—a Swimming; a Shallow Sea.

Sound, n. a strait, or a part of the sea between two headlands.
Sound'less, a. that cannot be fathomed.

Note.—Sound, anything audible; a noise; comes from the Latin (*sono.*)

Sur—Sour. Surelice—Surly.

Sour, a. acid; tart; harsh.
Sour'ish, a. somewhat sour.
Sour'ly, ad. with acidity.
Sour'ness, n. acidity; harshness of temper.
Sur'liness, n. moroseness.
Sor'rel, n. a plant, so named from its acid taste.
Sur'ly, a. gloomily; morose; uncivil.
Sur'lily, ad. in a surly manner.

Note.—Sorrel, a yellowish brown color, comes from the French (*saure.*)

Suth—South.

South, n. the point in which the sun is at noon to the inhabitants of the northern parts of the earth.
South'ward, ad. towards the south.
South'erly, a. lying towards the south.
South'ern, a. belonging to the south.

Span, spannan—to Measure; to Clasp; to Join.

Span, n. the space from the end of the thumb to the end of the little finger extended; nine inches; a brief period.
Span, v. to measure by the hand extended.
Span'ner, n. that which spans.

Sparran—to BAR; to STOP; to HINDER.

SPAR, *v.* to dispute; to fight with prelusive strokes; to box.

NOTE.—SPAR, a mast, boom, etc., comes from the Dutch (*spar*, a rafter,) and SPAR, a crystallized mineral, from the Dutch (*spaath*.)

Sparian—to SPARE.

SPARE, *v.* to use frugally; to do without.
SPARE'LY, *ad.* frugally.
SPARE'NESS, *n.* leanness.
SPARING'LY, *ad.* frugally.

Spearca—SPARK.

SPARK, *n.* a small particle of fire.
SPAR'KLE, *n.* a particle of fire.
SPAR'KLE, *v.* to emit sparks; to shine.
SPARK'LER, *n.* one that sparkles.
SPARK'LING, *a.* glittering; lively.
SPARK'LINGLY, *ad.* with twinkling lustre.

Sprǣcan—to SPEAK.

SPEAK, *v.* to express thoughts by words.
SPEAK'ABLE, *a.* that may be spoken.
SPEAK'ER, *n.* one who speaks.
SPEAK'ING, *n.* the act of expressing in words.
BESPEAK', *v.* to speak for beforehand.
SPEECH, *n.* the power of expressing thoughts by words.
SPEECH'LESS, *a.* deprived of speech; dumb.
SPOKE, *v.* did speak.
SPOKES'MAN, *n.* one who speaks for another.
SPO'KEN, *ppr.* expressed thoughts.

NOTE.—SPOKE, one of the bars of a wheel which extend from the hub to the rim, comes from the A.-S. (*spaca*.)

Specca—SPECK.

SPECK, *n.* a small spot; *v.* to spot.
SPEC'KLE, *v.* to mark with small spots.

Spedan—to SPEED; to PROSPER.

SPEED, *v.* to make haste; *n.* quickness.
SPEED'Y, *a.* quick; swift.
SPEED'ILY, *ad.* quickly.
SPEED'INESS, *n.* the quality of being speedy.

Spell—HISTORY; SPEECH; TIDINGS.

SPELL, *n.* a charm consisting of words.
SPELL'BOUND, *a.* under magic influence.
SPELL'-LAND, *n.* enchanted land.

Spelian— to TAKE ANOTHER'S PLACE.

SPELL, *n.* a turn of work; a short turn or time; season.
SPELL, *v.* to relieve by taking a turn at a piece of work.

Spǣtan—to THROW OUT.

SPIT, *v.* to eject from the mouth.
SPIT, *n.* what is ejected from the mouth.
SPIT'TLE, *n.* moisture of the mouth; saliva.
SPAT'TER, *v.* to sprinkle with dirt.
BESPAT'TER, *v.* to spot over with dirt.

NOTE.—SPIT, a long iron prong on which meat is roasted, comes from A.-S. (*spiter*.)

Spellian—to NARRATE.

SPELL, *v.* to form words with their proper letters.

SPELL'ING-BOOK, *n.* a book for teaching orthography.

Spendan—to CONSUME.

SPEND, *v.* to lay out; to waste.
SPEND'THRIFT, *n.* a prodigal; a lavisher.
SPEND'ING, *n.* the act of laying out.

Spinnan—to SPIN.

SPIN, *v.* to draw out and twist into threads; to protract; to move rapidly round.
SPIN'NER, *n.* one who spins.
SPIN'STER, *n.* a woman who spins; an unmarried woman.
SPIN'DLE, *n.* the pin on which the thread is formed; a long, slender stalk.
SPIN'DLE-LEGGED, *a.* having long, slender legs.
SPI'DER,* *n.* an insect.

* From *Spin*, *n* being dropped, so named, from spinning his web.

Spon—a CHIP.

SPOON, *n.* a utensil with a concave part for dipping liquids.
SPOON'FUL, *n.* as much as a spoon can hold.

Sprædan—to SPREAD.

SPREAD, *v.* to extend in all directions. | SPREAD'ING, *n.* the act of extending.

Springan—to SPRING.

SPRING, *v.* to rise out of the ground; to leap; to jump.
SPRING'Y, *a.* elastic.
SPRING, *n.* the season when plants begin to grow; a fountain.
SPRING'INESS, *n.* elasticity.

Sprengan—to SPRINKLE.

SPRIN'KLE, *v.* to scatter in drops. | SPRINK'LING, *n.* a small quantity scattered.

Spreot—a SPEAR; SPRIT.

SPRIT, *n.* a small boom used with some sails.
SPRIT'-SAIL, *n.* a sail extended by means of a sprit.

Gyllan—to YELL.

SQUALL, *v.* to scream violently.
SQUALL, *n.* a short, violent storm.
BEWAIL', *v.* to lament.
WAIL, *v.* to grieve audibly for.
WAIL'ING, *n.* audible sorrow.

Staef—a STICK.

STAFF, *n.* a stick used in walking.
STAVE, *n.* a thin, narrow piece of wood.
STAVE, *v.* to break in pieces.
STOVE, *ppr.* broken in as a boat or barrel.

NOTE.—STOVE, an iron box in which fire is made for heating and cooking, comes from the A.-S. (*stofa*, a stove; a bath.)

Stæger, stigan—to Go; to Ascend; to Mount.

STAGE, *n.* a raised floor; the theatre; a degree of advance.
STAGE'-COACH, *n.* a public coach.
STAIR, *n.* a step by which we ascend.
STAIRS, *n.* a series or flight of steps.
STILE, *n.* (*stigel,*) a set of steps for passing a fence or wall.

Stace, stician—to Stick.

STAKE, *n.* a stick fixed in the ground. | STAKE, *n.* that which is put at hazard.

Stal, steal—a Place; a Stand; a Stable.

STALE, *a.* old; long kept.
STALE'NESS, *n.* the state of being stale.
STALL, *n.* a crib for a horse or an ox.
STALL'FED, *a.* fed in a stall.
STALL, *n.* a bench or frame of shelves in the open air, on which anything is exposed for sale.
FORESTALL', *v.* to take beforehand.

Stælcan—to Stalk; to Go Softly or Warily.

STALK, *v.* to walk with lofty and proud steps.
STALK'ING-HORSE, *n.* a mask, a pretence.

Stælg—a Column.

STALK, *n.* the stem of a plant. | STALK'LESS, *a.* having no stem.

Standan—to Stand.

STAND, *v.* to be upon the feet in an erect position.
STAND, *n.* a station; a halt.
STAND'ARD, *n.* an ensign of war; a rule or measure.
STAND'ING, *a.* settled; lasting.

Stapel—a Prop; a Stake Set in the Ground.

STA'PLE, *n.* a loop of metal; a principal commodity. | STA'PLE, *a.* chief; principal.

Stearc—Rigid; Stiff.

STARCH, *n.* a substance used to stiffen linen.
STARCHED, *a.* stiffened; precise.
STARK, *ad.* completely; wholly.

Styran—to Stir; to Move; to Steer.

START, *v.* to move suddenly; to alarm.
START, *n.* a quick spring.
START'ING, *n.* the act of moving suddenly.
STAR'TLE, *v.* to alarm; to fright.
STAR, *n.* (*stearra,*) a luminous body in the heavens.
STAR'LESS, *a.* having no light of stars.
STAR'RY, *a.* abounding with stars.
STAR'LIGHT, *a.* lighted by the stars.
STAR'BOARD, *n.* the right hand side of a ship.
STEER, *v.* to direct; to guide.
STEER'AGE, *n.* an apartment in a ship.
STERN, *n.* the hind part of a ship where the rudder is placed.
STIR, *v.* to move; to agitate.
BESTIR', *v.* to put into brisk action.

NOTE.—STEER, a young bullock, comes from the A.-S. (*steor;*) and STEER, to guide, to direct, from the A.-S. (*styran,* to stir, to move).
STERN, severe of countenance, comes from the A.-S. (*starian,* to stare); and STERN, the hind part of a boat, from the A.-S. (*styran,* to stir, to steer).

Starian—to STARE.

STARE, *v* to look with fixed eyes.
STAR'ER, *n*. one who stares.

STERN, (*styrne,*) severe of countenance; harsh.
STERN'LY, severely.

Steorfan—to DIE; to PERISH.

STARVE, *v*. to kill with hunger or cold. | STARVA'TION, *n*. the act of starving.

Stede—PLACE.

STEAD, *n*. place; room.
STEAD'FAST, *a*. fast in place; firm; constant.

STEAD'Y, *a*. firm; fixed; constant.
STEAD'ILY, *ad*. with steadiness.
STEAD'INESS, *n*. firmness; constancy.

Stelan—to STEAL.

STEAL, *v*. to take by theft.
STEALTH, *n*. theft; secret act.

STAL'WORTH, *a*.(*stæl-weorth,*worth stealing,) stout; strong; robust.

Stæp—a STEP; a GOING.

STEP, *v*. to move the foot; to walk gravely.
STEEP, *a*. rising or descending with great inclination.

STIR'RUP, *n*. a step rope; a kind of hoop in which a horseman rests his foot.

NOTE.—STEEP, to soak, to imbue, comes from the German (*stippen*.)
STIRRUP, from A.-S. (*stige rapa*, from *stigan*, to step or ascend, and *rap*, a rope.) The first stirrups appear to have been ropes.

Steop from *steopan*—to DEPRIVE; to BEREAVE.

STEP, is a prefix denoting relationship arising out of orphanage.
STEP'CHILD, *n*. a child by marriage only.
STEP'FATHER, *n*. a father by marriage.

STEP'DAUGHTER, *n*. a daughter by marriage.
STEP'MOTHER, *n*. a mother by marriage.
STEP'SON, *n*. a son by marriage.

Stiward from ICEL. *Stia*—WORK; and *weard*—a GUARD or KEEPER.

STEW'ARD, *n*. one who manages the affairs of another.

STEW'ARDSHIP, *n*. the office of a steward.

Sticca—a STICK. *Sticce*—a PIECE; a PART.

STICK, *n*. a long, small piece of wood.
STIC'KLE, *v*. to contend; to contest.
STIC'KLER, *n*. an obstinate contender.

STEAK, *n*. a slice of meat for broiling or frying.

NOTE.—STICKLE, from the practice of prize-fighters, who placed seconds with staves, or *sticks*, to interpose occasionally.

Stillan—to STILL.

STILL, *v*. to make silent; to quiet.
STILL, *a*. silent; motionless.

STILL'NESS, *n*. calmness; silence.

NOTE.—STILL, a vessel for distillation, comes from the Latin (*stillo*.)

Stician—to STICK.

STICK, *v.* to pierce; to stab.
STICK'Y, *a.* adhesive; glutinous.

STICK, *v.* to cleave or adhere.

Stif—STIFF.

STIFF, *a.* not easily bent.
STIFF'EN, *v.* to make or grow stiff.

STIFF'LY, *ad.* rigidly; stubbornly.
STIFF'NESS, *n.* inflexibility.

Stingan—to STING.

STING, *v.* to pierce or wound with a sharp point.

STING, *n.* anything which gives pain.
STING'LESS, *a.* having no sting.

Stincan—to STINK.

STINK, *v.* to emit an offensive smell. | STENCH, *n.* a bad smell.

Stintan—to STOP.

STINT, *v.* to restrain within certain limits.

STUNT, *v.* to hinder from growth.

Stoc—a PLACE; THE STEM OF A TREE.

STOCK, *n.* the body of a plant; a lineage; shares of a public debt.

STOCK, *v.* to supply; to fill.
STOCKADE', *n.* an inclosure.

Stan—STONE.

STONE, *n.* earthy matter condensed into a hard state.
STON'INESS, *n.* the quality of being stony.

STON'Y, *a.* full of stones.
STONE'WORK, *n.* work consisting of stone.
STONE'BLIND, *a.* perfectly blind.

Stupian—to STOOP.

STOOP, *v.* to bend or lean forward; to descend.

STOOP, *n.* an inclination forward.

NOTE.—STOOP, the steps of a door, comes from the Dutch (*stoep*, a step,) and STOOP, a drinking-vessel, from the A.-S. (*stoppa*.)

Stor—GREAT; VAST.

STORE, *n.* a large quantity; plenty. | STORE, *v.* to lay up.

Storm—STORM. *Styrman*—to ASSAIL; to RAGE.

STORM, *n.* a violent commotion of the atmosphere.

STORM'Y, *a.* tempestuous.

Strac, stræc—STRAIGHT; RIGID. From *Streccan*—to STRETCH.

STRAIGHT, *a.* not crooked; direct.
STRAIGHT'EN, *v.* to make straight.
STRAIGHT'LY, *ad.* in a right line.
STRAIGHT'NESS, *n.* state of being straight.
STRAIGHT'FORTH, *ad.* directly.

STRAIGHT'WAY, *ad.* immediately.
STRETCH, *v.* to extend; to draw out; to strain.
STREET, *n.* (*stræt*,) a way between two rows of houses; a public road or place.

Streow—Straw.

Straw, *n.* the stalk or stem of grain. | Straw'y, *a.* like straw.

Straegan—to Spread; to Disperse.

Strag'gle, *v.* to wander; to rove; to be dispersed.
Strag'gler, *n.* one that straggles.
Stray, *v.* to wander away.
Astray', *ad.* out of the right way.
Stroll, *v.* to stray about.

Strica—a Line; Direction; Course.

Streak, *n.* a line or mark of a different color; a stripe. | Streak'y, *a.* striped.

Stream—Stream.

Stream, *n.* a current of water or other fluid.
Stream'er, *n.* an ensign; a pennon.
Stream'let, *n.* a small stream.
Stream'y, *a.* like a stream.

Astrican—to Strike.

Strike, *v.* to hit with force; to impress.
Strik'er, *n.* one that strikes.
Strik'ing, *a.* surprising; strong.
Stroke, *n.* a blow; a sound.
Stroke, *v.* to rub gently with the hand.
Stroke, *n.* sudden effect of forcible contact.
Strok'ing, *n.* the act of rubbing gently.

Streng—String; Sinew; Cord; Line.

String, *n.* a small rope or cord.
Stringed, *a.* having strings.
String'less, *a.* having no strings.
String'y, *a.* consisting of threads.
Strong, *a.* vigorous; powerful; firm.
Strength'less, *a.* wanting strength.
Strong'ly, *ad.* with strength; firmly.
Strength, *n.* force; firmness.
Strength'en, *v.* to make or grow strong.
Strung, *pp.* placed on a string.

Note.—Strung is the past participle of the verb to *string*.—"A *strong* man is a man well *strung*."

Bestrypan—to Strip.

Strip, *v.* to pull or tear off.
Stripe, *n.* a line, band, or mark of color.
Strip, *n.* a long, narrow piece.
Stri'ped, *a.* having stripes.
Strip'ling, *n.* a youth; a lad.

Styb or *steb*—Stub.

Stub, *n.* the stump of a tree.
Stub, *v.* to force up; to strike the toes against.
Stub'by, *a.* short and strong.
Stub'ble, *n.* the stumps of wheat etc., left in the ground.
Stub'born, *a.* hard to be moved; obstinate.
Stub'bornly, *ad.* obstinately.

Sucan—to Suck.

Suck, *v.* to draw with the mouth.
Suck'er, *n.* any thing that sucks.
Suck'le, *v.* to nurse at the breast.
Suck'ling, *n.* a young child or animal.
Suc'tion, *n.* the act of sucking.

Soden—SUDDEN.

SUD'DEN, *a.* happening without previous notice.
SUD'DENLY, *ad.* without notice.
SUD'DENNESS, *n.* the state of being sudden.

Solcen—SULKY; SLOTHFUL.

SUL'KY, *a.* sullen; sour; morose.
SULK'INESS, *n.* silent sullenness.

Swolath, swole—HEAT.

SUL'TRY, *a.* hot and close; warm and damp.
SUL'TRINESS, *n.* the state of being sultry.

Sunne—SUN.

SUN, *n.* the luminary which gives light and heat to the planets.
SUN'LESS, *a.* wanting sun.
SUN'NY, *a.* exposed to the sun.
SUN'BEAM, *n.* a ray of the sun.
SUN'BURN, *v.* to discolor by the sun.
SUN'BURNT, *a.* discolored by the sun.
SUN'DAY, *n.* the first day of the week; the Sabbath.
SUN'DIAL, *n.* an instrument which shows the hour by a shadow on a plate.
SUN'DRIED, *a.* dried in the rays of the sun.
SUN'LIGHT, *n.* the light of the sun.
SUN'RISE, *n.* morning.
SUN'SET, *n.* close of the day; evening.
SUN'SHINE, *n.* the light and heat of the sun.

Sundrian, syndrian—to SUNDER.

SUN'DER, *v.* to part; to sever; to divide.
SUN'DRY, *a.* several; more than one.
SUN'DRIES, *n.* several things.
ASUN'DER, *ad.* apart; separately.

Supan—to SUP.

SUP, *v.* to take or drink by mouthfuls.
SUP, *v.* to eat the evening meal.
SUP'PER, *n.* the evening meal.
SUP'PERLESS, *a.* without supper.

Swethel—to SWADDLE.

SWAD'DLE, *v.* to bind tight with clothes.
SWATHE, *n.* a band; a fillet.
SWAD'DLING, *ppr.* binding in tight clothes.
SWATHE, *v.* to bind; to confine.

Swegan—to SOUND or RATTLE.

SWAG'GER, *v.* to bluster; to bully.
SWAG'GERER, *n.* a turbulent fellow.

Swam—a FUNGUS or MUSHROOM.

SWAMP, *n.* spongy land; soft, wet ground.
SWAMP, *v.* to fill with water as a boat.
SWAMP'Y, *a.* low, wet and spongy.

Sweart—SWART. Swæthe—a TRACK; a PATH.

SWART, *a.* moderately black.
SWARTH'Y, *a.* dark of complexion.
SWATH, *n.* a line of grass or grain cut down by a mower.

Wæge—a Pair of Scales. Wæg—a Wave.

Sway, *v.* to wave in the hand; to govern. | Sway, *n.* power; rule.

Swerian—to Swear.

Swear, *v.* to utter an oath. | Forswear′, *v.* to swear falsely.

Swat—Sweat.

Sweat, *n.* the moisture which issues from the skin. | Sweat′y, *a.* covered with sweat.

Swapan—to Sweep.

Sweep, *v.* to brush with a broom; to carry off with a long stroke. | Sweep′ings, *n.* things swept away.
Sweep′stakes, *n.* the whole money staked. | Swab, *n.* a kind of mop.
| Swab′bing, *ppr.* cleaning with a mop.
Swoop, *v.* to fall on at once and seize.

Swet—Sweet.

Sweet, *a.* agreeable to the taste or smell; pleasing to any sense. | Sweet′ness, *n.* the quality of being sweet.
Sweet′en, *v.* to make or grow sweet. | Sweet′brier, *n.* a fragrant shrub.
Sweet′ish, *a.* somewhat sweet. | Sweet′heart, *n.* a lover or mistress.
Sweet′ly, *ad.* in a sweet manner.
Sweet′meat, *n.* fruit preserved with sugar.

Swellan—to Swell.

Swell, *v.* to grow larger. | Swell, *n.* increase; a billow.
Swell′ing, *n.* a morbid tumor.

Sweltan—to Swelt. Gothic, *swiltan*—to Die; to Perish.

Swelt, *v.* to swoon; to swelter. | Swel′ter, *v.* to sweat profusely.

Hweorfan—to Turn; to Warp.

Swerve, *v.* to turn aside; to deviate. | Swerv′ing, *n.* deviation from rule or duty.

Swift, from *swifan*—to Turn; to Whirl Round.

Swift, *n.* moving rapidly; quick. | Swiv′el, *n.* a ring which turns upon a staple.
Swift′ly, *ad.* rapidly; quickly.
Swift′ness, *n.* speed; quickness.

Swimman—to Swim.

Swim, *v.* to float; to be dizzy. | Swim′ming, *n.* act of floating.
Swim′mingly, *ad.* smoothly; with great success.

Swin—Swine.

Swine, *n.* a hog; a pig. | Swin′ish, *a.* like swine; gross; brutal.

Swelgan, swylgan—to SWALLOW; to SWILL.

SWILL, *v.* to drink grossly or greedily. | SWILL, *n.* liquid food for swine.
SWAL'LOW, *v.* to take down the throat.

NOTE.—SWALLOW, a bird, comes from the A.-S. (*swalewe.*)

Swengan—to SWING.

SWING, *v.* to move backward and forward. | SWING'ING, *a.* moving to and fro.

Aswanan—to LANGUISH; to PERISH; to SWOON.

SWOON, *v.* to faint; *n.* a fainting fit. | SWOON'ING, *n.* the act of fainting.

Swurd—SWORD.

SWORD, *n.* a warlike weapon. | SWORDS'MAN, *n.* one who fights with a sword.

To-eacan—to ADD TO.

TACK, *v.* to fasten; to join. | TACK, *v.* to change the course of a ship.

NOTE.—TACK, a small nail, comes from the Danish (*takke.*)

Tæcan—to TEACH. *Tacan*—to TAKE.

TAKE, *v.* to receive what is offered. | BETAKE', *v.* to have recourse to.
TAK'ING, *a.* pleasing; engaging. | TEACH, *v.* to impart knowledge.
TAK'INGNESS, *n.* quality of pleasing. | TEACH'ABLE, *a.* that may be taught.
TEACH'ER, *n.* one who teaches.

Tale—REPROACH; a RECKONING. *Tellan*—to TELL.

TALE, *n.* a story; a narrative; account; number reckoned. | TELL, *v.* to utter; to express in words.
TALE'BEARER, *n.* one who officiously tells tales. | TALK, *v.* to speak; to converse.
TALE'TELLER, *n.* one who tells tales. | TALK'ATIVE, *a.* given to talk.
TELL'TALE, *n.* one who officiously gives information. | TALK'ER, *n.* one who talks.
| TALK'ING, *n.* oral conversation.
| TAT'TLE, *v.* to use many words with little meaning.
TAT'TLER, *n.* an idle talker.

Tam—TAME.

TAME, *a.* not wild; subdued. | TAME'LESS, *a.* wild; untamable.
TAME'ABLE, *a.* that may be tamed. | TAME'LY, *ad.* not wildly; meanly.
TAME'NESS, *n.* the quality of being tame.

Tæppan—to BROACH, as a CASK.

TAP, *v.* to pierce a cask. | TAP'STER, *n.* one who draws liquor.
TAP'ROOT, *n.* the principal stem of a root.

NOTE.—TAP, to strike a very gentle blow, comes from the French (*taper*, to strike.)

Taper—TAPER.

TA'PER, *n.* a small wax candle. | TA'PER, *v.* to grow smaller towards the end.

Tare, tyr—TAR.

TAR, n. a thick substance obtained from pine trees by heat.

TAR'RY, a. covered with tar.
TAR'PAULIN, n. tarred canvas.

Teran—to TEAR; to REND.

TARE,* n. a weed growing among grain.
TAT'TER, n. a fluttering rag.

TAR'GET, n. (targ, a shield,) a mark set up to be shot at.
TAT'TERED, a. being in tatters.
TEAR, v. to separate by violence.

* TARE, because the weed destroys the grain.
NOTE —TARE, an allowance for weight of cask, etc., comes from the French (tare, loss, waste.)

Teart from tar—to PROVOKE.

TART, a. sour; sharp of taste.
TART, n. a kind of open pie.

TART'LY, ad. sourly; sharply.
TART'NESS, n. sourness; sharpness.

Team—a RACE; OFFSPRING.

TEAM, n. a number of things in a line.

TEAM, n. two or more horses or oxen yoked together.

Tear—TEAR.

TEAR, n. water from the eyes.

TEAR'FUL, a. full of tears.
TEAR'LESS, a. without tears.

Tæsan—to PLUCK or PULL.

TEASE, v. to comb or card, as wool or flax.

TEASE, v. to irritate with petty annoyances.

Teon, tugon—to TUG; TOW; PULL or DRAW TO.

TOUSE, v. to pull; to tear; to haul.
TOW'ZER, n. a name given to a dog.
TOW, n. the refuse of flax or hemp.
TOW, v. to draw through the water.

TOW'-LINE, n. a rope used for towing.
TUG, v. to pull with great effort.
TUG, n. a boat for drawing others.
TUG, n. a long, hard pull; a great effort.

Tyman—to BRING FORTH.

TEEM, v. to produce; to be full.
TEEM'LESS, a. unfruitful.

TEEM'FUL, a. prolific; brimful.

Thanne—THAN.

THAN, con. a particle used in comparison.
THEN, ad. at that time; afterward.

THENCE, ad. from that place; from that time.
THENCE'FORTH, ad. from that time.

Thær—THERE.

THERE, ad. in that place.
THERE-ABOUTS, ad. near that place.

THERE-AF'TER, ad. after that.
THEREFORE, ad. for that.

Thic—THICK.

THICK, *a.* dense; not thin.
THICK'EN, *v.* to make or grow thick.
THICK'ET, *n.* a close wood or copse.
THICK'NESS, *n.* the state of being thick.
THICK'LY, *ad.* densely; closely.
THICK'SET, *a.* closely planted.
THIGH, *n.* (*theoh*, thick,) the part of the limb between the knee and body.
THIGH'-BONE, *n.* (*thick-bone*,) the bone of the thigh.

Theof—THIEF.

THIEF, *n.* one who steals.
THEFT, *n.* the act of stealing.
THIEVE, *v.* to steal.
THIEV'ISH, *a.* given to stealing.

Thil—a STAKE; a PLANK.

THILL, *n.* the shafts of a wagon.
THILL'-HORSE, *n.* a shaft-horse.

Thyn—THIN.

THIN, *a.* having but little extent between two surfaces.
THIN'LY, *ad.* not thickly.
THIN'NESS, *n.* the state of being thin.
TI'NY, *a.* little; small; puny.

Thencan—to THINK; to REMEMBER; to THANK.

THANK, *v.* to express gratitude.
THANKS, *n.* expressions of gratitude.
THANK'FUL, *a.* full of gratitude.
THANK'LESS, *a.* ungrateful.
THANKS'GIVING, *n.* the act of giving thanks.
THINK, *v.* to employ the mind.
THINK'ER, *n.* one who thinks.
THINK'ING, *n.* having thought.
BETHINK', *v.* to call to mind.
THOUGHT, *n.* (*theaht*, from *thencan*,) the act of thinking; the image formed in the mind.
THOUGHT'FUL, *a.* attentive; careful.
THOUGHT'LESS, *a.* heedless; careless.

Thurst—THIRST.

THIRST, *n.* a desire to drink.
THIRST'Y, *a.* suffering for want of drink.
THIRST'INESS, *n.* the state of being thirsty.

Theah—THOUGH; YET; STILL; HOWEVER.

THOUGH, *con.* however; yet.
ALTHOUGH, *con.* notwithstanding.

Threscwald. Therscan—to BEAT; to THRESH; and wald—WOOD.

THRASH, *v.* to beat grain out of the husk.
THRASH'ER, *n.* one who thrashes.
THRESH'HOLD, *n.* the plank or step under the door.

NOTE.—This word is written *thrash* or *thresh* indifferently, *thrash* being preferred.

Thræd—THREAD.

THREAD, *n.* a small line or twist of any fibrous substance.
THREAD'EN, *a.* made of thread.
THREAD'Y, *a.* like thread.
THREAD'BARE, *a.* worn to the bare threads.

Thræl—THRALL.

THRALL, *n.* a slave; bondage.
INTHRALL', *v.* to reduce to servitude.
THRAL'DOM, *n.* slavery; bondage.

Threatian—to URGE; to REPROVE; to THREATEN.

THREAT'EN, *v.* to menace; to denounce evil.
THREAT'FUL, *a.* full of threats.
THREAT, *n.* a menace.
THREAT'ENING, *n.* foreboding evil.

Throte—THROAT.

THROAT, *n.* the fore part of the neck.
THROT'TLE, *v.* to choke; to suffocate; to strangle.
THROT'TLE, *n.* the windpipe.

Thurh—THROUGH. *Duru*—a DOOR; a GATE; a PASSAGE.

THROUGH, *prep.* from side to side, or from end to end.
THROUGH'OUT, *ad.* in every part.
THOR'OUGH, *a.* complete; perfect.
THOR'OUGHBRED, *a.* completely educated.
THOR'OUGHLY, *ad.* completely.
THOR'OUGHFARE, *n.* a passage through
DOOR, *n.* the entrance into a house.
WIN'DOW, *n.* door; an opening to let light and wind through.

Thrawan—to THROW.

THROW, *v.* to fling; to cast.
THROW, *n.* a cast.
THROW'ER, *n.* one who throws.
OVERTHROW', *v.* to turn upside down

Thuma—THUMB.

THUMB, *n.* the short, thick finger of the hand.
THUMB'ED, *pp.* handled awkwardly.

Thuner—THUNDER. *Thor*—the GOD OF THUNDER.

THUN'DER, *n.* the sound which follows a flash of lightning.
THUN'DERING, *n.* the emission of thunder.
THUN'DERBOLT, *n.* a shaft of lightning.
THUN'DERCLAP, *n.* a burst of thunder.
THUN'DERSHOWER, *n.* a shower with thunder.
THUN'DERSTRUCK, *pp.* or *a.* astonished; amazed.
THURS'DAY, (*Thors-dæg,*) *n.* the fifth day of the week.

Tinclan—to TICKLE.

TIC'KLE, *v.* to touch lightly and cause to laugh.
TICK'LISH, *a.* easily tickled; tottering; easy to be overthrown: critical.
TICK'LING, *n.* the act of one who tickles.

Tid—TIME; SEASON. *Tidan*—to HAPPEN.

TIDE, *n.* time; season; the flux and reflux of the sea.
TIDE'MILL, *n.* a mill put in motion by the tide.
TI'DY, *a.* clean and neat.
TI'DINGS, *n.* news; intelligence.
BETIDE', *v.* to happen; to befall.
TI'DILY, *ad.* neatly; readily.

Tian—to Tie. *Tied, ti'd*—Tight.

Tight, *a.* close; not loose.
Tight'en, *v.* to make tight.
Tie, *v.* to fasten with a cord or string.
Tight'ly, *ad.* closely.
Tight'ness, *n.* closeness.

Tilian—to Till.

Till, *v.* to cultivate.
Till'able, *a.* that may be cultivated.
Till'age, *n.* the act of cultivating.
Till'er, *n.* one who tills.
Tilth, *n.* culture.
Toil, *v.* (*tiolan,*) to work hard.
Toil'some, *a.* laborious.
Tool, *n.* any instrument.

Note.—Till, to the time of, comes from the A.-S. (*til,*) and Till, a money drawer, is of uncertain etymology.
Toil, a net, a snare, comes from the Latin (*tela.*)

Timber—Timber. *Timbrian*—to Build; Timber.

Tim'ber, *n.* wood fit for building. | Tim'bered, *a.* furnished with timber.

Tima—Time.

Time, *n.* the measure of duration.
Time'less, *a.* endless.
Time'ly, *a.* seasonable.
Betimes', *ad.* soon; early.

Tin—Tin.

Tin, *n.* a soft, white metal.
Tin'ner, *n.* one who works in a tin mine.
Tin'foil, *n.* (L. *folium,* a leaf,) tin reduced to a thin leaf.
Tin'man, *n.* a manufacturer of tin.

Tendan, tynan—to Kindle.

Tind, *v.* to set on fire. | Tin'der, *n.* any thing very inflammable.

Teorian, tirian—to Rub Away; to Fail; to Vex.

Tire, *n.* an iron band used to bind and protect the fellies of a wheel.
Tire'some, *a.* wearisome; tedious.
Tire, *v.* to fatigue; to weary.
Tired, *a.* fatigued; weary.

Note.—Tire, the outside band of a wheel, is so named because it is put there to protect the wheel, by receiving the wear and tear consequent to rolling on the ground.

Teotha—a Tenth.

Tithe, *n.* the tenth part.
Tithe, *v.* to take the tenth part of.
Tith'able, *a.* that may be tithed.
Tith'er, *n.* one who gathers tithes.

Toll—a Tribute.

Toll, *n.* a tax imposed for some service conferred.

Note.—Toll, to sound a bell slowly, comes from the Welsh (*tol.*)

Tunge—Tongue.

Tongue, *n.* the organ of speech and taste.
Tongue, *v.* to chide; to scold.
Tongue'less, *a.* speechless.
Tongue'tied, *a.* unable to speak freely.

Toth—Tooth.

Tooth, *n.* a bony substance growing out of the jaw.
Tooth'less, *a.* wanting teeth.
Tooth'some, *a.* pleasing to the taste.
Tooth'ache, *n.* pain in the teeth.

Top—Top.

Top, *n.* the highest part of anything.
Top'most, *a.* highest.
Top'ple, *v.* to fall forward; to tumble down.
Top'heavy, *a.* having the top too heavy.
Top'knot, *n.* a knot worn on the top of the head.
Top'sail, *n.* the highest sail.
Topsy-tur'vy, *ad.* (*tops*, or heads in the turf,) with the bottom upward.

Tealtian—to Totter; to Tilt.

Tot'ter, *v.* to shake so as to threaten a fall.
Tot'tering, *p. a.* shaking as if ready to fall.
Tilt, *v.* to incline; to raise one end.
Tilt, *v.* to raise and point, as a weapon.

Toh—Tough.

Tough, *a.* flexible without being brittle; strong.
Tough'en, *v.* to make or grow tough.
Tough'ly, *ad.* in a tough manner.
Tough'ness, *n.* the quality of being tough.

Tor—a Rock; a Peak; a Tower.

Tow'er, *n.* a lofty, narrow building. | Tow'er, *v.* to rise or fly high.

Tun—a Place Fenced Round. From *Tynan*—to Hedge In; to Inclose.

Town, *n.* a large collection of houses.
Towns'man, *n.* an inhabitant of a town.
Town'ship, *n.* the district belonging to a town.

Treppe—Trap.

Trap, *n.* an instrument for catching vermin or game; an ambush.
Trap'door, *n.* a door in a floor.
Trap'stick, *n.* a stick for playing at trap.
Entrap', *v.* to catch in a trap.

Trahtian—to Treat.

Treat, *v.* to behave to; to use.
Treat, *n.* an entertainment.
Treat'ise, *n.* a discourse.
Treat'ment, *n.* management.
Treat'y, *n.* negotiation; usage.

L. *Tres*, Three, and A.-S. *steal*, Stall, Trestle.

Tres'tle, *n.* the frame of a table; a three-legged stool.

Trifelan—to Reduce to Minute Parts.

Tri'fle, *v.* to act or talk with levity.
Tri'fler, *n.* one who trifles.
Tri'fle, *n.* any thing of very little importance.
Tri'fling, *a.* being of little value.

Tredan—to TREAD.

TREAD, *v.* to set the foot.
TREAD, *n.* a step.

TREAD′LE, *n.* the part of a machine which is moved by the foot.

Trum—FIRM; SOUND. *Trymian*—to PREPARE; to MAKE STRONG.

TRIM, *a.* of orderly form or shape; neat.
TRIM, *n.* dress; condition of a vessel.
TRIM, *v.* to set or put in order.

TRIM′LY, *ad.* neatly; nicely.
TRIM′MING, *n.* ornamental appendages.

Treowe, treowian—to TRUST; to CONFIDE IN; TRUE.

TRUE, *a.* conformable to fact.
TRUE′NESS, *n.* sincerely; reality.
TRUE′ISM, *n.* a self-evident truth.
TRU′LY, *ad.* according to truth.
TRUTH, *n.* true state of facts or things.
TRUTH′FUL, *a.* full of truth.
TRUTH′LESS, *a.* wanting truth.
TRUE′BORN, *a.* of genuine birth.
TRUE′HEARTED, *a.* honest; faithful.
TROTH, *n.* truth; belief; fidelity.
TROW, *v.* to think; to believe.
TRUCE, *n.* a temporary peace.
TRUST, *n.* confidence; reliance on another.

TRUE′PENNY, *n.* an honest fellow.
TRUST, *v.* to rely on; to commit to the care of.
TRUSTEE′, *n.* one intrusted with anything.
TRUST′LESS, *a.* not worthy of trust.
TRUST′Y, *a.* that may be trusted; honest.
TRUST′INESS, *n.* honesty.
MISTRUST′, *v.* to suspect; to doubt.
MISTRUST′, *n.* want of confidence.
MISTRUST′FUL, *a.* doubting.
MISTRUST′LESS, *a.* unsuspecting.
TRYST, *n.* an appointment to meet.

Trendel—a SPHERE; a CIRCLE; ANYTHING TURNED.

TREND, *v.* to turn; to diverge.
TREND′ING, *n.* a particular direction.
TRUN′DLE, *v.* to roll along, as a bowl or hoop.

TRUN′DLE, *n.* any round rolling thing.
TRUN′DLE-BED, *n.* a low bed that runs on wheels under a higher bed.

Tiwes-dæg, from *tig* or *tuisco*—the SAXON MARS, or GOD OF WAR, and *dæg*—a DAY.

TUES′DAY, *n.* the third day of the week.

Tumbian—to TUMBLE; to DANCE; TUMBLE.

TUM′BLE, *v.* to fall; to roll about. | TUM′BLER, *n.* a drinking glass.

NOTE.—TUMBLER, so called because originally it had a pointed base, and could not be set down with any liquor in it.

Tunne—a BUTT; a TUB; a VAT.

TUN, *n.* a large cask.
TUN′NEL, *n.* a conical vessel with a tube for conveying liquids into casks, bottles, etc.

TUN′NEL, *n.* an arched way under ground.
TON, *n.* a weight of 20 cwt.
TON′NAGE, *n.* weight; duty by the ton.

Turf—SOD.

TURF, *n.* a thin layer of soil held together by the roots of grass.

TURF, *n.* a race course.
TURF′Y, *a.* like turf.

Tyrnan, turnan—to Turn.

Turn, *v.* to move round; to revolve.
Turn′er, *n.* one who turns.
Turn′pike, *n.* a gate across a road.
Turn′stile, *n.* a turnpike in a footpath.
Overturn′, *v.* to throw down.

Tux—a Tooth.

Tusk, *n.* a long pointed tooth. | Tush, *n.* a tooth of a horse.

Twœdding—a Flattering; Twaddle.

Twad′dle, *n.* unmeaning talk; nonsense.
Twad′dle, *v.* to talk idly.

Twelf—Twelve.

Twelve, *a.* ten and two.
Twelfth′tide, *n.* twelfth day after Christmas.

Twentig, from *twend*, Two, and *tig*, Ten—Twenty.

Twen′ty, *a.* twice ten. | Twen′tieth, *a.* the ordinal of twenty.

Tweon-leoht. *Tweon*—Doubt, and *leoht*—Light; Doubtful Light.

Twi′light, *n.* the faint light before sunrise and after sunset.

Twin—Thread. *Twinan*—to Twine, from *Two*.

Twine, *v.* to twist so as to form one body out of two or more.
Entwine, *v.* to twist or wreath round.
Twin, *n.* one of two produced at a birth.

Note.—Thread or Twine has *two* or more fibers or strands twisted round each other.

Twiccian—to Twitch; to Pull; to Catch.

Twinge, *v.* to torment with sudden sharp pain.
Twitch, *v.* to pull with a sudden jerk.
Twitch, *n.* a sudden pull.

Twinclian—to Twinkle; to Glitter.

Twin′kle, *v.* to shine with a quivering light.
Twink′ling, *n.* a moment; an instant.

Getwysan—to Twist.

Twist, *v.* to unite by winding one thing round another.
Entwist′, *v.* to wreath round.

Edwitan. *Ed*—Again, and *witan*—to Blame; to Twit.

Twit, *v.* to tease by telling faults. | Twit′tingly, *ad.* so as to upbraid.

Twa, twi—Two.

Two, *a.* one and one.
Two′fold, *a.* double.
Twice, *ad.* two times.

Oga—GREAT FEAR; DREAD.

UG'LY, *a.* offensive to the sight. | UG'LINESS, *n.* total want of beauty.

Uncuth. Un—NOT, and cuth—KNOWN.

UNCOUTH', *a.* not known; awkward; clumsy. | UNCOUTH'LY, *ad.* awkwardly.

Under—UNDER.

UN'DER, *prep.* beneath; below. | UN'DERLING, *n.* an inferior agent.
UN'DERMOST, *a.* lowest in place.

Under, standan—UNDERSTAND.

UNDERSTAND', *v.* to know the meaning of. | UNDERSTAND'ING, *n.* the capacity of knowing.

Up—UP.

UP, *ad.* aloft; on high.
UP, *prep.* from a lower to a higher place.
UP'PER, *a.* higher in place.
UP'WARD, *a.* directed to a higher place.

UP'BRAID, *v.* (*gebrœdan,* to enlarge,) to charge contemptuously with something disgraceful.
UPBRAID'ING, *n.* the act of reproaching.

Wadan—to WADE.

WADE, *v.* to walk through water. | WAD'DLE, *v.* to move from side to side in walking.

Wægan—to DECEIVE; to FALSIFY; to CHEAT.

WAG, *n.* one who plays merry, frolicsome tricks. | WAG'GERY, *n.* mischievous merriment.
WAG'GISH, *a.* frolicsome.

NOTE.—WAG, to move from side to side, comes from the A.-S. (*wagian,* to move to and fro.)

Wægen—WAGON.

WAG'ON, *n.* a vehicle with four wheels. | WAG'ONER, *n.* one who drives a wagon.

Wealcan; p. weolc—to ROLL; to TUMBLE.

WALK, *v.* to move with moderate steps. | WALK'ER, *n.* one who walks.

Wann—PALE; LIVID. From Wanian—to DECREASE; to WANE.

WAN, *a.* pale; having a sickly hue.
WAN'NESS, *n.* paleness.
WANE, *v.* to decrease; to decline.
WANT'LESS, *a.* abundant; fruitful.

WANT, *v.* not to have; to lack.
WANT, *n.* need; necessity.
WANT'ING, *a.* deficient; lacking.

NOTE.—WANED, WAN'D, WANT, past participle of WANE.

Weard, weardes—TOWARDS.

WARD, *a.* suffix signifying direction to or from. | FRO'WARD, *a.* perverse; peevish.
FRO'WARDNESS, *n.* perverseness.

Weall—a SHORE; a BANK.

WALL, *n.* a work of stone or brick erected as a division or defence. | WALL'FRUIT, *n.* fruit raised against a wall.
WALL'EYED, *a.* having white eyes.

Wandrian—to WANDER.

WAN'DER, *v.* to ramble here and there. | WAN'DERER, *n.* one who wanders.
WAN'DERING, *n.* the act of roving.

Uuerre, wer—WAR.

WAR, *n.* a public contest carried on by force. | WAR'LIKE, *a.* relating to war; martial.
WAR'FARE, *n.* state of war; military service. | WAR'RIOR, *n.* a soldier.
| WAR'PROOF, *a.* able to resist a warlike attack.
WAR'WORN, *a.* worn with war.

Weard—a GUARD; WATCH; VIGILANCE.

WARD, *v.* to guard; to watch; to defend. | WAR'DEN, *n.* a keeper.
| WARD'ER, *n.* a keeper; a guard.
WARD, *n.* a division of a town; one under a guardian. | WARD'ROBE, *n.* a place where clothes are kept.
WARD'SHIP, *n.* guardianship.

Ware, from *waru*—MERCHANDISE.

WARE, *pl.* WARES, *n.* goods; merchandise. | WARE'HOUSE, *n.* a store-house for merchandise.
WARE'HOUSING, *n.* the act of depositing goods in a warehouse.

War, from *wær*—WARY; CAUTIOUS; PROVIDENT. *Warian*—to BEWARE; to GUARD. *Warnian*—to DEFEND.

WARE, *a.* cautious; *v.* to take heed. | WARN, *v.* to inform previously.
WARE'LESS, *a.* incautious. | WARN'ING, *n.* previous notice.
WARE'LY, *ad.* cautiously. | WAR'RANT, *v.* to authorize; to justify.
WA'RY, *a.* cautious; prudent. | WAR'RANT, *n.* authority; commission.
WAR'ILY, *ad.* cautiously; prudently. | WAR'RANTABLE, *a.* justifiable.
WAR'INESS, *n.* caution; prudence. | WAR'RANTY, *n.* promise; security.
BEWARE', *v.* to regard with caution. | WAR'REN, *n.* (*warian,*) a park, or inclosure for rabbits.
AWARE', *a.* apprised; conscious.
WAR'RENER, *n.* the keeper of a warren.

NOTE.—At present WARE is used only in composition.

Wearm—WARM.

WARM, *a.* heated in a moderate degree. | WARM'LY, *ad.* with moderate heat.
WARMTH, *n.* moderate or gentle heat. | WARM'NESS, *n.* moderate heat.

Waescan, wacsan—to WASH.

WASH, *v.* to cleanse with water. | WASH'ER, one who washes.
SWASH, *n.* impulse of water flowing with violence.

Weorpan, wurpan—to THROW; to CAST; to WARP.

WARP, v. to turn or twist out of shape.
WARP, n. the threads which are extended lengthwise in anything woven.

WARP, v. to move a vessel by means of a rope made fast to some fixed object.
WARP'ING, n. the act of turning aside.

Wæsp, wesp—a WASP.

WASP, n. a stinging insect.
WASP'ISH, a. peevish; petulant; having a slender shape.

WASP'ISHLY, ad. peevishly; snappishly.

Westan—to WASTE; to LAY WASTE; to RAVAGE.

WASTE, n. to diminish; to squander.
WASTE'FUL, a. destructive; prodigal.

WASTE'FULLY, ad. in a lavish manner.
WASTE'THRIFT, n. a spendthrift.

Wacian—to WAKE; to AROUSE.

WAKE, v. to rouse from sleep.
WAKE'FUL, a. not sleeping; watchful.
WAK'EN, v. to rouse from sleep.
WAK'ING, ppr. being awake; rousing from sleep.
AWAKE, v. to rouse from sleep.
AWAKE, a. not sleeping.
WATCH, v. to be awake; to keep guard.

WATCH'ER, n. one who watches.
WATCH'FUL, a. vigilant; attentive.
WATCH'ING, ppr. carefully observing.
WATCH'HOUSE, n. a house where a guard is placed.
WATCH'MAN, n. a man who keeps watch.
WATCH'WORD, n. the word given to sentinels to know their friends.

Wæter—WATER. Wæt, hwet—WET.

WA'TER, n. a well known fluid.
WA'TERING, ppr. supplying with water.
WA'TERISH, a. resembling water; moist.
WA'TERY, a. like water.

WET, a. containing water; moist.
WET'NESS, n. the state of being wet.
WHET, v. to stimulate; to incite; to excite.
WHET,* v. to rub for the purpose of sharpening.

WHET'STONE, n. a stone for sharpening.

* WHET, because while rubbing the stone is kept wet.

Wæg—a WAVE. Wagian—to WAG; to MOVE TO AND FRO.

WAVE, n. a moving swell of water.
WAVE, v. to undulate; to brandish; to put off.
WAVE'LESS, a. without waves; smooth.
WA'VER, v. to fluctuate.
WA'VING, ppr. moving to and fro.
WA'VY, a. rising in waves.
WAY, n. a road; a passage.

WAFT, v. to convey through the water or air.
WAY'LESS, a. having no road.
WAY'FARER, n. a traveler.
WAY'LAY, v. to beset by ambush.
WAY'WARD, a. liking his own way.
WAY'WARDNESS, n. perverseness.
WAG, v. to move from side to side.

WAG'GLE, v. to move from side to side.

Wodnesdæg. Wodnes, of Woden—the GOD OF WAR, and dæg—DAY.

WEDNES'DAY, n. the fourth day of the week.

Wac—INFIRM; WEAK.

WEAK, *a.* feeble; not strong; infirm.
WEAK'EN, *v.* to make weak.
WEAK'SIDE, *n.* a foible; a failing.
WEAK'LY, *ad.* feebly; faintly.
WEAK'NESS, *n.* want of strength.

Weax, from *wac*—PLIABLE.

WAX, *n.* (*weax,*) a tenacious substance formed by bees.
WAX'EN, *a.* made of wax.
WAX'Y, *a.* resembling wax.
WAX'WORK, *n.* a figure made of wax.
WAX, *v.* (*weaxan,*) to grow; to increase.

NOTE.—WAX, to grow, to increase, comes from the A.-S. (*weax,* the substance of which honeycomb is formed.) Bees are constantly adding to their store of honeycomb, thereby causing it to grow, to increase.

Werian—to WEAR. From *wer*—a GUARD; a PROTECTION.

WEAR, *v.* to waste by use or time; to carry on the body.
WEAR'ING, *ppr.* bearing on the person.
WEAR'ER, *n.* one who wears.
WEAR, *n.* (*wær,*) an enclosure; a fish pond; a dam to raise water.

Werig—FATIGUED; DEPRESSED.   *Werian*—to WEARY; to TEASE; to HARASS.

WEA'RY, *a.* tired; fatigued.
WEA'RIED, *p. a.* tired; fatigued.
WEA'RISOME, *a.* causing weariness; tedious.
WEA'RINESS, *n.* state of being weary.
WEA'RISOMENESS, *n.* tediousness.
WOR'RY, *v.* to tease; to trouble.
WOR'RY, *n.* trouble; perplexity.

Wefan—to WEAVE.   *Wacb*—WEB.

WEAVE, *v.* to unite threads so as to form cloth.
WEAV'ER, *n.* one who weaves.
WEB, *n.* any thing woven.
WEBBED, *a.* joined by a membrane.
WEB'FOOT, *a.* having the toes connected by a membrane.
WOOF, *n.* the threads which cross the warp.
WEFT, *n.* the threads which cross the warp.
WARP, *n.* (*wearp,*) the threads which are extended lengthwise in a loom.

Weddian—to COVENANT; to PROMISE; to PLEDGE.

WED, *v.* to marry; to unite.
WED'DED, *a.* closely attached.
WED'DING, *n.* marriage; nuptials.
WED'LOCK, *n.* marriage; matrimony.

Weod—WEED.

WEED, *n.* any useless or troublesome plant.
WEED'ER, *n.* one who weeds.
WEED'LESS, *a.* free from weeds.
WEED'Y, *a.* abounding with weeds.

NOTE.—WEEDS, a widow's mourning dress, comes from the A.-S. (*wæd,* a garment, clothing.)

Weoc—WEEK.

WEEK, *n.* the space of seven days.
WEEK'DAY, *n.* any day except the Sabbath.
WEEK'LY, *a.* done once a week.

Wenan—to Think, Suppose or Hope; to Ween.

Ween, v. to think; to imagine; to fancy.
Overween', v. to think too highly.
Overween'ing, ppr. a. arrogant; conceited.
Overween'ingly, ad. with arrogance.

Wepan—to Cry Out; to Weep.

Weep, v. to shed or drop tears.
Weep'er, n. one who weeps.
Weep'ingly, ad. in tears.

Wegan—to Bear; to Carry; to Weigh. *Weg*—a Balance.

Weigh, v. to examine by the balance.
Weigh'er, n. one who weighs.
Weight, n. (*wiht,*) quantity ascertained by the balance.
Weight'less, a. having no weight; light.
Weight'y, a. heavy; important.
Weight'ily, ad. heavily; with force.
Weight'iness, n. heaviness.

Wel—Well.

Well, a. being in health.
Well, ad. not ill; properly.
Well'-being, n. happiness.
Well'bred, a. elegant in manners; polite.
Weal, n. (*wela,*) happiness; prosperity.
Wealth, n. (*welig,*) riches; opulence.
Wealth'ily, ad. richly.
Welcome, n. (*wilcuma,* a good comer,) kind reception.

Note.—Well, a deep, narrow pit dug for the purpose of obtaining water, comes from the A.-S. (*wyl,* a spring; from *weallan,* to boil up.)

Wæltan—to Roll; Welt.

Welt, n. the edge of a garment turned over and sewed together.
Welt, v. to sew on a border.
Wel'ter, v. to roll or wallow in some foul matter.
Wel'tering, ppr. rolling; wallowing.

Wend—a Turn; a Change. *Wendæn*—to Go; to Come.

Wend, v. to go; to pass; to move.
Went, pret. of go; did go.

Note.—It will be observed that Went, now used as the preterit of the verb Go, has nothing at all to do with the verb Go, but belongs to the verb Wend.

West—West.

West, n. the region where the sun sets.
West'erly, a. towards the west.
West'ern, a. being in the west.
West'ward, ad. towards the west.

Hwæl—Whale.

Whale, n. a large animal.
Whale'bone, n. an elastic substance from the upper jaw of the whale.

Ahwylfan—to Overwhelm.

Whelm, v. to cover completely.
Overwhelm, v. to crush underneath

Hwær—Where.

Where, *ad.* at what place.
Where'abouts, *ad.* near what or which place.
Whereas', *ad.* when on the contrary.
Where'fore, *ad.* for which reason.

Wæflan—to Babble; to Whiffle.

Whif'fle, *v.* to turn or change with every wind.
Whiff, *n.* a slight blast; a puff.
Whif'fle-tree, *n.* a short bar to which the traces of a horse are fastened.

Note.—Whiffle-tree, sometimes, but erroneously, written Whipple-tree, gets its name from its constant change of position caused by the onward motion of the horse. See Whip.

Hwil—While.

While, *n.* space of time.
While, *v.* to draw out; to spend, as time.
While, *ad.* during the time that.

Wanian—to Deplore; Lament; Bewail.

Whine, *v.* to lament with a plaintive noise.
Whine, *n.* a drawling cry.
Whin'ing, *n.* complaining in drawling, plaintive tones.

Hweopan—to Whip.

Whip, *v.* to strike with a lash.
Whip'ping, *n.* correction with a lash.
Whip'hand, *n.* advantage over.
Whip'stock, *n.* the handle of a whip.

Hwyrfan—to Whirl; to Turn.

Whirl, *v.* to turn round rapidly.
Whirl'igig, *n.* a toy which turns round.
Whirl'pool, *n.* water moving circularly.
Whirl'wind, *n.* a revolving column of air.

Hwisprian—to Whisper.

Whis'per, *v.* to speak with the breath not made vocal.
Whis'perer, *n.* one who whispers.

Hwistlan—to Whistle.

Whis'tle, *v.* to form a kind of musical sound by the breath.
Whis'tler, *n.* one who whistles.

Wiht—a Creature; a Thing; Whit.

Whit, *n.* a point; a tittle; a very small part.
Wight, *n.* a being; a person.

Hwit—White.   *Hwitel*—to Make White.

White, *a.* having the color of snow.
Whit'en, *v.* to make or become white.
White'ness, *n.* the state of being white.
Whit'ish, *a.* somewhat white.
Whit'tle, *n.* (*hwitel,* to make white,) a knife; a white cloak.
Whit'tle, *v.* to cut with a knife.

Note.—To *whittle sticks,* to cut off the bark with a knife, to make them white.

Hwa—Who.

Who, *pro.* relating to persons.
Whoev'er, *pro.* any person whatever.

Whom, *pro.* the objective case of who.

Wicca—an Enchanter; Wicked.

Wick'ed, *a.* morally bad; vicious.
Wick'edly, *ad.* viciously.

Wick'edness, *n.* vice; sin; guilt.

Note.—Wiccian, to bewitch, is adopted by Tooke, who remarks that "all atrocious crimes were attributed by our ancestors to enchantment, sorcery, and *witchcraft*."

Wid—Wide.

Wide, *a.* extended far each way.
Wide'ly, *ad.* with great extent; far.
Width, *n.* extent from side to side.

Wid'en, *v.* to make or grow wide.
Wide'ness, *n.* breadth.

Wealdan—to Govern; Wield.

Wield, *v.* to use with full command or power.

Wield'y, *a.* manageable.

Wif—Wife.

Wife, *n.* a woman who is united to a man in marriage.
Wife'ly, *a.* becoming a wife.

Wife'hood, *n.* the state of a wife.
Wife'less, *a.* without a wife.

Wild—Wild.

Wild, *a.* not tame; desert; disorderly.
Wild'ly, *ad.* in a wild manner.
Bewil'der, *v.* to perplex; to confound.

Wild'ness, *n.* state of being wild.
Wil'der, *v.* to lose the way; to puzzle.
Wil'derness, *n.* an uncultivated tract.

Willa—Will.

Will, *n.* the power of mind by which we choose to do or forbear.
Will, *v.* to determine.
Will'ful, *a.* stubborn; perverse.

Will'fully, *ad.* stubbornly.
Will'ing, *a.* desirous; ready.
Will'ingly, *ad.* with free will.
Will'ingness, *n.* ready compliance.

Winnan—to Struggle; to Win.

Win, *v.* to gain in a contest.

Win'ning, *p. a.* attractive; charming.

Windan—to Wind.

Wind, *v.* to turn round; to twist; to blow.
Wind'ing, *n.* a turning.

Wind'lass, *n.* (*lace*, a cord,) a machine for raising weights.

Wincian—to Bend One's Self; to Nod; to Wink.

Wink, *v.* to close and open the eyelids.

Wink'ing, *n.* a rapid and repeated movement of the eyelids.

Note.—It is probable that Wing and Wink may be the same word differently applied—as *wings* and *eyelids* have somewhat similar motions.

Wind—WIND.

WIND, n. air in motion.
WIND'Y, a. consisting of wind.
WIND'INESS, n. state of being windy.
WIND'FALL, n. fruit blown from a tree; an unexpected benefit.
WIND'MILL, n. a mill turned by the wind.
WIN'NOW, v. (*windwian,* to wind,) to separate grain from chaff by the wind.
WIND'PIPE, n. the passage for the breath.
WIND'WARD, n. the point from which the wind blows.
WIN'DOW, n. (*door,*) an aperture for the admission of light and wind.
WIN'TER, n. the cold season of the year.*
WIND'ROW, n. grass laid in rows for drying.

NOTE.—From German *wehen,* to blow; *part. wehend,* blowing, contracted WIND The primary sense is, to move, flow, rush or drive along.
* SKINNER and others think it is so called because it is the *windy* season of the year.

Gehwing—a SIDE; a CORNER.

WING, n. the limb of a bird by which it flies.
WING'LESS, a. not having wings.

Witan—to WIST; to KNOW.

WIT, v. to know, or to be known; TO-WIT, ad. namely.
WIT'TINGLY, ad. knowingly; by design.
WIS, v. to think; to know; to wit.
WIST, *pret. of wis,* thought; knew.
WIST'FUL, a. full of thought; desirous; wishful.
WISE, a. (*wis,*) having knowledge; making a right use of knowledge.
WIST'FULLY, ad. attentively.
WIS'DOM, n. (*wis,* wise, and *dom,* judgment,) knowledge rightly used.
WISE'LY, ad. judiciously.
WISE'ACRE, n. (Ger. *sagen,* to say,) a simpleton; a dunce.
WIT'NESS, n. one who sees or knows personally.
WIZ'ARD, n. a conjurer; a sorcerer.
WOT, v. to know.

Wit, or ge-wit—WIT.

WIT, n. intellect; the power of associating ideas in new and unexpected relations.
WIT'LESS, n. wanting understanding.
WIT'LESSLY, ad. without judgment.
WIT'LING, n. pretender to wit.
WIT'TICISM, n. an attempt at wit.
WIT'TY, a. full of wit; ingenious.
WIT'TILY, ad. with wit; ingeniously.
WIT'TINESS, n. the quality of being witty.

Withan—to JOIN. Wyrthan—to BE.

WITH, *prep.* by; noting cause or means.
WITHAL', ad. along with the rest; likewise.
WITHIN', *prep.* in the inner part.
WITHOUT', *prep.* not with or by.
WITHDRAW', v. (*dragan,*) to take back or away.
WITHHOLD', v. (*healdan,*) to hold back.
WITHSTAND', v. (*standan,*) to oppose; to resist.

WITHE, n. (*withig,*) a twig used for a band, or to tie with.

NOTE.—WITH has descended to us from two different A.-S. verbs, viz.: (*withan,* to join, and *weorthan, wyrthan,* to be.) From the latter we have the compounds *within* and *without;* i. e., be in, be out.

Wa—Woe.

Woe, n. grief; sorrow; misery.
Wo'ful, a. sorrowful; wretched.
Wo'fully, ad. sorrowfully.
Wo'fulness, n. misery; calamity.
Woe'begone, a. far gone in woe.

Wulf—Wolf.

Wolf, n. a beast of prey. | Wolf'ish, a. like a wolf; savage.

Wifman—Woman.

Wom'an, n. the female of the human race.
Wom'anish, a. suitable to a woman.
Wom'anly, a. becoming a woman.
Wom'ankind, n. the female sex.

Note.—Man is a general term to include both sexes, and the specific name Wifman is given to the female, from her employment at the woof.

Wunian—Won.

Won, v. to dwell; to have abode. | Wont, n. custom; habit; practice.
Wont'ed, a. accustomed; usual.

Wunder—Wonder.

Won'der, n. the emotion excited by anything strange and inexplicable.
Won'derful, a. astonishing.
Won'derfully, ad. in a wonderful manner.
Won'drous, a. marvellous.

Wogan—to Woo.

Woo, v. to solicit in love; to court. | Woo'er, n. one who courts a woman.

Wudu—a Wood.

Wood, n. a large collection of trees; the substance of trees.
Wood'ed, a. covered with wood.
Wood'en, a. made of wood.
Wood'y, a. abounding with wood.
Wood'land, n. ground covered with woods.
Wood'man, n. one who cuts down timber.

Wull—Wool.

Wool, n. the soft hair which grows on sheep.
Wool'len, a. made of wool.
Wool'ly, a. consisting of wool.

Word—Word.

Word, n. an articulate sound which conveys an idea.
Word'less, a. without words; silent.
Word'y, a. full of words.
Word'ily, ad. with many words.

Woruld—World.

World, n. the whole system of created things.
World'ling, n. one devoted to this world.
World'ly, a. relating to this world.

Weorcan—to Work; to Labor.

Work, *v.* to labor; to act.
Work, *n.* labor; employment.
Work'er, *n.* one who works.
Work'man, *n.* a laborer.
Work'manlike, *a.* well performed.
Work'manly, *a.* skillful.
Work'manship, *n.* manufacture.
Work'shop, *n.* the place where work is done.
Wright, *n.* (*wyrhta,*) an artificer.
Wrought, *pp.* performed by work.

Wyrm—Worm.

Worm, *n.* a reptile; anything spiral.
Worm, *v.* to worm slowly and secretly.
Worm'y, *a.* full of worms.
Worm'eaten, *a.* gnawed by worms.
Worm'wood, *n.* a plant.

Wyrse—Worse.

Worse, *a.* more evil; more hurtful.
Worst, *a.* bad in the highest degree.

Weorth—Worth.

Worth, *n.* value; price.
Worth'less, *a.* having no worth or value.
Wor'thy, *a.* deserving; valuable.
Wor'thiness, *n.* merit; excellence.
Wor'ship, *v.* to adore; to honor.
Wor'shiper, *n.* one who worships.
Wor'ship, *n.* (*worth* and *ship,*) dignity; honor.

Wund—Wound.

Wound, *n.* a hurt given by violence.
Wound'less, *a.* free from hurt or injury.

Hweorfan—to Turn.

Wrap, *v.* to roll together; to inclose.
Wrap'per, *n.* that in which a thing is wrapped.

Wrath—Wrath.

Wrath, *n.* violent anger; rage.
Wrath'ful, *a.* very angry; furious.
Wroth, *a.* very angry.
Wrath'less, *a.* free from anger.
Wrath'y, *a.* extremely angry.

Wrecan—to Wreak.

Wreak, *v.* to do for a purpose of vengeance.
Wreak'ful, *a.* revengeful; angry.

Wræc—an Exile; a Wretch; Wreck.

Wreck, *n.* destruction by sea.
Wreck, *v.* to drive against the shore and destroy.
Wretch, *n.* a worthless creature.
Wretch'ed, *a.* miserable; worthless.
Wretch'edly, *ad.* miserably.
Wretch'edness, *n.* misery; meanness.

Writan—to Write. Gothic, *writs*, a letter.

Write, *v.* to express by letters.
Writ, *n.* a judicial writing.
Writ'er, *n.* one who writes.
Writ'ing, *n.* any thing written.

ANGLO-SAXON ROOTS AND DERIVATIVES.

Wringan—to WRING; to TWIST. *Wræstan*—to WRITHE; to TWIST.

WRING, *v.* to twist or turn around with violence.
WRING'ER, *n.* one who wrings.
WRAN'GLE, *v.* to dispute peevishly.
WRAN'GLE, *n.* a peevish dispute.
WRONG, *n.* a violation of right.
WRONG'FUL, *a.* injurious; unjust.
WRONG'LY, *ad.* unjustly; amiss.
WRENCH, *v.* to pull with a twist.
WRUNG, *ppr.* twisted.
WRIN'KLE, *n.* (*wrincle*,) a small ridge or furrow on any smooth surface.
WREATH, *n.* anything twisted; a garland.

WREATHE, *v.* to interweave; to twist.
WREATH'Y, *a.* twisted; curled.
WRITHE, *v.* to twist; to twist with agony.
WRY, *a.* twisted; crooked.
WRY'NESS, *n.* the state of being wry.
WREST, *v.* to twist by violence.
WRES'TLE, *v.* to strive who shall throw the other down.
WRES'TLER, *n.* one who wrestles.
WRES'TLING, *n.* contention.
WRIST, *n.* (from *wræstan*,) the joint which unites the hand to the arm.
WRIST'BAND, *n.* the band that passes round the wrist.

Gyard—a STAFF; a ROD; YARD.
YARD, *n.* a measure of three feet.

Geard, (from *gyrdan,* to GIRD)—YARD.
YARD, *n.* a small piece of enclosed ground.

Gear—YEAR.

YEAR, *n.* the time in which the earth moves round the sun.
YEAR'LING, *n.* an animal a year old.
YEAR'LY, *a.* happening every year.
YORE, *ad.* in time past; long ago.

Gearn—DESIROUS; EAGER.

YEARN, *v.* to feel a strong desire.
YEARN'ING, *n.* emotion of tenderness or pity.

Gelew—YELLOW.

YEL'LOW, *a.* being of the color of gold.
YEL'LOWISH, *a.* somewhat yellow.
YELK, YOLK, } *n.* the yellow part of an egg.

Gemæne—COMMON.

YEO'MAN, *n.* a man of small estate in land.
YEO'MANRY, *n.* the collective body of yeoman.

Gyrstan—YESTER.

YES'TER, *a.* last; last past.
YES'TERDAY, *n.* (*dæg,*) the day last past.

Gyldan—to PAY; to RESTORE; to RENDER.

YIELD, *v.* to produce; to afford; to give up.
YIELD'ANCE, *n.* concession.
YIELD'ING, *n.* the act of giving up.
YIELD'INGLY, *ad.* with compliance.

Eow, iu, inch—You.

You, *pro.* the nominative and objective plural of thou. | Your, *pro.* belonging to you.

Geong—Young.

Young, *a.* being in the first part of life. | Young'ish, *a.* somewhat young.

Geoguth—Youth.

Youth, *n.* the part of life which succeeds childhood.
Youth'ful, *a.* pertaining to early life.

Youth'fulness, *n.* state of being youthful.
Youth'ly, *a.* young; early in life.
Yule, *n.* (*geol*) Christmas.

FRENCH ROOTS AND DERIVATIVES.

Aboutir. *À*—To, and *bout*—End.

Abut', *v.* to end at.
Butt, *n.* the larger and blunt end of a thing; one who is the object of jests.

Abut'ment, *n.* that which receives the end of a thing.
Butt, *v.* to strike with the head or horns.

Butte, *n.* an abrupt hill.

Note.—Butt, a large vessel or cask, comes from the A.-S. (*butte.*)

Accoutrer—to Dress. From *coudre*—to Sew.

Accou'tre, *v.* to dress; to equip.
Accou'trement, *n.* military dress and arms.

Ajourner. *À*—To, and *jour*—Day.

Adjourn', *v.* to put off to another day.
Adjourn'ment, *n.* a putting off till another day.

Avant—Before.

Advance', *v.* to bring or put forward.
Advance'ment, *n.* progress.
Advan'tage, *n.* benefit; gain.
Advanta'geous, *a.* profitable.

Avaunt', *intj.* hence; begone.
Vant'age, *n.* gain; profit.
Van, *n.* the front of an army.
Van'guard, *n.* the first line of an army.

Aviser—to Advise; to Perceive; to See.

Advise', *v.* to counsel; to consult.
Advice', *n.* counsel; instruction.

Advis'able, *a.* prudent; expedient.
Advis'er, *n.* one who advises.

Agreer—to Concur. From *a gre*—at Will; at Concord.

Agree', *v.* to think or act in unison.
Agree'able, *a.* suitable to; pleasing.

Agreed', *p. a.* settled by consent.
Disagree', *v.* to differ; to vary.

Alarme, (Ital. *all'armi,*)—to Arms.

Alarm', *n.* a cry or notice of danger.
Alarm', *v.* to call to arms; to excite fear in.

Alarm'ing, *p. a.* terrifying; giving alarm.
Alarum, *n.* same as alarm.

Alerte—Alert.

Alert', *a.* being on the lookout; nimble.
Alert'ness, *n.* sprightliness.

Embuche. From *en*—In, and *bois*—a Wood, or Bushes.

Am'bush, *n.* the place or act of lying in wait.
Ambuscade', *n.* a station in which men lie to surprise others.

Piece—PIECE.

PIECE, n. a part; a fragment.
PIECE, v. to mend; to patch.
PIECE'MEAL, ad. in or by pieces.
APIECE, ad. to the part or share of each.

Apprendre—to LEARN.

APPRISE', v. to inform; to give notice.
APPREHEND', v. to lay hold on.
APPREHEN'SION, n. seizure; intellect; fear.
APPREHEN'SIVE, a. quick to understand; fearful.

Attacher—to ATTACH.

ATTACH', v. to fasten; to tie; to join. | ATTACH'MENT, n. fondness; love.

Beffler—to BEFOOL; to MOCK.

BAF'FLE, v. to elude by deceit or artifice.
BAF'FLER, n. one who baffles.

Bailler—to DELIVER; to GIVE.

BAIL, v. to release on security given for appearance in court.
BAIL, n. the sum given for security.
BAIL, v. (baille, a tub or bucket,) to free from water.
BAIL, n. the handle of a pail, bucket, etc.
BAIL'ABLE, a. that may be bailed.
BAIL'IFF, n. a law officer.

Balle—BALE.

BALE, n. a bundle, as of goods. | BALE, v. to make up in a bale or bundle.

Balustre—BALUSTER.

BAL'USTER, n. one of the supporters of a rail to a flight of stairs.
BAL'USTRADE, n. a row of balusters.
BAL'USTERED, p. a. having balusters.

Badiner—to TRIFLE; to JOKE.

BAN'TER, v. to ridicule pleasantly. | BAN'TERING, n. raillery; jesting.

Barre—BAR.

BAR, n. an obstruction to hinder entrance; the tribunal of justice.
BAR'RIER, n. an obstruction.
BARRICADE', n. an obstruction made in haste.
BAR'RISTER, n. a counsellor at law.

Baron—BARON.

BAR'ON, n. a rank of nobility.
BAR'ONESS, n. the wife of a baron.
BAR'ONY, n. the lands of a baron.
BAR'ONET, n. the title next below a baron.

Battre—BATTER.

BAT'TER, v. to beat with repeated blows.
BAT'TER, n. a mixture beaten together.
BAT'TERY, n. act of battering; a place for cannon.

FRENCH ROOTS AND DERIVATIVES.

Barguigner—to Higgle.

Bar'gain, *n.* a contract or agreement.
Bar'gaining, *n.* the act of making bargains.

Bataille—Battle.

Bat'tle, *n.* a fight; a contest.
Battal'ion, *n.* a division of the army.

Beau—Fair; Beautiful.

Beau, *n.* a man of dress; a fop.
Beau'teous, *a.* fair; elegant.
Beau'ty, *n.* that assemblage of graces which pleases the senses.
Beau'tify, *v.* to make beautiful.

Bœuf—a Bull; an Ox, or a Cow.

Beef, *n.* the flesh of bulls, oxen, or cows.
Beeves, *n.* oxen, etc., as fit for food.

Biais—Across; Athwart.

Bi'as, *n.* inclination; partiality.
Bi'as, *v.* to cause to incline to one side.

Billet—a Bill; a Handbill.

Bil'let, *n.* an account of money due; a proposed law.
Bil'let, *n.* a short letter.
Billet-doux, *n.* a love letter.
Bil'let, *v.* to quarter soldiers by ticket.

Blaspheme—Blame.

Blame, *v.* to charge with a fault.
Blam'able, *a.* faulty; culpable.
Blame'ful, *a.* deserving blame.
Blame'less, *a.* without blame.

Blanchir—to Make White; to Grow White.

Blanch, *v.* to whiten.
Blank, *a.* white; without writing.
Blench, *v.* to shrink; to start back.
Unblench'ed, *a.* not disgraced.

Botte—Boot.

Boot, *n.* a covering for the foot and leg.
Note.—Boot, profit, advantage, comes from A.-S. (*bot*, compensation.)

Bosse—a Hump or Knob.

Boss, *n.* a stud; a knob.
Emboss'ment, *n.* raised work.
Emboss', *v.* to form with protuberances.
Note.—Boss, a superintendent, comes from the Dutch (*baas*, a master.)

Branche—Branch; Bough.

Branch, *n.* the shoot or bough of a tree.
Branch'less, *a.* without branches or boughs.

Brigade—Brigade.

Brigade', *n.* a division of troops.
Brigadier', *n.* an army officer.

Bribe—a PIECE OF BREAD GIVEN TO A BEGGAR.

BRIBE, *n.* a reward given to corrupt the conduct. | BRI'BERY, *n.* the crime of giving or taking bribes.

Brigue—a LITTLE LOAF.

BRICK, *n.* a squared mass of clay burnt. | BRICK'KILN, *n.* a furnace for burning bricks.
BRICK'BAT, *n.* a piece of brick.

Brillant—SPARKLING. From *Briller*—to SHINE or SPARKLE.

BRILL'IANT, *a.* shining; sparkling. | BRILL'IANT, *n.* a diamond of the finest cut.
BRILL'IANCY, *n.* lustre; splendor.
BRILL'IANTLY, *ad.* splendidly.

Brouille—a BROIL. *Brouiller*—to EMBROIL.

BROIL, *n.* a noisy contention; a brawl. | EMBROIL', *v.* to disturb; to confuse.

Bruler—to BURN.

BROIL, *v.* to cook by laying on the coals. | BROILED, *p. a.* cooked over the coals.

Brunette, brun—BROWN.

BRUNETTE', *n.* a woman with a dark complexion.

Brosse—BRUSH.

BRUSH, *n.* an instrument for cleaning and sweeping. | BRUSH, *v.* to clean with a brush.

Boucher—BUTCHER.

BUTCH'ER, *n.* one who kills animals to sell their flesh. | BUTCH'ER, *n.* one who delights in slaughter.

Bouteillier—a BUTLER. From *Bouteille*—a BOTTLE.

BUT'LER, *n.* a servant who has charge of liquors.

Cabane—a CABIN; a COTTAGE.

CAB'IN, *n.* a small house or hut. | CAB'INET, *n.* a closet; a small room.
CAB'IN, *n.* an apartment in a ship. | CAB'INET, *n.* the ministers of state.

Caisse—a BOX or CHEST.

CASE, *n.* a covering; a sheath. | CAS'KET, *n.* a small elegant box for jewels, etc.
CASE'HARDEN, *v.* to harden on the outside. | CASQUE, *n.* a helmet; a case for the head.
CASE'KNIFE, *n.* a large table knife.
CASK, *n.* a close vessel for containing liquors. | CASH, *n.* money at command.
| CASHIER', *n.* one who has charge of money.

NOTE.—CASHIER, to dismiss from a post or office with reproach, comes from the Italian (*cassare*, to annul, to break.)

FRENCH ROOTS AND DERIVATIVES.   195

Cajoler—CAJOLE.

CAJOLE', *v.* to delude by flattery. | CAJOL'ERY, *n.* flattery; deceit.

Chauffer—to WARM.

CHAFE, *v.* to warm by rubbing; to make angry; to wear by rubbing. | CHAF'ING-DISH, *n.* a portable warming utensil.
CHAF'ING, *ppr.* heating or wearing by friction.

Charger—to LOAD; to BURDEN.

CHARGE, *v.* to intrust; to impute as debt; to accuse. | CHARGE'ABLE, *a.* imputable; expensive.
CHARGE, *n.* care; accusation; expense. | CHARGE'LESS, *a.* free from charge.
CAR'GO, *n.* the lading of a ship. | CHARG'ER, *n.* a large dish; a war-horse.

Chasser—to HUNT; to CHASE WILD ANIMALS.

CHASE, *n.* hunting; pursuit; the thing hunted. | CHASE, *v.* to pursue; to drive.

NOTE.—CHASE, to emboss, as metals, comes from the French (*chasse*, a frame.)

Échec—a CHECK.   *Echiquier*—a CHESS-BOARD.

CHECK, *n.* an order for money; cloth woven into squares of different colors. | CHECK, *v.* to stop; to restrain; to curb.
 | CHECK'ER, *v.* to form into squares of different colors.

Chere—ENTERTAINMENT.

CHEER, *v.* to encourage; to comfort. | CHEER'LESS, *a.* gloomy.
CHEER, *n.* a shout of applause; entertainment. | CHEER'ILY, *ad.* cheerfully.
CHEER'FUL, *a.* lively; gay. | CHEER'FULLY, *ad.* in a cheerful manner; willingly.
CHEER'FULNESS, *n.* gayety; alacrity.

Chef—the HEAD, *i. e.*, the TOP or HIGHEST POINT.

CHIEF, *n.* a commander; a leader. | ACHIEVE'MENT, *n.* a performance.
CHIEF, *a.* principal; most important. | KER'CHIEF, *n.* the head dress of a woman.
CHIEF'LY, *ad.* principally. |
CHIEF'TAIN, *n.* a leader of a clan. | MIS'CHIEF, *n.* (Saxon *mis*,) harm; hurt; injury.
ACHIEVE', *v.* to perform; to finish. |
MIS'CHIEVOUS, *a.* hurtful; wicked.

Chevalier—a KNIGHT.   *Cheval*—a HORSE.

CHEVALIER', *n.* a gallant horseman. | CHIV'ALRY, *n.* a military dignity; knighthood.
CHIV'ALROUS, *a.* gallant; warlike. |

Cotte—COAT.

COAT, *n.* an outside garment worn by men. | COAT, *v.* to cover the outside.

Combattre—to Fight Against.

Com'bat, *v.* to fight; to oppose. | Com'batant, *n.* one who combats.

Controle. Contre—Against. Role—a Roll, or Register.

Control', *n.* a register kept to verify another account.
Control', *n.* restraint; check.
Control', *v.* to have power over.
| Control'ler, *n.* one who controls.
Comptrol'ler, *n.* an officer who examines the accounts of collectors of public money.

Coquet—a Beau; a General Lover.

Coquet', *v.* to practise deceit in love.
Coquette', *n.* a vain female.
| Coquet'ry, *n.* trifling in love.
Coquet'tish, *a.* practising coquetry.

Costume—Custom; Manners; Costume.

Costume', *n.* style or mode of dress. | Cos'tumer, *n.* one who prepares dress.

Coucher, couche—a Bed.

Couch, *v.* to lie down; to stoop.
Couch'ant, *a.* lying down; squatting.
| Couch'ing, *n.* the act of bending.
Couch'-fellow, *n.* a bed-fellow.

Fr. Cour, from L. Cortis—a Yard or Enclosed Place; a Company of Soldiers.

Court, *n.* a palace; a hall of justice; an enclosed place in front of a house.
Court, *v.* to endeavor to please; to flatter.
Court'ier, *n.* one who courts favor.
Court'like, *a.* elegant; polite.
Cour'tesan, *n.* a lewd woman.
| Court'ly, *a.* elegant; flattering.
Court'liness, *n.* elegance of manners.
Court'ship, *n.* the act of making love.
Cour'teous, *a.* polite; well bred; civil.
Cour'tesy, *n.* civility; act of civility made by women.

Écraser—to Crush.

Crash, *v.* to make a sudden, loud noise, as of many things falling at once.
Crash, *n.* a sudden, loud noise.
Crash'ing, *n.* a violent mixed noise.
Crush, *v.* to break by pressure.
| Craze, *v.* to break; to crush; to disorder the intellect.
Cra'zy, *a.* broken; feeble; disordered in intellect.
Cra'ziness, *n.* weakness; disorder of the mind.

Craie—Chalk.

Cray'on, *n.* a pencil for drawing. | Cray'on, *v.* to design with a crayon.

Courbe—to Bend.

Curb, *n.* any thing that restrains or checks. | Curb, *v.* to restrain; to control.

Danger—Danger.

Dan'ger, *n.* exposure to death, loss or injury.
| Dan'gerous, *a.* full of danger.
Dan'gerously, *ad.* perilously.

Dame—a LADY.

DAME, n. the mistress of a house.
DAM, n. a female parent of beasts.
BEL'DAM, n. on old woman; a hag.
MAD'AM, n. a term of address to a lady.

NOTE.—DAM, a bank to confine water, comes from the Dutch (*dam.*)

Debaucher—DEBAUCH.

DEBAUCH', v. to corrupt; to vitiate. | DEBAUCHEE', n. a libertine; a rake.
DEBAUCH'ERY, n. excess; lewdness.

Des mœurs—of GOOD MANNERS.

DEMURE', a. of serious or pensive look; affectedly modest.
DEMURE'LY, ad. with affected modesty.
DEMURE'NESS, n. soberness.

Draper—to CLOTHE.

DRAPE, v. to cover or ornament with cloth.
DRA'PER, n. one who sells cloth.
DRA'PERY, n. curtains, hangings, etc.

Dresser—to MAKE STRAIGHT.

DRESS, v. to set or put in order; to clothe.
DRESS, n. clothes; garments.

Drole—DROLL.

DROLL, a. comical; odd; merry. | DROLL'ERY, n. idle jokes.

Gage—a PLEDGE.

GAGE, n. a pledge; a measure.
ENGAGE', v. to bind; to enlist.
ENGAGE'MENT, n. obligation; employment.
DISENGAGE', v. to separate; to withdraw.
ENGA'GING, p. a. winning; attractive.
MORT'GAGE, n. the pledge of an estate as security.
WAGE, n. pledge; gage; wages.
WAGES, n. hire; reward for service.
WA'GER, n. a bet; v. to bet.

NOTE.—WAGE, to venture, to make, to carry on as war, is from the German (*wagen.*)

Enticer—to ENTICE.

ENTICE', v. to allure to evil. | ENTICE'MENT, n. allurement.

Equiper—to EQUIP.

EQUIP', v. to fit out.
EQUIP'MENT, n. complete outfit.
EQUIP'AGE, n. a carriage with its accompaniments.

Fin—FINE.

FINE, a. small; thin; not coarse.
FINE'LY, ad. beautifully; well.
FINE'NESS, n. elegance; purity.
FIN'ERY, n. show; gaiety.
FINESSE', n. artifice; stratagem.
FIN'ICAL, a. nice in trifles.
FINE'SPUN, a. minute.
REFINE', v. to purify.
REFINE'MENT, n. polish of manners.
SUPERFINE', a. very or most fine.

Foible—Feeble.

Fee'ble, *a.* weak; infirm.
Fee'bleness, *n.* weakness; infirmity.
Enfee'ble, *pp.* made weak.
Fee'bly, *ad.* weakly; without strength.
Foi'ble, *n.* a moral weakness.

Finance—Finance.

Finance', *n.* revenue; income.
Finan'cial, *a.* relating to finance.
Financier', *n.* one who understands revenue.

Flatter, from L. *Flato*—to Blow.

Flat'ter, *v.* to soothe with praises.
Flat'terer, *n.* one who flatters.
Flat'tering, *p. a.* exciting hope.
Flat'tery, *n.* false praise.

Flair—Scent.

Fla'vor, *n.* fragrance; relish; taste.
Fla'vored, *a.* having a fine taste.

Affoler—to Foil.

Foil, *v.* to baffle; to defeat.

Note.—Foil, a leaf, gilding, comes from the Latin (*folium.*)

Fol—Mad; Foolish. *Fou*—a Madman; a Fool.

Fool, *n.* one of weak understanding.
Fool'ish, *a.* unwise.
Fool'ishness, *n.* want of wisdom.
Fool'hardy, *a.* foolishly bold.
Fool'hardiness, *n.* courage without sense.
Fol'ly, *n.* want of understanding.

Fourrager—to Forage.

For'age, *v.* to wander in search of spoil.
Foraging, *n.* roving in search of provisions.

Forge, from L. *Ferrum*—Iron.

Forge, *n.* a furnace for heating iron.
Forge, *v.* to form by furnace and hammer.
Forge, *v.* to counterfeit; to falsify.
Forg'er, *n.* one who forges; a falsifier.
Forg'ery, *n.* the crime of falsifying.

Franc—Frank.

Frank, *a.* free; open; sincere.
Frank'ly, *ad.* openly; freely.
Frank'lin, *n.* a freeholder; a steward.
Frank'ness, *n.* plainness; openness.
Fran'chise, *n.* privilege; right.

Friser—to Frizz.

Frizz, *v.* to curl; to crisp.
Friz'zle, *v.* to curl in short curls.
Frieze, *n.* a coarse woolen cloth with a nap on one side.

Fournir—to Furnish.

Fur'nish, *v.* to supply; to fit up.
Fur'nished, *p. a.* supplied; fitted up.
Fur'niture, *n.* goods in a house for use.

Froncer—to WRINKLE.

FROWN, *v.* to express displeasure by contracting the brow.
FROWN, *n.* a look of displeasure.

FROWN'ING, *p. a.* expressing displeasure by a frown.
FROWN'INGLY, *ad.* with a look of displeasure.

Galant—GALLANT.

GAL'LANT, *a.* gay; splendid; brave.
GAL'LANTLY, *ad.* bravely; nobly.
GAL'LANTRY, *n.* bravery; nobleness.

GALLANT', *a.* polite and attentive to ladies.

Garnir—to FURNISH; to ADORN.

GAR'NISH, *v.* to adorn; to beautify. | GAR'MENT, *n.* a covering for the body.

Gai—GAY.

GAY, *a.* cheerful; merry; showy.
GAY'ETY, *n.* cheerfulness; finery.

GAY'LY, *ad.* merrily; cheerfully.
GAY'NESS, *n.* cheerfulness; finery.

Genievre—a JUNIPER BERRY.

GIN, *n.* a distilled spirit flavored with juniper berries.

NOTE.—GIN, a trap; a snare; an instrument for cleaning cotton; is a contraction of the word *engine*.

Glaner, glane—a HANDFUL OF CORN GATHERED.

GLEAN, *v.* to gather what is left by reapers; to gather what is thinly scattered.

GLEAN'ER, *n.* one who gleans.
GLEAN'ING, *n.* anything gleaned.

Gourmand—GORMAND.

GOR'MAND, *n.* a greedy eater; a glutton. | GOR'MANDIZE, *v.* to eat to excess.

Garantir—to WARRANT.

GRANT, *v.* to give; to admit.
GRANTEE', *n.* one to whom a grant is made.

GRANT'OR, *n.* one by whom a grant is made.

Grappe—a BUNCH; a CLUSTER.

GRAPE, *n.* the fruit of the vine.
GRAPE'STONE, *n.* the seed of the grape.

GRAPE'SHOT, *n.* shot so arranged as to resemble a bunch of grapes.

Gratter—to SCRAPE.

GRATE, *v.* to wear away; to rub hard. | GRAT'ING, *a.* rubbing; harsh.

NOTE.—GRATE, a frame for holding coals; and GRATING, lattice work; are from the Latin (*crates*, a crate; a hurdle.) GRATEFUL is from the Latin (*gratus*.)

Graisse—FAT.

GREASE, *n.* animal fat in a soft state.
GREAS'Y, *a.* smeared with grease.
GREAS'ILY, *ad.* with grease.

GREAS'INESS, *n.* the state of being greasy.

Groupe—GROUP.

GROUP, *n.* a cluster; a collection. | GROUP, *v.* to collect together.

Guider—to GUIDE.

GUIDE, *v.* to direct or lead in a way. | GUIDANCE, *n.* direction; government

Guise—GUISE.

GUISE, *n.* manner; garb; dress. | DISGUISE', *v.* to conceal by an unusual dress, etc.

Hardi—BOLD; DARING.

HAR'DY, *a.* firm; strong; bold. | HAR'DIHOOD, *n.* boldness; stoutness.
HAR'DINESS, *n.* firmness; courage.

Hasard—HAZARD.

HAZ'ARD, *n.* chance; danger. | HAZ'ARDOUS, *a.* dangerous.

Haineux, haine—HATRED.

HEI'NOUS, *a.* wicked in a high degree. | HEI'NOUSLY, *ad.* wickedly.

Hideux—FRIGHT; DREAD.

HID'EOUS, *a.* frightful to the sight. | HID'EOUSLY, *ad.* horribly.

Jaloux—JEALOUS.

JEAL'OUS, *a.* apprehensive of rivalship. | JEAL'OUSY, *n.* suspicious fear.

Nor. Fr. *Juele*, Fr. *Joyau*—JEWEL.

JEW'EL, *n.* any ornament of great value. | JEW'ELRY, *n.* jewels collectively.

Jour—DAYLIGHT. *Journee*—DAY.

JOUR'NAL, *n.* a daily register. | JOUR'NEY, *n.* the travel of a day.
JOUR'NALIZE, *v.* to enter in a journal. | JOUR'NEYMAN, *n.* a man hired by the day.

Joie—JOY.

JOY, *n.* gladness; delight. | JOY'LESS, *a.* giving no pleasure.
JOY'FUL, *a.* full of joy; glad. | JOY'OUS, *a.* glad; merry.

Jus—JUICE.

JUICE, *n.* the sap of vegetables. | JUI'CINESS, *n.* abundance of juice.
JUI'CY, *a.* abounding with juice. | JUICE'LESS, *a.* destitute of juice.

Laver—LAVE.

LAVE, *v.* to throw up or out. | LAV'ISHLY, *ad.* profusely.
LAV'ISH, *a.* profuse; wasteful. | LAV'ISH, *v.* to expend in profusion.

Loiser—LEISURE.

LEI′SURE, *n.* freedom from occupation. | LEI′SURELY, *ad.* done without hurry.

Longis—a SLOW FELLOW; a LINGERER.

LOUNGE, *v.* to spend time lazily. | LOUNG′ER, *n.* an idler.

Maniere, from L. *Manus*—the HAND.

MAN′NER, *n.* method; peculiar way. | MAN′NERLY, *ad.* civil; courteous.

Manoir, from L. *Maneo* –to ABIDE.

MAN′OR, *n.* the land of a lord. | MANO′RIAL, *a.* pertaining to a manor.

Marauder—to PLAY THE ROGUE. *Maraud*—a ROGUE.

MARAUD′, *v.* to rove in quest of plunder. | MARAUD′ER, *n.* a plunderer.

Macher—to CHEW.

MASH, *v.* to mix or beat into a confused mass. | MASH, *n.* a mixture.

Masque, from Sp. *Mascara. Mas*—MORE, and *Cara*—VISAGE, *i. e.,* a SECOND VISAGE.

MASK, *n.* a cover to disguise the face. | MASQUERADE′, *n.* an assemblage of persons wearing masks.

Merci, from L. *Misericordia.*

MER′CY, *n.* tenderness towards an offender. | MER′CIFUL, *a.* willing to pity and spare.
MER′CILESS, *a.* void of mercy. | MER′CILESSNESS, *n.* want of mercy.

Mine—MINE.

MINE, *n.* a pit from which minerals are dug. | MINE, *v.* to sap; to undermine.
| MI′NER, *n.* one who digs in a mine.
MIN′ERAL, *n.* a substance found in the earth.

NOTE.—MINE, of, or belonging to me, comes from the A.-S. (*min.*)

Moderne, from L. *Modo*—JUST NOW.

MOD′ERN, *a.* of the present time. | MOD′ERNIZE, *v.* to render modern.

Moite—MOIST; DAMP.

MOIST, *a.* wet in a small degree. | MOIST′NESS, *n.* wetness in a small degree.
MOIST′EN, *v.* to make damp. |
MOIST′URE, *n.* a moderate degree of wetness.

Moule—a MOULD or a MATRIX.

MOULD, *n.* that in which anything is shaped. | MOULD′ER, *n.* one who casts or shapes.

NOTE.—MOULD, the upper or surface soil, comes from the A.-S. (*molde, myl,* earth.)

Moisir—to Must; to Mould.

Must, *v.* to make mouldy.
Mus'tiness, *n.* mouldiness.

Mus'ty, *a.* spoiled with damp or age.

Note.—Must, to be obliged, comes from the A.-S. (*mast,*) and Must, new wine, from A.-S. (*must.*)

Mutiner—to Mutiny.

Mu'tiny, *n.* a rising against authority.

Mutineer', *n.* one guilty of mutiny.
Mu'tinous, *a.* turbulent.

Net—Entirely.

Net. *a.* clear after all deductions.

Note.—Net, a texture of twine, etc., comes from the A.-S. (*net.*)

Noise—Strife; Quarrel; Dispute.

Noise, *n.* a loud sound; an outcry.
Noi'sy, *a.* sounding loud.

Noise'less, *a.* without sound.

Panteler—to Gasp for Breath.

Pant, *v.* to beat, as the heart.

Pant'ing, *n.* rapid breathing.

Parler—to Speak.

Parle, *v.* to talk; to converse.
Par'lance, *n.* conversation; talk.
Par'ley, *v.* to discuss orally.
Parole', *n.* a verbal promise.

Par'liament, *n.* the British legislative council.
Par'lor, *n.* a sitting-room.

Pate—Paste; Dough.

Paste, *n.* a cement made of flour and water.
Pas'try, *n.* things made of baked paste.

Pas'ty, *n.* a pie baked without a dish.
Paste'board, *n.* a kind of thick paper.
Pas'tel, *n.* a kind of crayon.

Petit, from L. *Petilus*—Slender; Delicate.

Pet'it, *a.* small; little.
Pet, *n.* a little favorite.
Pet, *n.* a slight fit of peevishness.
Ped'dle, *v.* to travel about and sell goods in small quantities.
Ped'ler, *n.* a traveling dealer in small wares.
Pet'tiness, *n.* smallness.

Pet'tish, *a.* fretful; peevish.
Pet'ticoat, *n.* a woman's lower garment.
Pet'tifog, *v.* to do small business as a lawyer.
Pet'tifogger, *n.* an inferior lawyer.
Pet'ty, *a.* small; trifling.

Percer, from L. *Pertundo, pertusus*—to Beat, Push, or Thrust Through.

Pierce, *v.* to thrust a pointed instrument into.
Pierc'er, *n.* one that pierces.
Pierc'ingly, *ad.* sharply; keenly.

Pierce'able, *a.* that may be penetrated.
Pierc'ing, *p. a.* cutting; keen.

FRENCH ROOTS AND DERIVATIVES.

Payer, from L. *Paco, pacare*—to PACATE; to PACIFY.

PAY, *v.* to discharge, as a debt.
PAY, *n.* compensation for service.

PAY'ABLE, *a.* that may or can be paid.
PAY'MENT, *n.* that which is paid.

Paysan—a COTTAGER.

PEAS'ANT, *n.* a countryman.

PEAS'ANTRY, *n.* country people.

Peler, piller—to PLUNDER. From L. *Pilo,* to deprive of hair.

PEEL, *v.* to strip off; to plunder.
PILL, *v.* to strip; to rob; to pillage.
PIL'LAGE, *v.* to strip of property by violence.

PIL'LAGE, *n.* plunder; spoil.
PIL'FER, *v.* to steal by petty theft.
PIL'FERER, *n.* one who pilfers.
PIL'FERING, *n.* petty theft.

Pelerin, from L. *Peregrinus*—ONE WHO COMES FROM ABROAD.

PIL'GRIM, *n.* one who travels on a religious account.

PIL'GRIMAGE, *n.* a journey to a holy place.

Épingle, from L. *Spina*—a PRICKLE; a THORN.

PIN, *n.* a small pointed instrument.
PIN'CASE, *n.* a case for pins.
PIN'HOLE, *n.* a very small hole.
PIN'FEATHERED, *a.* not fully feathered.

PIN'CUSHION, *n.* a cushion to stick pins in.
PIN'MONEY, *n.* a wife's pocket money.

Pincer—to PINCH.

PINCH, *v.* to squeeze between two sharp points.

PIN'CERS, *n.* an instrument for gripping.

Piquer—to PRICK; to STING.

PIQUE, *n.* ill will; offence.
PIQ'UANCY, *n.* sharpness; tartness.

PIQ'UANT, *a.* sharp; pungent.
PIQ'UANTLY, *ad.* sharply; tartly.

Pitie—COMPASSION, from L. *Pietas*—DUTIFUL CONDUCT.

PIT'Y, *n.* the feeling excited by the distress of another.
PIT'EOUS, *a.* sorrowful.

PIT'EOUSLY, *ad.* in a piteous manner.
PIT'IABLE, *a.* deserving pity.
PIT'IFUL, *a.* full of pity.

PIT'ILESS, *a.* without pity.

Plaider—to PLEAD.

PLEA, *n.* that which is advanced in pleading.

PLEAD, *v.* to argue before a court.
PLEAD'ER, *n.* one who pleads.

PLEAD'ING, *pp.* supporting by arguments.

Pocher—to BRUISE, as the eyes.

POKE, *v.* to feel in the dark; to search for with a long instrument.

POK'ER, *n.* an instrument for stirring the fire.

POK'ING, *a.* drudging; servile.

NOTE.—POKE, a pouch, a pocket, etc., comes from the A.-S. (*pocca.*)

Peser—to Weigh.

Poise, *n.* weight; balance.
Coun'terpoise, *n.* equivalence of weight.
Overpoise', *v.* to outweigh.
Outpoise', *v.* to outweigh.
Unpoised', *a.* not balanced.

Poudre—Dust.

Pow'der, *n.* any dry substance composed of minute particles.
Pow'dery, *a.* dusty.
Pow'derflask, *n.* a case in which gunpowder is kept.
Pow'dermill, *n.* a mill for making gunpowder.

Pourchasser—to Pursue; to Seek.

Pur'chase, *v.* to buy; to acquire.
Pur'chaser, *n.* one who buys.

Pouvoir—to Be Able.

Pow'er, *n.* ability; strength.
Pow'erful, *a.* having power.
Pow'erless, *a.* without power.
Empow'er, *v.* to give power to.

Old Fr. *Prim*—Prime; First.

Prim, *a.* straight; precise; affectedly nice.
Prim, *v.* to deck with great nicety.
Prim'ness, *n.* affected formality or niceness.

Provigner—to Layer the Vine for Propagation.

Prune, *v.* to cut off superfluous branches.
Prun'er, *n.* one who prunes.

Note.—Prune, a dried plum, comes from the Latin (*prunum*.)

Puisne. Puis—Since, and *ne*—Born.

Pu'ny, *a.* small and feeble.
Po'ny, *n.* a small horse.

Old Fr. *Quarrier*—to Square, *i. e.*, to Hew and Prepare them for the Builders.

Quar'ry, *n.* a place from which stones are dug.
Quar'ry, *v.* to dig from a quarry.

Note.—To quarry stones, means properly to *square*.

Querir—to Seek.

Quar'ry, *n.* the game flown at by a hawk.

Quitter, from L. *Quieto*—to Make Quiet.

Quit, *v.* to leave; to forsake.
Quit, *a.* free; clear.
Quit'rent, *n.* a small rent reserved.
Quit'tance, *n.* discharge.
Quit'claim, *n.* the release of a claim

Railler—to Banter; to Jest.

Ral'ly, *v.* to treat with satirical merriment.
Rail'lery, *n.* jesting language.
Rail, *v.* to use insolent language.

Note.—Rally, to reunite, to come back to order, comes from the French (*rallier*.)

Ramper—to CREEP.

RAMP, *v.* to climb; to leap; to sport.
RAM'PANT, *a.* exuberant; rank.
ROMP, *v.* to play rudely.
ROMP, *n.* a noisy, boisterous girl.
ROMP'ISH, *a.* inclined to romp.

Rang—ROW; LINE.

RANGE, *v.* to place in order.
RANK, *n.* a line; a row; a class.

Arriere—REAR.

REAR, *n.* that which is behind.
REAR, *a.* in the rear; hindermost.

NOTE.—REAR, to raise, to elevate, comes from the A.-S. (*ræran*.)

Refuser, from L. *Refuto*—to REPRESS; to REFUTE.

REFUSE', *v.* to deny a request.
REF'USE, *n.* what remains.
REFUS'AL, *n.* denial; option.
REFUS'ABLE, *a.* that may be refused.

Regarder—to LOOK AT.

REGARD', *v.* to observe; to respect.
REGARD, *n.* attention; respect.
REGARD'FUL, *a.* attentive.
REGARD'LESS, *a.* heedless.

Old Fr. *Rewerdon*—RECOMPENSE.

REWARD', *v.* to give in return; recompense.
REWARD'ABLE, *a.* worthy of reward.

Riote—a BRAWL; a TUMULT.

RI'OT, *n.* a tumult; an uproar.
RI'OTOUS, *a.* turbulent.

River, from L. *Gyro*—to TURN or WHEEL ROUND.

RIV'ET, *v.* to fasten by bending down the point.
RIV'ET, *n.* a nail clinched at both ends.

Roc—ROCK.

ROCK, *n.* a large mass of stone.
ROCK'LESS, *a.* without rocks.
ROCK'Y, *a.* full of rocks.
ROCK'INESS, *n.* the state of being rocky.

NOTE.—ROCK, to move backwards and forwards, comes from the Danish (*rokker*,) and ROCK, a distaff, from the Danish (*rok*.)

Rond, from L. *Rotundus*—ROUND. *Rota*—a WHEEL.

ROUND, *a.* circular; spherical.
ROUND'ISH, *a.* somewhat round.
ROUND'LY, *ad.* in a round form.
ROUND'NESS, *n.* the quality of being round.
ROUND'ABOUT, *a.* indirect.
ROUND'ROBIN, *n.* a writing signed by names in a circle.
ROUTE, *n.* a road; a way.
ROUTINE', *n.* a round or course of business.

Écouter—to LISTEN; to HEAR.

SCOUT, *n.* one who is sent privily to observe the motions of an enemy.
SCOUT, *v.* to act the spy; to reject with contempt.

Sauce, from L. *Salsus*—SALT.

SAUCE, *n.* something to give relish to food.
SAU'CER, *n.* a platter for a tea cup.
SAU'CY, *a.* insolent; impudent.
SAU'CILY, *ad.* impudently.
SAU'CINESS, *n.* impudence.
SAUCE'BOX, *n.* an impudent person.
SAUCE'PAN, *n.* a small pan.

Saison—SEASON.

SEA'SON, *n.* one of the four divisions of the year.
SEA'SON, *n.* a fit or suitable time.
SEA'SON, *v.* to give relish to.
SEA'SON, *v.* to prepare for use by time.
SEA'SONABLE, *a.* at the proper time.
SEA'SONING, *n.* something added to give relish.

Saisir—to SEIZE.

SEIZE, *v.* to take hold of; to grasp.
SEIZ'ABLE, *a.* that may be seized.
SEIZ'URE, *n.* the act of seizing.

Sevrer—to SEPARATE.

SEV'ER, *v.* to part by violence; to divide.
SEV'ERAL, *a.* different; separate.
SEV'ERALLY, *ad.* separately.
SEV'ERANCE, *n.* separation.

Sire, from L. *Senior*—an AGED PERSON.

SIRE, *n.* a father.
SIR, *n.* a word of respect.
SIR'RAH, *n.* or *interj.* a term of reproach or insult.

Teindre, from L. *Tingo*—to TINGE; to DYE.

STAIN, *v.* to discolor; to spot; to disgrace.
STAIN'LESS, *a.* free from stain.

Étancher, from L. *Stagno*—to MAKE STAGNANT.

STANCH, *v.* to stop from flowing.
STANCH, *a.* strong; firm; sound.
STAN'CHION, *n.* a prop; a support.
STANCH'LESS, *a.* that cannot be stanched.
STANCH'NESS, *n.* stoutness; firmness.

Surflot—the RISING OF BILLOW UPON BILLOW.

SURF, *n.* the swell of the sea breaking on the shore.

Surprise—SURPRISE.

SURPRISE', *v.* to come or fall upon suddenly.
SURPRISE', *n.* the act of taking unawares.
SURPRIS'AL, *n.* the act of surprising.

Tailleur, tailler—to CUT.

TAI'LOR, *n.* one who makes clothes.
TAL'LY, *n.* a stick with notches cut to mark numbers.

Étang—a POND; a POOL.

TANK, *n.* a large cistern.
TANK'ARD, *n.* a large drinking vessel.

Tanner—to TAN.

TAN, *v.* to impregnate with bark; to make brown.
TAN'NING, *n.* the process of making leather.
TAN'NER, *n.* one who tans leather.
TAN'NIN, *n.* the astringent principle in bark.
TAW'NY, *a.* of a yellowish dark color.

Tater—to FEEL; to TASTE.

TASTE, *v.* to perceive by the palate.
TASTE, *n.* the sense by which we perceive the relish of a thing.
TAST'ABLE, *a.* that may be tasted.
TASTE'FUL, *a.* having good taste.
TASTE'LESS, *a.* having no taste.

Tancer—to REBUKE.

TAUNT, *v.* to reproach with insulting words.
TAUNT'INGLY, *ad.* scoffingly.

Tete—the HEAD.

TES'TY, *a.* fretful; peevish.
TES'TINESS, *n.* fretfulness.

Etiquette—a LITTLE NOTE, BREVIATE or BILL.

TICK'ET, *n.* a token of any right or debt. | TICK, *n.* trust; credit.

NOTE.—TICK, a small animal, comes from the French (*tique*.) TICK, to make a small noise, from the Dutch (*tikken*,) and TICK, the case of a bed, from the Dutch (*teek*.)

Torche, from L. *Torqueo*—to TWIST.

TORCH, *n.* a large light carried in the hand.
TORCH'LIGHT, *n.* the light of a torch.

NOTE.—Because they are made with twisted thread.

Toucher—to TOUCH.

TOUCH, *v.* to perceive by the sense of feeling; to come in contact with.
TOUCH'Y, *a.* peevish; irritable.
TOUCH'ING, *a.* affecting; pathetic.
TOUCH'INESS, *n.* peevishness.

Tramail, from L. *Trama*—the WEFT, or FILLING OF A WEB.

TRAM'MEL, *n.* a net; a kind of shackle. | TRAM'MEL, *v.* to shackle; to hamper.

Travailler—to TRAVEL.

TRAV'AIL, *v.* to labor; to toil.
TRAV'EL, *v.* to make journeys.
TRAV'ELED, *a.* having made journeys.
TRAV'ELER, *n.* one who travels.

Tricherie, tricher—to CHEAT; to TRICK.

TREACH'ERY, *n.* breach of faith.
TREACH'EROUS, *a.* faithless.
TRICK, *n.* a sly fraud.
TRICK'ERY, *n.* artifice.
TRICK'ISH, *a.* artful; knavish.
TRICK'STER, *n.* one who practises tricks.

Trancher, from L. *Trans*—ACROSS, and *Scindo*—to CUT.

TRENCH, *v.* to cut or dig into ditches. | TRENCH'ANT, *a.* cutting; sharp.

Troubler, from L. *Turbo, turbatus*—to THROW INTO DISORDER.

TROUB'LE, *v.* to disturb; to afflict; to vex

TROUB'LESOME, *a.* giving trouble.
TROUB'LOUS, *a.* disordered.

Truand—a VAGABOND; a BEGGAR.

TRU'ANT, *n.* one who neglects his duty.

TRU'ANCY, *n.* the act of playing truant.

Tromper—to DECEIVE.

TRUMP, *v.* to impose upon.

TRUMP'ERY, *n.* worthless finery.

NOTE.—To TRUMP UP, to forge, to get together by all sorts of expedients. TRUMP, a winning card, comes from the Latin (*triumphus,*) and TRUMP, a musical instrument, from the Italian (*tromba.*)

Trier—to CULL OUT.

TRY, *v.* to prove by experiment.

TRI'AL, *n.* the act of trying; test.

Vanter, from L. *Vano, vanatum*—to UTTER EMPTY WORDS.

VAUNT, *v.* to boast; to brag.

VAUNT'ER, *n.* a boaster.

Viver, from L. *Gyro, gyratus*—to TURN IN A CIRCLE.

VEER, *v.* to turn; to change direction.

VEER'ING, *n.* the act of turning.

Vis—to TURN ABOUT; to TWIST.

VICE, *n.* an iron press with a screw for holding fast.

NOTE.—VICE, depravity, wickedness, comes from the Latin (*vitium,*) and VICE, in the place of, from the Latin (*vi'ce.*)

Voyage, from L. *Via*—a Way, and *Ago*—to Pursue.

VOY'AGE, *n.* a journey by sea.

VOY'AGER, *n.* one who travels by sea.

Guichet—a GRATING; a LATTICE-WORK DOOR.

WICK'ET, *n.* a small door made in a gate.

DUTCH ROOTS AND DERIVATIVES.

Schuin—AWRY; OBLIQUE.

ASKANCE', *ad.* sidewise; obliquely. | ASKANT', *ad.* sidewise; obliquely.

Bancket—BANQUET.

BAN'QUET, *n.* a grand entertainment of eating and drinking.

NOTE.—BANCKET, in the sense of bench or table, at which messmates sit and feast together. BANQUET, a raised footpath across a bridge, comes from the French (*banquette*, a covered bench.)

Barg—a BARK.

BARGE, *n.* a large row boat. | BARGE'MAN, *n.* the manager of a barge.

Babbelen—to PRATTLE; to BLAB.

BLAB, *v.* to tattle; to tell tales. | BLAB'BER, *n.* a tell-tale.

Blaer—a PUSTULE; a BLISTER.

BLEAR, *a.* dim with rheum or water. | BLEAR'-EYED, *a.* having sore eyes.

Block—BLOCK.

BLOCK, *n.* a heavy, thick piece of wood or stone.

NOTE.—To BLOCK, to shut up, to obstruct, comes from the French (*bloquer*, to blockade.)

Donder—to THUNDER.

BLUN'DER, *v.* to mistake grossly. | BLUN'DERBUSS, *n.* a gun with a large
BLUN'DERER, *n.* one who blunders. | bore.
BLUN'DERHEAD, *n.* a stupid fellow.

Blaar—a BLISTER; a PUSTULE.

BLUR, *n.* something that obscures or | BLUR, *v.* to obscure by some blot,
soils. | soil, or stain.
BLURT, *v.* to utter suddenly.

Byster—FURIOUS.

BOIS'TEROUS, *a.* stormy; violent; | BOIS'TEROUSLY, *ad.* in a boisterous
noisy. | manner.

• *Baas*—MASTER.

BOSS, *n.* a master among mechanics.

NOTE.—This word originated in New York among the Dutch.

Blosen—to BLUSH.

BLOWZE, *n.* a ruddy fat-faced girl. | BLOW'ZY, *a.* fat and ruddy; sunburnt.

Brak—SALTISH.

BRACK'ISH, *a.* rather salt. | BRACK'ISHNESS, *n.* saltness in a small degree.

Braggeren—to BRAG.

BRAG, *v.* to boast; to vaunt. | BRAG'GART, *n.* a vain boaster.
BRAG'GER, *n.* a boaster. | BRAG'GING, *p. a.* praising one's self.

Bobbel—BUBBLE.

BUB'BLE, *n.* a small bladder of water; anything empty; a cheat. | BUB'BLE, *v.* to rise in bubbles.
| BUB'BLY, *a.* consisting of bubbles.

Bulle—BULL.

BULL, *n.* the male of bovine animals. | BUL'LOCK, *n.* an ox.

NOTE.—BULL, an edict or mandate issued by the pope, comes from the Latin (*bulla*, a boss, a knob,) so named from the seal affixed to it having raised work on it. BULL, a gross contradiction or blunder, was so named from OBADIAH BULL, a lawyer in the time of Henry VII., noted for his blunders.

Bolwerk—BULWARK.

BUL'WARK, *n.* a mound to protect from an enemy. | BUL'WARK, *n.* the woodwork round a vessel above her deck.

Boei—BUOY.

BUOY, *n.* a floating mark. | BUOY'ANT, *a.* tending to rise or float.

Koek—CAKE.

CAKE, *n.* sweetened dough baked. | CAKE, *n.* any mass of matter concreted.

Kouten—to JABBER.

CHAT, *v.* to talk freely or at ease. | CHAT'TER, *v.* to talk idly; to make a noise by collision of the teeth.
CHAT'TERBOX, *n.* an incessant talker. |

Kappen—to CHOP.

CHOP, *v.* to cut with a quick blow. | CHIP, *n.* a small piece cut off.

Circken—to CHIRP.

CHIRP, *v.* to make a noise like a bird. | CHIRP'ING, *n.* the gentle noise of birds.

Klatteren—to CLATTER.

CLAT'TER, *v.* to make a confused noise. | CLAT'TERING, *n.* noise; clamor.

Klinken—to KLINK; to RIVET.

CLINCH, *v.* to grasp in the hand. | CLINK, *v.* to make a small sharp sound.
CLINCH'ER, *n.* a holdfast. |

Klomp—Clump.

Clump, n. a shapeless mass; a cluster of trees.
Clump'y, a. shapeless; ill-shaped.
Clum'sy, a. without grace of form; awkward.
Clum'sily, ad. in a clumsy manner.
Clum'siness, n. awkwardness.
Lump, n. a small mass; the gross.
Lump'ish, a. heavy; dull; gross.
Lump'y, a. full of lumps.

Koets—a Coach; a Couch.

Coach, n. a four-wheeled pleasure carriage.
Coach'hire, n. money for the use of a coach.
Coach'horse, n. a horse for drawing a coach.
Coach'maker, n. one who makes coaches.
Coach'man, n. the driver of a coach.

Kost—Cost.

Cost, n. price; charge; expense.
Cost'less, a. without expense.
Cost'ly, a. of a high price.
Cost'liness, n. expensiveness.

Kraek—Crack.

Crack, n. a narrow breach; a fissure.
Crack, v. to break partially; to cause to sound sharply and suddenly.
Crack'le, v. to make slight and frequent cracks.
Crack'ling, n. a slight frequent noise.
Crack'brained, a. crazy.

Kramp—Cramp.

Cramp, n. a spasmodic contraction of the muscles.
Cramp, v. to restrain; to hinder.

Kricken—to Creak, derived from the sound.

Creak, v. to make a sharp, harsh grating sound.
Creak'ing, n. a harsh grating noise.

Komberen—to Cumber.

Cum'ber, v. to oppress with a load or burden.
Cum'bersome, a. burdensome.
Cum'brance, n. burden; hindrance.
Cum'brous, a. burdensome.
Encum'ber, v. to clog; to load.

Krullen—to Curl.

Curl, n. a ringlet of hair.
Cur'ly, a. having curls
Curl, v. to form into curls.

Dabben—to Dab.

Dab, v. to strike suddenly.
Dab'ble, v. to dip a little or often.
Bedab'ble, v. to wet; to besprinkle.
Dab'bler, n. one who dips slightly into anything.
Daub, v. to smear; to paint coarsely.
Dab'ster, n. one who is expert at anything.
Daub'er, n. one who daubs.
Daub'ed, a. smeared with soft, adhesive matter.
Bedaub'ed, pp. daubed over.

Dollen—to TRIFLE.

DAL'LY, *v.* to lose time in trifles. | DAL'LIANCE, *n.* acts of fondness.

Damp—DAMP.

DAMP, *a.* moist; slightly wet.
DAMP, *v.* to moisten; to check or abate.
DAMP'EN, *v.* to make damp.
DAMP'ER, *n.* that which checks or abates.
DAMP'ISH, *a.* somewhat damp.
DAMP'NESS, *n.* moisture.

Koyen, kooi—a CAGE or DECOY.

DECOY', *v.* to lure into a net, cage or snare. | DECOY', *n.* an artifice to entrap.

Drek—DIRT.

DIRT, *n.* any thing that renders foul or unclean.
DIRT'Y, *a.* foul; nasty; filthy.
DIRT'ILY, *ad.* filthily.
DIRT'INESS, *n.* filthiness.

Droom—DREAM.

DREAM, *n.* thoughts of a person in sleep.
DREAM'ER, *n.* one who dreams.
DREAM'INGLY, *ad.* sluggishly; negligently.
DREAM'LESS, *a.* free from dreams.

Trom—DRUM.

DRUM, *n.* an instrument of military music. | DRUM-MAJOR, *n.* the chief drummer.

Dom—DULL; BLUNT; STUPID.

DUMP, *n.* sorrow; sadness.
DUMP'ISH, *a.* sad; melancholy.
DUM'PY, *a.* sullen; short and thick.
DUM'PLING, *n.* a sort of pudding.

Vlak—a SPOT.

FLECK, *v.* to spot; to streak.
FREAK, *v.* to variegate; to checker.
FREC'KLE, *n.* a yellowish spot in the skin.

NOTE.—FREAK, a whim, a fancy, comes from the German (*frech*, impudent, bold.)

Vragt—FREIGHT.

FREIGHT, *n.* the cargo of a ship. | FREIGHT'AGE, *n.* money for freight.

Frisch—FRESH; LIVELY; GAY.

FRISK, *v.* to leap; to skip.
FRISK'FUL, *a.* full of gayety.
FRISK'Y, *a.* frolicsome; gay.
FRISK'ILY, *ad.* gayly.

Fommelen—to FUMBLE.

FUM'BLE, *v.* to feel or grope about. | FUM'BLING, *p. a.* doing anything awkwardly.

Gantelope. *Gant*—a Passage. *Loopen*—to Run.

Gant'let, *n.* a military punishment, in which the criminal, running between two ranks, receives a lash from each man.

Note.—Gauntlet, an iron glove, comes from the French (*gantelet.*)

Glaren—to Glare.

Glare, *v.* to shine with a dazzling light.
Glare, *n.* a bright, dazzling light.
Glar'ing, *a.* bright; notorious; barefaced.
Glar'ingly, *ad.* notoriously.

Glimmen—to Glimmer.

Glim'mer, *v.* to shine faintly.
Glim'mering, *n.* a faint view.
Glimpse, *n.* a faint light; a short view.

Grof—Gruff.

Gruff, *a.* surly; harsh.
Gruff'ness, *n.* harshness of manner or look.

Gissen—to Guess.

Guess, *v.* to judge at random.
Guess'work, *n.* work done by guess.

Kullen—to Gull.

Gull, *v.* to trick; to cheat.
Gull, *n.* one easily cheated.

Note.—Gull, a sea bird, comes from the Welsh (*gwylan.*)

Oxhoofd—Oxhead.

Hogs'head, *n.* a large cask.

Note.—The English orthography is grossly corrupt.

Hoog—Huge.

Huge, *a.* very large in size.
Huge'ly, *ad.* immensely.
Huge'ness, *n.* enormous bulk.

Hulzen—Husks.

Husk, *n.* the covering of certain fruits.
Husk'y, *a.* rough in tone.

Lasigh—Lazy.

La'zy, *a.* disposed to be idle.
La'zily, *ad.* idly; indolently.
La'ziness, *n.* disposition to be idle.

Lek—a Leak.

Leak, *n.* a hole which lets water in or out.
Leak'age, *n.* the quantity that escapes by leaking.
Leak'y, *a.* letting water in or out.
Leach, *v.* to cause a fluid to percolate through.

Note.—Leech, a physician, a kind of worm, comes from the A.-S. (*lece.*)

Loopen—Because it is Easily Slipped Off.

Loop, *n.* a double in a string. | Loop'hole, *n.* a hole for escape or evasion.

Laag—Low.

Low, *a.* not high; humble.
Low'er, *v.* to bring low; to lessen.
Low'er, *v.* to appear dark or gloomy.
Low'land, *n.* land which is low.
Low'ly, *a.* humble; meek; mild.
Low'liness, *n.* humility.
Low'ness, *n.* state of being low.

Geluk, luk—Luck.

Luck, *n.* that which happens; fortune.
Luck'y, *a.* successful by chance.
Luck'less, *a.* unfortunate.
Luck'ily, *ad.* fortunately.
Luck'iness, *n.* good fortune.

Note.—The sense is, that which comes, falls, or happens.

Middelen—to Mediate.

Med'dle, *v.* to act in the concerns of others in which one's interposition is not necessary.
Med'ley, *n.* a mixture.
Med'dler, *n.* one who meddles.
Med'dlesome, *a.* given to meddling.
Med'dling, *n.* officious interposition.

Moppen—to Pout.

Mope, *v.* to be very dull and spiritless. | Mo'pish, *a.* spiritless.

Modder—Mud.

Mud, *n.* moist and soft earth.
Mud'dy, *a.* foul with mud.
Mud'dily, *ad.* with foul mixture.
Moth'ery, *a.* full of mother; concreted.
Mud'dle, *v.* to make confused.
Moth'er, *n.* a thick, slimy substance in liquors.

Note.—Mother, the female parent, comes from the A.-S. (*moder*.)

Mof—Muff.

Muff, *n.* a cover for the hands. | Muf'fle, *v.* to cover; to conceal.
Muf'fler, *n.* a cover for the face.

Mommelen—to Speak Like One Wearing a Mask. *Mom*—a Mask.

Mum'ble, *v.* to speak inwardly; to mutter. | Mum'bler, *n.* one who mumbles.

Knippen—to Nip.

Nip, *v.* to pinch; to blast. | Nip'pers, *n.* small pincers.

Pak—Pack.

Pack, *n.* a bundle; a bale.
Pack, *v.* to press close.
Pack'thread, *n.* thread for packing.
Pack'age, *n.* a parcel of goods packed.
Pack'et, *n.* a small bundle.

Note.—Packet, a vessel for conveying the mails, etc., comes from the French (*paquet*.)

Piloot. *Piil*—a PLUMMET LINE, and *Loot*—LEAD.

PI′LOT, *n.* one who steers a ship. | PI′LOTAGE, *n.* the duty or pay of a pilot.

Pinken—to TWINKLE WITH THE EYES.

PINK, *v.* to pierce with small holes; to stab. | PINK, *n.* an eye; a flower; a color.

Plots—DULL; HEAVY.

PLOD, *v.* to toil; to travel or work slowly. | PLOD′DER, *n.* one who plods.
| PLOD′DING, *n.* slow motion or study.

Ploeg—PLOUGH.

PLOUGH, *n.* an instrument for turning up the ground. | PLOUGH′BOY, *n.* a boy who ploughs.
| PLOUGH′MAN, *n.* one who ploughs.
PLOUGH′SHARE, *n.* part of a plough.

Bol—a BALL; a BULB.

POLL, *n.* the head; the place of an election. | POLL, *v.* to lop or cut the top off; to register, as a vote.
POL′LARD, *n.* anything polled, or having the top cut off.

Pot—POT.

POT, *n.* a hollow vessel used for boiling meat, holding liquids, etc. | POT′HERB, *n.* an herb fit for cookery.
POT′TAGE, *n.* anything boiled for food. | POT′HOOK, *n.* a hook on which pots are hung.
POT′TER, *n.* one who makes earthen vessels. | POT′HOUSE, *n.* an alehouse.
| POT′LID, *n.* the cover of a pot.
POT′TERY, *n.* the place where earthen vessels are made. | POT′VALIANT, *a.* courageous from strong drink.
POT′SHERD, *n.* a fragment of a broken pot.

NOTE.—SHERD, from A.-S. (*sceard*,) a fragment.

Praaten—to PRATE.

PRATE, *v.* to talk idly. | PRAT′ING, *n.* idle talk; tattle.
PRAT′ER, *n.* an idle talker. | PRAT′TLE, *n.* trifling talk.
PRAT′TLER, *n.* a chatterer.

Pof—a BOUNCE.

PUFF, *n.* a small blast of wind. | PUFF′ER, *n.* one who puffs.
PUFF, *v.* to swell with wind. | PUFF′Y, *a.* windy; tumid.

Ratelan—to RATTLE.

RAT′TLE, *v.* to make a sharp noise rapidly repeated. | RAT′TLING, *n.* a rapid succession of sharp sounds.

Reef—REEF.

REEF, *n.* a portion of a sail. | REEF, *v.* to reduce as a sail.

NOTE.—REEF, a chain of rocks, comes from the German (*riff*.)

Ras—to Go.

RACE, *n.* a contest in running. | RACE'COURSE, *n.* the ground on which races are run.

NOTE.—RACE, the lineage of a family, comes from the Latin (*radix.*)

Rot—ROUT.

ROUT, *n.* a clamorous multitude; a select company. | ROW, *n.* a riotous disturbance.
 | ROW'DY, *n.* a riotous fellow.

NOTE.—ROUT, to defeat and throw into confusion, comes from the Latin (*ruptum.*) ROUTE, (*rout*,) course traveled, road, way, etc., comes from the Latin (*rota*, a wheel.)

Schelden—to RAIL.

SCOLD, *v.* to find fault with rude clamor. | SCOLD'ING, *n.* clamorous, rude language.

Schop—SCOOP.

SCOOP, *n.* a large ladle. | SCOOP, *v.* to make hollow.

Krabbelen—to SCRAPE; to SCRATCH.

SCRAB'BLE, *v.* to scrape or scratch with the hands. | SCRAM'BLE, *v.* to catch at anything eagerly with the hands.
SCRAWL, *v.* to write clumsily. | SCRAW'LER, *n.* an inelegant writer.

Zweemen—to RESEMBLE.

SEEM, *v.* to appear; to present the appearance. | SEEM'INGLY, *ad* in appearance.
 | SEEM'LESS, *a.* indecorous.
SEEM'ING, *n.* appearance; show. | SEEM'LY, *a.* becoming decent.
BESEEM', *v.* to be come; to be fit.

Schyf, Ger. Scheiden—to DIVIDE; to SEPARATE.

SHIVE, *n.* a little piece; a splinter. | SHIV'ERING, *n.* the act of breaking into pieces.
SHIV'ER, *v.* to break into many small pieces. | SKIV'ER, *n.* a sheepskin split by a machine.

NOTE.—SHIVER, to shudder, as with cold or fear, comes from the German (*schauren.*)

Schuw—SHY.

SHY, *a.* reserved; cautious. | SHY'LY, *ad.* in a shy manner.
SHY'NESS, *n.* reserve; coyness.

Slabben—SLABBER.

SLAB'BER, *v.* to let saliva fall from the mouth. | SLAV'ER, *n.* spittle running from the mouth.

Slinder—SLENDER.

SLEN'DER, *a.* thin; slight. | SLEN'DERLY, *ad.* slightly; without bulk.
SLEN'DERNESS, *n.* thinness; slightness. |

DUTCH ROOTS AND DERIVATIVES.

Slecht—Bad; Mean; Worthless.

Slight, *a.* small; weak; trifling.
Slight, *n.* neglect; disregard.
Slight'er, *n.* one who disregards.

Slight'ingly, *ad.* without respect.
Slight'ly, *ad.* weakly; negligently.
Slight'ness, *n.* weakness.

Slof—Careless; Negligent.

Slov'en, *n.* one carelessly dressed. | Slov'enly, *a.* negligent of neatness.

Slordig—Sluttish; Bad.

Slur, *v.* to pass lightly. | Slur, *n.* slight reproach or disgrace.

Snappen, from Ger. *Schnebbe*—the Beak of a Bird.

Snap, *v.* to bite or catch suddenly.
Snap, *v.* to break suddenly.

Snap'per, *n.* one who snaps.
Snap'pish, *a.* eager to bite; peevish.

Note.—A bird *snaps* or seizes its prey with its beak.

Snoer—a String or Cord.

Snore, *n.* a string with which a boy spins his top.

Snare, *n.* anything which entraps.
Snarl, *n.* entanglement.

Note.—Snore, to breathe audibly through the nose in sleep, comes from the A.-S. (*snora*, a snoring.) Snarl, to growl, as a surly dog; to speak roughly, comes from the German (*schnarren*, to speak in the throat.)

Snuif—Snuff. *Snuiven*—to Snuff.

Snuff, *n.* the burnt part of a candle-wick; powdered tobacco.
Snuff'ers, *n.* a utensil for snuffing candles.
Snuf'fle, *v.* to speak through the nose.

Snuff'er, *n.* one who snuffs.
Sniff, *v.* to draw air audibly up the nose.
Sniv'el, *v.* to cry as children with snuffling; to run at the nose.
Sniv'eler, *n.* one who snivels.

Spang—Spang.

Spang, *n.* a shining ornament.
Span'gle, *n.* a small plate of shining metal.

Bespan'gle, *v.* to adorn with spangles.

Spar—a Rafter.

Spar, *n.* a general term for masts, booms, yards, etc.

Note.—Spar, a crystallized mineral, comes from the German (*spath*,) and Spar, to dispute, to box, comes from the A.-S. (*spirian*, to dispute.)

Spyt—Vexation.

Spite, *n.* malice; hate. | Spite'ful, *a.* filled with spite.

Splinter, splijten—to Split.

Split, *n.* a fragment split off. | Splin'ter, *n.* a thin piece split off.
Split, *v.* to divide lengthwise.

Boertig—MERRY; JOCULAR.

SPORT, *n.* play; diversion; mirth.
SPORT'FUL, *a.* merry; done in jest.
SPORT'FULLY, *ad.* in jest; in mirth.
SPORT'IVE, *a.* playful; frolicsome.

SPORT'LESS, *a.* joyless; sad.
SPORTS'MAN, *n.* one who pursues field sports.

Staggeren—to STAGGER.

STAG'GER, *v.* to move from side to side in walking.

STAG'GERING, *n.* the act of reeling.

Stampen—to STAMP.

STAMP, *v.* to stride downward with the foot; to impress with a mark.

STAMP, *n.* an instrument for making an impression.

Staen—to STAND.

STAY, *v.* to continue in a place; to prop; to support.
STAYS, *n.* a woman's waistcoat.

STAYED, *p. a.* propped; supported.
STAID, *a.* sober; grave; steady.
STAID'NESS, *a.* sobriety; gravity.

Stoep—a STEP.

STOOP, *n.* the steps before a door.

NOTE.—STOOP, to bend down, to lean forward, comes from the A.-S. (*stupian,* to stoop.)

Stoppen—to STOP.

STOP, *v.* to hinder; to obstruct.

STOP'PAGE, *n.* the act of stopping.

Stout—BOLD; STOUT.

STOUT, *a.* strong; lusty; brave.
STOUT'NESS, *n.* strength; boldness.

STOUT'LY, *ad.* lustily; boldly.

Streven—to STRIVE.

STRIVE, *v.* to make efforts.
STRIFE, *n.* contention; discord.

STRIFE'FUL, *a.* contentious.
STRIV'ING, *n.* contest; contention.

Stof—STUFF.

STUFF, *n.* any matter or body.
STUFF, *v.* to fill very full.
STUFF'ING, *n.* that by which any thing is filled.

STI'FLE, *v.* to stop the breath by crowding something into the windpipe.

Stomp—STUMP.

STUMP, *n.* the part which is left when the main body is taken away.

STUMP, *v.* to lop; to puzzle.
STUMP'Y, *a.* full of stumps.

Zwendelen—to SWINDLE.

SWIN'DLE, *n.* to cheat by false pretense.

SWIN'DLER, *n.* a cheat; a rogue.

Tintelen—to TINGLE.

TIN'GLE, *v.* to feel a kind of thrilling sound or pain.
TIN'GLING, *n.* a thrilling sound or pain.
TIN'KLE, *v.* to make a sharp, quick noise.
TINK'LING, *n.* a sharp, quick noise.
TINK'ER, *n.* one who mends old pans, etc.

Tip—TIP.

TIP, *n.* the end; the point. | TIP'TOE, *n.* the end of the toe.
TIP'TOP, *n.* the highest degree.

Tassen—to HEAP UP.

TOSS, *v.* to throw; to fling; to agitate. | TOSS'ING, *n.* violent commotion.

Tooijen—to ATTIRE; to ADORN.

TOY, *n.* a plaything; a bauble.
TOY, *v.* to play; to trifle.
TOY'MAN, *n.* one who deals in toys.
TOY'SHOP, *n.* a shop where toys are sold.

Treilen—to DRAW; to PULL.

TRAIL, *n.* a track left by anything that has passed along.
TRAIL, *v.* to draw along the ground.

Trappen—to TREAD.

TRAMP, *v.* to walk with a heavy tread.
TRAMP'ER, *n.* one who tramps.
TRAM'PLE, *v.* to tread under foot.

Trippelen—to TRIP.

TRIP, *v.* to strike from under the body. | TRIP, *v.* to run or step lightly.

Kwetteren—to TWITTER.

TWIT'TER, *v.* to make a succession of small tremulous noises.
TWIT'TER, *v.* to feel a tremulous motion of the nerves.

Wachten—to WATCH; to WAIT; to STAY.

WAIT, *v.* to stay in expectation; to remain. | WAIT'ER, *n.* one who waits.

Wals—a ROLLER; a CYLINDER.

WALTZ, *n.* a kind of whirling dance. | WALTZ, *v.* to dance a waltz.

Jagten—to HASTEN; to PURSUE EAGERLY.

YACHT, *n.* a small vessel for pleasure.

GERMAN ROOTS AND DERIVATIVES.

Bannen—to BANISH.

BAN′ISH, *v.* to compel to leave one's country. | BAN′ISHMENT, *n.* act of banishing.

Begehren—to DESIRE.

BEG, *v.* to ask for with humility.
BEG, *v.* to assume without proof.
BEG′GARY, *n.* great want. | BEG′GAR, *n.* one who begs.
BEG′GARLY, *ad.* meanly; poorly.

Boll—BOWL.

BOWL, *n.* a round mass or ball of wood.
BOWL, *v.* to roll as a bowl.
BOWL′ER, *n.* one who plays at bowls. | BOUL′DER, *n.* a large round stone.
BOWL′ING-GREEN, *n.* a level piece of ground for bowling.

NOTE.—BOWL, a vessel to hold liquids; the hollow part of anything; comes from the A.-S. (*bolla*, a round vessel.)

Brav—BOLD; HONEST.

BRAVE, *a.* courageous; valiant. | BRAVE′LY, *ad.* in a brave manner.
BRA′VERY, *n.* courage; heroism.

Klatschen—to CLAP.

CLASH, *v.* to strike against; to act in opposition. | CLASH′ING, *n.* opposition.

Dotteren—to TREMBLE; to TOTTER.

DOTE, *v.* to have the mind impaired by age or passion; to be over-fond. | DOT′AGE, *n.* silly fondness.
DO′TARD, *n.* one whose mind is impaired by age.

Dogge—DOG.

DOG, *n.* a domestic animal.
DOG, *v.* to follow in a sly manner.
DOG′GED, *a.* sullen; sour; morose.
DOG′GEREL, *n.* irregular kind of verse. | DOG′S-EARS, *n.* the corners of leaves of books folded down.
DOG′SLEEP, *n.* pretended sleep.
DOG′TROT, *n.* a gentle trot.

NOTE.—DOG prefixed to other words denotes meanness, degeneracy, or worthlessness.

Dut. Dan. and Sw. *Daler.* Ger. *Thaler,* so called from the Ger. *Thal*—a DALE, a VALLEY, WHERE THEY WERE FIRST COINED.

DOL′LAR, *n.* a coin of the United States; 100 cents.

Frech—Impudent; Bold.

FREAK, n. a sudden and causeless change of mind. | FREAK'ISH, a. capricious.

Fliessen—to Flow.

FLUSH, v. to redden suddenly.
FLUSH, a. fresh; full of vigor. | FLUS'TER, v. to make hot and rosy with confusion.
FLUS'TERED, a. heated and confused.

Futter—a Lining; Fur; Furring.

FUR, n. the finer hair on animals.
FUR'RY, a. consisting of fur.
FUR'RIER, n. a dealer in furs. | FUR'RING, n. strips of wood nailed to joists, etc., to bring them to an even surface for lathing and plastering.

Glanzen—to Glisten; to Shine.

GLANCE, v. to look with a rapid cast of the eye; to fly off obliquely. | GLANCE, n. a quick view.

Grollen—Growl.

GROWL, v. to snarl like an angry dog. | GROWL, n. a deep snarl or murmur.

Harsch—Harsh.

HARSH, a. rough to the touch, ear, or taste. | HARSH'LY, ad. in a harsh manner.
HARSH'NESS, n. roughness; severity.

Hast—Haste.

HASTE, n. hurry; speed.
HAST'EN, v. to make haste. | HAS'TY, a. quick; speedy.
HAST'ILY, ad. with haste.
HAS'TINGS, n. early peas; early fruit.

Herold—Herald.

HER'ALD, n. a proclaimer. | HER'ALDRY, n. the art of a herald.

Hucken—to Take on the Back.

HUCK'STER, n. a retailer; a pedlar. | HAWK, v. to offer for sale by crying in the streets.

Hummen—Hum.

HUM, v. to utter the sound of bees. | HUM'MING, n. the sound of bees.
HUM'-DRUM, a. dull; stupid.

Kind—a Child. Nap—to Steal.

KID'NAP, v. to steal a human being. | KID'NAPPER, n. a man stealer.

Latte—Lath.

LATH, n. a thin slip of wood. | LAT'TICE, n. a network of laths.

Lullen—to LULL.

LULL, *v.* to quiet; to become calm. | LUL'LABY, *n.* a song to lull asleep.

Nass—WET.

NAS'TY, *a.* disgustingly dirty. | NAS'TILY, *ad.* dirtily; filthily.
NAS'TINESS, *n.* dirt; filth.

Ode—SOLITARY.

ODD, *a.* not even; strange. | ODD'LY, *ad.* not evenly; strangely.
ODD'ITY, *n.* singularity. | ODD'NESS, *n.* strangeness.
ODDS, *n.* inequality; advantage.

Plump—RUDE; COARSE; CLUMSY

PLUMP, *a.* full; round; *v.* to fall heavily. | PLUMP'NESS, *n.* fullness; roundness.

Prangen—to SHINE; to MAKE A SHOW.

PRANK, *v.* to dress ostentatiously. | PRANCE, *v.* to spring; to bound.
PRANK, *n.* a frolic; a trick. | PRAN'CING, *n.* the act of bounding.

Punsch—PUNCH.

PUNCH, *n.* a drink composed of spirits, water and sugar. | PUNCH'BOWL, *n.* a bowl to hold punch.

NOTE.—PUNCH, to perforate by driving, comes from the Latin (*pungo,*) and PUNCH, the buffoon of a puppet show, from the Italian (*punchinello.*)

Quaken—to QUACK.

QUACK, *v.* to cry like a duck. | QUACK'ERY, *n.* false pretenses to skill.

Reiben—to RUB.

RUB, *v.* to move along the surface with pressure. | RUB'BER, *n.* one that rubs; a majority of three games.
RUB'BISH, *n.* anything worthless.

NOTE.—RUBBISH, that which comes off by rubbing.

Rummeln—RUMBLE.

RUM'BLE, *v.* to make a low, heavy continued noise. | RUM'BLING, *n.* a low continued noise.

Schirmen—to COVER; to PROTECT.

SCREEN, *n.* something that affords shelter or concealment. | SCREEN, *v.* to protect; to hide.

NOTE.—SCREEN, a kind of sieve, comes from the Latin (*excerno,* to separate,) through the French (*escran.*)

Schlich—TRICK; CUNNING.

SLEIGHT, *n.* an artful or adroit trick. | SLEIGHT'FUL, *a.* artful; cunning.

Sclave—SLAVE.

SLAVE, *n.* one held in bondage; a drudge.

SLAV'ERY, *n.* the state of being a slave.
SLAV'ISH, *a.* servile; mean.
SLAV'ISHNESS, *n.* servility; meanness.

NOTE.—SLAVE, in its present application, is from the SLAVI or SCLAVI, (*Slavonians*,) reduced to servitude by the Germans.

Storrig—STURDY.

STUR'DY, *a.* hardy; stout; strong. | STUR'DILY, *ad.* hardily; obstinately.
STUR'DINESS, *n.* hardiness; stoutness.

Wirbeln—to WHIRL.

WAB'BLE, *v.* to move from side to side.
WAR'BLE, *v.* to sing with vibrations of tone.
WAR'BLER, *n.* a singer.

Watte—WAD.

WAD, *n.* a mass of a loose substance pressed together.
WAD'DING, *n.* a soft stuff used for quilting.

Wisch—a WISP.

WHISK, *n.* a kind of brush or broom.
WHISK, *v.* to sweep with a light rapid motion.
WHISK'ER, *n.* hair growing on the cheek.
WHISK'ING, *a.* sweeping along lightly.

WELSH ROOTS AND DERIVATIVES.

Bicre—a CONFLICT; to PECK LIKE BIRDS.

BICK'ER, *v.* to keep up a noisy altercation.
BICK'ERING, *n.* a quarrel; a skirmish.

Bostio—to BOAST; to VAUNT.

BOAST, *v.* to brag; to exalt one's self. | BOAST'ER, *n.* one who boasts.
BOAST'FUL, *a.* given to boasting.

Boch—the CHEEK.

BOX, *n.* a blow on the head or ear, given by the hand.
BOX'ER, *n.* one who boxes.
BOX'ING, *n.* fighting with the fists.

NOTE.—BOX, an evergreen shrub whose wood is very useful, comes from the Greek, through the Latin (*buxus*, a box-tree,) and BOX, a case made of wood, from the A.-S. (*box*.)

Brol—BRAGGING.

BRAWL, n. a noisy quarrel. | BRAWL'ING, p. a. quarreling noisily.

Bonglera—to BUNGLE.

BUN'GLE, v. to perform clumsily. | BUN'GLER, n. a bad or clumsy workman.

Clog—a LARGE STONE.

CLOG, v. to load with so as to hinder motion. | CLOG'GING, n. an obstruction; a hinderance.
CLOG'GY, a. thick; adhesive.

Clwpa—a KNOB or LUMP.

CLUB, n. a heavy stick. | CLUB'FISTED, a. having a large fist.
CLUBBED, a. collected into one sum. | CLUB'FOOTED, a. having crooked feet.

NOTE.—CLUB, to combine for one purpose; to contribute to a common expense; comes from the A.-S. (cleofan, to divide.)

Darnio—to PIECE.

DARN, v. to mend a rent or hole. | DARN'ING, n. the act of mending holes.

Gwn—a CONTRACTION OF ENGINE.

GIN, n. any machine. | GUN'POWDER, n. the powder put in guns.
GUN, n. a general name for firearms. |
GUN'NER, n. one who manages guns. | GUN'SHOT, n. the distance a gun will shoot.
GUN'NERY, n. the art of managing artillery. | GUN'SMITH, n. one who makes guns.

NOTE.—GIN, a kind of ardent spirits distilled from rye and malted barley and flavored with juniper berries, comes from the Latin (juniperus, the juniper tree; junior, younger, and pario, to produce;—so called because it puts forth younger berries while the others are ripening.)—MINSHEU.

Hap—LUCK; CHANCE.

HAP, n. chance; fortune; accident. | HAPHAZ'ARD, n. chance; accident.
HAP'LESS, a. unhappy; unfortunate. | MISHAP', n. ill luck; misfortune.
HAP'LY, ad. perhaps; by chance. | PERHAPS, ad. it may be.
HAP'PEN, v. to come to pass. | UNHAP'PY, a. miserable; unfortunate.
HAP'PY, a. lucky; in a state of felicity. | UNHAP'PILY, ad. unfortunately.
HAP'PINESS, n. good fortune; felicity. | UNHAP'PINESS, n. misery; misfortune.

Hwt—HOOT.

HOOT, v. to shout in contempt. | HOOT'ING, n. shouting; clamor.

Cic—the FOOT.

KICK, v. to strike with the foot. | KICK'ER, n. one that kicks.

Llan—Land.

Lawn, *n.* a grassy plain.

Note.—Lawn, a sort of fine linen, comes from the Latin (*linum*.)

Leech—a Flat Stone.

League, *n.* a distance of three miles.

Note.—League, an alliance; a combination; comes from the Latin (*ligo.*)

Moel—Bald; Bare.

Moult, *v.* to shed or change the feathers. | Moult'ing, *n.* the act of changing feathers or hair.

Pert—Pert.

Pert, *a.* lively; saucy. | Pert'ly, *ad.* briskly; saucily.
Pert'ness, *n.* briskness; sauciness.

Syth—Stiffening; Glue.

Size, *v.* to cover with glutinous matter. | Size, *n.* a glutinous substance.

Note.—Size, bulk; magnitude; is an abbreviation of Assize, a court, or the sitting of a court, from Latin (*assideo*, to sit by or near,) formerly anything reduced to certainty in respect to time, number, quantity, etc.

Swyf—Sweet.

Su'et, *n.* hard fat. | Su'ety, *a.* resembling suet.

Tal—Tall.

Tall, *a.* high in stature; lofty. | Tall'ness, *n.* height of stature.

Twc—Tuck.

Tuck, *n.* a horizontal fold made in a garment to shorten it. | Tuck, *v.* to gather into a narrow compass.
Tuck'er, *n.* a small piece of linen over a woman's bosom.

Gwasg—Pressure; Squeeze.

Waist, *n.* the middle part of the body. | Waist'band, *n.* the band which encircles the waist.
Waist'coat, *n.* a coat over the waist.

Chwim—Quick Motion

Whim, *n.* a sudden turn or start of the mind. | Whim'sical, *a.* full of whims.

Gwingo—to Wriggle; to Twist.

Wince, *v.* to shrink; to start back. | Winch, *n.* a crank or handle to turn.

DANISH ROOTS AND DERIVATIVES.

Bark—BARK.

BARK, *n.* the rind or covering of a tree. | BARK, *v.* to strip off bark.

NOTE.—BARK, the noise of a dog, comes from the A.-S. (*beorcan,* to bark,) and BARK, a kind of ship, comes from the Dutch (*bark.*)

Plet—a BLOT.

BLOT, *v.* to spot; to stain; to blur. | BLOT, *n.* a spot or stain.
BLOTCH, *n.* a spot upon the skin.

Bolk—BULK.

BULK, *n.* size; magnitude. | BULK'Y, *a.* of great size.
BULK'HEAD, *n.* a partition across a ship.

Kaste—CAST.

CAST, *v.* to throw; to fling; to compute. | CAST, *n.* a throw; a mould.
| CAST'ER, *n.* one who casts.
CAST'AWAY, *n.* an abandoned person.

Dingle—DANGLE.

DAN'GLE, *v.* to hang loose and swinging in the air. | DAN'GLER, *n.* one who hangs about women only to waste time.

Duun—DOWN.

DOWN, *n.* the fine soft feathers of fowls. | DOWN'Y, *a.* covered with down; soft.

Dvaeler—to STAY.

DWELL, *v.* to live in a place. | DWELL'ER, *n.* one who lives in a place.
DWELL'ING, *n.* place of residence.

Myg—SOFT; PLIABLE.

MEEK, *a.* mild; soft; gentle. | MEEK'LY, *ad.* mildly; gently.
MEEK'NESS, *n.* mildness; gentleness.

Skaane—to SPARE.

SCANT, *v.* to limit; to stint. | SCANT'Y, *a.* small; not ample.
SCANT, *a.* not plentiful; scarce. | SCANT'ILY, *a.* sparingly.
SCANT'NESS, *n.* smallness. | SCANT'INESS, *n.* want of fullness.

Skrige—SCREAK.

SCREAK, *v.* to make a shrill, loud noise. | SCREECH, *v.* to cry out as in terror.

Sky—a Cloud.

Sky, *n.* the aerial region which surrounds the earth.
Sky′ish, *a.* like the sky.
Sky′lark, *n.* a bird which mounts and sings.
Sky′light, *n.* a window in a roof.

Trives—to Increase.

Thrive, *v.* to increase; to grow.
Thriv′ing, *n.* prosperity; growth.
Thrift, *n.* frugality; gain
Thrift′y, *a.* thriving by industry and frugality.

Vigre—a Twig. From *Viger*—to Yield.

Wick′er, *a.* made of twigs or osiers.
Wick′erwork, *n.* a texture of twigs or osiers.

GOTHIC ROOTS AND DERIVATIVES.

Kuef—a Catarrh. *Kof*—Suffocation.

Cough, *n.* a convulsion of the lungs.
Cough′er, *n.* one who coughs.

Greitan—to Cry.

Cry, *v.* to utter a loud noise.
Cry′ing, *n.* clamor.

Daddjan—to Milk.

Dai′ry, *n.* a place where milk is kept.
Dai′rymaid, *n.* a female servant in a dairy.

Thinsan—to Dance.

Dance, *v.* to move with regulated steps.
Dan′cing, *n.* act of moving with regulated steps.

Gruds—Loath.

Grudge, *v.* to grant with reluctance.
Begrudge, *v.* to envy the possession of.

Giutan—to Pour Out.

Gush, *v.* to flow or rush out with violence.
Gust, *n.* a sudden violent blast, as of wind.

Note.—Gust, taste; relish; comes from the Latin (*gustus*.)

***Hurra*—to Drive; to Move Violently.**

Hurl, *v.* to throw with violence.
Hur'ly-bur'ly, *n.* tumult; *a.* tumultuous.
Hur'ry, *v.* to hasten; to drive.
Hur'ry-skur'ry, *ad.* confusedly.

***Mes*—a Table.**

Mess, *n.* a portion of food.
Mess'mate, *n.* one who eats at the same table.

***Klander*—Infamy.**

Slan'der, *n.* false censure.
Slan'derer, *n* one who slanders.
Slan'derous, *a.* uttering false reproach.

SWEDISH ROOTS AND DERIVATIVES.

***Krok, kroka*—to Curve; to Bend.**

Crook, *n.* a bend; a curvature.
Crook, *v.* to bend; to curve.
Crook'ed, *a.* bent; not straight.

***Daska*—to Strike.**

Dash, *v.* to strike or throw violently.
Dash, *n.* anything that comes with sudden violence.

***Drabba*—to Hit.**

Drub, *v.* to beat; to thrash.
Drub'bing, *n.* a beating.

***Myra*—Marshy Ground.**

Mire, *n.* soft, wet earth; mud.
Mi'ry, *a.* full of mire.

***Slinta*—to Slip.**

Slant, *a.* sloping; inclined from a direct line.
Slant'ing, *p. a.* inclining from a right line.

***Vir*—Wire.**

Wire, *n.* a metallic thread.

GAELIC ROOTS AND DERIVATIVES.

Apran—APRON.
A'PRON, *n.* a cloth to keep the dress clean.

Bog—BOG.
BOG, *n.* a soft, marshy place covered with grass. | BOG'GY, *a.* marshy; swampy.

Bran—BRAN.
BRAN, *n.* the husks of wheat or other grain.

Brisg—BRISK.
BRISK, *a.* lively; active. | BRISK'LY, *ad.* actively.
BRISK'NESS, *n.* liveliness.

Brisgear—GRISTLE.
BRIS'KET, *n.* the breast of an animal.

Craos—a WIDE MOUTH; REVELRY.
CAROUSE', *v.* to drink freely and with jollity. | CAROU'SAL, *n.* a noisy drinking bout.
CAROUS'ER, *n.* one who carouses.

Clann—CLAN.
CLAN, *n.* a family; a race; a tribe. | CLAN'NISH, *a.* disposed to unite in clans.

Craig—CRAG.
CRAG, *n.* a rough, steep rock. | CRAG'GY, *a.* rugged; rocky; rough.

Dud—a RAG.
DUDS, *n.* old worn clothes. | DOW'DY, *n.* an awkward, ill-dressed woman.

ITALIAN ROOTS AND DERIVATIVES.

Bozza—a BUNCH.

BOTCH, *n.* a work ill finished. | BOTCH, *n.* a clumsy workman.

Brezza—BREEZE.

BREEZE, *n.* a gentle gale. | BREEZE'LESS, *a.* without a breeze.

Broccata—BROCADE.

BROCADE', *n.* embroidered silk. | BROCAD'ED, *a.* woven as brocade.

Buffone, buffo—COMIC.

BUFFOON', *n.* a low jester. | BUFFOON'ERY, *n.* low jests.

Ruffiano—a PIMP.

RUFF'IAN, *n.* a brutal fellow. | RUFF'IANLY, *a.* brutal; violent.

Salvia, from L. *Salvo*—to SAVE.

SAGE, *n.* a plant.

NOTE.—SAGE, wise; prudent; comes from the Latin (*sagus.*)

Scarso—SCARCE.

SCARCE, *a.* not plentiful; rare. | SCARCE'LY, *ad.* hardly; with diffi-
SCARC'ITY, *n.* want of plenty. | culty.
SCARCE'NESS, *n.* want of plenty.

Scorare—to DISHEARTEN.

SCARE, *v.* to terrify suddenly. | SCARE'CROW, *n.* an image to frighten birds.

Scherno—SCORN.

SCORN, *v.* to despise; to disdain. | SCORN'ER, *n.* one who scorns.
SCORN, *n.* extreme contempt. | SCORN'FUL, *a.* disdainful.
SCORN'ING, *ppr.* treating with contempt.

LATIN ROOTS AND DERIVATIVES.

PRONUNCIATION.

LATIN words are usually pronounced in this country, in accordance with the general principles of English pronunciation. It is important, however, to bear in mind:

1st. That every vowel or diphthong in a Latin word must be enunciated; *i. e.*, every word has as many syllables as there are vowels or diphthongs in it. Thus, *miles* is pronounced *mi-les; mare, mar-e*.

2d. Words of two syllables have the accent always on the first syllable; as, *a'cer, a'go, ar'bor*.

3d. When a word of more than one syllable ends with *a*, that letter is sounded as *a* in *ah*.

4th. That the diphthongs æ and œ are sounded as simple *e* would be in the same place; thus, *fæ'dus*, fe'dus; *pœ'na*, pe'na; *œm'ulus*, em'ulus.

5th. That *ch* is always sounded like *k*.

6th. That *c* and *g* are hard before *a, o,* and *u*, and soft before *e, i*, and *y*, thus, in the words *ca'lo, co'lo* and *cu'ra*, the *c* has the sound of *k;* in *ce'do* and *ci'vis* it has the sound of *s*. So *g*, in the words *li'go, lon'gus* and *gut'ta*, has the sound of *g* in *go;* in the words *ge'ro, gig'no*, it has the sound of *j*.

Ac'idus—SOUR.

ACID'ITY, *n.* sourness; tartness. | ACID'ULATE, *v.* to make slightly sour.

Ac'ris—SHARP; SOUR.

AC'RID, *a.* biting to the taste. | AC'RIMONY, *n.* ill nature.

A'cu-o, acu't-um—to SHARPEN.

ACU'MEN, *n.* sharpness of intellect. | ACUTE', *a.* sharp; pointed.

A'go, ac'tum—to DO; to PERFORM; to DRIVE.

ACT, *v.* to do; to perform.
AC'TION, *n.* a performance.
AGIL'ITY, *n.* quickness of motion.
AG'ILE, *a.* moving easily.
AC'TUATE, *v.* to put in action.
A'GENT, *n.* a person acting for another.
AG'ITATE, *v.* to put in motion.
CO'GENT, *a.* forcible; powerful.
COG'ITATE, *v.* to think.

ENACT', *v.* to perform; to decree.
EXACT', *v.* to take by force.
EXACT', *a.* accurate; strict.
EX'IGENCY, *n.* pressing necessity.
PROD'IGAL, *a.* driving forth recklessly.
TRANSACT', *v.* to perform through.
NAVIGATE, *v.* to drive a ship to sail.
REACT', *v.* to act back.

Ag'ger—a Heap; a Mound.

Exag'gerate, v. to enlarge beyond the truth.

A'ger, a'gri—a Field.

Agra'rian, a. relating to lands.

Ag'riculture, n. the cultivation of fields.

A'lius—Other; Another.

A'lien, n. a foreigner.
A'lias, ad. otherwise.

A'lienate, v. to transfer to another.
Aliena'tion, n. estrangement.

A'lo, ali'tum—to Feed; to Nourish.

Al'iment, n. food.
Al'imony, n. the allowance to a divorced woman.

Al'moner, n. one who distributes alms.
Alms, n. gifts to the poor.
Coalesce, v. to grow together.

Coali'tion, n. union; league.

Alter'nus—by Turns; One After the Other.

Alter'nate, v. to do by turns.

Alter'native, n. a choice of two things.

Al'tus—High; Lofty.

Al'titude, n. height; elevation.

Exalt', v. to raise up.

Am'bulo—to Walk; to Pace.

Am'ble, v. to pace, as a horse.

Peram'bulate, v. to walk through.

A'mo—to Love. Ami'cus—a Friend.

Am'atory, a. relating to love.
Amateur', n. a lover of the fine arts.
A'miable, a. worthy of love.
Am'orous, a. affected by love.
Am'icable, a. friendly.

Am'ity, n. friendship.
En'mity, n. hatred.
En'emy, n. a foe.
Inim'ical, a. unfriendly; opposed.
Amour', n. a love affair.

Am'plus—Large; Extensive; Plentiful.

Am'ple, a. large; full; wide.
Am'ply, ad. largely.

Am'plify, v. to enlarge.
Amplifica'tion, n. enlargement.

Am'plitude, n. largeness.

An'glia—England. An'glicus—English.

An'glican, a. of England; English.
An'glo-Amer'ican, n. an American of English descent.

An'glo-Da'nish, a. belonging to the English Danes.
An'glo-Sax'on, a. belonging to the English Saxons.

An'go, anx'i—to Vex.

An'guish, n. intense pain.
An'ger, n. wrath; rage.

Anxi'ety, n. solicitude.
Anx'ious, a. troubled in mind.

LATIN ROOTS AND DERIVATIVES. 233

An'gulus—a CORNER; an ANGLE.

AN'GLE, n. a corner.
AN'GULAR, a. having corners.
MULTAN'GULAR, a. many cornered.
PENTAN'GULAR, a. five cornered.
QUAD'RANGLE, n. a square.

RECT'ANGLE, n. a right angled four-sided figure.
SEPTAN'GULAR, a. having seven corners.
EQUIAN'GULAR, a. having equal angles.

TRI'ANGLE, n. a three cornered figure.

An'imus—MIND; COURAGE.   An'ima—WIND; BREATH; LIFE.

AN'IMAL, n. a living creature.
ANIMAL'CULE, n. a minute animal.
AN'IMATE, v. to make alive.
ANIMADVERT', v. to pass censure.
INAN'IMATE, a. lifeless.
ANIMA'TION, n. liveliness.
ANIMOS'ITY, n. violent hatred.

UNANIM'ITY, n. agreement.
UNAN'IMOUS, a. of one mind.
EQUANIM'ITY, n. evenness of mind.
MAGNANIM'ITY, n. greatness of mind.
MAGNAN'IMOUS, a. brave; noble.
PUSILLANIM'ITY, n. cowardice.
REAN'IMATE, v. to restore to life.

An'nus—a CIRCLE; a YEAR.

AN'NALS, n. yearly records.
ANNIVER'SARY, n. a stated day coming once in every year.
AN'NUAL, a. yearly.
ANNU'ITY, n. a yearly allowance.
BIEN'NIAL, a. in every two years.
MILLEN'NIUM, n. a thousand years.

CENTEN'NIAL, a. in every hundred years.
OCTEN'NIAL, a. in every eighth year.
PEREN'NIAL, a. perpetual.
SEPTEN'NIAL, a. in every seven years.
TRIEN'NIAL, a. in every third year.
SUPERAN'NUATE, v. to impair by age.

Anti'quus—OLD or ANCIENT.

AN'TIQUARY, n. one who studies ancient things.
ANTIQUA'RIAN, a. relating to antiquity.

AN'TIQUATE, v. to make obsolete.
ANTIQUE', a. ancient.
ANTIQ'UITY, n. old times.
AN'CIENT, a. old.

AN'TIC, a. odd; fanciful.

Ape'rio, aper'tum—to OPEN.

APE'RIENT, a. gently purgative. | AP'ERTURE, n. an opening; a hole.

Ap'tus—FIT; MEET.

ADAPT', v. to fit; to adjust.
APT, a. fit; ready.
AP'TITUDE, n. tendency.

APT'NESS, n. quickness of apprehension.

A'qua—WATER.

AQUAT'IC, a. pertaining to water.
A'QUEDUCT, n. a channel for water.
A'QUEOUS, a. watery.

TERRA'QUEOUS, a. composed of land and water.

Ar'biter—an UMPIRE or JUDGE.

AR'BITRATE, v. to decide.
ARBITRA'TION, n. determination by an arbitrator.

AR'BITRATOR, n. a decider; an umpire.
AR'BITRARY, a. despotic.

Ar′bor—a Tree.

Ar′bor, *n.* a bower.	Ar′borary, *a.* belonging to trees.

Ar′ceo—to Keep; to Drive; to Restrain.

Coerce, *v.* to restrain by force.	Coer′cion, *n.* restraint.

Arc′us—a Bow.

Arch, *n.* a curved structure.	Arch′er, *n.* he that shoots with a bow.

Ar′deo, ar′sum—to Burn.

Ar′dent, *a.* hot; passionate.	Ar′dor, *n.* passion; zeal.
Ar′dency, *n.* eagerness; heat.	Ar′son, *n.* the crime of house burning.

Ar′guo—to Argue.

Ar′gue, *v.* to reason; to dispute.	Ar′gument, *n.* a reason offered.

Ar′ma—Arms; Weapons.

Arm, *v.* to furnish with arms.	Ar′mistice, *n.* a cessation of hostilities.
Arms, *n.* weapons.	Ar′mory, *n.* a place for arms.
Arma′da, *n.* a fleet of war.	Ar′my, *n.* a number of armed men.
Ar′mament, *n.* a naval warlike force.	Disarm′, *v.* to deprive of weapons.
Ar′mor, *n.* defensive arms.	

Ars, ar′tis—Art; Skill; Trick.

Art, *n.* skill; cunning; trade.	Ar′tifice, *n.* trick; fraud.
Art′ist, *n.* a professor of an art.	Art′ful, *a.* cunning.
Art′isan, *n.* a workman.	Art′less, *a.* unskillful; without fraud.
Artifi′cial, *a.* made by art; not genuine.	Inert′, *a.* dull; motionless.

Ar′tus—a Joint. *Artic′ulus*—a Little Joint.

Ar′ticle, *n.* a single thing.	Artic′ulate, *v.* to speak distinctly.
Artic′ular, *a.* belonging to the joints.	Artic′ulate, *a.* distinct; jointed.
	Inartic′ulate, *a.* not distinct.

As′per—Rough; Harsh; Severe.

Asper′ity, *n.* roughness.	Exas′perate, *v.* to enrage.

At′rox, atro′cis—Cruel; Fierce.

Atro′cious, *a.* extremely wicked.	Atroc′ity, *n.* great wickedness.

Au′dio, audi′tum—to Hear; to Listen; to Obey.

Au′dible, *a.* that can be heard.	Au′ditory, *n.* an assembly of hearers.
Au′dience, *n.* the persons assembled to hear.	Obey′, *v.* to comply with commands.
Au′dit, *v.* to examine an account.	Obe′dience, *n.* submission.
Au′ditor, *n.* a hearer.	Obe′dient, *a.* obeying.
	Disobey′, *v.* to break commands.
Inau′dible, *a.* not to be heard.	

LATIN ROOTS AND DERIVATIVES.

Au′deo—to DARE. Au′dax—VERY DARING.

AUDA′CIOUS, *a.* bold and impudent. | AUDAC′ITY, *n.* effrontery.

Au′geo, auc′tum—to INCREASE.

AUGMENT′, *v.* to increase.
AUC′TION, *n.* a sale to the highest bidder.
AU′THOR, *n.* an originator.
AU′THORIZE, *v.* to give authority.
AUTHOR′ITY, *n.* legal power.
AUXIL′IARY, *a.* helping.

Augur—a SOOTHSAYER.

AU′GUR, *v.* to foretell; to predict.
INAU′GURATE, *v.* to lead into office with suitable ceremonies.
AU′GURY, *n.* prediction by omens.
AUSPIC′IOUS, *a.* favorable.
INAUSPI′CIOUS, *a.* unfortunate.

Bac′chus—in heathen mythology, the GOD OF WINE.

BACCHANA′LIAN, *a.* pertaining to drunken revelry.
DEBAUCH′, *v.* to corrupt; to ruin.
DEBAUCHEE′, *n.* a rake; a drunkard.
DEBAUCH′ERY, *n.* intemperance.

Bar′barus—RUDE; SAVAGE; CRUEL.

BAR′BAROUS, *a.* rude; uncivilized.
BARBA′RIAN, *n.* a savage.
BARBAR′IC, *a.* foreign; rude.
BAR′BARISM, *n.* inhumanity.
BARBAR′ITY, *n.* brutality.

Bea′tus—HAPPY; BLESSED.

BEAT′IFY, *v.* to make happy. | BEAT′ITUDE, *n.* blessedness.

Bel′lum—WAR.

BELLIG′ERENT, *a.* waging war. | REB′EL, *n.* one who revolts.
REBEL′LION, *n.* insurrection.

Be′ne—GOOD; WELL.

BENEDIC′TION, *n.* a blessing.
BENEFAC′TION, *n.* a blessing conferred.
BENEFAC′TOR, *n.* he who confers a benefit.
BENEF′ICENT, *a.* kind; doing good.
BENEFI′CIAL, *a.* advantageous.
BENEV′OLENCE, *n.* good will; charity.
BEN′EFIT, *n.* advantage.

Benig′nus—KIND; LIBERAL.

BENIGN,′ *a.* kind; generous. | BENIG′NITY, *n.* actual kindness.

Bi′bo—to DRINK.

BIB′BER, *n.* a tippler. | BIB′ULOUS, *a.* absorbing.
IMBIBE′, *v.* to drink in.

Blandus—GENTLE; WINNING.

BLAND, *a.* gentle; mild.
BLAND′ISH, *v.* to smooth; to soften.
BLAN′DISHMENT, *n.* winning words or actions.

Bis—Twice. *Bi'ni*—Two by Two.

Bi'furcated, *a.* having two prongs.
Big'amy, *n.* having two wives at once.
Bi'nary, *a.* composed of two.
Bi'ped, *n.* an animal with two feet.
Bisect', *v.* to cut into two equal parts.
Combine', *v.* to join or unite.
Bien'nial, *a.* in every two years.
Bis'cuit, *n.* a kind of bread, (twice baked.)

Bre'vis—Short; Brief.

Brief, *a.* short; concise.
Brev'ity, *n.* shortness.
Brev'iary, *n.* an abridgement.
Abbre'viate, *v.* to shorten.
Abridge', *v.* to shorten.

Bru'tus—Brute; Senseless.

Bru'tal, *a.* unfeeling.
Bru'tish, *a.* like a brute.

Ca'do, ca'sum—to Fall; to Happen.

Ca'dence, *n.* the fall of the voice.
Deca'dence, *n.* fall; decay.
Case, *n.* condition; state.
Cas'ual, *a.* accidental.
Cas'ualty, *n.* accident.
Ac'cident, *n.* that which happens unforeseen.
Cascade', *n.* waterfall.
Coincide', *v.* to agree.
Coin'cidence, *n.* concurrence.
Decay', *v.* to rot; to fall away.
Decid'uous, *a.* falling; dying.
In'cident, *n.* an event.
Occa'sion, *v.* to cause.
Oc'cident, *n.* the west.

Cœ'do, cœ'sum—to Cut; to Kill.

Incis'ion, *n.* a cut into any thing.
Excis'ion, *n.* a cutting out.
Excise, *n.* a tax on goods.
Concise', *a.* short; brief.
Decide', *v.* to determine.
Decis'ion, *n.* determination.
Deci'sive, *a.* conclusive; final.
Precise', *a.* exact; strict.
Precis'ion, *n.* exactness.
Frat'ricide, *n.* the murder of a brother.
Hom'icide, *n.* a manslayer.
Infan'ticide, *n.* the murder of an infant.
Par'ricide, *n.* the murder of a parent.
Su'icide, *n.* self-murder.
Reg'icide, *n.* the murder of a king.

Cal'culus—a Small Stone; a Pebble.

Cal'culate, *v.* to compute.
Cal'culus, *n.* a disease.

Ca'leo—to be Warm or Hot. *Ca'lor*—Heat.

Calefac'tion, *n.* the act of heating.
Cal'dron, *n.* a pot; a boiler.
Calor'ic, *n.* the element of heat.
Calorif'ic, *a.* making hot.
Incales'cence, *n.* warmth.
Scald, *v.* to burn with a hot fluid.

Camp'us—a Plain; a Tented Field.

Camp, *n.* the ground on which an army pitches its tents.
Campaign', *n.* a military year.
Decamp, *v.* to change a camp; to move off.
Encamp', *v.* to pitch tents.

Calum'nia—CALUMNY.

CAL'UMNY, n. false accusation.
CALUM'NIATE, v. to accuse falsely.
CALUM'NIOUS, a. slanderous.

Can'deo—to GLOW WITH HEAT; to be BRIGHT or WHITE.

CAN'DOR, n. frankness; sincerity.
CAN'DID, a. fair; open.
CAN'DIDATE, n. one proposed for office.
CAN'DLE, n. a light made of tallow.
INCEN'DIARY, n. one who sets on fire.
EXCANDES'CENCE, n. white heat.
CHANDELIER', n. a branch for candles.
IN'CENSE, n. perfume burnt.
INCENSE', v. to enrage; to provoke.
INCEN'TIVE, n. a motive; inducement.

Ca'no, can'tum—to SING; to SOUND.

CHANT, n. a kind of sacred music.
CAN'TICLE, n. a song.
CAN'TO, n. a section of a poem.
CANT, n. affected manner of speech.
DESCANT', v. to discourse.
AC'CENT, n. a stress of voice.
ENCHANT', v. to delight highly.
INCANTA'TION, n. the act of enchanting by singing.
RECANT', v. to recall; to retract.

Ca'pio, cap'tum—to TAKE; to TAKE INTO THE MIND.

ACCEPT', v. to take; to receive.
ACCEPT'ABLE, a. pleasing.
ANTIC'IPATE, v. to take beforehand.
CA'PABLE, a. able to do or take.
CAPA'CIOUS, a. wide; large.
CAPAC'ITATE, v. to qualify.
CAPAC'ITY, n. power of holding.
CAP'TIOUS, a. peevish; caviling.
CAP'TIVATE, v. to take prisoner; to charm.
CAP'TIVE, n. a prisoner.
CAP'TOR, n. he who takes prisoners.
CAP'TURE, n. a seizure.
CONCEIT', n. fancy; opinion.
CONCEIVE', v. to think.
CONCEP'TION, n. notion; idea.
DECEIVE', v. to cheat; to mislead.
DECEIT', n. a fraud; a cheat.
DECEP'TION, n. act of deceiving.
EMAN'CIPATE, v. to set at liberty.
EXCEPT, v. to leave out.
INCIP'IENT, a. commencing.
INTERCEPT', v. to stop on the way.
MISCONCEP'TION, n. a false opinion.
OCCUPA'TION, n. employment.
OC'CUPY, v. to possess.
PARTIC'IPATE, v. to share.
PERCEIVE', v. to notice; to see.
PRE'CEPT, n. a rule given.
PRIN'CIPAL, a. chief; capital.
PRIN'CIPLE, n. cause; motive.
RECEIVE', v. to take; to admit.
RECEIPT', n. acknowledgment for money paid.
RECEP'TACLE, n. that which receives or contains.
RECEP'TION, n. a receiving.
REC'IPE, n. a medical prescription.
RECIP'IENT, n. one who receives.
SUSCEP'TIBLE, a. sensitive.

Cap'ut, cap'itis—the HEAD; LIFE.

CAP, n. a covering for the head.
CAP'ITAL, a. chief; principal.
CAPITA'TION, n. counting by heads.
CAPIT'ULATE, v. to surrender by treaty.
CAPE, n. a headland.
CAP'TAIN, n. a chief commander.
CHAP'TER, n. a division or head.
DECAP'ITATE, v. to behead.
PRE'CIPICE, n. a headlong steep.
PRECIP'ITANCE, n. headlong hurry.
PRECIP'ITATE, v. to tumble headlong.
PRECIP'ITATE, a. headstrong; hasty.
PRECIP'ITATE, n. a sediment.
RECAPIT'ULATE, v. to repeat.
CHIEF'TAIN, n. a headman.
OC'CIPUT, n. the hinder part of the head.

Car'bo, carbo'nis— a Coal.

Car'bon, n. the essential ingredient of coal.
Carbon'ic, a. containing carbon.
Car'buncle, n. a little coal; a gem; a tumor.

Ca'ro, car'nis—Flesh.

Car'nage, n. slaughter.
Car'nal, a. fleshly; lustful.
Carniv'orous, a. feeding on flesh.
Incar'nate, a. clothed with flesh.
Car'nival, n. a feast before Lent.
Car'rion, n. putrid flesh.
Car'cass, n. a dead body.
Carnel'ian, n. a red stone.
Carna'tion, n. the natural flesh color.

Cas'tus—Chaste; Pure; Correct.

Chaste, a. pure; uncorrupt.
Chas'tity, n. purity.

Cav'us—Hollow.

Cav'ern, n. a deep, hollow place.
Cav'ity, n. a hollow place.
Con'cave, a. hollow.
Ex'cavate, v. to hollow out.

Cau'sa—a Cause; a Reason.

Cause, n. that which produces an effect.
Accuse', v. to charge with a crime.
Excuse', v. to pardon.
Because', con. for the reason that.

Ca'veo, cau'tum—to Beware; to Take Care.

Cau'tion, n. prudence in respect to danger.
Ca'veat, n. a warning.
Incau'tious, a. heedless.
Precau'tion, n. previous care.

Ce'do, ces'sum—to Yield; to Go Away.

Cede, v. to yield or give up.
Ces'sion, n. the act of yielding.
Cease, v. to stop; to leave off.
Cessa'tion, n. a stop.
Accede', v. to assent to.
Access', n. approach.
Acces'sion, n. an increase.
An'cestor, n. a forefather.
An'cestry, n. a series of ancestors.
Antece'dent, a. going before.
Concede', v. to yield; to grant.
Conces'sion, n. the act of granting.
Decease', n. death.
Exceed', v. to go beyond.
Excess', n. more than enough.
Inces'sant, a. without pause.
Intercede', v. to go between.
Precede', v. to go before.
Prec'edent, n. an example.
Proceed', v. to go forward.
Recede', v. to go back.
Proc'ess, n. a method.
Proces'sion, n. a ceremonious march.
Recess', n. a place of retreat.
Secede', v. to withdraw from.
Seces'sion, n. a withdrawing from.
Succeed', v. to follow; to prosper.
Success', n. fortune; prosperity.
Succes'sive, a. following in order.

Cel'la—a Cell; a Small, Close Room.

Cell, n. a small, close room.
Cel'lar, n. a room under a house.
Cel'lular, a. having little cells.

Cel'ebris—Renowned; Famous.

Cel'ebrate, v. to praise; to extol. | Celeb'rity, n. fame; renown.

Ce'ler—Swift.

Celeb'ity, n. swiftness; speed. | Accel'erate, v. to hasten.

Cel'sus—High; Lifted Up.

Excel', v. to outdo; to surpass. | Ex'cellent, a. surpassing.

Ce'lo—to Cover; to Hide.

Conceal', v. to hide. | Conceal'ment, n. the act of hiding.

Cen'seo—to Think; to Judge; to Blame.

Cen'sor, n. one who judges. | Cen'sus, n. a numbering of the people.
Cen'sure, n. blame; reproach. |
Censo'rious, a. apt to censure.

Cen'trum—the Center.

Cen'ter, n. the middle point of any thing. | Concen'tric, a. having the same center.
Cen'tral, a. relating to the center. | Concen'trate, v. to bring together.
Eccen'tric, a. going from the center.

Cen'tum—a Hundred.

Cent, n. the one-hundredth part of a dollar. | Cen'tiped, n. an insect with many feet.
Cen'tury, n. a hundred years. | Centu'rion, n. an officer over a hundred men.
Centen'nial, a. occurring every hundred years. |

Ce'ra—Wax.

Cere, v. to cover with wax. | Sincere', a. pure; true.
Ce'rate, n. an ointment of wax, etc. | Sincer'ity, n. honesty; purity.

Cer'no, cre'tum—to Sift; to Distinguish; to Decree.

Concern', v. to affect or disturb. | Discrim'inate, v. to distinguish.
Decree', v. to ordain or command. | Discrimina'tion, n. distinction.
Discern', v. to see; to distinguish. | Indiscrim'inate, a. not making any distinction.
Discern'ment, n. judgment. |
Discreet', a. discerning; prudent. | Se'cret, a. hidden; private.
Discre'tion, n. prudence. | Secrete', v. to hide or conceal.
Sec'retary, n. one who writes for another.

Note.—Secretary, so called from the secret affairs entrusted to him.

Cer'to—to Contend; to Strive.

Concert', v. to contrive together. | Disconcert', v. to disturb.
Con'cert, n. a musical entertainment. | Preconcert'ed, a. contrived beforehand.

Cer′tus—Certain; Sure.

Cer′tain, *a.* sure; undoubted.	Certif′icate, *n.* a testimony in writing.
Ascertain′, *v.* to make certain.	
Cer′tify, *v.* to assure.	Uncer′tain, *a.* doubtful.

Cho′rus—a Dance Accompanied with Song.

Choir, *n.* a band of singers.	Cho′ral, *a.* belonging to a choir.
Cho′rus, *n.* a number of singers.	Chor′ister, *n.* a leader of a choir.

Cin′go, cinc′tum—to Gird; to Surround.

Pre′cinct, *n.* a district.	Succinct′, *a.* short; compact.

Cir′cus—a Circle. *Cir′culus*—a Little Circle.

Cir′cle, *n.* a ring; a round space.	Cir′cuit, *n.* extent round about.
Cir′clet, *n.* a little circle.	Circu′itous, *a.* not direct.
Cir′cular, *a.* round, like a circle.	Cir′cus, *n.* an open space for sports.
Cir′culate, *v.* to move in a circle.	Encir′cle, *v.* to surround.

Ci′to—to Call or Summon; to Stir Up.

Cite, *v.* to summon; to quote.	Incite′ment, *n.* impulse.
Excite′, *v.* to stir up.	Recite′, *v.* to repeat; to tell over.
Excite′ment, *n.* agitation.	Recita′tion, *n.* a telling over of something learned.
Incite′, *v.* to urge on.	

Resus′citate, *v.* to bring back to life.

Ci′vis—a Citizen.

Civ′ic, *a.* relating to a city.	Unciv′il, *a.* impolite; rude.
Civ′il, *a.* gentle; well bred.	Civ′ilize, *v.* to reclaim from a savage state.
Cit′y, *n.* a large corporate town.	
Cit′izen, *n.* an inhabitant of a city.	Civil′ity, *n.* politeness.

Cla′mo, clama′tum—to Cry Out; to Shout.

Clam′or, *n.* outcry; noise.	Disclaim′, *v.* to disown; to deny.
Clam′orous, *a.* noisy.	Exclaim′, *v.* to cry out.
Claim, *v.* to demand.	Proclaim′, *v.* to publish.
Claim′ant, *n.* one that demands.	Reclaim′, *v.* to recall; to reform.

Cla′rus—Clear; Bright.

Clear, *a.* bright; evident.	Clar′ion, *n.* a shrill trumpet.
Clar′ify, *v.* to purify.	Declare′, *v.* to make known.

Clau′do, clau′sum—to Shut; to Close; to Finish.

Clause, *n.* a part of a sentence.	Exclude′, *v.* to shut out.
Close, *v.* to shut.	Seclude′, *v.* to shut apart.
Clos′et, *n.* a small private room.	Preclude′, *v.* to shut before.
Conclude′, *v.* to finish.	Include′, *v.* to shut in.
Disclose′, *v.* to reveal; to tell.	Seclu′sion, *n.* retirement.
Enclose′, *v.* to shut in.	Recluse′, *n.* a solitary person.

Cle′mens, clemen′tis—MILD; MERCIFUL.

CLEM′ENT, *a.* merciful; kind.
INCLEM′ENT, *a.* severe; rough.
CLEM′ENCY, *n.* mercy.
INCLEM′ENCY, *n.* severity.

Cli′no—to BEND; to LEAN.

INCLINE′, *v.* to bend; to lean.
DECLINE′, to lean downwards.
RECLINE′, *v.* to lean back.

Co′lo, cul′tum—to TILL; to CULTIVATE.

COL′ONY, *n.* a settlement in a new country.
CUL′TIVATE, *v.* to improve by labor.
CUL′TURE, *n.* cultivation.
AG′RICULTURE, *n.* cultivation of the ground.
HOR′TICULTURE, *n.* gardening.

Co′mes, com′itis—a COMPANION.

COM′ITY, *n.* kindness of manner.
CONCOM′ITANT, *a.* going with.
COUNT, *n.* the companion of a king.
COUN′TY, *n.* a district under a count.

Concil′io, concilia′tum—to UNITE; to MAKE FRIENDS.

REC′ONCILE, *v.* to make friends again.
CONCIL′IATE, *v.* to win to friendship.

Cop′ula—SOMETHING THAT JOINS TOGETHER.

COUP′LE, *n.* two things together.
COUP′LET, *n.* two verses.

Co′quo, coc′tum—to BOIL; to COOK; to DIGEST.

CONCOCT′, *v.* to prepare by digesting.
COOK, *v.* to prepare food by heat.
DECOC′TION, *n.* a liquor in which something has been boiled.

Cor, cor′dis—the HEART, MIND, or COURAGE.

CORE, *n.* the heart or central part.
COR′DIAL, *a.* warm; hearty.
COR′DIAL, *n.* any thing that gladdens the heart.
CON′CORD, *n.* agreement.
COUR′AGE, *n.* the state of having heart; bravery.
DIS′CORD, *n.* disagreement.
RECORD′, *v.* to register.
ENCOUR′AGE, *v.* to animate.
DISCOUR′AGE, *v.* to depress; to deter.

Co′rium—a SKIN or HIDE.

CUR′RIER, *n.* one who dresses hides.
EXCO′RIATE, *v.* to take off the skin.

Cor′pus, cor′poris—a BODY.

COR′PORAL, *n.* an army officer.
COR′PORAL, *a.* relating to the body.
CORPO′REAL, *a.* having a body.
COR′PORATE, *a.* united into a body.
COR′PULENT, *a.* having a bulky body.
CORPS, *n.* a body of soldiers.
CORPSE, *n.* a dead body.

Cras—TO-MORROW.

PROCRAS′TINATE, *v.* to put off.
PROCRAS′TINATION, *n.* deferring.

Cre'do, cred'itum—to Trust; to Believe.

Creed, n. articles of belief.
Cre'dence, n. belief; credit.
Cred'it, n. belief; trust.
Cred'ible, a. worthy of belief.
Cred'itor, n. a truster.
Cred'ulous, a. apt to believe.
Discred'it, v. to disbelieve.
Incred'ible, a. not to be believed.
Credu'lity, n. easiness of belief.

Cre'o, crea'tum—to Create.

Create', v. to cause to exist.
Crea'ture, n. a thing created.
Rec'reant, a. cowardly; false.
Recrea'tion, n. amusement.

Cres'co, cre'tum—to Grow; to Increase.

Cres'cent, n. the increasing or new moon.
Decrease', v. to grow less.
Increase', v. to grow larger.
Recruit', v. to repair; to supply.

Cri'men, crim'inis—an Accusation; a Crime.

Crime, n. a great fault.
Crim'inal, a. guilty of a crime.
Recrim'inate, v. to retort a charge.

Cru'dus—Raw; Unripe. Crude'lis—Unfeeling; Cruel.

Crude, a. raw; unripe.
Crude'ness, n. unripeness.
Cru'el, a. unfeeling.
Cru'elty, n. inhumanity.

Crus'ta—a Crust; the Tough Shell of a Lobster.

Crust, n. an outer coat; a case.
Incrust', v. to cover with a crust.

Cu'bo, or cum'bo—to Lie Down.

Cum'ber, v. to burden; to hinder.
Encum'ber, v. to burden.
Incum'bent, a. resting upon.
Recum'bent, a. leaning.
Cub, n. the young of a beast.
Succumb', v. to sink under a difficulty.

Cul'pa—a Fault; Blame.

Cul'pable, a. worthy to be blamed.
Cul'prit, n. an accused person.
Excul'pate, v. to clear from blame.
Incul'pate, v. to put into blame.

Cu'mulus—a Heap.

Accu'mulate, v. to heap up.
Cu'mulative, a. heaping up.

Cu'ra—Care. Cu'ro—to Take Care Of; to Heat.

Cure, v. to restore to health.
Cu'rable, a. that may be cured.
Cu'rate, n. a parish priest.
Cu'racy, n. the office of a curate.
Care, n. anxiety.
Cu'rious, a. prying; inquisitive.
Ac'curate, a. exact; correct.
Ac'curacy, n. exactness.
Secure', a. free from care; safe.
Secu'rity, n. safety.
In'secure, a. not safe.
Procure', v. to obtain.
Prox'y, n. a substitute.
Si'necure, n. an office of profit without employment.

LATIN ROOTS AND DERIVATIVES.

Cur'ro, cur'sum—to RUN; to PASS SWIFTLY.

CUR'RENT, *n.* a running stream.
CUR'SORY, *a.* hasty; slight.
CAREER', *n.* a course; a race.
COU'RIER, *n.* a messenger sent in haste.
COURSE, *n.* career; progress.
CONCUR', *v.* to agree.
CON'COURSE, *n.* a gathering.
DISCOURSE', *n.* conversation.
EXCUR'SION, *n.* a ramble.
INCUR', *v.* to become liable to.
INCUR'SION, *n.* inroad; invasion.
OCCUR', *v.* to happen.
OCCUR'RENCE, *n.* an event.
RECUR', *v.* to happen again; to return.
PRECUR'SOR, *n.* a forerunner.
RECOURSE', *n.* a running to something for protection or aid.
SUC'COR, *v.* to help; to relieve.

Cur'vus—BENT; WINDING.

CURVE, *n.* a bent line.
CURV'ATURE, *n.* crookedness.
CURVILIN'EAR, *a.* composed of curved lines.

Cu'tis—the SKIN.

CU'TICLE, *n.* the thin outer skin.
CUTA'NEOUS, *a.* affecting the skin.

Dam'num—LOSS; HURT; DAMAGE.

DAM'AGE, *n.* loss; injury.
CONDEMN', *v.* to give sentence against.
INDEM'NIFY, *v.* to relieve from loss.
INDEM'NITY, *n.* security from loss.

Deb'ilis—WEAK.

DEBIL'ITY, *n.* weakness; languor.
DEBIL'ITATE, *v.* to weaken.

Deb'eo, deb'itum—to OWE.

DEBT, *n.* that which is due.
DEB'IT, *v.* to charge with debt.
DEBT'OR, *n.* one who is in debt.
DEBENT'URE, *n.* a writing acknowledging a debt.
DUE, *a.* that ought to be paid.
DU'TY, *n.* that which one ought to do.

De'cet—to be BECOMING or PROPER.

DE'CENT, *a.* becoming; fit.
DE'CENCY, *n.* propriety of manner.
DECO'RUM, *n.* propriety.
DEC'ORATE, *v.* to adorn.
DECO'ROUS, *a.* observing propriety.
INDECO'RUM, *n.* impropriety.

Deli'ciæ—PLEASURES; DELIGHT; NICENESS.

DELI'CIOUS, *a.* pleasant to the taste.
DELEC'TABLE, *a.* delightful.
DEL'ICATE, *a.* nice; fine; soft.
DELIGHT', *n.* pleasure; joy.

Den'sus—THICK; CLOSE.

CONDENSE', *v.* to thicken.
DENSE, *a.* close; thick.

Dens, den'tis—a TOOTH.

DEN'TAL, *a.* pertaining to the teeth.
DEN'TIST, *n.* a tooth doctor.
DEN'TIFRICE, *n.* tooth powder.
INDENT', *v.* to impress, as with teeth.
INDENTA'TION, *n.* a notch.
TRI'DENT, *n.* Neptune's scepter.

***De'us*—God.   *Di'vus*—a God.**

DE'IST, *n.* one who believes in God but denies revelation.
DE'ITY, *n.* the Divine Being.
DIVIN'ITY, *n.* the nature of God.
DIVINE', *a.* godlike; heavenly.
DIVINE', *v.* to predict.
DIVINA'TION, *n.* foretelling.

***Dex'ter*—Right-handed; Ready; Expert.**

DEX'TEROUS, *a.* expert; ready. | DEXTER'ITY, *n.* readiness.

***Di'co, dicta'tum*—to Devote; to Set or Put Apart.**

DED'ICATE, *v.* to devote.
AB'DICATE, *v.* to give up right.
IN'DICATE, *v.* to point out.
PRED'ICATE, *v.* to show before the people.

***Di'co, dic'tum*—to Say; to Speak; to Tell.**

DIC'TION, *n.* language; style.
DIC'TIONARY, *n.* a word book.
DIC'TATE, *v.* to give commands.
ADDICT', *v.* to devote to.
BENEDIC'TION, *n.* a blessing.
E'DICT, *n.* a proclamation.
INDICT', *v.* to accuse in writing.
INTERDICT', *v.* to prohibit.
INDITE', *v.* to put into words.
MALEDIC'TION, *n.* a curse.
PREDICT', *v.* to foretell.
VER'DICT, *n.* the decision of a jury.

***Di'es*—a Day.**

DI'ARY, *n.* a daily account.
DI'AL, *n.* a plate upon which are marked the hours of the day.
DIUR'NAL, *a.* daily.
MERID'IAN, *n.* midday or noon.
DIS'MAL, *a.* sad; gloomy.

***Dig'nus*—Worthy; Deserving.**

DIG'NITY, *n.* true honor.
DIG'NIFY, *v.* to make worthy.
DEIGN, *v.* to condescend.
CONDIGN', *a.* suitable; merited.
INDIG'NANT, *a.* angry and disgusted.
INDIG'NITY, *n.* unworthy treatment.
DISDAIN', *v.* to despise; to scorn.
INDIGNA'TION, *n.* anger with contempt.

***Dis'co*—to Learn.**

DISCI'PLE, *n.* a follower. | DIS'CIPLINE, *n.* instruction.

***Div'ido*—to Divide.**

DIVIDE', *v.* to separate into parts.
DIVIS'ION, *n.* a dividing.
DIVIS'OR, *n.* the number to divide by.
INDIVID'UAL, *n.* a single being.
DIV'IDEND, *n.* the number divided; a share.
DIVIS'IBLE, *a.* that may be divided.

NOTE.—A single person is indivisible.

***Do, da'tum*—to Give; to Put or Place.**

ADD, *v.* to put to; to join to.
ADDI'TION, *n.* the act of adding.
CONDI'TION, *n.* quality; state.
DATE, *n.* a point of time.
ED'IT, *v.* to give forth; to publish.
PERDI'TION, *n.* destruction.
REN'DER, *v.* to give back.
SURREN'DER, *v.* to give up.

Do'ceo, doc'tum—to TEACH.

DOC'TOR, *n.* a teacher.
DOC'UMENT, *n.* a paper containing evidence.
DOC'TRINE, *n.* that which is taught.
DOC'ILE, *a.* easily taught.
DOCIL'ITY, *n.* aptness to be taught.

Do'leo—to GRIEVE.

DOLE'FUL, *a.* sorrowful.
DO'LOROUS, *a.* full of grief.
CONDOLE', *v.* to lament with others.
IN'DOLENCE, *n.* laziness.

Dom'inus—MASTER; LORD.

DOMIN'ION, *n.* supreme power; territory.
DOMINA'TION, *n.* arbitrary power.
DOM'INANT, *a.* ruling.
DOMAIN', *n.* empire; estate.
DOMINEER', *v.* to rule with insolence.
PREDOM'INATE, *v.* to prevail over the rest.

Do'mus—a HOUSE.

DOME, *n.* a house; a spherical roof.
DOMES'TICATE, *v.* to tame.
DOMES'TIC, *a.* belonging to the house or family.
DOM'ICIL, *n.* a mansion or abode.

Do'num—a GIFT. *Do'no, dona'tum*—to GIVE; to PRESENT.

DO'NOR, *n.* a giver.
DONA'TION, *n.* a gift.
DON'ATIVE, *a.* giving.
DONEE', *n.* one who receives a gift.

Dor'mio, dormi'tum—to SLEEP.

DOR'MANT, *a.* sleeping.
DOR'MITORY, *n.* a place to sleep in.

Dor'sum—the BACK.

DOR'SAL, *a.* relating to the back.
ENDORSE', *v.* to write on the back.

Du'bito—to HESITATE TO BELIEVE.

DOUBT, *v.* to hesitate to believe.
DOUBT, *n.* uncertainty of mind.
DU'BIOUS, *a.* doubtful.

Du'co, duc'tum—to LEAD; to BRING; to CARRY.

DUCT, *n.* a little channel.
ADDUCE', *v.* to bring forward.
A'QUEDUCT, *n.* a tube for conveying water.
CONDUCT', *v.* to lead or guide.
CON'DUCT, *n.* behavior.
CONDUCE', *v.* to lead or tend.
CON'DUIT, *n.* a water pipe.
DEDUCE', *v.* to draw from.
DEDUCT', *v.* to substract.
DUKE, *n.* a leader; a noble.
EDUCE', *v.* to bring out.
ED'UCATE, *v.* to bring up; to instruct.
INDUCE', *v.* to lead by motives.
INDUCE'MENT, *n.* a motive.
INDUCT', *v.* to bring in.
INDUC'TION, *n.* a leading in.
INTRODUCE', *v.* to usher in.
PRODUCE', *v.* to bring forth.
PRODUC'TIVE, *a.* capable of producing.
PROD'UCT, *n.* a thing produced.
REDUCE', *v.* to bring down.
SEDUCE', *v.* to entice; to corrupt.
SEDUC'TIVE, *a.* fitted to entice.
TRADUCE', *v.* to calumniate.

Duo—Two.

Du′al, *a.* relating to two.
Du′el, *n.* a combat between two.
Duet′, *n.* a piece of music.
Doub′le, *a.* consisting of two.
Dupli′cate, *a.* double; twofold.
Duplic′ity, *n.* double; dealing.

Du′rus—Hard; Solid.

Du′rable, *a.* lasting.
Du′rance, *n.* imprisonment.
Dura′tion, *n.* continuance.
Du′ring, *prep.* as long as.
Endure′, *v.* to bear.
Ob′durate, *a.* stubborn.

E′brius—Drunken.

Ebri′ety, *n.* drunkenness.
Inе′briate, *n.* a drunkard.
Sobri′ety, *n.* soberness.

Æ′des, œ′dis—a House or Building.

Ed′ifice, *n.* a building.
Ed′ify, *v.* to instruct; to improve.

E′go—I.

E′gotism, *n.* talking much of one's self.
E′gotist, *n.* one who talks much of himself.

E′mo, emp′tum—to Buy.

Exempt′, *a.* not liable.
Exempt′, *v.* to free from.
Exemp′tion, *n.* freedom from.
Per′emptory, *a.* absolute.
Prompt, *a.* ready; quick.
Pre-emp′tion, *n.* a right of buying before others.
Redeem′, *v.* to buy back; to rescue.
Redemp′tion, *n.* deliverance; rescue.

Ens, en′tis—Being. Es′se—To Be.

Ab′sent, *a.* not present.
Es′sence, *n.* the best part.
In′terest, *v.* to concern.
Pres′ent, *a.* within sight; near.

E′o, i′tum—to Go or Pass.

Ambi′tion, *n.* desire of honor.
Cir′cuit, *n.* extent round about.
Ex′it, *n.* a departure.
Per′ish, *v.* to die; to decay.
Pret′erite, *a.* past; gone by.
Sedi′tion, *n.* a going aside.
Tran′sient, *a.* passing quickly.
Tran′sit, *n.* a passing over.
Transi′tion, *n.* change from one condition to another.

E′quus, for Æ′quus—Even; Equal; Just.

E′qual, *a.* of the same size or importance.
E′qualize, *v.* to make equal.
E′quable, *a.* not varying.
Coe′qual, *a.* of the same rank.
Ad′equate, *a.* equal to.
Equanim′ity, *n.* evenness of mind.
Equa′tion, *n.* making equal.
Equilib′rium, *n.* equal weight.
E′quinox, *n.* the time of equal day and night.
Eq′uity, *n.* justice.
Iniq′uity, *n.* injustice.
Equiv′alent, *a.* equal in value.
Equiv′ocal, *a.* ambiguous.
Equiv′ocate, *v.* to use words of doubtful meaning.

E′quus—a Horse.

Eques′trian, *a.* pertaining to horsemanship.
E′query, *n.* a stable for horses.
Equip′, *v.* to furnish; to dress.

Er′ro, erra′tum—to Wander; to Err.

Err, *v.* to mistake.
Er′ror, *n.* a mistake.
Err′ing, *a.* irregular; vicious.
Erro′neous, *a.* wrong; incorrect.

Æ′stimo—to Value.

Es′timate, *v.* to compute the value.
Estima′tion, *n.* computation.
Es′timable, *a.* worthy of esteem.
Es′teem, *n.* high regard.

Æ′vum—Life; Time.

Coe′val, *a.* of the same age.
Longev′ity, *n.* length of life.
Prime′val, *a.* of the first age.

Exem′plum—an Example; a Copy.

Exam′ple, *n.* model; pattern.
Exem′plar, *n.* a model; a copy.
Ex′emplary, *a.* worthy of imitation.
Exem′plify, *v.* to show by example.
Sam′ple, *n.* specimen.
Sam′pler, *n.* a pattern of needlework.

Ex′terus—Outward; Foreign; Strange.

Exte′rior, *n.* the outside.
Exter′nal, *a.* relating to the outside.
Extra′neous, *a.* not belonging to the subject.
Extreme′, *a.* utmost; last.
Extrem′ity, *n.* the utmost point.
Extrin′sic, *a.* outward; external.
Strange, *a.* foreign; unusual.

Fab′rico, fabrica′tum—to Make; to Frame.

Fab′ric, *n.* something made.
Fab′ricate, *v.* to make or form.

Fab′ula—a Feigned Story.

Fa′ble, *n.* a feigned story.
Fab′ulous, *a.* fictitious.

Fa′cies—the Face.

Face, *n.* the surface of a thing.
Deface′, *v.* to disfigure.
Efface′, *v.* to blot out.
Sur′face, *n.* the outside.
Fea′ture, *n.* cast of the face.
Fash′ion, *n.* form; custom.
Superfi′cial, *a.* lying on the outside; shallow.

Fac′ilis—Easy to Do.

Fac′ile, *a.* easily led; yielding.
Facil′ity, *n.* easiness.
Facil′itate, *v.* to make easy.
Dif′ficult, *a.* hard to be done.

Fal′lo, fal′sum—to Deceive.

False, *a.* not true.
Fal′sity, *n.* an untruth.
Fal′lacy, *n.* a deceitful argument.
Falla′cious, *a.* fitted to deceive.
Fal′lible, *a.* liable to error.
Fal′sify, *v.* to make false.

Fa'cio, fac'tum—to MAKE; to DO; to ACT.

FACT, *n.* a thing done; a reality.
AFFECT', *v.* to act upon.
AFFEC'TION, *n.* love; kindness.
AFFECTA'TION, *n.* assumed feeling.
COUN'TERFEIT, *n.* a forgery.
DEFEAT', *v.* to undo; to overthrow.
DEFEC'TION, *n.* desertion.
DEFECT', *n.* a fault; a blemish.
DEFI'CIENT, *a.* faulty; wanting.
EFFECT', *v.* to bring to pass; to do.
EFFI'CIENT, *a.* active; able.
EFFECT'UAL, *a.* producing decisive effect.
EFFEC'TIVE, *a.* producing effect.
INFECT', *v.* to taint with disease.
INFEC'TION, *n.* a tainting.
PER'FECT, *a.* complete; pure.
PROFI'CIENCY, *n.* a making forwards.
PROFI'CIENT, *n.* one advanced in any pursuit.
REFEC'TION, *n.* refreshment after fatigue.
REFEC'TORY, *n.* an eating room.
SUFFICE', *v.* to make enough.
SUFFI'CIENT, *a.* making enough.
SUR'FEIT, *v.* to feed to excess.

Fa'ma—FAME; RENOWN; REPUTATION.

FAME, *n.* celebrity; renown.
FA'MOUS, *a.* full of renown.
DEFAME', *v.* to slander.
DEFAMA'TION, *n.* calumny.
IN'FAMY, *n.* utter disgrace.
IN'FAMOUS, *a.* openly censured.

Fa'mes—HUNGER; SCARCITY OF FOOD.

FAM'INE, *n.* scarcity of food.
FAM'ISH, *v.* to starve.

Famil'ia—a FAMILY.

FAM'ILY, *n.* the persons living in a house.
FAMIL'IAR, *a.* affable; well known.

Fa'num—a TEMPLE; a HOLY PLACE.

FANE, *n.* a temple.
FANAT'IC, *n.* an enthusiast.
PROFANE', *v.* to pollute.
PROFANE', *a.* irreverent; common.

Fe'lix, feli'cis—HAPPY.

FELIC'ITY, *n.* happiness.
FELIC'ITOUS, *a.* happy; fortunate.
FELIC'ITATE, *v.* to congratulate.
INFELIC'ITY, *n.* misfortune.

Fe'ra—a WILD BEAST.

FERO'CIOUS, *a.* cruel; savage.
FIERCE, *a.* savage; furious.

Fe'ro, la'tum—to BEAR; to CARRY; to BRING.

FER'TILE, *a.* bearing plentifully.
CIRCUM'FERENCE, *n.* a carrying round.
CONFER', *v.* to consult.
COLLATE', *v.* to bring together.
DEFER', *v.* to put off.
DEF'ERENCE, *n.* regard; respect.
DIF'FER, *v.* to be unlike.
DIL'ATORY, *a.* tardy; slow.
INFER', *v.* to draw a conclusion.
IN'FERENCE, *n.* a conclusion.
OF'FER, *v.* to present for acceptance.
PREFER', *v.* to like better.
PROF'FER, *v.* to offer.
REFER', *v.* to give to another for decision.
RELATE', *v.* to tell; to pertain to.
SUF'FER, *v.* to bear; to allow.
TRANSFER', to convey; to remove.

Fen'do, fen'sum—to STRIKE; to WARD.

FEND, v. to ward off.
FENCE, n. a security.
DEFEND', v. to protect.

DEFENCE', n. guard; security.
OFFEND', v. to displease.
OFFENCE', n. crime; injury.

Fer'veo—to be HOT; to BOIL.

FER'VOR, n. heat; zeal.

FER'VENT, a. hot; ardent.

Fes'tum—a FEAST.

FES'TAL, a. belonging to a feast.
FES'TIVE, a. joyful; gay.
FEAST, n. a sumptuous entertainment.

FES'TIVAL, n. a time of feasting.
FESTIV'ITY, n. joyfulness.

Fi'des—FAITH; TRUST.

FIDEL'ITY, n. faithfulness.
CONFIDE', v. to trust in.
CON'FIDENCE, n. trust; boldness.
DEFY', v. to challenge; to dare.

DIF'FIDENT, a. distrusting one's self.
IN'FIDEL, n. an unbeliever.
PER'FIDY, n. treachery.
AFFI'ANCE, v. to pledge faith to.

Fi'go, fix'um—to FIX or FASTEN; to PIERCE.

FIX, v. to make fast.
FIX'TURE, n. anything fixed to a place or house.
TRANSFIX', v. to pierce through.

AFFIX', v. to join to.
PREFIX', v. to put before.
SUFFIX', v. to add to the end.

Fi'nis—the END; BORDER; LIMIT.

FIN'ISH, v. to complete; to end.
FI'NITE, a. having an end.
IN'FINITE, a. unlimited.
DEFINE', v. to limit; to explain.
DEF'INITE, a. certain; limited.

FI'NAL, a. last; conclusive.
CONFINE', v. to shut up; to limit.
INDEF'INITE, a. not limited.
REFINE', v. to improve; to polish.
SUPERFINE', a. eminently fine.

Fir'mus—STRONG.

FIRM, a. hard; strong.
AFFIRM', v. to declare positively.

CONFIRM', v. to establish.
INFIRM', a. weak; feeble.

Fis'cus—a BAG or BASKET.

FIS'CAL, a. pertaining to the public treasury.

CONFIS'CATE, v. to seize as a forfeit.

Fla'gro—to BURN; to BE IN FLAMES.

FLA'GRANT, a. burning; notorious.

CONFLAGRA'TION, n. an extensive fire.

Flam'ma—a FLAME; a FIRE.

FLAME, n. a burning vapor.
INFLAME', v. to set on fire.

FLAM'BEAU, n. a kind of torch.
INFLAM'MABLE, a. easily set on fire.

Fla'tus—a BLAST; a PUFF OF WIND.

FLAT'ULENT, *a.* windy; vain. | INFLATE', *v.* to puff up.

Flec'to, flex'um—to BEND; to TURN.

CIR'CUMFLEX, *a.* moving round.
FLEX'IBLE, *a.* ductile; pliant.
DEFLEC'TION, *n.* turning from the true course.
INFLEX'IBLE, *a.* not to be bent.
REFLECT', *v.* to cast back; to think.
INFLECT', *v.* to bend.
INFLEC'TION, *n.* a bending inward.

Fli'go, flic'tum—to BEAT; to DASH.

AFFLICT', *v.* to pain; to grieve.
AFFLIC'TION, *n.* calamity.
CON'FLICT, *n.* contest; struggle.
INFLICT', *v.* to beat in or on.

Flos, flo'ris—a FLOWER.

FLO'RA, *n.* the goddess of flowers.
FLO'RAL, *a.* relating to flowers.
FLOR'IST, *n.* a cultivator of flowers.
FLOR'ID, *a.* flushed with red.
FLOW'ER, *n.* a blossom.
FLOW'ER, *v.* to blossom.
FLOUR'ISH, *v.* to thrive; to grow.

Flu'o, flux'um—to FLOW.

FLUX, *n.* the act of moving, as a fluid.
FLUID, *n.* anything that flows.
FLU'ENT, *a.* flowing; voluble.
FLU'ENCY, *n.* readiness of speech.
EF'FLUX, *n.* a flowing out.
AF'FLUENCE, *n.* riches; plenty.
CON'FLUENCE, *n.* a flowing together.
IN'FLUX, *n.* a flowing in.
RE'FLUX, *n.* backward course.
IN'FLUENCE, *n.* power.
INFLUEN'TIAL, *a.* exerting power.
SUPER'FLUOUS, *a.* overflowing.
SUPERFLU'ITY, *n.* more than enough
FLUC'TUATE, *v.* to move as waves.
FLUCTUA'TION, *n.* wavering.

Fo'cus—a HEARTH; a FIRE-PLACE.

FO'CUS, *n.* the place of fire. | FO'CAL, *a.* belonging to the focus.

NOTE.—The place of heat when a burning glass is held in the sun.

Fo'lium—a LEAF; a SHEET, (as of paper.)

FOIL, *n.* a thin leaf of metal.
FO'LIAGE, *n.* a growth of leaves.
FO'LIO, *n.* a large book.
PORTFO'LIO, *n.* a case for loose leaves.

For'ma—a FORM; BEAUTY.

FORM, *n.* shape; figure.
FORM'AL, *a.* ceremonious.
FORMAL'ITY, *n.* ceremony.
CONFORM', *v.* to make like; to comply with.
DEFORM', *v.* to disfigure.
INFORM', *v.* to instruct.
PERFORM', *v.* to do or act.
PERFORM'ANCE, *n.* action; work.
REFORM', *v.* to grow better.
TRANSFORM', *v.* to change.
U'NIFORM, *a.* even; regular.

Fors, for'tis—CHANCE; LUCK.

FOR'TUNE, *n.* chance; wealth.
FOR'TUNATE, *a.* successful.
UNFOR'TUNATE, *a.* unlucky.
MISFOR'TUNE, *n.* calamity.
FORTU'ITOUS, *a.* accidental.

For'tis—BRAVE; STRONG.

FOR'TITUDE, *n.* courage; bravery.
FOR'TIFY, *v.* to strengthen.
FOR'TRESS, *n.* a fortified place.
FORCE, *n.* strength.

FORCE, *v.* to compel.
COM'FORT, *v.* to cheer.
EF'FORT, *n.* exertion.
ENFORCE', *v.* to put in execution.

Fran'go, frac'tum—to BREAK.

FRAC'TION, *n.* a broken part.
FRAC'TURE, *n.* a breaking.
FRAG'MENT, *n.* a broken part.
FRAG'ILE, *a.* easily broken.

FRAIL, *a.* easily broken.
FRAIL'TY, *n.* weakness.
INFRAC'TION, *n.* a violation.
INFRINGE', *v.* to break in upon.

Fra'ter, fra'tris—a BROTHER.

FRATER'NAL, *a.* brotherly.

FRAT'RICIDE, *n.* the murder of a brother.

Fraus, frau'dis—DECEIT; CHEAT.

FRAUD, *n.* deceit.
DEFRAUD', *v.* to cheat.

FRAUD'ULENT, *a.* deceitful.
FRAU'DULENCE, *n.* deceitfulness.

Fri'gus, fri'goris—COLD.

FRIG'ID, *a.* cold.
FRIGID'ITY, *n.* coldness.

REFRIG'ERATE, *v.* to cool.
REFRIG'ERATOR, *n.* a cooler.

Frons, fron'tis—the FOREHEAD; the FACE.

FRONT, *n.* the face; the forepart.
AFFRONT', *v.* to offend.

CONFRONT', *v.* to meet face to face.
EFFRONT'ERY, *n.* impudence.

Fru'or, fru'itus—to ENJOY.

FRUI'TION, *n.* enjoyment.
FRUIT, *n.* the produce of a tree or plant.

FRUC'TIFY, *v.* to make fruitful.

Fu'gio, fu'gitum—to FLY or FLEE.

FU'GITIVE, *a.* running away.
SUB'TERFUGE, *n.* an evasion.
REF'UGE, *n.* shelter.

REFUGEE', *n.* one who flies for protection.
VER'MIFUGE, *n.* a worm medicine.

Fu'mus—SMOKE; FUME.

FUME, *n.* smoke; vapor.
FU'MIGATE, *v.* to smoke.

FU'MING, *a.* raging; smoking.
PERFUME', *v.* to scent.

Fun'do, fu'sum—to POUR OUT; to MELT.

FUSE, *v.* to melt.
FU'SION, *n.* the act of melting.
FU'SIBLE, *a.* that may be melted.
CONFOUND', *v.* to mingle.
CONFUSE', *v.* to confound; to mix.
DIFFUSE', *v.* to spread.
EFFU'SION, *n.* a pouring out.

INFUSE', *v.* to pour in.
PROFUSE', *a.* lavish.
PROFU'SION, *n.* abundance.
REFUND', *v.* to pour back.
SUFFUSE', *v.* to spread over.
REFUSE', *v.* to deny; to decline.
REFU'SAL, *n.* a denial.

Fun'dus—a Bottom or Basis.

FOUND, v. to lay the basis of.
FOUN'DERY, n. a casting house.
FOUNDA'TION, n. basis.

FUNDAMEN'TAL, a. lying at the base.
PROFOUND', a. deep; thorough.
PROFUND'ITY, n. depth.

Fu'ria—Madness.

FU'RIOUS, a. mad; raging.
FU'RY, n. rage; frenzy.
INFU'RIATE, v. to make furious.

Ge'lu—Frost; Ice.

CONGEAL', v. to freeze.
CONGELA'TION, n. a freezing.
GEL'ID, a. extremely cold.
GELAT'INOUS, a. like gelatine.

GEL'ATINE, n. an animal substance resembling jelly.
JEL'LY, n. a kind of sweetmeat.

Ge'nus, gen'eris—Birth; Family; Race.

CON'GENIAL, a. agreeing in temper and tastes.
DEGEN'ERATE, v. to grow worse.
ENGEN'DER, v. to produce.
GEN'DER, n. kind; sex.
GEN'ERAL, a. public; extensive.
GEN'ERATE, v. to beget; to produce.
GEN'EROUS, a. noble; liberal.
GENEROS'ITY, n. liberality.
GE'NIAL, a. causing production.
GE'NIUS, n. mental power.

GENTEEL', a. elegant in manners.
GENTIL'ITY, n. dignity of birth.
GEN'TILE, n. a pagan.
GEN'TLE, a. soft; mild; tame.
GEN'UINE, a. pure; real.
INGE'NIOUS, a. witty; skillful.
INGEN'UOUS, a. open; frank.
INGENU'ITY, n. wit; acuteness.
PROGEN'ITOR, n. a forefather.
PROG'ENY, n. offspring; race.
REGEN'ERATE, v. to renew.

Ge'ro, ges'tum—to Bear; to Carry.

GES'TURE, n. action.
GESTIC'ULATE, v. to use gestures.
DIGEST', v. to arrange; to dissolve.
SUGGEST', v. to hint.

CONGES'TION, n. a carrying together.
INDIGES'TION, n. want of power to digest food.

Glo'ria—Glory; Honor.

GLO'RIFY, v. to give glory to.
GLO'RY, n. praise; renown.
INGLO'RIOUS, a. shameful.

Gra'dior, gres'sus—to Go Step by Step.

GRADE, n. rank; degree.
GRAD'UAL, a. advancing by steps.
GRADA'TION, n. regular progress.
GRAD'UATE, v. to mark degrees.
DEGREE', n. a step; a rank.
DEGRADE', v. to put in a lower rank.
DEGRADA'TION, n. a low condition.
DIGRESS', v. to turn aside.
TRANSGRESS', v. to violate.

E'GRESS, n. a going out.
IN'GRESS, n. entrance.
CON'GRESS, n. a coming together.
AGGRES'SION, n. an attack.
DIGRES'SION, n. a deviation.
PROGRESS', v. to advance.
PROGRES'SIVE, a. advancing.
RET'ROGRADE, a. going backward.

Glu'tio—to Gulp Down.

Glut, *v.* to overfill; to stuff.
Deglutition, *n.* the act of swallowing.
Glut'ton, *n.* an excessive eater.

Gran'dis—Great; Grand.

Grand, *a.* great; high in power.
Grandee', *n.* a man of high rank.
Grand'eur, *n.* state; splendor.
Ag'grandize, *v.* to make great.

Gra'num—a Grain of Corn.

Grain, *n.* a seed of corn.
Gran'ary, *n.* a storehouse for grain.
Gran'ite, *n.* grain stone.
Gran'ule, *n.* a small grain.
Gran'ulate, *v.* to form into grains.
Gran'ular, *a.* consisting of grains.

Gra'tus—Pleasing; Thankful.

Grate'ful, *a.* thankful; pleasing.
Grat'itude, *n.* thankfulness.
In'grate, *a.* unthankful.
In'grate, *n.* an ungrateful person.
Grat'is, *ad.* for nothing.
Gratu'itous, *a.* given without reward.
Gratu'ity, *n.* a free gift.
Grat'ify, *v.* to indulge; to please.
Congrat'ulate, *v.* to wish joy to.
Grace, *n.* favor; kindness.
Gra'cious, *a.* merciful; kind.
Disgrace', *v.* to dishonor.
Ingra'tiate, *v.* to put or wind into favor.

Gra'vis—Heavy; Grievous.

Grave, *a.* serious; weighty.
Grav'ity, *n.* weight; seriousness.
Grief, *n.* sorrow; trouble.
Griev'ous, *a.* mournful; sad.
Grieve, *v.* to mourn.
Griev'ance, *n.* an injury.
Aggrieve', *v.* to vex; to trouble.
Ag'gravate, *v.* to make worse.

Grex, gre'gis—a Herd or Flock.

Grega'rious, *a.* going in flocks.
Con'gregate, *v.* to assemble.
Congrega'tion, *n.* an assembly.
Egre'gious, *a.* remarkably bad.
Ag'gregate, *v.* to gather into a mass.
Ag'gregate, *n.* a mass.

Grus, gru'is—a Crane.

Con'gruous, *a.* going together as cranes in a flock.
Incon'gruous, *a.* unsuitable.
Congru'ity, *n.* agreement; fitness.

Gus'tus—Taste; Relish.

Gust, *n.* taste; relish.
Disgust', *n.* distaste; dislike.

Note.—Gust, a blast of wind, comes from the Danish (*gust*.)

Ha'beo, hab'itum—to Have; to Hold.

Have, *v.* to possess.
Hab'it, *n.* custom; use.
Habita'tion, *n.* a dwelling.
Habit'ual, *a.* customary.
Habit'uate, *v.* to accustom.
A'ble, *a.* having power.
Abil'ity, *n.* power.
Habil'iment, *n.* a garment.
Disa'ble, *v.* to deprive of force.
Ena'ble, *v.* to empower.
Exhib'it, *v.* to show; to display.
Debil'itate, *v.* to enfeeble.
Inhab'it, *v.* to dwell in.
Prohib'it, *v.* to forbid.

Hæ′reo, hæ′sum—to STICK FAST; to STOP.

ADHERE′, *v.* to stick to.
COHE′SIVE, *a.* sticking.
COHE′SION, *n.* state of union.
HES′ITATE, *v.* to delay; to pause.
COHE′RENT, *a.* sticking together.
INCOHE′RENT, *a.* unconnected.
INHE′RENT, *a.* existing in.

Hæ′res, hære′dis—an HEIR.

HEIR, *n.* one who inherits.
INHER′IT, *v.* to possess by descent.
COHEIR′, *n.* an heir with another.
HER′ITAGE, *n.* property inherited.
INHER′ITANCE, *n.* patrimony.
DISINHER′IT, *v.* to cut off from succession.
HERED′ITARY, *a.* that has descended from an ancestor.
HEIR′LOOM, *n.* any movable owned by inheritance.

Ha′lo—to BREATHE.

EXHALE′, *v.* to breathe out.
EXHALA′TION, *n.* vapor.
INHALE′, *v.* to breathe in.

Hau′rio, haus′tum—to DRAW, as water.

EXHAUST′, *v.* to draw out until nothing is left.
INEXHAUST′IBLE, *a.* that cannot be exhausted.

Hil′aris—CHEERFUL; MERRY.

EXHIL′ARATE, *v.* to make cheerful.
HILAR′ITY, *n.* cheerfulness.

Ho′mo, hom′inis—a MAN.

HU′MAN, *a.* belonging to mankind.
HUMANE′, *a.* kind; tender.
HU′MANIZE, *v.* to render humane.
HUMAN′ITY, *n.* the nature of man.
INHU′MAN, *a.* barbarous; cruel.
HOM′ICIDE, *n.* manslaughter.

Ho′nor, hones′tus—HONORABLE; HONEST.

HON′OR, *n.* dignity; respect.
HON′ORARY, *a.* done in honor.
HON′ORABLE, *a.* worthy of honor.
DISHON′OR, *n.* disgrace; shame.
HON′EST, *a.* without fraud; upright.
HON′ESTY, *n.* justice; truth.
DISHON′EST, *a.* unjust; wicked.

Hos′pes, hos′pitis—a HOST or GUEST.

HOS′PITABLE, *a.* kind to strangers.
HOS′PITAL, *n.* a building for the sick.
HOST, *n.* one who entertains another.
HOTEL′, *n.* an inn.
HOST′LER, *n.* a man who takes care of horses.

Hos′tis—an ENEMY.

HOST, *n.* an army; a multitude.
HOS′TILE, *a.* adverse; opposite.
HOSTIL′ITY, *n.* open war.

Hu′mus—the GROUND. *Hu′milis*—OF THE GROUND; LOW; HUMBLE.

INHUME′, *v.* to bury.
EXHUME′, *v.* to take out of the ground.
HUM′BLE, *a.* modest; submissive.
HUM′BLE, *v.* to crush; to subdue.
HUMIL′ITY, *n.* freedom from pride.
HUMILIA′TION, *n.* abasement of pride.

I'dem—the SAME.

IDEN'TITY, *n.* sameness.
IDEN'TIFY, *v.* to prove to be the same.
IDEN'TICAL, *a.* the very same.

Ig'nis—FIRE.

IGNITE', *v.* to set on fire.
IG'NEOUS, *a.* containing fire.
IGNI'TION, *n.* the state of red heat.
IGNI'TIBLE, *ppr.* capable of being set on fire.

Ima'go, imag'inis—an IMAGE.

IM'AGE, *n.* a picture; an idol.
IMAG'INE, *v.* to form an idea in the mind.
IMAGINA'TION, *n.* fancy; idea.
IMAG'INARY, *a.* existing only in fancy.

Im'pero, impera'tum—to COMMAND.

EM'PEROR, *n.* a commander; a monarch.
IMPER'ATIVE, *a.* commanding.
IMPE'RIOUS, *a.* overbearing.
EM'PIRE, *n.* the dominion of an emperor, or of a mighty nation.
IMPE'RIAL, *a.* royal; regal.

In'sula—an ISLAND.

IN'SULAR, *a.* belonging to an island.
IN'SULATE, *v.* to detach from surrounding objects.
I'SOLATED, *a.* placed by itself.
PENIN'SULA, *n.* land almost surrouded by water.

In'teger—WHOLE; ENTIRE; UNBROKEN.

IN'TEGER, *n.* a whole number.
IN'TEGRAL, *a.* whole; complete.
INTEG'RITY, *n.* honesty: purity.
IN'TEGRATE, *v.* to make entire.

In'tus—WITHIN.

INTE'RIOR, *a.* inner; inland.
INTER'NAL, *a.* inward; within.
IN'TIMATE, *a.* inmost; familiar.
IN'TIMATE, *v.* to hint.
IN'TIMACY, *n.* close familiarity.
INTRIN'SIC, *a.* internal; real.

I'ra—ANGER.

IRE, *n.* anger; rage.
IRAS'CIBLE, *a.* easily made angry.
IR'RITABLE, *a.* easily provoked.
IR'RITATE, *v.* to tease; to fret.

Ja'cio, jac'tum—to THROW or CAST.

AB'JECT, *a.* thrown away; mean.
AD'JECTIVE, *n.* a describing word.
CONJEC'TURE, *v.* to guess.
DEJECT', *v.* to cast down.
DEJEC'TION, *n.* lowness of spirits.
EJECT', *v.* to throw out.
INJECT', *v.* to throw in.
EJAC'ULATE, *v.* to utter abruptly.
INTERJEC'TION, *n.* an exclamation.
OBJECT', *v.* to oppose.
OB'JECT, *n.* purpose; design.
PRO'JECT, *n.* scheme; contrivance.
PROJECT', *v.* to cast forward; to plan.
PROJEC'TILE, *n.* a body thrown forward.
REJECT', *v.* to refuse.
SUBJECT', *v.* to put under.

Ja'ceo—to Lie.

Ja'cent, *a.* lying at length.
Adja'cent, *a.* lying next.
Circumja'cent, *a.* lying round.
Interja'cent, *a.* lying between.

Jo'cus—a Joke; Sport.

Jocose', *a.* merry; waggish.
Joke, *n.* a merry trick.
Joc'ular, *a.* sportive; merry.
Joc'und, *a.* gay; lively.

Ju'dico, judica'tum—to Judge; to Decide.

Judi'cial, *a.* pertaining to courts of justice.
Judi'ciary, *n.* the system of courts of justice.
Adjudge', *v.* to pass a sentence.
Adju'dicate, *v.* to try and decide.
Judge, *v.* to decide.
Judi'cious, *a.* guided by judgment.
Prej'udice, *n.* a prejudgment.

Ju'gum—a Yoke.

Con'jugal, *a.* pertaining to marriage.
Sub'jugate, *v.* to put under the yoke.
Con'jugate, *v.* to join together.

Jun'go, junc'tum—to Join.

Junc'tion, *n.* union.
Join, *v.* to unite; to combine.
Joint, *n.* a joining; a connection allowing motion.
Adjoin'ing, *a.* next; contiguous.
Ad'junct, *n.* something joined.
Conjoin', *v.* to unite; to associate.
Disjoin', *v.* to separate.
Enjoin', *v.* to direct; to order.
Injunc'tion, *n.* precept; order.
Subjoin', *v.* to add at the end.
Subjunc'tive, *a.* conditional.

Ju'ro—to Swear.

Abjure', *v.* to renounce upon oath.
Adjure', *v.* to charge solemnly.
Conjure', *v.* to summon in a solemn manner.
Con'jure, *v.* to practice secret arts.
Ju'ry, *n.* a set of men sworn to give a true verdict.
Ju'ror, *n.* a member of a jury.
Per'jury, *n.* false swearing.

Jus, ju'ris—Right; Justice; Law.

Just, *a.* equitable; honest.
Just'ice, *n.* right.
Injust'ice, *n.* wrong.
Jus'tify, *v.* to clear from guilt.
Adjust', *v.* to set right.
In'jure, *v.* to treat unjustly.
Inju'rious, *a.* hurtful.
Jurisdic'tion, *n.* legal authority.

Ju'venis—Young.

Ju'venile, *a.* youthful.
Ju'nior, *n.* one younger.

Ju'vo, ju'tum—to Help or Aid.

Ad'jutant, *n.* a major's aid.
Coadju'tor, *n.* a fellow helper.

La'bor, lap'sus—to Fall; to Slip; to Glide.

Lapse, *n.* a slip; a fault.
Collapse', *v.* to fall inward.
Elapse', *v.* to pass away.
Relapse', *v.* to fall back again.

La′bor—LABOR.

LA′BOR, n. work; toil.
LABO′RIOUS, a. fatiguing.
ELAB′ORATE, a. much labored upon.
LAB′ORATORY, n. a chemist's workroom.

Lac, lac′tis—MILK.

LAC′TEAL, a. pertaining to milk. | LACTIF′EROUS, a. bearing milk.

Lan′gueo—to DROOP; to LANGUISH.

LAN′GUID, a. drooping; weak.
LAN′GUOR, n. faintness; weakness.
LAN′GUISH, v. to grow feeble.

La′pis, lap′idis—a STONE.

LAP′IDARY, n. a worker in precious stones. | DILAPIDA′TION, n. ruin; decay.

La′tus—a SIDE.

LAT′ERAL, a. pertaining to the side. | COLLAT′ERAL, a. placed by the side.

La′tus—WIDE; BROAD.

DILATE′, v. to widen apart. | LAT′ITUDE, n. breadth.

Laus, lau′dis—PRAISE.

LAUD, v. to praise; to extol.
LAU′DATORY, a. bestowing praise.
LAU′DABLE, a. praiseworthy.

La′vo, lo′tum—to WASH.

LAVE, v. to wash; to bathe. | LO′TION, n. a medicinal wash.

Lax′us—LOOSE; SLACK.

LAX, a. loose; dissolute.
PROLIX′, a. loosened out; lengthy.
RELAX′, v. to slacken; to remit.
RELAXA′TION, n. ease; remission.

Le′go, lega′tum—to SEND AS AN AMBASSADOR; to BEQUEATH.

ALLEGE′, v. to affirm.
ALLEGA′TION, n. affirmation.
COL′LEAGUE, n. a partner.
ALLE′GIANCE, n. the duty of a subject.
DEL′EGATE, n. a deputy.
DEL′EGATE, v. to send on an embassy.
LEG′ACY, n. a gift made by will.
LEG′ATE, n. an ambassador of the Pope.

Le′vis—LIGHT; EASY.

LEV′ITY, n. lightness; gayety.
ALLE′VIATE, v. to make easy to.
EL′EVATE, v. to raise up.
LEAV′EN, n. a substance to make bread light.
RELIEF′, n. ease; assistance.
LEAV′EN, v. to make light, as bread.
LE′VER, n. a mechanical power.
LEV′Y, v. to raise; to collect.
REL′EVANT, a. applicable.
RELIEVE′, v. to ease; to succor.

Le'go, lec'tum—to GATHER; to READ; to CHOOSE.

COLLECT', *v.* to gather together.
DI'ALECT, *n.* subdivision of a language.
DIL'IGENT, *a.* industrious.
ELEC'TION, *n.* the act of choosing.
EL'IGIBLE, *a.* fit to be chosen.
IN'TELLECT, *n.* understanding.
INTEL'LIGENT, *a.* able to understand.
INTEL'LIGENCE, *n.* information.
LEC'TURE, *n.* a discourse.
LE'GEND, *n.* a wild narrative.
LEG'IBLE, *a.* that can be read.
LE'GION, *n.* a body of soldiers.
NEGLECT', *v.* to pass over carelessly.
NEGLECT', *n.* inattention; slight.
NEG'LIGENT, *a.* careless; heedless.
PREDILEC'TION, *n.* a liking before hand.
RECOLLECT', *v.* to bring to mind.
SELECT', *v.* to choose out.
SELEC'TION, *n.* choice.

Le'nis—MILD; GENTLE.

LE'NIENT, *a.* mild; soothing.
LEN'ITY, *n.* mildness of temper.

Lex, le'gis—a LAW or RULE.

LE'GAL, *a.* lawful.
ILLE'GAL, *a.* unlawful.
LEGAL'ITY, *n.* lawfulness.
LE'GALIZE, *v.* to make lawful.
LEG'ISLATE, *v.* to make laws.
LEG'ISLATURE, *n.* the law making power.
LEGIT'IMATE, *a.* lawful; genuine.
LEGIT'IMACY, *n.* lawfulness of birth.
PRIV'ILEGE, *n.* a special advantage.

Li'ber, lib'ri—a BOOK.

LI'BRARY, *n.* an apartment for books.
LI'BEL, *n.* a defamatory writing.
LIBRA'RIAN, *n.* one who has charge of a library.
LI'BELOUS, *a.* defamatory.

Li'ber—FREE.

LIB'ERAL, *a.* free; generous.
LIB'ERTY, *n.* freedom.
LIB'ERATE, *v.* to set free.
ILLIB'ERAL, *a.* mean; suspicious.

Li'bra—a POUND; a BALANCE.

DELIB'ERATE, *v.* to weigh mentally.
EQUILIB'RIUM, *n.* an equal balancing.

Li'ceo, lic'itum—to be LAWFUL or PERMITTED.

ILLIC'IT, *a.* unlawful.
LI'CENSE, *n.* permission.
LI'CENSE, *v.* to grant authority to.
LICEN'TIOUS, *a.* unrestrained.

Li'go, liga'tum—to BIND; to TIE.

ALLE'GIANCE, *n.* the binding of a subject to his government.
LEAGUE, *n.* a binding or union.
LI'ABLE, *a.* bound; responsible.
OB'LIGATE, *v.* to bind by contract.
OB'LIGATORY, *a.* binding.
OBLIGE', *v.* to gratify; to compel.
RELIG'ION, *n.* duty to God.

Li'men, lim'inis—a THRESHOLD.

ELIM'INATE, *v.* to put out of doors.
PRELIM'INARY, *a.* introductory.

Li′nea—a Linen Thread.   Li′num—Flax.

Delin′eate, *v.* to describe.
Interline′, *v.* to write between lines.
Line, *n.* a rank; a row; extension in length.
Lin′eal, *a.* descending in a line.

Lin′eament, *n.* feature; outline.
Lin′eage, *n.* race; progeny.
Lin′en, *n.* cloth made of flax.
Lin′seed, *n.* the seed of flax.
Lint, *n.* down scraped from linen.

Lin′gua—the Tongue; a Language.

Lan′guage, *n.* a using the tongue; speech.

Lin′go, *n.* corrupt language.
Lin′guist, *n.* one skilled in languages.

Lin′quo, lic′tum—to Leave; to Forsake.

Delin′quent, *a.* failing in duty.
Delin′quent, *n.* an offender.
Derelic′tion, *n.* a forsaking.

Rel′ic, *n.* something left.
Rel′ict, *n.* a widow.
Relin′quish, *v.* to forsake; to quit.

Li′queo—to Melt; to Flow, as water.

Liq′uefy, *v.* to make liquid.
Liq′uor, *n.* a liquid substance.
Liq′uidate, *v.* to clear away; to pay.

Liq′uid, *n.* a fluid.
Liq′uid, *a.* flowing like water.

Lis, li′tis—Strife; a Lawsuit.

Lit′igate, *v.* to contest in law.
Litig′ious, *a.* given to litigation.

Litiga′tion, *n.* a suit at law.
Lit′igant, *n.* one engaged in a lawsuit.

Lit′era—a Letter.

Let′ter, *n.* a character representing some sound; an epistle.
Lit′eral, *a.* exact to the letter.
Lit′erary, *a.* relating to letters.

Lit′erature, *n.* learning.
Litera′ti, *n.* men of learning.
Illit′erate, *a.* unlearned.
Oblit′erate, *v.* to rub out.

Lo′cus—a Place.

Lo′cal, *a.* relating to place.
Lo′cate, *v.* to place; to fix.
Local′ity, *n.* situation; place.
Col′locate, *v.* to place together.
Dis′locate, *v.* to put out of joint.

Locomo′tion, *n.* the power of changing place.
Locomo′tive, *n.* a steam engine on wheels.

Lo′quor, locu′tus—to Speak.

Circumlocu′tion, *n.* a circuit of words.
Col′loquy, *n.* a speaking together.
Collo′quial, *a.* relating to conversation.
El′oquent, *a.* having the power of oratory.

Elocu′tion, *n.* a speaking out.
Loquac′ity, *n.* talkativeness.
Ob′loquy, *n.* blame; slander.
Solil′oquy, *n.* a speech to one's self.
Ventril′oquism, *n.* the act of speaking from the stomach.

Note.—Ventriloquism is the art of modifying the natural voice so that it seems to come from a greater or less distance, and from different directions.

Lon'gus—Long.

Long, *a.* having length.
Long, *v.* to desire earnestly.
Elon'gate, *v.* to lengthen.
Longev'ity, *n.* length of life.

Ob'long, *a.* longer than broad.
Prolong', *v.* to lengthen out.
Lon'gitude, *n.* length; distance east or west.

Lu'crum—Gain; Profit.

Lu'cre, *n.* gain; money.
Lu'crative, *a.* profitable.

Lu'do, lu'sum—to Play; to Deceive; to Cheat.

Allude', *v.* to refer to.
Allu'sion, *n.* a reference to.
Collu'sion, *n.* dishonest agreement.
Delude', *v.* to deceive; to mislead.
Delu'sive, *a.* deceptive.

Elude', *v.* to escape by deception.
Illu'sion, *n.* a deceptive appearance.
Lu'dicrous, *a.* laughable.
Prel'ude, *n.* something introductory.
In'terlude, *n.* a play between.

Lu'men, lu'minis—Light.

Lu'minous, *a.* giving light.
Lu'minary, *n.* anything that gives light.
Illumina'tion, *n.* a lighting up.

Lu'cid, *a.* bright; shining.
Lu'cifer, *n.* the morning star; Satan.
Elu'cidate, *v.* to clear up.
Pellu'cid, *a.* clear.

Translu'cent, *a.* transparent.

Lu'na—the Moon.

Lu'nar, *a.* relating to the moon.
Luna'tion, *n.* a month.

Lu'nacy, *n.* madness.
Lu'natic, *n.* a madman.

Sub'lunary, *a.* beneath the moon.

Lu'o, lu'tum—to Wash.

Ablu'tion, *n.* a washing.
Allu'vium, *n.* soil deposited by water.
Allu'vial, *a.* deposited by water.

Dilute', *v.* to make thin or weak.
Dil'uent, *a.* that which dilutes.
Pollute', *v.* to make unclean.

Lus'tro, lustra'tum—to Purify; to Make Clean or Bright.

Lus'tre, *n.* brightness; splendor.
Illus'trious, *a.* very distinguished.

Illus'trate, *v.* to explain.
Lustra'tion, *n.* a cleansing.

Luxu'ria—Luxury.

Lus'cious, *a.* sweet to excess.
Lux'ury, *n.* a great or excessive pleasure.

Luxu'riant, *a.* growing rank.
Luxu'rious, *a.* voluptuous.
Luxu'riate, *v.* to revel; to wanton.

Luxu'riance, *n.* rank growth.

Magis'ter—a Master; a Ruler.

Mag'istrate, *n.* a civil officer.
Mag'istracy, *n.* the office of a magistrate.

Magiste'rial, *a.* having the air of authority.
Mas'ter, *n.* one who controls.

LATIN ROOTS AND DERIVATIVES.

Mag'nes, magne'tis—LOADSTONE.

MAG'NET, *n.* the loadstone.
MAGNET'IC, *a.* attractive.
MAG'NETISM, *n.* the power of attraction.

Mag'nus—GREAT; LARGE; GRAND.

MAG'NITUDE, *n.* size; greatness.
MAG'NIFY, *v.* to make greater.
MAGNAN'IMOUS, *a.* of noble mind.
MAGNIF'ICENCE, *n.* grandeur.
MAGNIF'ICENT, *a.* splendid.
MA'JOR, *a.* greater.
MA'JOR, *n.* a military officer.
MAJOR'ITY, *n.* the greater number.
MAY'OR, *n.* the chief magistrate of a city.
MAJ'ESTY, *n.* dignity.
MAJES'TIC, *a.* grand; stately.

Ma'gus—a DIVINE or ENCHANTER; a PRIEST.

MA'GI, *n.* a wise man.
MAG'IC, *n.* enchantment.
MAG'ICAL, *a.* produced by enchantment.
MAGI'CIAN, *n.* a sorcerer.

Ma'le—BADLY; ILL.

DIS'MAL, *a.* sorrowful; gloomy.
MALEDIC'TION, *n.* a curse.
MALEFAC'TOR, *n.* a criminal.
MALEV'OLENCE, *n.* ill will.

Malig'nus—ENVIOUS; FATAL TO LIFE.

MALIGN, *a.* having malice and envy.
MALIG'NANT, *a.* hostile to life.
MALIG'NITY, *n.* violent hatred.
MALIG'NANTLY, *ad.* with ill intention.
MAL'ICE, *n.* desire to injure.
MALI'CIOUS, *a.* ill disposed.

Mal'leus—a HAMMER. *Mal'leo*—to BEAT.

MALL, *n.* a large wooden hammer; a beetle.
MAL'LET, *n.* a little mall.
MAL'LEABLE, *a.* that may be spread by hammering.

Man'do, manda'tum—to COMMIT; to COMMAND.

MAN'DATE, *n.* a command.
COMMAND', *v.* to govern; to order.
COMMEND', *v.* to praise.
COMMENDA'TION, *n.* praise.
COUNTERMAND', *v.* to revoke a command.
DEMAND', *v.* to ask with authority.
DEMAND', *n.* a call of authority.
REMAND', *v.* to send back.
RECOMMEND', *v.* to commend to another.

Ma'neo, man'sum—to STAY; to ABIDE.

MAN'SION, *n.* a house; a residence.
PER'MANENT, *a.* durable; lasting.
REMAIN', *v.* to stay; to continue.
REM'NANT, *n.* that which is left.

Ma're—the SEA.

MARINE', *a.* belonging to the sea.
MAR'INER, *n.* a seaman.
MAR'ITIME, *a.* near the sea.
SUBMARINE', *a.* under the sea.
TRANSMARINE', *a.* across the sea.
ULTRAMARINE', *a.* across the sea.
ULTRAMARINE', *n.* a very fine blue.

Manifes'tus—CLEAR; EVIDENT.

MAN'IFEST, *a.* plain; open.
MANIFES'TO, *n.* a declaration.
MAN'IFEST, *n.* a list of a cargo.

Ma'nus—the HAND. Manip'ulus—a HANDFUL.

MAN'UAL, *a.* performed by the hand.
MANUFAC'TURE, *n.* anything made by art.
MAINTAIN', *v.* to support.
MAN'ACLE, *v.* to handcuff.
MAN'AGE, *v.* to conduct.
MANIP'ULATE, *v.* to handle.
EMAN'CIPATE, *v.* to set free.
MANUMIS'SION, *n.* giving liberty to slaves.
MANUMIT', *v.* to set free.
MANURE', *v.* to fertilize.
MAN'USCRIPT, *n.* a writing.
MANŒU'VRE, *n.* a skillful movement.

Mar'go, mar'ginis—a BRINK or EDGE.

MAR'GIN, *n.* the border; the edge.
MAR'GINAL, *a.* on the margin.

Ma'ter, mat'ris—a MOTHER; a MATRON.

MATER'NAL, *a.* motherly.
MAT'RIMONY, *n.* marriage.
MA'TRON, *n.* an elderly woman.
MAT'RICIDE, *n.* the murder of a mother.

Matu'rus—RIPE; MATURE.

MATURE', *a.* ripe; complete.
MATU'RITY, *n.* ripeness.
IMMATURE', *a.* not ripe.
PREMATURE', *a.* ripe too soon.

Me'deor—to HEAL; to CURE. Med'icus—a PHYSICIAN.

MED'ICINE, *n.* any substance used in curing disease.
MEDIC'INAL, *a.* having the power of healing.
MED'ICAL, *a.* relating to medicine.
MED'ICATED, *a.* tinctured with medicine.
REM'EDY, *n.* a cure.
REME'DIAL, *a.* affording remedy.

Me'dius—MIDDLE; BETWEEN. Medioc'ris—MIDDLING.

ME'DIUM, *n.* the middle point.
ME'DIATE, *v.* to interpose.
ME'DIATE, *a.* put between.
IMME'DIATE, *a.* instant; direct.
INTERME'DIATE, *a.* coming between.
MEDIOC'RITY, *n.* middle rate.
MEDITERRA'NEAN, *a.* between lands.

Med'itor, medita'tus—to MUSE; to THINK UPON.

MEDITA'TION, *n.* deep thought.
PREMED'ITATE, *v.* to think beforehand.

Me'mor—MINDFUL; KEEPING IN MIND.

MEM'ORY, *n.* the faculty of recollecting.
MEM'ORABLE, *a.* worthy to be remembered.
MEMO'RIAL, *n.* something to keep in memory.
MEMOIR', *n.* a short account.
IMMEMO'RIAL, *a.* beyond memory.
MEMEN'TO, *n.* a memorial.
MEN'TION, *v.* to speak of.
REMEM'BER, *v.* to bear in mind.
REMINIS'CENCE, *n.* recollection.
COMMEM'ORATE, *v.* to hold in memory.

Mens, men'tis—the MIND; REASON.

MEN'TAL, *a.* relating to the mind.
DEMEN'TATE, *v.* to make insane.
DEMENT'ED, *p. a.* insane.

COM'MENT, *n.* note; explanation.
COM'MENTARY, *n.* a writing to explain another.

VE'HEMENCE, *n.* force; ardor.

Mensu'ra—a MEASURE. *Me'tior*—to MEASURE.

METE, *v.* to measure.
ME'TER, *n.* a measure.
MEAS'URE, *v.* to compute quantity by a rule.
COMMEN'SURATE, *a.* equal.

MENSURA'TION, *n.* the art of measuring.
DIMEN'SION, *n.* bulk; extent.
IMMENSE', *a.* very great; vast.
IMMEN'SITY, *n.* unlimited extent.

Mer'cor, merca'tus—to BUY; to TRADE.

COM'MERCE, *n.* trade; intercourse.
COMMER'CIAL, *a.* relating to commerce.
MER'CHANT, *n.* a trader.
MER'CHANDISE, *n.* things bought and sold.

MER'CANTILE, *a.* relating to trade.
MAR'KET, *n.* a place of sale.
MER'CENARY, *n.* one who is bought; actuated by the hope of gain.
MER'CER, *n.* a dealer in silks.
MER'CURY, *n.* the god of commerce.

NOTE.—MERCURY, an ancient heathen deity, the messenger of the gods, and the god of eloquence, commerce, travelers, etc.

Mer'go, mer'sum—to PLUNGE or DIP; to SINK.

MERGE, *v.* to swallow up; to sink.
EMERGE', *v.* to rise out of.
EMER'GENCY, *n.* sudden occasion.
IMMERSE', *v.* to put under water.
SUBMERGE', *v.* to put under water.

IMMER'SION, *n.* the act of putting below the surface of a fluid.
SUBMER'SION, *n.* the state of being wholly covered by a fluid.

Me'reo, mer'itum—to EARN; to DESERVE.

DEMER'IT, *n.* fault; vice.
MER'IT, *v.* to deserve.

MERITO'RIOUS, *a.* full of merit.

Mi'gro, migra'tum—to CHANGE ONE'S ABODE or DWELLING.

MI'GRATE, *v.* to remove from one place to another.
EM'IGRATE, *v.* to remove out of a country.

MIGRA'TION, *n.* change of residence.
IM'MIGRATE, *v.* to remove into a country.
EM'IGRANT, *n.* one who removes.

Mi'les, mil'itis—a SOLDIER.

MIL'ITANT, *a.* fighting.
MIL'ITARY, *a.* relating to soldiers.

MIL'ITATE, *v.* to operate against.
MILI'TIA, *n.* citizen soldiers.

Minister—a SERVANT; a HELPER.

MIN'ISTER, *n.* a servant of the church.
MIN'ISTRY, *n.* the body of ministers.

ADMIN'ISTER, *v.* to supply to; to manage or rule.

ADMINISTRA'TION, *n.* government.

Mi'neo—to Jut Out; to Hang Over.

Em'inent, *a.* distinguished; high.
Im'minent, *a.* near; at hand.

Prom'inence, *n.* distinction.
Prom'inent, *a.* standing out.

Min'uo, minu'tum—to Lessen or Diminish.

Dimin'ish, *v.* to lessen.
Diminu'tion, *n.* a growing less.
Dimin'utive, *a.* small.
Min'iature, *n.* a small portrait.
Min'imum, *n.* the smallest quantity.
Mi'nor, *n.* one under age.

Minor'ity, *n.* the less number.
Min'uend, *n.* the number to be diminished.
Mi'nus, *a.* diminished by.
Minute', *a.* very small.
Min'ute, *n.* a portion of time.

Minu'tiæ, *n.* small particulars.

Mi'rus—Strange; Wonderful.

Admire', *v.* to regard with wonder or esteem.
Mir'acle, *n.* a supernatural event.

Admira'tion, *n.* affection mingled with wonder.
Mirac'ulous, *a.* supernatural.

Mis'ceo, mix'tum—to Mix; to Mingle.

Mix, *v.* to mingle.
Mix'ture, *n.* a mixed mass.
Min'gle, *v.* to mix; to join.
Commix', *v.* to mingle; to blend.
Intermix', *v.* to mingle together.

Mis'cellany, *n.* a collection of various things.
Miscella'neous, *a.* of various kinds.
Promis'cuous, *a.* mingled indiscriminately.

Mit'to, mis'sum—to Send; to Let Go or Come.

Admit', *v.* to suffer to enter.
Admit'tance, *n.* entrance.
Commit', *v.* to intrust.
Commis'sion, *n.* a trust; authority given.
Commit'tee, *n.* persons selected to examine or manage any matter.
Com'promise, *n.* an adjustment by concessions on each side.
Demise', *n.* death; decease.
Demise', *v.* to grant at one's death.
Dismiss', *v.* to send away.
Dismis'sion, *n.* discharge.
Em'issary, *n.* one sent out as a secret agent.
Emis'sion, *n.* a sending out.
Emit', *v.* to send forth.
Intermis'sion, *n.* cessation for a time.
Intermit'tent, *a.* ceasing at intervals.
Manumis'sion, *n.* sending away from bondage.
Manumit', *v.* to release from slavery.

Mis'sive, *n.* a letter sent.
Mis'sile, *n.* that may be thrown.
Mis'sion, *n.* a being sent by authority.
Mis'sionary, *n.* one sent to propagate religion.
Omit', *v.* to leave out.
Omis'sion, *n.* neglect; failure.
Per'mit, *n.* a written permission.
Permit', *v.* to grant permission.
Permis'sion, *n.* leave granted.
Premise', *v.* to state beforehand.
Prom'ise, *v.* to engage to do.
Prom'issory, *a.* containing a promise.
Remiss', *a.* slack; careless.
Remit', *v.* to relax; to forgive.
Remis'sion, *n.* abatement; pardon.
Remit'tance, *n.* a sum sent back.
Submit', *v.* to yield to authority.
Submis'sive, *a.* humble; yielding.
Surmise', *n.* a suspicion.
Transmit', *v.* to send over.
Transmis'sion, *n.* a sending over.

Mo'lior, moli'tus—to Heap; to Build.

Demol'ish, *v.* to destroy.

Demoli'tion, *n.* destruction.

LATIN ROOTS AND DERIVATIVES.

Mi′ser—Wretched.

Mis′ery, *n.* wretchedness.
Mi′ser, *n.* one who is wretched through covetousness.
Mi′serly, *a.* very covetous.
Mis′erable, *a.* unhappy.
Commis′erate, *v.* to pity.

Mo′dus—a Measure; a Limit; a Mode or Manner.

Mode, *n.* a manner or fashion.
Mood, *n.* temper of mind.
Mod′el, *n.* a copy to be imitated.
Mod′ify, *v.* to alter; to soften.
Mod′ulate, *v.* to vary sound.
Mod′erate, *a.* temperate; not violent.
Mod′est, *a.* restrained by a sense of propriety.
Mod′esty, *n.* decency; diffidence.
Mod′icum, *n.* a small portion.
Commo′dious, *a.* convenient.
Commod′ity, *n.* an article of merchandise.
Accom′modate, *v.* to make convenient to.
Discommode′, *v.* to put to trouble.
Incommode′, *v.* to disturb; to annoy.
Immod′erate, *a.* excessive.
Immod′est, *a.* wanting modesty.
Remod′el, *v.* to model anew.

Mol′lis—Soft. Mol′lio—to Soften.

Emol′lient, *a.* softening.
Mol′lify, *v.* to assuage; to soften.

Mo′neo, mon′itum—to Remind; to Warn.

Mon′itor, *n.* one who warns.
Mon′ument, *n.* a memorial.
Admon′ish, *v.* to warn; to reprove.
Admoni′tion, *n.* gentle reproof.
Premon′itory, *a.* giving warning beforehand.
Sum′mon, *v.* to call by authority.

Mons, mon′tis—a Mountain; a High Hill.

Mount, *n.* a hill.
Moun′tain, *n.* a very large hill.
Mound, *n.* a heap or bank of earth.
Amount′, *n.* the sum.
Dismount′, *v.* to alight from a horse.
Par′amount, *a.* above all others.
Prom′ontory, *n.* high land jutting into the sea.
Remount′, *v.* to mount again.
Surmount′, *v.* to rise above.
Tan′tamount, *a.* equal in value or meaning.

Mon′stro, monstra′tum—to Show; to Declare.

Demon′strate, *v.* to show plainly.
Mon′ster, *n.* something unnatural.
Mon′strous, *a.* unnatural; huge.
Remon′strate, *v.* to present reasons against.

Mor′deo, mor′sum—to Bite.

Mor′sel, *n.* a little bite.
Remorse′, *n.* a biting again; sorrow for a fault.
Mor′dant, *n.* any substance to hold colors in dyeing.

Mors, mor′tis—Death.

Mor′tal, *a.* subject to death.
Mor′tify, *v.* to lose vitality; to shame or vex.
Mortal′ity, *n.* death.
Mur′der, *v.* to put to death.
Immor′tal, *a.* exempt from death.
Immor′talize, *v.* to make immortal.

Mos, mo'ris—Manner; Custom.

Mor'al, *a.* conformed to law and rectitude.
Moral'ity, *n.* correctness of life.
Demor'alize, *v.* to make immoral.
Mor'alize, *v.* to apply to moral subjects.
Immor'al, *a.* vicious.

Mo'veo, mo'tum—to Move.

Move, *v.* to put out of one place into another.
Move'ment, *n.* change of place.
Mo'tion, *n.* change of place.
Mo'tive, *n.* cause; reason.
Mob, *n.* a disorderly multitude.
Momen'tum, *n.* force of motion.
Commo'tion, *n.* tumult.
Emo'tion, *n.* disturbance of mind.
Promote', *v.* to advance; to exalt.
Promo'tion, *n.* advancement to higher rank.
Remote', *a.* at a distance.
Remove', *v.* to put from its place.

Mul'tus—Many; Numerous; Much.

Multi'tude, *n.* a great number.
Mul'tiply, *v.* to increase in number.
Multifa'rious, *a.* having great variety.

Mu'nus, mu'neris—a Gift; an Office.

Munif'icent, *a.* very liberal.
Commune', *v.* to talk together.
Commu'nicate, *v.* to impart.
Com'mon, *a.* shared by all.
Commu'nion, *n.* intercourse.
Commu'nity, *n.* the commonwealth.
Immu'nity, *n.* exemption.
Remu'nerate, *v.* to reward.

Mu'rus—a Wall.

Mu'ral, *a.* pertaining to a wall.
Immure', *v.* to imprison.

Mu'to, muta'tum—to Change.

Mu'table, *a.* changeable.
Muta'tion, *n.* change.
Commute', *v.* to exchange.
Mu'tual, *a.* reciprocal.
Mu'tiny, *v.* to rise against authority.
Permuta'tion, *n.* exchange.
Transmute', *v.* to change from one nature into another.

Nas'cor, na'tus—to be Born; to Spring Up; to Grow.

Na'tal, *a.* relating to one's birth.
Na'tion, *n.* a distinct people.
Na'tive, *a.* conferred by birth.
Na'tive, *n.* one who is born in a country.
Nativ'ity, *n.* birth.
Nat'ural, *a.* made by nature.
Supernat'ural, *a.* above nature.
Na'ture, *n.* original quality; the power which produces or causes things to grow.
Innate', *a.* born with us.
Nat'uralist, *n.* a student of nature.
Nat'uralize, *v.* to intrust with the rights of a native.

Na'vis—a Ship or Vessel.

Na'vy, *n.* the ships of war of a nation.
Na'val, *a.* relating to ships.
Naviga'tion, *n.* traveling by ships.
Nav'igable, *a.* passable by ships.
Nau'tical, *a.* pertaining to sailors or sailing.
Nau'sea, *n.* sea-sickness.
Nau'seous, *a.* loathsome.
Nau'tilus, *n.* the sailor-fish.

LATIN ROOTS AND DERIVATIVES.

Neces'se—NECESSARY; INEVITABLE.

NEC'ESSARY, *a.* needful.
NECES'SITATE, *v.* to make necessary.
NECES'SITOUS, *a.* needy.

NECES'SITY, *n.* compulsion; want.
NEFA'RIOUS, *a.* wicked.
UNNEC'ESSARY, *a.* not needed.

Nec'to, nex'um—to TIE or BIND; to KNIT.

CONNECT', *v.* to join together.
CONNEC'TION, *n.* a joining; relation.

DISCONNECT', *v.* to sever.
ANNEX', *v.* to unite at the end.

Ne'go, nega'tum—to DENY; to REFUSE.

NEGA'TION, *n.* a denial.
NEG'ATIVE, *a.* denying.

NEG'ATIVE, *n.* that which denies.
DENY', *v.* to contradict; to refuse.

Neu'ter, neu'trum—NEITHER.

NEU'TRAL, *a.* of neither side or party.
NEU'TRALIZE, *v.* to destroy the peculiar properties of.

NEU'TER, *a.* neither one or the other.
NEUTRAL'ITY, *n.* the state of being neutral.

No'ceo—to HURT; to OFFEND.

NO'CENT, *a.* hurtful.
NOX'IOUS, *a.* hurtful.
INNO'CENT, *a.* guiltless.

OBNOX'IOUS, *a.* hateful; offensive.
IN'NOCENCE, *n.* purity; simplicity.
NUI'SANCE, *n.* something offensive.

Nor'ma—a RULE or SQUARE.

NOR'MAL, *a.* according to rule.

ENOR'MOUS, *a.* beyond rule or measure.

No'men, nom'inis—a NAME.

DENOM'INATE, *v.* to name down.
DENOM'INATION, *n.* a name; a class.
IG'NOMINY, *n.* disgrace; shame.
NAME, *n.* the term by which we distinguish things.
NOM'INAL, *a.* in name only.

NO'MENCLATURE, *n.* a system of names.
NOM'INATE, *v.* to name; to propose.
RENOWNED', *a.* named again and again.

Nos'co, no'tum—to UNDERSTAND; to KNOW. *No'bilis*—NOBLE.

NO'BLE, *a.* high in rank; generous.
NOBIL'ITY, *n.* dignity; rank.
IGNO'BLE, *a.* of low birth.
NO'TICE, *v.* to observe.

NO'TIFY, *v.* to give notice to.
NO'TION, *n.* thought; idea.
NOTO'RIOUS, *a.* known or famous (in a bad sense.)

REC'OGNIZE, *v.* to know again.

No'vus—NEW.

NOV'EL, *a.* new; unusual.
NOV'EL, *n.* a tale; a romance.
NOV'ELIST, *n.* a writer of novels.
NOV'ELTY, *n.* newness.
NOVI'TIATE, *n.* the time of learning rudiments.

NOV'ICE, *n.* one new in the business.
RENEW', *v.* to make again.
RENOVA'TION, *n.* renewal.
IN'NOVATE, *v.* to introduce novelties or change.

No′ta—a Mark.

Denote′, v. to mark down.
No′table, a. worthy to be noted.
No′tice, n. observation.
No′tary, n. one who notes.

Nox, noc′tis—Night.

Noctur′nal, a. nightly.
Night, n. the time of darkness.
E′quinox, n. the time of equal day and night.
Equinoc′tial, a. pertaining to the equinox.

Nu′bo, nup′tum—to Marry.

Connu′bial, a. pertaining to marriage.
Nup′tial, a. pertaining to marriage.

Nu′dus—Naked; Bare.

Denude′, v. to strip; to make bare.
Nu′dity, n. nakedness.

Nul′lus—None; Null or Void.

Null, a. void; of no force.
Nul′lity, n. nothingness.
Nul′lify, v. to make null or void.
Annul′, v. to make void.

Nu′merus—a Number.

Num′ber, n. more than one thing.
Num′ber, v. to count; to reckon.
Nu′merous, a. containing many.
Numera′tion, n. the art of numbering.
Numer′ical, a. denoting number.
Num′eral, a. relating to number.
Enu′merate, v. to reckon up singly.
Innu′merable, a. too many to be counted.

Nun′cio, nuncia′tum—to Bring News; to Tell.

Announce′, v. to give notice.
Denounce′, v. to declare against.
Denuncia′tion, n. public threat.
Enun′ciate, v. to tell or speak out.
Pronounce′, v. to tell or speak out.
Pronuncia′tion, n. mode of utterance.
Renounce′, v. to disown.

Nu′trio, nu′tritum—to Nourish; to Suckle.

Nour′ish, v. to support by food.
Nurse, n. a person who has the care of infants or sick persons.
Nu′triment, n. food.
Nutri′tion, n. the act of nourishing.
Nutri′tious, a. nourishing.

Oc′ulus—an Eye; a Bud.

Oc′ular, a. known by the eye; evident.
Oc′ulist, n. an eye doctor.
Binoc′ular, a. having two eyes.
Inoc′ulate, v. to insert an eye or bud of one tree in another.

O′leo, ol′itum—to Emit Odor; to Grow.

Abol′ish, v. to do away with.
Aboli′tion, n. a doing away.
Adult′, n. one full grown.
Ob′solete, a. out of use.
Olfac′tory, a. pertaining to smell.
Red′olent, a. diffusing odor.

LATIN ROOTS AND DERIVATIVES.

O'di—to HATE.

O'DIOUS, *a.* hateful. | O'DIUM, *n.* hatred; dislike.

O'men, om'inis—a SIGN; an OMEN.

O'MEN, *n.* a sign; a prognostic. | ABOM'INATE, *v.* to loathe extremely
OM'INOUS, *a.* foreboding evil. | ABOM'INABLE, *a.* hateful.

Om'nis—ALL; EVERY.

OMNIP'OTENT, *a.* having all power. | OMNIS'CIENT, *a.* knowing all things.
OMNIPRES'ENT, *a.* present everywhere. | OM'NIBUS, *n.* a public coach.

O'nus, on'eris—a BURDEN or LOAD.

ON'EROUS, *a.* burdensome. | EXON'ERATE, *v.* to disburden.

Op'era—WORK.

OP'ERATE, *v.* to work or act. | OPERA'TION, *n.* action; effect.
COOP'ERATE, *v.* to work together. | OP'ERATOR, *n.* one who works.
OP'ERA, *n.* a dramatic work set to music.

Opi'nor—to THINK; to BELIEVE.

OPINE', *v.* to think. | OPIN'ION, *n.* belief; judgment.

Op'to—to WISH; to CHOOSE.

OP'TION, *n.* choice; preference. | ADOPT', *v.* to choose or take to one's self.
OP'TATIVE, *a.* expressing desire. |
ADOP'TION, *n.* the act of adopting.

Or'bis—a CIRCLE; a WHEEL; an ORB.

ORB, *n.* a circle; a globe. | EXOR'BITANT, *a.* going beyond the regular path or limit; enormous.
OR'BIT, *n.* the track or path of a planet. |

Or'do, or'dinis—ORDER; RANK.

OR'DER, *n.* regularity. | COÖR'DINATE, *a.* holding the same rank.
ORDAIN', *v.* to appoint; to decree. |
OR'DINAL, *a.* noting order. | INOR'DINATE, *a.* excessive.
OR'DINANCE, *n.* a public law. | EXTRAOR'DINARY, *a.* beyond the usual course.
OR'DINARY, *a.* common; usual. |
SUBOR'DINATE, *a.* in a lower rank. | DISOR'DER, *v.* to confuse.

O'rior—to RISE or SPRING FROM.

O'RIENT, *n.* the east; the rising sun. | OR'IGIN, *n.* source; beginning.
O'RIENTAL, *a.* eastern. | ORIG'INAL, *a.* first; primary.
ORIG'INATE, *v.* to bring into being.

Or'no, orna'tum—to DECK; to ADORN.

ADORN', *v.* to decorate. | SUBORN', *v.* to induce a person to swear falsely.
OR'NAMENT, *n.* that which adorns. |
OR'NATE, *a.* beautiful. |

O'ro, ora'tum—to PRAY; to BEG.

ORA'TION, *n.* a formal speech.
OR'ATOR, *n.* a public speaker.
OR'ISON, *n.* a prayer.
OR'ACLE, *n.* one famed for wisdom.
O'RAL, *a.* delivered by mouth.

ADORE', *v.* to worship.
ADORA'TION, *n.* worship.
OR'IFICE, *n.* an opening.
INEX'ORABLE, *a.* not to be moved by entreaty.

Os, os'sis—a BONE.

OS'SEOUS, *a.* bony.

OS'SIFY, *v.* to change into bone.

O'tium—EASE; REPOSE; RETIREMENT FROM BUSINESS.

EASE, *n.* quiet; facility.

NEGO'TIATE, *v.* to transact business.
DISEASE', *n.* malady.

O'vum—an EGG.

O'VAL, *a.* shaped like an egg.

O'VARY, *n.* the seat of eggs.
OVIP'AROUS, *a.* producing eggs.

Pal'leo—to be PALE.

PAL'LID, *a.* pale; not bright.

PAL'LOR, *n.* paleness.

Pal'lium—MANTLE or CLOAK; a COVERING.

PALL, *n.* a covering for the dead.
PALLIA'TION, *n.* mitigation.

PAL'LIATE, *v.* to put a cloak upon; to cover with excuse.

Pal'po—to TOUCH GENTLY; to FEEL.

PAL'PABLE, *a.* that may be felt.

PAL'PITATE, *v.* to beat; to flutter.

Pan'do, pan'sum—to OPEN; to SPREAD.

EXPAND', *v.* to spread; to open.
EXPAN'SION, *n.* a spreading out.
EXPANSE', *n.* a wide extent.

EXPAN'SIVE, *a.* having power to expand.

Pa'nis—BREAD.

COMPAN'ION, *n.* one who eats bread with another; an associate.
COM'PANY, *n.* a number of companions.
ACCOM'PANY, *v.* to go with.

PANA'DA, *n.* bread boiled and sweetened.
PAN'TRY, *n.* the place where bread is kept.

Pan'nus—CLOTH; a PATCH or PIECE OF CLOTH.

PAN'EL, *n.* a patch or piece; a piece of parchment on which the names of jurors were written; a piece of board inserted into a frame.

IMPAN'EL, *v.* to enrol as jurors.
PANE, *n.* a piece of thin cloth used in windows; a piece or square of glass for windows.

Pa'rio, par'tum—to BRING FORTH; to GENERATE; to PRODUCE.

PA'RENT, *n.* that which produces; a father or mother.

Par—Like; Equal.

Pair, *n.* two things like each other.
Par'ity, *n.* likeness; equality.
Dispar'ity, *n.* inequality.
Compare', *v.* to examine together.
Dispar'age, *v.* to cause disgrace.
Peer, *n.* an equal; a nobleman.
Peer'less, *a.* without an equal.
Peer'age, *n.* the rank of a peer.
Compeer', *n.* an equal.

Pa'reo, par'itum—to Become Visible; to Appear.

Appear', *v.* to become visible to.
Appar'ent, *a.* visible; evident.
Appari'tion, *n.* a spectre; a ghost.
Disappear', *v.* to become invisible.
Transpa'rent, *a.* that can be seen through.

Pa'ro, para'tum—to Get Ready or Prepare.

Appara'tus, *n.* necessary instruments for any trade or art.
Appar'el, *n.* dress; clothing.
Sev'er, *v.* to separate.
Dissev'er, *v.* to part in two.
Insep'arable, *a.* not to be parted.
Sev'eral, *a.* many; distinct.
Irrep'arable, *a.* not to be repaired.
Prepare', *v.* to make ready.
Repair', *v.* to mend; to restore.
Parade', *n.* military preparation.
Prepara'tion, *n.* act of getting ready.
Sep'arate, *v.* to divide; to part.

Pars, par'tis—a Part; a Share.

Part, *n.* a portion; a share.
Par'ticle, *n.* a little part.
Partic'ipate, *v.* to take part.
Par'ty, *n.* a set of persons engaged in one design.
Par'tisan, *n.* a party man.
Par'tial, *a.* inclined to favor one party.
Apart', *ad.* separately; asunder.
Part'ner, *n.* a sharer.
Copart'ner, *n.* a sharer.
Depart', *v.* to go away; to leave.
Depart'ure, *n.* a going away.
Impart', *v.* to give.
Impar'tial, *a.* just; equitable.
Par'cel, *n.* a small package.
Por'tion, *n.* a part; a share.
Partic'ular, *a.* pertaining to a part; exact.
Propor'tion, *n.* the portion or measure of one thing considered in comparison with some other thing.

Pas'sus—a Pace; a Step.

Pass, *v.* to move in space; to go.
Pace, *v.* to measure by steps.
Com'pass, *v.* to go round; to grasp.
Encom'pass, *v.* to surround.
Pas'sage, *n.* a way or channel.
Pas'senger, *n.* one who goes.
Pass'port, *n.* a permission of passage.
Pas'time, *n.* amusement.
Surpass', *v.* to excel; to exceed.
Tres'pass, *v.* to pass beyond; to transgress.

Pa'ter, pa'tris—a Father.

Pater'nal, *a.* fatherly.
Pat'rimony, *n.* an inherited estate.
Pa'triot, *n.* a lover of one's country.
Compa'triot, *n.* a fellow countryman.
Expa'triate, *v.* to put out of one's country.
Par'ricide, *n.* the murder of a parent.
Patri'cian, *n.* a nobleman.
Pa'triarch, *n.* the father and ruler of a family.
Pa'tron, *n.* a protector.
Pa'tronize, *v.* to protect; to support.

Pas'co, pas'tum—to FEED; to EAT.

PAS'TOR, *n.* a shepherd; a clergyman.
PAS'TORAL, *a.* relating to shepherds.
REPAST', *n.* an eating again; a meal.

PAS'TURE, *n.* land on which cattle graze.

Pa'tior, pas'sus—to SUFFER; to ENDURE.

PA'TIENCE, *n.* calm endurance.
PA'TIENT, *a.* enduring without complaint.
PA'TIENT, *n.* a sick person.
IMPA'TIENT, *a.* hasty; fretful.
PAS'SION, *n.* anger; zeal.

PAS'SIVE, *a.* suffering without resistance.
PAS'SIONATE, *a.* easily moved to anger.
COMPAS'SION, *n.* pity; sympathy.
DISPAS'SIONATE, *a.* calm.

Pau'per—POOR.

PAU'PER, *n.* a poor person.
POOR, *a.* indigent; lean.

POV'ERTY, *n.* indigence; want.
IMPOV'ERISH, *v.* to make poor.

Pax, pa'cis—PEACE.

PEACE, *n.* quiet; rest.
PACIF'IC, *a.* mild; gentle.

PAC'IFY, *v.* to calm; to quiet.
APPEASE', *v.* to quiet; to still.

Pec'tus, pec'toris—the BREAST; the CHEST.

PEC'TORAL, *a.* belonging to the breast.
EXPEC'TORATE, *v.* to cough up.

Pel'lo, pul'sum—to DRIVE; to STRIKE or BEAT.

PULSE, *n.* the throbbing of the arteries.
PULSA'TION, *n.* a throbbing.
COMPEL', *v.* to force; to drive.
COMPUL'SORY, *a.* forcing.
DISPEL', *v.* to drive away.
EXPEL', *v.* to drive out.
EXPUL'SION, *n.* a driving out.

IMPEL', *v.* to urge forward.
IM'PULSE, *n.* force given.
IMPUL'SIVE, *a.* moved by sudden thought.
PROPEL', *v.* to drive forward.
REPEL', *v.* to drive back.
REPULSE', *n.* a rejection.
REPUL'SIVE, *a.* forbidding in manners.

Pen'deo—to HANG; to LEAN.   *Perpendic'ulum*—a PLUMB LINE.

PEN'DENT, *a.* hanging.
PEN'DULUM, *n.* a body to swing to and fro.
PEND'ING, *a.* remaining undecided.
APPEND', *v.* to hang or join to.
APPEND'IX, *n.* something added at the end.
DEPEND', *v.* to hang from; to rely on.
DEPEND'ENCE, *n.* trust.

IMPEND', *v.* to hang over.
INDEPEN'DENT, *a.* free.
PROPEN'SITY, *n.* inclination.
SUSPEND', *v.* to hang; to delay.
SUSPENSE', *n.* uncertainty.
SUSPEN'SION, *n.* a hanging up; a stop.
PERPENDIC'ULAR, *a.* directly downwards.

NOTE.—A PLUMB LINE is a line perpendicular to the horizon, or a line directed to the center of gravity of the earth.

Pen'na—a FEATHER; a WING.

PEN, *n.* an instrument of writing.
PEN'NATE, *a.* winged.

LATIN ROOTS AND DERIVATIVES.

Pen'do, pen'sum—to WEIGH; to LAY OUT.

COMPEND'IUM, *n.* an abridgment.
COM'PENSATE, *v.* to give an equivalent.
DISPENSE', *v.* to distribute. To DISPENSE WITH, to do without.
EXPEND', *v.* to spend; to lay out.

EXPEND'ITURE, *n.* amount expended.
EXPANSE', *n.* cost; charges.
EXPEN'SIVE, *a.* costly.
PEN'SIVE, *a.* thoughtful; sad.
PEN'SION, *n.* annual allowance.
REC'OMPENSE, *n.* reward.

STI'PEND, *n.* wages; stated pay.

Pœ'na—PUNISHMENT.

PE'NAL, *a.* enacting punishment.
PEN'ALTY, *n.* suffering or loss in consequence of crime.
PENITEN'TIARY, *n.* a prison.

PEN'ANCE, *n.* voluntary suffering on account of sin.
PEN'ITENT, *a.* contrite for sin.
REPENT', *v.* to sorrow for sin.

Perpet'uus—UNCEASING; PERPETUAL.

PERPET'UAL, *a.* never ceasing. | PERPET'UATE, *v.* to make perpetual.
PERPETU'ITY, *n.* duration to all futurity.

Perso'na—the MASK WORN BY PLAYERS.

PER'SON, *n.* a human being.
PER'SONATE, *v.* to represent by action.

PERSON'IFY, *v.* to make or regard as a person.

PER'SONALLY, *ad.* in person.

Pes, pe'dis—a FOOT.

PED'AL, *n.* a key designed to be moved by the foot.
PED'ESTAL, *n.* the foot of a column or statue.
PEDES'TRIAN, *a.* going on foot.
PED'IGREE, *n.* lineage.
BI'PED, *n.* a two footed animal.
QUAD'RUPED, *n.* a four footed animal.

EXPE'DIENT, *a.* facilitating or helping.
EXPE'DIENT, *n.* contrivance.
EXPEDI'TION, *n.* a hastening; an enterprise on which one undertakes a journey.
EX'PEDITE, *v.* to hasten.
EXPEDI'TIOUS, *a.* quick.
IMPEDE', *v.* to hinder; to retard.

IMPED'IMENT, *n.* hindrance.

Pe'to, peti'tum—to SEEK; to STRIVE FOR; to ASK.

PETI'TION, *n.* an asking.
AP'PETITE, *n.* hunger; desire.
COMPAT'IBLE, *a.* suitable to.
COMPETE', *v.* to strive for together.
COMPET'ITOR, *n.* one who strives with another.

COM'PETENT, *a.* fit; capable.
COM'PETENCE, *n.* sufficiency.
INCOM'PETENT, *a.* not capable.
IM'PETUS, *n.* force from motion.
IMPET'UOUS, *a.* violent; fierce.
REPEAT', *v.* to do again.

Pin'go, pic'tum—to PAINT.

PICT, *n.* a painted person.
PIC'TURE, *n.* a painting.
PICTURESQUE', *a.* like a picture.

PIG'MENT, *n.* paint; color.
DEPICT', *v.* to paint; to describe.
PAINT, *v.* to describe; to color.

PICTO'RIAL, *a.* containing pictures.

Pi'o, pia'tum—to ATONE FOR.

EX'PIATE, *v.* to atone for. | EX'PIATORY, *a.* atoning.

Pis'cis—a FISH.

PISCATO'RIAL, *a.* relating to fishermen. | PIS'CATORY, *a.* relating to fishes.

Pla'ceo—to PLEASE.

PLAC'ID, *a.* pleasing to one's self; serene; gentle.
COMPLA'CENCE, *n.* satisfaction.
COM'PLAISANT, *a.* desirous to please.
PLEASE, *v.* to delight; to gratify.
DISPLEASE', *v.* to make angry.
PLEAS'ANT, *a.* gay; agreeable.
PLEAS'ANTRY, *n.* gayety; mirth.
PLEAS'URE, *n.* that which pleases or delights.

Plan'go, planc'tum—to BEAT; to BEMOAN.

COMPLAIN', *v.* to murmur; to lament.
COMPLAINT', *n.* a lamentation.
PLAINT, *n.* a lamentation.
PLAIN'TIFF, *n.* the one who begins a lawsuit.
PLAIN'TIVE, *n.* lamenting.

Plan'ta—the BOTTOM OF THE FOOT; a PLANT.

PLANT, *n.* a vegetable.
PLANT, *v.* to put into the ground to grow.
DISPLANT', *v.* to pluck up.
IMPLANT', *v.* to set; to insert.
SUPPLANT', *v.* to displace.
TRANSPLANT', *v.* to move and plant in another place.

PLANTA'TION, *n.* a place planted.

Pla'nus—SMOOTH; PLAIN; EVIDENT.

PLANE, *v.* to make smooth.
PLAIN, *n.* a level region; evident.
EXPLAIN', *v.* to make plain or clear.
EXPLANA'TION, *n.* act of explaining.

Plau'do, plau'sum—to PRAISE BY CLAPPING HANDS.

PLAU'DIT, *n.* loud praise.
APPLAUD', *v.* to praise; to extol.
APPLAUSE', *n.* approbation.
PLAUS'IBLE, *a.* right in appearance.
EXPLODE', *v.* to burst with a loud report.
EXPLO'SION, *n.* violent bursting.
EXPLO'SIVE, *a.* causing explosion.

Ple'o, ple'tum—to FILL. *Ple'nus*—FULL.

PLE'NARY, *a.* full; complete.
PLEN'TY, *n.* abundance.
PLEN'ITUDE, *n.* fullness.
PLEN'TEOUS, *a.* abundant.
REPLEN'ISH, *v.* to fill again.
ACCOM'PLISH, *v.* to finish entirely.
COMPLETE', *a.* full; perfect.
COM'PLEMENT, *n.* full quantity.
COM'PLIMENT, *n.* an act of civility.
EX'PLETIVE, *n.* a word added to fill up.
IM'PLEMENT, *n.* a tool; a utensil.
INCOMPLETE', *a.* not finished.
DEPLE'TION, *n.* an emptying.
REPLETE', *a.* completely full.
SUPPLY, *v.* to fill up; to furnish.

SUP'PLEMENT, *n.* an addition.

Plu'ma—a FEATHER; a PLUME.

PLUME, *n.* a feather. | PLU'MAGE, *n.* feathers.

Pli'co, plica'tum—to FOLD; to KNIT.

ACCOM'PLICE, *n.* one united with another in a crime.
APPLY', *v.* to put one thing to another; to seek or ask for.
AP'PLICANT, *n.* one who applies.
APPLICA'TION, *n.* the thing applied.
COM'PLEX, *a.* twined or knit together.
COMPLEX'ION, *n.* the texture and color of the skin.
COM'PLICATE, *v.* to entangle.
COMPLY', *v.* to yield to.
COMPLI'ANCE, *n.* submission.
DISPLAY', *v.* to unfold; to exhibit.
DOUB'LE, *v.* to make twice as much.
DUPLIC'ITY, *n.* doubleness of intention.
DU'PLICATE, *n.* a second thing of the sort.
EXPLIC'IT, *a.* unfolded; plain.
IMPLY', *v.* to express indirectly.
IM'PLICATE, *v.* to involve.
IMPLIC'IT, *a.* trusting without reserve.
MUL'TIPLY, *v.* to make many fold.
MULTIPLIC'ITY, *n.* a great variety.
PERPLEX', *v.* to entangle; to vex.
PLI'ANT, *a.* yielding; easily bent.
PLI'ABLE, *a.* flexible; pliant.
PLY, *v.* to keep busy.
REPLY', *v.* to answer.
SIM'PLE, *a.* plain; artless.
SIMPLIC'ITY, *n.* innocence.
SIM'PLIFY, *v.* to make easier.
SUP'PLICATE, *v.* to entreat.
SUP'PLIANT, *n.* a petitioner.
TRIP'LE, *a.* three-fold.
TREB'LE, *v.* to multiply by three.
TRIP'LET, *n.* three together.

NOTE.—SUPPLICATE, to *fold* or *bend* the knees under.

Plo'ro, plora'tum—to WEEP; to LAMENT.

DEPLORE', *v.* to lament about.
DEPLOR'ABLE, *a.* lamentable; sad.
EXPLORE', *v.* to search out carefully.
IMPLORE', *v.* to weep or lament to.

Plum'bum—LEAD.

PLUMB, *n.* a piece of lead attached to a line.
PLUM'MET, *n.* a little plumb.
PLUMBA'GO, *n.* black lead.
PLUMB, *a.* perpendicular to the horizon.

Plus, plu'ris—MORE.

PLU'RAL, *a.* containing more than one.
SUR'PLUS, *n.* that which remains over the necessary quantity.
PLURAL'ITY, *n.* the greater number.
NON'PLUS, *n.* a situation in which no more can be done.
NON'PLUS, *v.* to confound; to puzzle.

Po'mum—an APPLE.

POM'ACE, *n.* the substance of ground apples.
POMEGRAN'ATE, *n.* a fruit.
POM'MEL, *n.* a knob or ball.

NOTE.—POMEGRANATE, an apple having many grains or seeds.

Pop'ulus—the PEOPLE.   *Pub'licus*—COMMON TO ALL.

PEO'PLE, *n.* persons; a nation.
POPULA'TION, *n.* the whole number of inhabitants.
POP'ULACE, *n.* the common people.
POP'ULAR, *a.* liked by the people.
POP'ULOUS, *a.* full of people.
POPULAR'ITY, *n.* favor of the people.
DEPOP'ULATE, *v.* to deprive of people.
PUB'LIC, *a.* open to all.
PUBLIC'ITY, *n.* open to the knowledge of all.
PUB'LISH, *v.* to make known.

Pon′dus, pon′deris—a Weight; a Pound.

Pound, *n.* a weight.
Pon′derous, *a.* heavy.
Pon′der, *v.* to weigh in the mind.
Prepon′derate, *v.* to outweigh.
Poise, *v.* to weigh; to balance.

Po′no, pos′itum—to Put; to Place.

Posi′tion, *n.* place; attitude.
Pos′itive, *a.* set; certain.
Post, *n.* a place; office.
Postpone′, *v.* to put off; to delay.
Pos′ture, *n.* attitude; condition.
Compose′, *v.* to put together.
Compos′itor, *n.* one who sets types.
Com′post, *n.* a putting together; a mixture.
Compo′sure, *n.* tranquillity.
Decompose′, *v.* to separate into original elements.
Depo′nent, *n.* a witness on oath.
Depose′, *v.* to put down.
Depot′, *n.* a place of deposit.
Depos′it, *n.* to lay down; to place.
Discompose′, *v.* to disorder; to vex.
Dispose′, *v.* to place in order.
Dispos′al, *n.* control.
Disposi′tion, *n.* management; temper of mind.
Expose′, *v.* to lay open.
Expos′itor, *n.* an explainer.
Expound′, *v.* to explain; to clear.
Impose′, *v.* to put upon; to cheat.
Imposi′tion, *n.* a cheat.
Im′post, *n.* a tax on imported goods.
Impos′tor, *n.* a deceiver.
Impos′ture, *n.* a fraud; a cheat.
Interpose′, *v.* to put between.
Oppose′, *v.* to act against.
Oppo′nent, *n.* an adversary.
Op′posite, *a.* on the other side; facing.
Propound′, *v.* to offer for consideration.
Propose′, *v.* to offer for consideration.
Propo′sal, *n.* an offer.
Proposi′tion, *n.* a thing proposed.
Pur′pose, *n.* intention; design.
Repose′, *v.* to rest; to place out of the way.
Repos′itory, *n.* a place for laying up things.
Suppose′, *v.* to imagine.
Transpose′, *v.* to put each into the place of the other.

Pons, pon′tis—a Bridge.

Pon′tiff, *n.* a high priest; the pope.
Pontoon′, *n.* a boat used for making floating bridges.

Note.—The first bridge over the Tiber was constructed and consecrated by the chief priest.

Pos′sum, pot′ui—to be Able.

Pos′sible, *a.* that can be done.
Po′tent, *a.* powerful.
Im′potent, *a.* powerless.
Omnip′otent, *a.* having infinite power.
Impos′sible, *a.* that cannot be.
Pos′se, *n.* an armed power.
Po′tentate, *n.* one having great power.
Poten′tial, *a.* relating to power.

Pos′terus—After; Coming After.

Poste′rior, *a.* coming after.
Poster′ity, *n.* succeeding generations.
Post′ern, *n.* a back door or gate.
Prepos′terous, *a.* absurd.

Po′to, pota′tum—to Drink.

Po′tion, *n.* a draught; a dose.
Pota′tion, *n.* a drinking.

Por'to, porta'tum—to Carry; to Bear; to Bring.

Por'ter, *n.* a carrier; a doorkeeper.
Port'able, *a.* easily carried.
Port'ly, *a.* bulky; corpulent.
Por'tal, *n.* a gate; a door.
Por'tico, *n.* a covered walk.
Portman'teau, *n.* a portable bag.
Port'hole, *n.* a gun hole in a ship.
Port, *n.* a harbor.
Portfo'lio, *n.* a case for loose papers.
Pur'port, *n.* meaning.
Comport', *v.* to suit; to bear.
Deport'ment, *n.* conduct.
Export', *v.* to carry out.
Import', *v.* to bring in.
Impor'tant, *a.* weighty.
Importune', *v.* to solicit earnestly.
Opportu'nity, *n.* fit time.
Opportune', *a.* well timed.
Report', *n.* a rumor.
Support', *v.* to bear; to uphold.
Transport', *v.* to carry from place to place.

Pra'vus—Crooked; Wicked.

Deprave', *v.* to make wicked. | Deprav'ity, *n.* corruption.

Pre'cium—a Price, Value or Worth.

Appraise', *v.* to set a price upon.
Pre'cious, *a.* of great value.
Price, *n.* value; rate.
Prize, *v.* to value highly.

Pre'cor, preca'tus—to Entreat; to Pray.

Dep'recate, *v.* to dread or regret.
Im'precate, *v.* to pray curses upon.
Preca'rious, *a.* uncertain.
Preach, *v.* to proclaim.

Pre'da—Prey; Plunder.

Prey, *n.* plunder.
Pred'atory, *a.* plundering.
Dep'redate, *v.* to rob; to pillage.
Dep'redator, *n.* a robber.

Prehen'do, prehen'sum—to Take Hold Of; to Seize.

Apprehend', *v.* to seize; to suspect with fear.
Apprehen'sion, *n.* seizure; fear.
Apprise', *v.* to give notice.
Appren'tice, *n.* one bound to learn an art or trade.
Comprehend', *v.* to understand; to include.
Comprehen'sive, *a.* capacious; full.
Comprise', *v.* to include.
En'terprise, *n.* an undertaking.
Surprise', *v.* to astonish.
Impreg'nable, *a.* not to be taken.
Incomprehen'sible, *a.* not to be understood.
Pris'on, *n.* a place of confinement.
Impris'on, *v.* to confine.
Misapprehend', *v.* to misunderstand.
Prize, *n.* something taken or won.
Repri'sal, *n.* a seizure in retaliation.
Reprehend', *v.* to blame.
Reprehen'sible, *a.* blame-worthy.
Reprieve', *v.* to respite.

Pre'mo, pres'sum—to Press.

Press, *v.* to squeeze; to urge.
Impress', *v.* to imprint.
Impres'sion, *n.* a mark made by pressure.
Compress', *v.* to force together.
Depress', *v.* to bear down.
Depres'sion, *n.* dejection.
Oppress', *v.* to crush by severity.
Express', *v.* to squeeze out; to declare.
Expres'sive, *a.* showing with force.
Print, *v.* to stamp with letters.
Imprint', *v.* to press on.
Repress', *v.* to force back.
Suppress', *v.* to subdue; to conceal.

Pre′tium—Price; Reward.

Price, *n.* the money asked or paid for anything.
Pre′cious, *a.* valuable; costly.
Appre′ciate, *v.* to set a just value on.
Depre′ciate, *v.* to undervalue.

Pri′mus—First. Prin′ceps, prin′cipis—Original; Chief.

Prime, *a.* first rate; highest.
Prime, *v.* to apply a first coat of paint.
Prim′er, *n.* a child's first book.
Prime′val, *a.* original.
Prim′itive, *a.* original.
Prince, *n.* a king's son.
Pri′mate, *n.* an archbishop.
Prem′ier, *n.* a prime minister.
Prim, *a.* formal; precise.
Pri′mary, *a.* first; chief.
Prin′ciple, *n.* original cause; element.
Prin′cipal, *a.* chief; main.
Pri′or, *a.* preceding in time.
Prior′ity, *n.* state of being first.
Pris′tine, *a.* first; original.

Pri′vus—Single; Belonging to One's Self Alone.

Pri′vate, *a.* secret; belonging to one's self alone.
Pri′vacy, *n.* secrecy.
Priva′tion, *n.* loss; absence.
Priv′ilege, *n.* a peculiar advantage.
Priv′y, *a.* sharing in a secret; secret.
Priv′ily, *ad.* in a secret manner.
Deprive′, *v.* to take from.
Privateer′, *n.* a private ship of war.

Pro′bo, proba′tum—to Prove; to Try. Pro′bus—Honest.

Prob′ity, *n.* honesty; integrity.
Probe, *v.* to search into.
Prob′able, *a.* likely.
Proba′tion, *n.* trial.
Prove, *v.* to confirm by experiment.
Proof, *n.* that which renders certain.
Approve′, *v.* to like; to be pleased with.
Appro′val, *n.* the act of approving.
Approba′tion, *n.* the act of approving.
Disprove′, *v.* to show to be false.
Disapprove′, *v.* to account deserving censure.
Improve′, *v.* to make better.
Reprove′, *v.* to blame; to chide.
Reprobate′, *a.* lost to virtue.
Reproof′, *n.* open censure.

Pro′pe—Near. Prox′imus—Nearest or Next.

Propin′quity, *n.* nearness.
Prox′imate, *a.* nearest; next.
Approx′imate, *v.* to come near.
Approach′, *v.* to draw near to.
Proxim′ity, *n.* nearness.
Propi′tious, *a.* favorable.
Propi′tiate, *v.* to conciliate.
Reproach′, *v.* to censure.

Pro′prius—One's Own; Peculiar; Fit.

Appro′priate, *v.* to take for one's own use.
Appro′priate, *a.* peculiar; suitable.
Prop′er, *a.* suitable; fit.
Improp′er, *a.* unbecoming.
Impropri′ety, *n.* unfitness.
Propri′ety, *n.* fitness; justness.
Prop′erty, *n.* that which is one's own.
Propri′etor, *n.* an owner.

Pug′nus—the Fist. Pug′no—to Fight or Contend.

Pu′gilist, *n.* one who fights with his fist.
Pugna′cious, *a.* quarrelsome.
Impugn′, *v.* to attack; to oppose.
Repug′nance, *n.* opposition of mind.

Pun'go, punc'tum—to PRICK; to STING.

PUN'GENT, *a.* pricking; sharp.
PUNCT'URE, *n.* a hole pierced.
PUNCT'UAL, *a.* exact; precise.
PUNCTIL'IOUS, *a.* exact to excess.
COMPUNC'TION, *n.* sting of conscience.
EXPUNGE', *v.* to rub out.

POIG'NANT, *a.* severe; intense.
POINT, *n.* the sharp end of anything.
POINT, *v.* to aim; to direct.
PON'IARD, *n.* a dagger.
POUNCE, *v.* to fall on and seize.
PUNCH, *v.* to perforate.

Pu'nio, puni'tum—to PUNISH.

PUN'ISH, *v.* to inflict pain for evil conduct.
IMPU'NITY, *n.* freedom from punishment.

Pur'go—to CLEANSE; to CLEAR.

PURGE, *v.* to make clear or pure.
PUR'GATIVE, *n.* a purging medicine.
EXPUR'GATE, *v.* to cleanse from.

Pu'rus—CLEAN; PURE.

PURE, *a.* free from mixture.
PU'RIFY, *v.* to make pure.

PU'RITY, *n.* cleanness.
IMPURE', *a.* not pure; unholy.

Pu'to, puta'tum—to CUT or PRUNE; to THINK; to RECKON.

ACCOUNT', *n.* a reckoning; a narrative.
AM'PUTATE, *v.* to cut off.
COMPUTE', *v.* to count or reckon.
COUNT, *v.* to number.
DEP'UTY, *n.* one appointed to act for another.

DEPUTE', *v.* to empower to act.
DIS'COUNT, *v.* to count off; to deduct.
DISPUTE', *v.* to contend in argument.
REPUTE', *n.* character; name.
REPUTA'TION, *n.* character by report.
DISREP'UTABLE, *a.* dishonorable.
IMPUTE', *v.* to charge upon.

RECOUNT', *v.* to relate.

Pu'tris—ROTTEN. Pu'treo—to be ROTTEN.

PU'TRID, *a.* rotten.
PUTRID'ITY, *n.* rottenness.

PU'TREFY, *v.* to make rotten.
PUTRES'CENT, *a.* growing rotten.

Qua'lis—of WHAT SORT; SUCH AS.

QUAL'ITY, *n.* degree of excellence.
QUAL'IFY, *v.* to render fit.

QUALIFICA'TION, *n.* fitness.
DISQUAL'IFY, *v.* to render unfit.

Qua'tuor—FOUR. Quad'ra—a SQUARE.

QUAD'RANT, *n.* a quarter of a circle.
QUADRILLE', *n.* a dance.
QUADROON', *n.* a person quarter blooded.
QUAD'RUPLE, *a.* fourfold.
QUAD'RUPED, *n.* a fourfooted animal.

QUART, *n.* one-fourth of a gallon.
QUAR'TER, *n.* the fourth part.
SQUAD'RON, *n.* part of a fleet.
SQUARE, *n.* a figure of four equal sides and four right angles.
QUAR'ANTINE, *n.* forty days.

Que'ror, ques'tus—to COMPLAIN.

QUAR'REL, *v.* to contend angrily.
QUER'ULOUS, *a.* full of complaint.

Quæ′ro, quæsi′tum—to Seek; to Ask.

Quest, *n.* search; inquiry.
Que′ry, *n.* an inquiry.
Ques′tion, *n.* something asked.
Que′rist, *n.* an inquirer.
Acquire′, *v.* to obtain.
Acquisi′tion, *n.* the thing acquired.
Con′quer, *v.* to gain by force.
Con′quest, *n.* victory.
Ex′quisite, *a.* excellent; fine.
In′quest, *n.* a judicial inquiry.
Inquire′, *v.* to seek out.
Inquisi′tion, *n.* search; trial.
Inquis′itive, *a.* curious; prying.
Per′quisite, *n.* a fee of office.
Request′, *v.* to ask; to solicit.
Require′, to demand; to claim.
Req′uisite, *a.* necessary.

Qui′es, quie′tis—Rest; Ease.

Qui′et, *a.* still; calm.
Qui′etude, *n.* rest; repose.
Acquiesce′, *v.* to quietly assent.
Disqui′et, *v.* to make uneasy.
Re′quiem, *n.* a hymn for the dead.

Quot—How Many; So Many.

Al′iquot, *a.* measuring without a remainder.
Quo′rum, *n.* a competent number to do business.
Quo′ta, *n.* a just part or share.
Quo′tient, *n.* the number which shows how many times the divisor is contained in the dividend.

Ra′dius—the Spoke of a Wheel; a Beam or Ray of Light.

Ra′dius, *n.* the semi-diameter of a circle.
Ray, *n.* a line of light.
Ra′diate, *v.* to emit rays.
Ra′diance, *n.* sparkling luster.
Irra′diate, *v.* to illumine.

Ra′dix, rad′icis—a Root; a Foundation.

Rad′ical, *a.* pertaining to the root.
Erad′icate, *v.* to root out.

Ra′do, ra′sum—to Shave; to Scrape.

Abrade′, *v.* to rub or wear off.
Abra′sion, *n.* the act of rubbing off.
Ra′zor, *n.* a tool for shaving.
Erase′, *v.* to rub out.
Raze, *v.* to destroy utterly.

Ra′mus—a Bough or Branch.

Ram′ify, *v.* to branch out.
Ramifica′tion, *n.* a branch.

Ran′ceo—to be Stale; Strong Scented.

Ran′cid, *a.* having a rank smell.
Ran′cor, *n.* spite; malice.
Rank, *a.* strong to the taste.
Ran′kle, *v.* to fester.

Ra′pio, rap′tum—to Snatch; to Seize; to Hurry Away.

Rap′ine, *n.* plunder.
Rapa′cious, *a.* plundering; greedy.
Rav′enous, *a.* hungry to rage.
Rapt, *a.* seized with rapture.
Rap′ture, *n.* extreme delight.
Enrap′ture, *v.* to delight highly.
Rap′id, *a.* hurrying away; swift.
Rav′age, *v.* to lay waste.
Rav′ish, *v.* to take away by violence.

Ra'rus—Scattered; Scarce; Thin.

Rar'efy, v. to make thin. | Rar'ity, n. thinness.

Re'go, rec'tum—to Govern; to Rule.

Re'gal, a. royal; kingly.
Correct', v. to make right.
Direct', v. to guide; to order.
Direct', a. straight.
Direct'ly, ad. immediately.
Direc'tion, n. aim; order.
Erect', a. upright.
Incor'rigible, a. bad beyond correction.
Incorrect', a. not exact; wrong.
Indirect', a. not direct.
Irreg'ular, a. not regular.
Rec'tify, v. to make right.
Rec'titude, n. uprightness; virtue.
Re'gent, n. a governor.
Rec'tor, n. a minister of a parish.
Reg'icide, n. the murderer of a king.
Reg'imen, n. course of diet.
Reg'ular, a. agreeable to rule.
Reg'ulate, v. to adjust by rule.
Regular'ity, n. conformity to rule.
Regula'tion, n. method; rule.
Reign, v. to rule, as a king.
Right, a. just; true; not wrong.
Right, n. freedom from error; justice
Rule, v. to govern; to control.
Rega'lia, n. ensigns of royalty.

Re'or, ra'tus—to Think; to Judge.

Rate, n. a fixed price.
Rate, v. to appraise.
Rat'ify, v. to confirm.
Ratifica'tion, n. confirmation.
Ra'tional, a. agreeable to reason.
Ra'tion, n. a fixed allowance.
Ra'tio, n. proportion; rate.
Rea'son, n. the faculty of judging.
Rea'son, v. to examine by arguments.

Re'po, rep'tum—to Creep.

Rep'tile, n. a creeping animal.

Res—a Thing.

Re'al, a. actually existing.
Real'ity, n. actual existence.
Re'alize, v. to feel strongly, or consider as real.

Re'te—a Net.

Ret'icule, n. a small bag.
Ret'iform, a. having the form of a net.
Ret'ina, n. one of the coats of the eye, like a net.

Ri'deo, ri'sum—to Laugh; to Smile.

Rid'icule, a. to make sport of.
Ridic'ulous, v. worthy of ridicule.
Ris'ible, a. laughable.
Deride', v. to laugh at; to mock.
Deris'ion, n. contempt.

Ri'geo—to be Cold or Stiff.

Rig'id, a. stiff; strict.
Rigid'ity, n. stiffness; harshness.
Rig'or, n. stiffness; severity.
Rig'orous, a. severe; exact.

Ro'bur, ro'boris—an Oak; Strength.

Corrob'orate, v. to confirm. | Robust', a. strong; vigorous.

Ri'vus—a STREAM or RIVER.

RIV'ER, *n.* a large stream.
RIV'ULET, *n.* a little stream.
ARRIVE', *v.* to come to.
DERIVE', *v.* to deduce; to draw.
RI'VAL, *n.* a competitor.
RI'VAL, *v.* to try to equal or excel.

Ro'do, ro'sum—to GNAW; to EAT AWAY.

CORRODE', *v.* to eat away slowly.
CORRO'SION, *n.* the act of corroding.

Ro'go, roga'tum—to ASK; to DEMAND or CLAIM.

AB'ROGATE, *v.* to repeal; to annul.
AR'ROGATE, *v.* to claim proudly.
AR'ROGANT, *a.* haughty; conceited.
DER'OGATE, *v.* to detract.
DEROG'ATORY, *a.* tending to lessen.
INTER'ROGATE, *v.* to question.
PREROG'ATIVE, *n.* an exclusive privilege.
PROROGUE', *v.* to put off.

Ro'ta—a WHEEL; a CIRCLE.

RO'TARY, *a.* turning on its axis, as a wheel.
ROTE, *a.* a mere repetition of words without attending to the sense.
ROUTINE', *n.* a round of business.
ROTA'TION, *n.* a turning round.
ROTUND', *a.* round; circular.
ROTUND'ITY, *n.* roundness.
ROTUND'O, *n.* a round building.

Ru'dis—RUDE; UNWROUGHT; UNTAUGHT.

RUDE, *a.* rough; coarse; unfinished.
ER'UDITE, *a.* learned.
ERUDI'TION, *n.* learning.
RU'DIMENT, *n.* a first principle.

Ru'ga—a WRINKLE.

COR'RUGATE, *v.* to wrinkle.
COR'RUGATED, *p. a.* furrowed.

Rum'po, rup'tum—to BREAK; to BURST.

RUP'TURE, *n.* a breaking.
ABRUPT', *a.* broken off short.
BANK'RUPT, *n.* one who cannot pay his debts.
CORRUPT', *v.* to deprave.
CORRUP'TION, *n.* depravity.
ERUP'TIVE, *a.* a bursting forth.
ERUP'TION, *n.* a bursting out.
IRRUP'TION, *n.* a bursting in.
INTERRUPT', *v.* to stop; to hinder.

Rus, ru'ris—the COUNTRY.

RU'RAL, *a.* relating to the country.
RUS'TIC, *a.* plain; rude.
RUSTIC'ITY, *n.* want of refinement.
RUS'TICATE, *v.* to reside in the country.

Sa'cer, sa'cri—SACRED; HOLY.

SA'CRED, *a.* holy; inviolable.
CON'SECRATE, *v.* to make sacred.
DES'ECRATE, *v.* to pervert from a sacred purpose.
DESECRA'TION, *n.* a profaning.
SACERDO'TAL, *a.* belonging to the priesthood.
EX'ECRATE, *v.* to make hateful.
SAC'RAMENT, *n.* the Lord's supper.
SAC'RIFICE, *n.* a religious offering.
SAC'RIFICE, *v.* to offer to heaven.
SAC'RILEGE, *n.* a violation of sacred things.

LATIN ROOTS AND DERIVATIVES.

Sa'gio—to Perceive Quickly; to Foresee.

Sage, *a.* wise; prudent; solemn.
Sage, *n.* a wise man.
Saga'cious, *a.* discerning quickly.
Sagac'ity, *n.* quick discernment.
Presage', *v.* to foretell.

Sal—Salt; Seasoning; Wit.

Sal'ad, *n.* raw herbs eaten as a relish to other food.
Sal'ary, *n.* yearly wages.
Saline', *a.* like salt.
Sauce, *n.* something to give relish to food.

Sa'lio, sal'tum—to Leap; to Jump; to Spring.

Assail', *v.* to attack.
Assault', *n.* an attack.
Des'ultory, *a.* jumping from one thing to another.
Exult', *v.* to leap for joy.
Insult', *v.* to leap upon; to abuse.
Result', *v.* to spring back.
Sal'ly, *v.* to issue out.
Sa'lient, *a.* leaping; projecting.
Salm'on, *n.* a leaping fish.
Salta'tion, *n.* a leaping or jumping.

Sa'lus, salu'tis—Safety; Health; Welfare.

Sal'utary, *a.* healthful.
Safe, *a.* free from danger.
Salu'brity, *n.* healthfulness.
Salute', *v.* to wish health to.
Sal'vage, *n.* an allowance for saving goods from a wreck.
Saluta'tion, *n.* a greeting.
Salva'tion, *n.* preservation from destruction.
Sal'vo, *n.* an exception.
Salve, *n.* an ointment.
Save, *v.* to preserve; to rescue.
Sav'iour, *n.* a deliverer.

San'cio, sanc'tum—to Make Sacred; to Confirm.

Saint, *n.* a holy person.
Sanc'tify, *v.* to make holy.
Sanc'timony, *n.* holiness.
Sanc'tion, *n.* confirmation.
Sanc'tity, *n.* holiness.
Sanc'tuary, *n.* a sacred place.

San'guis, san'guinis—Blood.

San'guinary, *a.* bloody.
San'guine, *a.* full of blood; ardent.
Consanguin'ity, *n.* relationship.
Ensan'guine, *v.* to stain with blood.

Sa'nus—Sound; Healthy.

Sane, *a.* sound; having reason.
San'ity, *n.* soundness of mind.
Insane', *a.* disordered in mind.
Insan'ity, *n.* madness.

Sa'pio—to Savor or have Taste; to be Wise.

Sa'pient, *a.* wise; knowing.
Sa'pience, *n.* wisdom.
Sap'id, *a.* having taste.
Saporif'ic, *a.* producing taste.
Insip'id, *a.* tasteless.
Sa'vor, *n.* taste or oder.
Sa'vory, *a.* pleasing to the taste or smell.

Sca'la—a Ladder; a Stair.

Escalade', *n.* an assault of a fortress by means of ladders.
Scale, *v.* to mount by a ladder.

Sa'tis—Enough; Sufficient.

Sate, *v.* to give enough.
Sa'tiate, *v.* to fill beyond natural desire.
Sati'ety, *n.* an excess of gratification.
Sat'urate, *v.* to supply fully.
Sat'isfy, *v.* to make or give enough.
Insa'tiable, *a.* not to be satisfied.

Scan'do, scan'sum—to Climb; to Mount.

Ascend', *v.* to climb or go up.
Ascent', *n.* an eminence.
Descend', *v.* to go down.
Descent, *n.* declivity.
Condescend', *v.* to stoop.
Transcend', *v.* to rise beyond.
Scan, *v.* to examine nicely.
Condescen'sion, *n.* a voluntary stooping from dignity.

Scin'do, scis'sum—to Cut; to Divide.

Scis'sors, *n.* small shears.
Rescind', *v.* to revoke.

Sci'o—to Know. Scien'tia—Knowledge.

Sci'ence, *n.* knowledge.
Scientif'ic, *a.* relating to science.
Sci'olist, *n.* a smatterer.
Con'scious, *a.* knowing.
Con'science, *n.* the knowledge of right and wrong.
Conscien'tious, *a.* obedient to the dictates of conscience.
Omnis'cient, *a.* all-knowing.

Scri'bo, scrip'tum—to Write; to Draw or Paint.

Scribe, *n.* a writer; a secretary.
Scrib'ble, *v.* to write carelessly.
Script'ure, *n.* a writing; the Bible.
Scrip, *n.* a small writing.
Subscribe', *v.* to sign; to attest.
Subscrip'tion, *n.* the act of subscribing.
Ascribe', *v.* to attribute to.
Circumscribe', *v.* to limit.
Describe', *v.* to give an account of.
Inscribe', *v.* to write upon.
Inscrip'tion, *n.* an address.
Man'uscript, *n.* a paper written.
Prescribe', *v.* to give a written direction.
Prescrip'tion, *n.* a medical receipt.
Proscribe', *v.* to censure and condemn.
Transcribe', *v.* to copy.
Tran'script, *n.* a copy.
Superscrip'tion, *n.* a writing on the outside.
Post'script, *n.* something written afterwards.

Scru'tor, scruta'tus—to Search Closely.

Scru'tiny, *n.* close examination.
Scru'tinize, *v.* to examine closely.
Inscru'table, *a.* unsearchable.

Scur'ra—a Scoffer; a Buffoon.

Scurril'ity, *n.* abusive language.
Scur'rilous, *a.* vulgar; indecent.

Se'co, sec'tum—to Cut; to Divide or Separate.

Sec'tion, *n.* a part.
Sect, *n.* a division; a party.
Seg'ment, *n.* a part cut off.
Sec'tary, *n.* one of a sect.
Dissect', *v.* to cut in pieces.
Bisect', *v.* to divide into two equal parts.
In'sect, *n.* a small animal.
Intersect', *v.* to cut mutually.
Venesec'tion, *n.* blood-letting.

Scul'po, sculp'tum—to CARVE.

SCULP'TOR, *n.* a carver of wood or stone.
SCULP'TURE, *n.* the art of carving.

Se'deo, ses'sum—to SIT; to LIGHT or SETTLE.

SED'ENTARY, *a.* sitting; inactive.
SES'SION, *n.* a sitting.
SEDATE', *a.* settled; calm.
SED'IMENT, *n.* that which settles.
SED'ULOUS, *a.* diligent.
ASSID'UOUS, *a.* constant in application.
ASSESS', *v.* to set a tax or duty.
INSID'IOUS, *a.* sly; deceitful.
POSSESS', *v.* to hold; to own.
PRESIDE', *v.* to direct or control.
RESIDE', *v.* to live in a place.
RES'IDUE, *n.* that which is left.
SUBSIDE', *v.* to settle down; to sink away.
SUBSID'IARY, *a.* aiding.
SUB'SIDIZE, *v.* to hire with a subsidy.
SUB'SIDY, *n.* aid in money.
SUPERSEDE', *v.* to take the place of.

Se'men, sem'inis—SEED.

SEM'INAL, *a.* pertaining to seed.
SEM'INARY, *n.* a place of education.
DISSEM'INATE, *v.* to scatter apart, as seed.

Se'nex, se'nis—an OLD PERSON.

SE'NIOR, *n.* one older than another.
SE'NILE, *a.* pertaining to old age.
SEN'ATE, *n.* a body of senators.
SEIGN'IOR, *n.* a nobleman.

Sen'tio, sen'sum—to PERCEIVE; to FEEL; to THINK.

SEN'TIMENT, *n.* thought; opinion.
SENTIMEN'TAL, *a.* reflective.
SENSE, *n.* perception; meaning.
SENS'UAL, *a.* pleasing the senses.
SEN'SITIVE, *a.* easily affected.
SEN'SIBLE, *a.* intelligent.
ASSENT', *v.* to agree to.
CONSENT', *v.* to yield.
DISSENT', *v.* to differ in opinion.
DISSEN'SION, *n.* strife; quarrel.
PRESENT'IMENT, *n.* a perceiving beforehand.
RESENT', *v.* to be angry at.
SCENT, *v.* to perceive by the smell.

Se'quor, secu'tus—to FOLLOW.

SE'QUEL, *n.* that which follows.
SE'QUENCE, *n.* a following.
SUB'SEQUENT, *a.* coming after.
CONSEC'UTIVE, *a.* following in regular order.
CON'SEQUENT, *a.* following as an effect.
ENSUE', *v.* to follow.
EX'ECUTE, *v.* to carry into effect.
OBSE'QUIOUS, *a.* servilely obedient.
OB'SEQUIES, *n.* funeral solemnities.
PER'SECUTE, *v.* to pursue with hatred.
PROS'ECUTE, *v.* to follow with a view to accomplish.
PURSUE', *v.* to follow; to chase.
SUE, *v.* to prosecute by law.
SUIT, *n.* a petition; a set.
SUITE, *n.* attendants following.

Se'ro, ser'tum—to KNIT; to JOIN.

SE'RIES, *n.* a succession of things.
SER'MON, *n.* a religious discourse.
ASSERT', *v.* to declare; to affirm.
DESERT', *v.* to forsake.
DISSERTA'TION, *n.* a treatise.
INSERT', *v.* to set in or among.

Ser′po—to Creep.

Ser′pent, *n.* a creeping animal.
Ser′pentine, *a.* winding; spiral.

Ser′vio, servi′tum—to Serve; to Obey.

Serve, *v.* to assist; to wait on.
Ser′vant, *n.* one who serves.
Serf, *n.* a kind of slave.
Ser′vile, *a.* meanly submissive.
Ser′vitude, *n.* slavery.
Deserve′, *v.* to be worthy of.
Subserve′, *v.* to serve slightly.

Ser′vo, serva′tum—to Keep; to Save.

Conserve′, *v.* to preserve entire.
Con′serve, *n.* a sweetmeat.
Conserv′ative, *a.* opposing injury.
Observe′, *v.* to watch; to keep.
Preserve′, *v.* to keep; to save.
Reserve′, *v.* to hold back.
Res′ervoir, *n.* a place where any thing is stored.

Seve′rus—Severe.

Severe′, *a.* sharp; harsh.
Persever′ance, *n.* constancy in a pursuit.
Sever′ity, *n.* harshness; strictness.
Persevere′, *v.* to persist in an attempt.

Si′dus, sid′eris—a Star.

Side′real, *a.* relating to the stars.
Consid′er, *v.* to think of.
Desire′, *v.* to request; to wish.
Desidera′tum, *n.* something needed.

Sig′num—a Mark or Sign.

Sign, *n.* a token; a mark.
Sign, *v.* to mark with one's name.
Sig′nal, *n.* a sign to give notice.
Sig′nal, *a.* remarkable; eminent.
Sig′nify, *v.* to express; to mean.
Insignif′icant, *a.* unimportant.
Sig′nalize, *v.* to make eminent.
Sig′nature, *n.* a sign or mark impressed.
Significa′tion, *n.* meaning.
Sig′net, *n.* a seal.
Assign′, *v.* to mark out.
Assign′ment, *n.* a making over.
Consign′, *v.* to commit to another's care.
Design′, *v.* to purpose; to plan.
Des′ignate, *v.* to point out.
Resign′, *v.* to give up; to yield.

Sim′ilis—Like.

Sim′ilar, *a.* like; resembling.
Sim′ile, *n.* a comparison.
Assim′ilate, *v.* to make like to.
Dissem′ble, *v.* to hide under a false appearance.
Dissim′ilar, *a.* unlike.
Dissimula′tion, *n.* hypocrisy.
Simil′itude, *n.* resemblance.
Fac sim′ile, *n.* an exact imitation.
Resem′ble, *v.* to be like.
Simula′tion, *n.* a counterfeiting.

Sis′to—to Stand; to Stop.

Assist′, *v.* to help.
Consist′, *v.* to be composed of.
Desist′, *v.* to cease from; to stop.
Exist′, *v.* to have being.
Consis′tent, *a.* agreeing together.
Insist′, *v.* to stand upon; to be unyielding.
Persist′, *v.* to stand to the end.
Resist′, *v.* to make opposition.

Si′nus—the Bosom; a Bend.

Si′nus, n. a bay.
Sinuos′ity, n. a bending in and out.
Insin′uate, v. to introduce slowly and artfully.
Insinua′tion, n. a hint.

So′cius—a Companion.

So′ciable, a. familiar; friendly.
So′cial, a. relating to society.
Soci′ety, n. a collection of persons.
Asso′ciate, v. to unite.

Sol—the Sun.

So′lar, a. belonging to the sun.
Sol′stice, n. the tropical point.

Solic′itus—Uneasy; Anxious.

Solic′it, v. to ask with earnestness.
Solicita′tion, n. entreaty.
Solic′itous, a. anxious.
Solic′itude, n. anxiety.

Sol′idus—Solid; Firm; Entire.

Sol′id, a. hard; firm; not liquid.
Solid′ity, n. hardness; firmness.
Consol′idate, v. to unite into a solid mass.
Solid′ify, v. to make solid.
Sol′der, v. to unite by metallic cement.
Sol′dier, n. a warrior.

So′lor, sola′tus—to Cheer; to Comfort; to Soothe.

Console′, v. to comfort; to cheer.
Sol′ace, n. a comfort; ease.
Discon′solate, a. sad; hopeless.

So′lus—Alone.

Sole, a. single; only.
Sol′itary, a. alone; lonely.
Sol′itude, n. a lonely place.
Des′olate, a. without inhabitants.
Solil′oquy, n. a speech to one's self.

Sol′vo, solu′tum—to Loose; to Free; to Melt.

Solve, v. to explain.
Solu′tion, n. explanation.
Sol′uble, a. capable of being dissolved.
Sol′vency, n. ability to pay.
Sol′vent, a. able to pay all debts.
Sol′vent, n. a fluid which dissolves a substance.
Insol′vent, a. unable to pay.
Absolve′, v. to acquit of a crime.
Ab′solute, a. unlimited.
Absolu′tion, n. acquittal.
Dissolve′, v. to melt.
Dis′solute, a. loose in morals.
Resolve′, v. to determine.
Resolu′tion, n. determination.
Res′olute, a. fixed in purpose.

Som′nus—Sleep.

Somnam′bulist, n. one who walks in sleep.
Somnif′ic, a. causing sleep.
Som′nolency, n. drowsiness.

Sor′beo, sorp′tum—to Suck or Imbibe.

Absorb′, v. to suck up.
Absorp′tion, n. a sucking up.

So′nus—a Sound.

Sound, n. a noise.
Sono′rous, a. loud sounding.
Con′sonant, n. a letter.
Con′sonant, a. consistent.
Dis′sonant, a. discordant.
Resound′, v. to send back sound.
U′nison, n. agreement of sound.
Res′onant, a. resounding.

Sors, sor′tis—a Lot; a Kind or Sort.

Assort′, v. to separate into classes.
Con′sort, n. a companion; a wife or husband.
Consort′, v. to associate.
Resort′, v. to turn to.
Sort, n. a kind; a species.

Spar′go, spar′sum—to Scatter.

Sparse, a. thinly spread.
Asperse′, v. to bespatter with calumny.
Asper′sion, n. calumny.
Disperse′, v. to scatter.
Intersperse′, v. to scatter between.

Spa′tium—Space; Room.

Space, n. room; extension.
Expa′tiate, v. to enlarge upon a subject.
Spa′cious, a. roomy; extensive.

Spe′cio, spec′tum—to Look; to See.

As′pect, n. look; appearance.
Cir′cumspect, a. watchful; cautious.
Conspic′uous, a. in full view.
Despise′, v. to look down upon.
Des′picable, a. base; mean.
Espe′cial, a. particular.
Expect′, v. to look for.
Inspect′, v. to look into.
Perspec′tive, n. a view through; a prospect.
Perspicu′ity, n. clearness.
Pros′pect, n. view within reach of the eye.
Prospec′tive, a. looking forward.
Retrospec′tive, a. looking back.
Respect′, n. regard; honor.
Disrespect′, n. want of respect.
Respect′able, a. worthy of regard.
Respec′tive, a. particular.
Spe′cial, a. particular; uncommon.
Spe′cies, n. a sort or kind.
Specif′ic, a. naming the particular properties.
Specif′ic, n. an unfailing agent.
Spec′ify, v. to mention particulars.
Spec′imen, n. a sample.
Spe′cious, a. apparently right.
Spec′tacle, n. a show; a sight.
Specta′tor, n. a looker on.
Spec′ter, n. an apparition.
Spec′ulate, v. to meditate.
Suspect′, v. to mistrust.
Suspi′cion, n. act of suspecting.

Spi′ro, spira′tum—to Breathe.

Spir′it, n. the soul; the life.
Spir′itual, a. belonging to the spirit.
Sprite, n. a spirit.
Spir′itualize, v. to refine.
Spir′acle, n. a breathing hole.
Aspire′, v. to aim at something elevated.
As′pirant, n. one who aspires.
Aspira′tion, n. a breathing after.
Conspir′acy, n. a plot; treason.
Conspire′, v. to combine for some evil purpose.
Dispir′it, v. to discourage.
Expire′, v. to die.
Inspire′, v. to breathe into.
Inspir′it, v. to animate.
Perspire′, v. to emit by the pores.
Respire′, v. to breathe.
Transpire′, v. to pass out; to become known.

Spe′ro—to Hope.

Despair′, n. hopelessness.
Des′perate, a. reckless; hopeless.
Despera′do, n. a reckless villain.

Pros′per, v. to be successful.
Prosper′ity, n. success; fortune.
Pros′perous, a. thriving.

Spi′na—a Thorn; the Spine or Back Bone.

Spine, n. the back bone.
Spi′nous, a. full of thorns.

Spi′nal, a. pertaining to the back bone.

Splen′deo—to Shine.

Splen′did, a. shining; showy.
Splen′dor, n. luster; elegance.
Resplen′dent, a. very bright.

Spo′lium—Spoil; Booty.

Spoil, n. plunder; pillage.
Despoil, v. to rob; to strip.

Spon′deo, spon′sum—to Promise; to Hope.

Spon′sor, n. one who promises for another.
Spon′sal, a. relating to marriage.
Spouse, n. a husband or wife.
Espouse′, v. to take to one's self.

Correspond′, v. to suit; to answer.
Despond′, v. to lose courage.
Despond′ent, a. not hoping.
Respond′, v. to answer.
Response′, n. a reply.
Respon′sible, a. answerable.

Stel′la—a Star.

Constella′tion, n. a cluster of stars.
Stel′late, a. like a star.
Stel′lar, a. starry.

Ster′ilis—Barren.

Ster′ile, a. barren; unfruitful.
Steril′ity, n. barrenness.

Ster′no, stra′tum—to Strew; to Lay Flat.

Stra′tum, n. a layer, as of earth.
Strat′ified, a. composed of layers.
Strat′ify, v. to arrange in layers.

Substra′tum, n. a lower layer.
Pros′trate, a. lying flat.
Consterna′tion, n. great terror.

Sti′go—to Prick; to Spur.

In′stigate, v. to stir up; to urge.
Instiga′tion, n. a spurring on.

Stil′lo, stilla′tum—to Drop or Trickle Down.

Distill′, v. to fall drop by drop.
Instill′, v. to drop in; to teach slowly.

Stim′ulus—a Spur.

Stim′ulus, n. something that excites.
Stim′ulate, v. to spur; to urge.
Stim′ulative, a. exciting.

Stim′ulant, n. something that excites.

Stin'guo, stinc'tum—to MARK; to THRUST.

DISTIN'GUISH, *v.* to mark difference; to make eminent.
DISTINCT', *a.* separate; clear.
EXTINCT', *a.* put out; destroyed.
INDISTINCT', *a.* not plain; confused.
EXTIN'GUISH, *v.* to quench; to destroy.

Sti'no, stina'tum—to FIX; to SET.

DES'TINE, *v.* to fix unalterably.
DESTINA'TION, *n.* a purpose or end.
OB'STINATE, *a.* stubborn.
PREDES'TINE, *v.* to foredoom.

Stirps, stir'pis—a ROOT or STEM.

EXTIR'PATE, *v.* to take out the roots; to destroy utterly.
EXTIRPA'TION, *n.* total destruction.

Sto, sta'tum—to STAND; to PLACE; to SET UP.

STATE, *n.* rank; condition.
STA'TION, *n.* a standing place.
STA'TIONARY, *a.* standing still.
STAT'URE, *n.* the height of a person.
STAT'UE, *n.* a standing image.
STA'BLE, *a.* able to stand.
STABIL'ITY, *n.* firmness.
AR'MISTICE, *n.* a short truce.
ARREST', *v.* to stop; to seize.
CIR'CUMSTANCE, *n.* a fact or event attending something else.
CIRCUMSTAN'TIAL, *a.* detailing all the circumstances.
CON'STANT, *a.* unvaried.
CON'STABLE, *n.* a police officer.
CONSIST', *v.* to be composed of.
CON'STITUTE, *v.* to set or build together.
CONSTITU'TION, *n.* a building together; the fundamental laws of a nation or society.
CONTRAST', *v.* to set in opposition.
DESIST', *v.* to stand off; to stop.
DES'TITUTE, *a.* being in want.
DESTITU'TION, *n.* utter want.
DIS'TANT, *a.* not near.
DIS'TANCE, *n.* space between two objects.
ESTAB'LISH, *v.* to settle firmly.
EXIST', *v.* to be.
EX'TANT, *a.* now in being.
INSIST', *v.* to stand upon.
IN'STANCE, *n.* urgency; example.
IN'STANT, *a.* pressing; urgent.
IN'STANT, *n.* a moment.
INSTANTA'NEOUS, *a.* done in an instant.
IN'STITUTE, *v.* to establish.
IN'TERSTICE, *n.* a space between.
OB'STACLE, *n.* something standing in the way.
PERSIST', *v.* to persevere.
RESIST', *v.* to withstand.
PROS'TITUTE, *v.* to devote to a base purpose.
RESTITU'TION, *n.* a placing back.
SUB'STANCE, *n.* being; body.
SUBSTAN'TIAL, *a.* real; solid.
SUPERSTI'TION, *n.* false religion.

Strin'go, stric'tum—to BIND; to DRAW TIGHT.

STRICT, *a.* exact; severe.
ASTRIN'GENT, *a.* drawing together.
CONSTRAIN', *v.* to bind or oblige.
CONSTRAINT', *n.* compulsion.
DISTRAIN', *v.* to lay hold on.
RESTRAIN', *v.* to draw or hold back.
RESTRAINT', *n.* hinderance of the will.
RESTRICT', *v.* to limit.
RESTRIC'TION, *n.* limitation.
STRAIN, *v.* to extend with force.

Stu'deo—to STUDY.

STU'DENT, *n.* a person studying.
STU'DIOUS, *a.* devoted to study.
STUD'Y, *v.* to apply the mind.
STU'DIO, *n.* the workshop of an artist.

LATIN ROOTS AND DERIVATIVES.

Stru'o, struc'tum—to BUILD; to PLACE IN ORDER.

STRUC'TURE, *n.* a building.
CONSTRUCT', *v.* to build; to form.
CON'STRUE, *v.* to interpret.
INSTRUCT', *v.* to teach; to inform.

IN'STRUMENT, *n.* a tool.
OBSTRUCT', *v.* to block up.
DESTROY', *v.* to put an end to.
DESTRUC'TION, *n.* waste; ruin.

Stu'peo—to BE DULL or SENSELESS.

STU'PID, *a.* dull; senseless.
STU'PEFY, *v.* to make stupid.

STUPEFAC'TION, *n.* dullness.
STUPEN'DOUS, *a.* to be wondered at.

Sua'deo, sua'sum—to ADVISE.

PERSUADE', *v.* to advise strongly.
DISSUADE', *v.* to advise against.

PERSUA'SIVE, *a.* having the power to persuade.

Sua'vis—SWEET; PLEASANT.

SUAV'ITY, *n.* sweetness; softness.

SUAV'IFY, *v.* to render agreeable.

Su'do, suda'tum—to SWEAT.

EXUDE', *v.* to sweat out.

SUDORIF'IC, *a.* causing sweat.

Su'go, suc'tum—to SUCK or DRAW IN.

SUCK, *v.* to draw into the mouth.
SUCK'LE, *v.* to nurse at the breast.

SUC'TION, *n.* the act of drawing in.
SUC'CULENT, *a.* juicy; moist.

Su'i—of ONE'S SELF.

SU'ICIDE, *n.* self-murder.

SUICI'DAL, *a.* self-destroying.

Sum'ma—the CHIEF PART; the WHOLE.

CONSUM'MATE, *a.* complete; finished.
SUM, *n.* the whole; the amount.
SUM'MIT, *n.* the utmost height.

SUM'MARY, *n.* an abridgment.
SUM'MARY, *a.* short; brief.

Su'mo, sump'tum—to TAKE; to SPEND or CONSUME.

ASSUME', *v.* to take upon one's self.
ASSUMP'TION, *n.* the act of taking upon one's self.
CONSUME', *v.* to use; to waste.
CONSUMP'TION, *n.* a using or wasting.

PRESUME', *v.* to take for granted.
PRESUMP'TUOUS, *a.* too bold.
RESUME', *v.* to begin again.
SUMP'TUARY, *a.* relating to expense.
SUMP'TUOUS, *a.* costly; magnificent.

Su'per—ABOVE; OVER; HIGH.

SUPE'RIOR, *a.* higher in place or excellence.
SUPER'LATIVE, *a.* highest in degree.
SUPREME', *a.* highest; greatest.
SUPREM'ACY, *n.* highest power.
SUPERB', *a.* grand; magnificent.

SU'PERABLE, *a.* that may be overcome.
INSU'PERABLE, *a.* that cannot be overcome.
SUPERCIL'IOUS, *a.* haughty; overbearing.

Sur'go, surrec'tum—to RISE.

SOURCE, *n.* origin; first cause.
SURGE, *n.* a rising mass of water.
INSUR'GENT, *n.* a rebel.

INSURREC'TION, *n.* a rebellion.
RESURREC'TION, *n.* a rising again.
SURGE'LESS, *a.* smooth; calm.

Taber'na—a SHED or SHOP; an INN.

TAB ERNACLE, *n.* a temporary dwelling. | TAV'ERN, *n.* a drinking place.

Tab'ula—a BOARD; a GAMING TABLE.

TA'BLE, *n.* a board for holding dishes, etc.

TAB'ULAR, *a.* in the form of a table.
TAB'LET, *n.* a little table.

Ta'ceo, tac'itum—to be SILENT.

TAC'IT, *a.* silent; implied. | TAC'ITURN, *n.* habitually silent.

Tan'go, tac'tum—to TOUCH.

TAN'GENT, *n.* a line touching a curve.
TAN'GIBLE, *a.* that may be touched.
TACT, *n.* peculiar skill; nice perception.
INTACT', *a.* untouched.
CON'TACT, *n.* touch; close union.
CONTA'GION, *n.* communication of disease by touch.

CONTIG'UOUS, *a.* touching.
CONTIGU'ITY, *n.* contact.
CONTIN'GENT, *a.* accidental.
ENTIRE', *a.* whole; unbroken.
IN'TEGER, *n.* a whole number.
IN'TEGRAL, *a.* whole.
INTEG'RITY, *n.* honesty; purity.

Tar'dus—SLOW.

RETARD', *v.* to stay or keep back. | TAR'DY, *a.* slow; not swift.

Te'go, tec'tum—to COVER.

INTEG'UMENT, *n.* a covering.
TEG'UMENT, *n.* a natural covering.

PROTECT', *v.* to cover; to defend.
DETECT', *v.* to find out.

DETEC'TION, *n.* discovery.

Tem'no, temp'tum—to SCORN.

CONTEMN', *v.* to despise; to scorn. | CONTEMPT', *n.* scorn; disregard.

Tem'pero—to TEMPER; to REGULATE.

TEM'PER, *n.* disposition.
TEM'PER, *v.* to moderate.
TEM'PERANCE, *n.* moderation.
INTEM'PERANCE, *n.* excess.

TEM'PERATE, *a.* moderate.
TEM'PERAMENT, *n.* constitution.
TEM'PERATURE, *n.* state as regards heat or cold.

DISTEM'PER, *n.* disease.

Tem'pus, tem'poris—TIME; OCCASION.

TEM'PORAL, *a.* relating to time.
TEM'PORARY, *a.* lasting only a time
TEM'PORIZE, *v.* to comply with times and occasions.

CONTEM'PORARY, *a.* living at the same time.
EXTEM'PORE, *ad.* without premeditation.

EXTEMPORA'NEOUS, *a.* uttered without previous study.

Ten'do, ten'sum, or ten'tum—to STRETCH; to GO TOWARDS.

TEND, v. to move towards; to watch.
TEND'ENCY, n. direction towards.
ATTEND', v. to listen; to regard.
ATTEN'TION, n. regard; care.
CONTEND', v. to strive.
CONTEN'TION, n. strife.
DISTEND', v. to expand.
EXTEND', v. to spread; to enlarge.
EXTENT', n. size; compass.
EXTEN'SIVE, a. large; wide spread.
INTEND', v. to mean; to design.
INTEN'TION, n. design.
INTENT', a. eager in pursuing.
INTENSE', a. strained; ardent.
INTEN'SITY, n. ardor; violence.

OSTEN'SIBLE, a. seeming; plausible.
OSTENTA'TION, n. vain show.
PORTEND', v. to foreshow.
PORTEN'TOUS, a. foretokening ill.
PORTENT', n. an omen of ill.
PRETEND', v. to feign.
PRETENSE', n. a feigning.
PRETEN'SION, n. a claim.
SUBTEND', v. to extend under.
SUPERINTEND', v. to have the direction of.
TEN'DON, n. a sinew.
TENSE, a. stretched to stiffness.
TEN'SION, n. tightness.
TENT, n. a portable dwelling.

Te'neo, ten'tum—to HOLD; to KEEP.

ABSTAIN', v. to keep from.
AB'STINENCE, n. the act of keeping from.
ABSTE'MIOUS, a. temperate; sober.
APPERTAIN', v. to belong to.
CONTAIN', v. to hold; to comprise.
CONTENT', a. satisfied.
CONTIN'UE, v. to remain; to last.
CONTIN'UAL, a. uninterrupted.
CONTINU'ITY, n. unbroken connection.
COUN'TENANCE, n. features; look.
DETAIN', v. to keep back.
DETEN'TION, n. a detaining.
ENTERTAIN', v. to receive into one's house.
MAINTAIN', v. to support; to persist in.
OBTAIN', v. to gain; to get.

PERTAIN', v. to belong to.
PER'TINENT, a. to the purpose.
IMPER'TINENT, a. not pertinent; ill mannered.
PERTINA'CIOUS, a. obstinate.
PERTINAC'ITY, n. obstinacy.
RETAIN', v. to keep; to hold.
RETEN'TIVE, a. having the power to retain.
SUSTAIN', v. to hold up; to support.
SUS'TENANCE, n. support.
TEN'ANT, n. an occupier.
TEN'DRIL, n. the clasper of a vine.
TENA'CIOUS, a. holding fast.
TEN'EMENT, n. a dwelling.
TEN'ET, n. an opinion; a principle.
TEN'URE, n. a holding.
TEN'OR, n. continued course; meaning.

Ten'to, tenta'tum—to TRY.

ATTEMPT', n. a trial; an effort.
TEN'TATIVE, a. trying.
TEMPT, v. to solicit to an evil act.

Ten'uis—THIN; FINE.

TEN'UOUS, a. thin; small.
TENU'ITY, n. thinness.

ATTEN'UATE, v. to make thin.
EXTEN'UATE, v. to lessen; to palliate.

Te'ro, tri'tum—to WEAR BY RUBBING.

TRITE, a. worn out by use.
ATTRI'TION, n. a wearing away by rubbing.
TRIT'URATE, v. to grind to a powder.

CON'TRITE, a. bruised in spirit.
DET'RIMENT, n. loss; damage.
DETRI'TUS, n. matter worn off.

Ter'minus—an END; a LIMIT or BOUNDARY.

TERM, *n.* an end or limit.
TER'MINATE, *v.* to put an end to.
INTER'MINABLE, *a.* having no end.
DETER'MINE, *v.* to fix; to decide.
EXTER'MINATE, *v.* to destroy utterly.

Ter'ra—the EARTH or GROUND.

INTER', *v.* to bury in the earth.
DISINTER', *v.* to unbury.
TER'RACE, *n.* a platform of earth.
TERRES'TRIAL, *a.* earthly.
TER'RITORY, *n.* a tract of land.
TERRA'QUEOUS, *a.* composed of land and water.
MEDITERRA'NEAN, *a.* encircled with land.
SUBTERRA'NEAN, *a.* beneath the surface of the earth.
TER'RIER, *n.* a dog that hunts under ground.

Ter'reo—to MAKE AFRAID; to FRIGHTEN.

DETER', *v.* to stop by fear.
TER'ROR, *n.* extreme fear.
TERRIF'IC, *a.* causing fear.
TER'RIBLE, *a.* frightful.
TER'RIFY, *v.* to frighten.

Tes'tis—a WITNESS.

ATTEST', *v.* to bear witness.
CONTEST', *v.* to dispute; to struggle.
DETEST', *v.* to abhor.
DETESTA'TION, *n.* abhorrence.
TESTA'TOR, *n.* one who makes a will.
TES'TAMENT, *n.* a will.
TES'TIMONY, *n.* evidence.
INTES'TATE, *a.* not having made a will.
PROTEST', *v.* to declare against.
PROT'ESTANT, *n.* one who protests.
TESTIMO'NIAL, *n.* a certificate.
TES'TIFY, *v.* to bear witness.

Tex'o, tex'tum—to WEAVE; to KNIT.

CONTEXT', *a.* knit or woven together.
CON'TEXT, *n.* the connected passages.
TEXT'URE, *n.* the thing woven.
PRE'TEXT, *n.* pretence.
TEXT, *n.* a passage of Scripture.

Tim'eo—to FEAR.

TIM'ID, *a.* fearful.
INTIM'IDATE, *v.* to make fearful.
TIM'OROUS, *a.* cowardly.

Tin'go, tinc'tum—to DIP or STEEP; to DYE; to STAIN.

TINGE, *v.* to color slightly.
TINT, *n.* a slight coloring.
TAINT, *n.* a stain or blemish.
TAINT, *v.* to corrupt; to infect.
TINC'TURE, *n.* a steeping or dyeing.
ATTAINT', *v.* to fix a stain upon.
ATTAIN'DER, *n.* a putting a stain upon.

Tol'ero, tolera'tum—to BEAR WITH or SUFFER.

TOL'ERATE, *v.* to bear with that which is not approved.
TOLERA'TION, *n.* allowance of that which is not approved.
INTOL'ERABLE, *a.* that can not be borne.
INTOL'ERANT, *a.* that can not tolerate.

Tit'ulus—a TITLE; an INSCRIPTION.

TI'TLE, *n.* a name; a claim of right.
ENTI'TLE, *v.* to give a claim to.

TIT'ULAR, *a.* relating to a title.
UNTI'TLED, *a.* having no title.

Tor'peo—to BE NUMB or TORPID.

TOR'PID, *a.* inactive; numbed.
TOR'POR, *n.* numbness.

TOR'PITUDE, *n.* sluggishness.
TORPE'DO, *n.* an electric fish.

Tor'reo—to PARCH; to ROAST; to BOIL.

TOR'RID, *a.* dried by heat.
TOR'RENT, *n.* a rapid stream.

TOR'REFY, *v.* to dry by a fire.

Tor'queo, tor'tum—to TWIST; to WRITHE.

CONTOR'TION, *n.* a twisting.
DISTORT', *v.* to twist out of shape.
EXTORT', *v.* to wrest from one.
EXTOR'TION, *n.* illegal exaction.
RETORT', *n.* a severe reply.

RETORT', *v.* to throw back a charge or argument.
TOR'MENT, *n.* extreme pain.
TORT'URE, *n.* extreme pain.
TORT'UOUS, *a.* twisted; winding.

To'tus—the WHOLE; ALL.

TO'TAL, *a.* whole; entire; full.
TO'TALLY, *ad.* wholly; entirely.
SURTOUT', *n.* an overcoat.

FACTO'TUM, *n.* a person for all kinds of work.

Tra'ho, trac'tum—to DRAW; to TAKE.

ABSTRACT', *v.* to draw from.
AB'STRACT, *a.* existing in the mind only.
ABSTRAC'TION, *n.* absence of mind.
ATTRACT', *v.* to draw to; to allure.
ATTRAC'TIVE, *a.* having power to attract.
CONTRACT', *v.* to draw together.
DETRACT', *v.* to take from.
DISTRACT', *v.* to draw apart.
DISTRAC'TION, *n.* derangement of reason.
EXTRACT', *v.* to draw out.
PORTRAY', *v.* to draw forth or exhibit.
TREAT'Y, *n.* a contract or league.

POR'TRAIT, *n.* a likeness.
PROTRACT', *v.* to draw out or lengthen in time.
RETRACT', *v.* to draw back.
SUBTRACT', *v.* to take a part from the rest.
TRACE, *n.* a mark left.
TRACK, *n.* a footprint; a path.
TRACT, *n.* a region; a treatise.
TRACT'ABLE, *a.* docile.
TRACT'ILE, *a.* ductile.
TRAIL, *v.* to draw along the ground.
TRAIT, *n.* a feature; a line.
TREAT, *v.* to use; to discuss.

Tre'mo—to SHAKE; to TREMBLE.

TREM'BLE, *v.* to quake; to quiver.
TRE'MOR, *n.* a trembling.
TREM'ULOUS, *a.* shaking; quivering.

TREMEN'DOUS, *a.* to be trembled at or feared.

Trep'idus—AGITATED; TREMBLING.

INTREP'ID, *a.* not trembling; fearless.
TREPIDA'TION, *n.* fear; tremor.

Tres, tri'a—THREE.

TREB'LE, *a.* threefold.
TRIP'LE, *a.* threefold.
TRI'AD, *n.* the union of three.
TRI'ANGLE, *n.* a figure with three angles.
TRI'UNE, *n.* three in one.

TRI'POD, *n.* a three legged stool.
TRI'DENT, *n.* an instrument having three prongs.
TRIN'ITY, *n.* a union of three in one.
TRIV'IAL, *a.* unimportant.
TRISECT', *v.* to divide into three parts.

TRI'O, *n.* three united.

Trib'uo, tribu'tum—to GIVE; to PAY.

TRIB'UTE, *n.* a tax paid to a conqueror.
TRIB'UTARY, *a.* paying tribute.
ATTRIB'UTE, *v.* to ascribe.

CONTRIB'UTE, *v.* to give with others.
DISTRIB'UTE, *v.* to deal out.
DISTRIBU'TION, *n.* a giving to several.
RETRIB'UTIVE, *a.* repaying.

RETRIBU'TION, *n.* a paying back.

Tri'bus—a TRIBE.

TRIBE, *n.* a distinct body of people. | TRIB'UNE, *n.* a Roman officer.

TRIBU'NAL, *n.* a court of justice.

NOTE.—TRIBUS, originally a third part of the Roman people, afterwards a *tribe;* TRES, three. TRIBUNE, an officer chosen by the common people to protect them from the oppression of the nobles.

Tru'do, tru'sum—to THRUST; to PUSH.

ABSTRUSE', *a.* difficult to be understood.
DETRUDE', *v.* to thrust down.
INTRUDE', *v.* to thrust in.
EXTRU'SION, *n.* the act of thrusting out.

INTRU'SION, *n.* the act of intruding.
OBTRUDE', *v.* to thrust on.
OBTRU'SION, *n.* act of obtruding.
OBTRU'SIVE, *a.* bold; coming uninvited.
INTRU'SIVE, *a.* entering without right.

PROTRUDE', *v.* to thrust forward.

Tu'ber—a SWELLING.

TU'BER, *n.* a knob in roots.
TU'BERCLE, *n.* a small tumor.

PROTU'BERANCE, *n.* a swelling out.
TU'BEROUS, *a.* having tubes.

NOTE.—TUBER, a thickened portion of a subterranean stem or branch, having eyes or buds, as a potato.

Tu'eor, tui'tus—to WATCH; to GUARD.

TUI'TION, *n.* instruction.
INTUI'TION, *n.* immediate perception of truth.
TU'TELAGE, *n.* guardianship.

INTU'ITIVE, *a.* having the power to discover things untaught.
TU'TELAR, *a.* protecting.
TU'TOR, *n.* a teacher; a guardian.

u'meo—to SWELL.

TU'MID, *a.* swollen; pompous.
TU'MOR, *n.* swelling.
TU'MULT, *n.* a commotion.
TUMULT'UARY, *a.* disorderly.
CON'TUMELY, *n.* haughty behavior.

CON'TUMACY, *n.* contempt of authority.
CONTUMA'CIOUS, *a.* stubborn.
TOMB, *n.* a grave; a burial place.
ENTOMB', *v.* to put in a tomb.

LATIN ROOTS AND DERIVATIVES.

Tun'do, tu'sum—to BEAT; to BRUISE.

CONTU'SION, *n.* a bruise. | OBTUSE', *a.* dulled or blunted.

Tur'ba—a CROWD; CONFUSION.

DISTURB', *v.* to disquiet.
DISTURB'ANCE, *n.* confusion.
PERTURBA'TION, *n.* agitation of mind.
TUR'BULENCE, *n.* violence.
TROUB'LE, *n.* perplexity.
TUR'BID, *a.* muddy; not clear.
TUR'BULENT, *a.* full of confusion.

Tur'geo—to SWELL; to be INFLATED.

TUR'GID, *a.* bloated; swollen. | TUR'GENT, *a.* swelling; tumid.

U'ber—FRUITFUL; PLENTIFUL.

EXU'BERANT, *a.* very plentiful. | U'BERTY, *n.* fruitfulness.

Ulte'rior—FURTHER. *Ul'timus*—FURTHEST or LAST.

ULTE'RIOR, *a.* further.
UL'TIMATE, *a.* furthest; final; last.
UL'TIMATELY, *ad.* in the end.
ULTIMA'TUM, *n.* a final proposition.

Um'bra—a SHADOW or SHADE.

UM'BRAGE, *n.* suspicion of injury; offence.
UMBRA'GEOUS, *a.* shady.
UMBREL'LA, *n.* a shade or screen carried in the hands.

Un'da—a WAVE.

UN'DULATE, *v.* to move like waves.
UN'DULATING, *a.* rising and falling.
UN'DULATORY, *a.* moving like waves.
ABOUND', *v.* to be in great plenty.
ABUN'DANT, *a.* plentiful.
REDUN'DANT, *a.* full to overflowing.
ABUN'DANCE, *n.* more than enough.
INUN'DATE, *v.* to flow upon.
INUNDA'TION, *n.* a flood.
REDOUND', *v.* to be sent back, as a wave; to result.

Un'guo, unc'tum—to ANOINT.

UNC'TION, *n.* an anointing.
UNC'TUOUS, *a.* oily; greasy.
UN'GUENT, *n.* ointment.
OINT'MENT, *n.* a salve.

U'nus—ONE; ALONE.

U'NIT, *n.* a single thing.
U'NITY, *n.* oneness.
UNITE', *v.* to make one; to join.
DISUNITE', *v.* to separate.
REUNITE', *v.* to unite again.
UNANIM'ITY, *n.* agreement in opinion.
UNAN'IMOUS, *a.* of one mind.
U'NIFORM, *a.* even; regular.
U'NION, *n.* concord; agreement.
UNIQUE', *a.* the only one of its kind.
U'NISON, *n.* concord of sounds.
U'NIVERSE, *n.* the whole system of things.
UNIVER'SAL, *a.* pertaining to all.

NOTE.—UNION, the upper, inner corner of a flag, the rest being called the *fly*. The *union* of the U. S. flag is a blue field with white stars, representing the confederation of the States, one for each State, and the fly is composed of thirteen alternate white and red stripes, representing the original thirteen states.

Urbs, ur'bis—a City.

UR'BAN, *a.* pertaining to a city.
URBANE', *a.* civil; polite; refined.
URBAN'ITY, *n.* politeness.
SUB'URBS, *n.* the out part of a city.

U'tor, u'sus—to Use.

USE, *v.* to employ.
USE'FUL, *a.* serviceable.
U'SUAL, *a.* customary.
U'SAGE, *n.* established custom.
ABUSE', *v.* to use improperly.
DISUSE', *v.* to cease to use.
MISUSE', *v.* to treat ill.
UTIL'ITY, *n.* usefulness.
INUTIL'ITY, *n.* uselessness.
PERUSE', *v.* to read.
U'SURY, *n.* illegal interest.
USURP', *v.* to seize without right.
UTEN'SIL, *n.* that which is used.

Va'co, vaca'tum—to Be Empty; to Be at Leisure.

VA'CANT, *a.* empty.
VACA'TION, *n.* being at leisure; recess.
VAC'UUM, *n.* an empty space.
EVAC'UATE, *v.* to make empty.

Va'do, va'sum—to Go.

EVADE', *v.* to go from or shun.
EVA'SION, *n.* an artifice to elude.
INVADE', *v.* to enter, as an enemy.
INVA'SION, *n.* a hostile entrance.
PERVADE', *v.* to pass through.

Va'gus—Wandering.

VA'GRANT, *n.* an idle wanderer.
VA'GRANT, *a.* wandering; unsettled.
VAGUE, *a.* indefinite; uncertain.
VAGA'RY, *n.* a whim; a caprice.
VAG'ABOND, *n.* a worthless person.
EXTRAV'AGANT, *a.* wasteful; excessive.
EXTRAV'AGANCE, *n.* excess.

Va'leo—to Be Well or Strong; to Be Worth.

AVAIL', *v.* to take advantage of; to be of use to.
IN'VALID, *n.* a sick person.
INVAL'ID, *a.* of no force.
INVAL'IDATE, *v.* to make weak or null.
CONVALES'CENT, *a.* recovering health and strength.
EQUIV'ALENT, *a.* equal in value.
PREVAIL', *v.* to overcome; to have effect.
PREV'ALENT, *a.* widely existing.
PREV'ALENCE, *n.* general existence.
VALEDIC'TION, *n.* a farewell.
VAL'IANT, *a.* brave; strong.
VAL'ID, *a.* of full force; good in law.
VALID'ITY, *n.* soundness; strength.
VAL'OR, *n.* bravery.
VAL'UE, *n.* worth; price.
INVAL'UABLE, *a.* precious above estimation.

Va'nus—Vain; Empty.

VAIN, *a.* empty; worthless.
VAN'ITY, *n.* petty or empty pride.
VAN'ISH, *v.* to disappear.
EVANES'CENT, *a.* fleeting.

Va'rius—Changeable; Diverse; Different.

VA'RY, *v.* to make different.
VA'RIANCE, *n.* disagreement.
VA'RIEGATE, *v.* to diversify.
VARI'ETY, *a.* change; diversity.

Va'por—Steam; Fume.

Va'por, n. fume, steam; mist; fog. | Evap'orate, v. to pass away in vapor.

Vas'tus—Very Large; Desert.

Vast, a. very large; great.
Devas'tate, v. to lay waste.

Devasta'tion, n. waste; havoc.
Waste, n. a desolate country.

Ve'ho, vec'tum—to Carry; to Bear.

Convey', v. to carry.
Convey'ance, n. that which conveys.
Invec'tive, n. angry abuse.
Ve'hicle, n. a carriage.

Inveigh', v. to carry or bring charges against.
Ve'hemence, n. ardor; violence.

Vel'lo, vul'sum—to Pull; to Pluck.

Convulse', v. to give violent motion to. | Revul'sion, n. a drawing back.

Ve'lo—to Cover; to Conceal.

Veil, v. to hide; to cover.
Veil, n. a curtain.
Devel'op, v. to unfold; to unclose.
Devel'opment, n. an unfolding.

Envel'op, v. to wrap up.
Reveal', v. to draw back the veil; to make known.
Revela'tion, n. discovery.

Ven'do—to Sell.

Vend, v. to sell.
Vend'er, n. one who sells.

Vendue', n. an auction.
Ve'nal, a. that may be bought or sold.

Vene'num—Poison; Venom.

Ven'om, n. poison.
Enven'om, v. to poison.

Ven'omous, a. poisonous.

Ve'nio, ven'tum—to Come; to Go.

Ad'vent, n. a coming.
Advent'ure, n. a hazard or risk.
Adventi'tious, a. accidental.
Av'enue, n. a passage.
Circumvent', v. to come round.
Contravene', v. to hinder.
Convene', v. to assemble.
Conven'tion, n. a coming together.
Conve'nient, a. fit; suitable.
Conven'tional, a. customary.
Cov'enant, n. a mutual agreement.

Event', n. that which happens.
Event'ual, a. happening as a result.
Event'ually, ad. in the event.
Event'uate, v. to terminate.
Intervene', v. to come between.
Invent', v. to devise.
Prevent', v. to hinder.
Rev'enue, n. the income of a state.
Ven'ture, v. to run a hazard; to dare.
Ven'turous, a. daring; bold.

Ver'bum—a Word.

Verb, n. a part of speech.
Ver'bal, a. uttered by the mouth.
Ver'biage, n. an unnecessary profusion of words.

Verbose', a. full of words.
Prov'erb, n. a maxim.
Ad'verb, n. a part of speech.
Verba'tim, ad. word for word.

Ven'tus—the WIND.

VENT, *n.* an air hole.
VEN'TIDUCT, *n.* a passage for air.
VEN'TILATE, *v.* to cause a circulation of air.

Ve'reor—to FEAR; to STAND IN AWE OF.

REVERE', *v.* to respect greatly.
REV'ERENCE, *n.* great respect; awe.
REV'EREND, *a.* worthy of reverence.
REVEREN'TIAL, *a.* expressing reverence.

Ver'go—to TURN or TEND TOWARDS.

VERGE, *n.* brink; border; edge.
VERGE, *v.* to bend towards.
CONVERGE', *v.* to tend to one point.
DIVERG'ENT, *a.* going apart.

Ver'mis—a WORM.

VER'MIN, *n.* noxious animal.
VER'MIFUGE, *n.* a medicine to destroy worms.
VERMIC'ULAR, *a.* resembling a worm.
VERMICEL'LI, *n.* a paste in the form of worms.

Ver'to, ver'sum—to TURN.

ADVERT', *v.* to turn to.
INADVER'TENCE, *n.* heedlessness.
AD'VERSE, *a.* opposed; hostile.
AD'VERSITY, *n.* misfortune.
AD'VERSARY, *n.* an enemy.
ADVERTISE', *v.* to publish a notice.
ANIMADVER'SION, *n.* censure.
AVERT', *v.* to turn away.
AVER'SION, *n.* dislike.
CONTROVERT', *v.* to dispute.
CON'TROVERSY, *n.* disputation.
CONVERT', *v.* to change from one condition to another.
CONVERSE', *v.* to discourse with.
CON'VERSE, *n.* an opposite proposition.
DIVERT', *v.* to turn off; to amuse.
DIVER'SION, *n.* amusement.
DI'VERS, *a.* several; more than one.
DI'VERSE, *a.* varied; unlike.
DIVER'SITY, *n.* variety; difference.
DIVER'SIFY, *v.* to vary.
INVERT', *v.* to turn upside down.
PERVERT', *v.* to turn to a wrong use.
PERVERSE', *a.* obstinately wrong.
PERVER'SION, *n.* a wrong use.
REVERT', *v.* to turn back.
REVERSE', *v.* to turn the front part back.
REVER'SION, *n.* a turning or falling back.
SUBVERT', *v.* to overthrow.
SUBVER'SIVE, *a.* tending to overthrow.
TRANSVERSE', *a.* lying across.
TRAV'ERSE, *v.* to pass over.
VER'SATILE, *a.* easily turning to a new task.
VERSE, *n.* a line of poetry.
VER'SIFY, *v.* to make verse.
VER'SION, *n.* a translation.
VER'TEBRA, *n.* a joint of the spine.
VER'TEX, *n.* the top.
VER'TICAL, *a.* overhead.
VER'TIGO, *n.* giddiness.
VOR'TEX, *n.* a whirlpool.

Ve'rus—TRUE.

VER'ITY, *n.* truth.
VERAC'ITY, *n.* habitual observance of truth.
VERA'CIOUS, *a.* observant of truth.
VER'DICT, *n.* the report of a jury.
VER'IFY, *v.* to prove true.
VER'ILY, *ad.* in truth.
VER'ITABLE, *a.* true; genuine.
AVER', *v.* to declare positively.

LATIN ROOTS AND DERIVATIVES.

Vesti'gium—a Footstep; a Track or Trace.

Ves'tige, *n.* a track; a trace.
Inves'tigate, *v.* to search into.

Ves'tis—a Garment; Clothing.

Invest', *v.* to clothe in.
Vest, *n.* an outer garment.
Ves'ture, *n.* a garment; a robe.
Divest', *v.* to strip; to deprive.
Ves'try, *n.* a room in a church for the sacred garments, etc.

Ve'tus, vet'eris—Old.

Vet'eran, *n.* an old soldier.
Invet'erate, *a.* fixed by long continuance.

Vi'a—a Way.

De'viate, *v.* to turn aside.
De'vious, *a.* wandering.
En'voy, *n.* a public messenger.
Per'vious, *a.* penetrable.
Imper'vious, *a.* not admitting a passage through.
Ob'viate, *v.* to remove.
Ob'vious, *a.* plain to be seen.
Pre'vious, *a.* antecedent.
Vi'aduct, *n.* a structure supporting a passage way.

Vi'cis—a Change; in Stead.

Vic'ar, *n.* a substitute.
Vicege'rent, *n.* a deputy.
Vice'roy, *n.* a king's deputy governor.
Vicis'situde, *n.* change.

Vi'deo, vi'sum—to See.

Vis'ion, *n.* sight.
Vis'ible, *a.* that can be seen.
Vis'ionary, *a.* not real.
Vis'it, *v.* to go to see.
Vis'ual, *a.* pertaining to sight.
Vi'sor, *n.* a mask.
Vis'ta, *n.* a view; a prospect.
Vis'age, *n.* the countenance.
View, *n.* a seeing or sight.
Ev'ident, *a.* plain; apparent.
Invis'ible, *a.* not to be seen.
Provide', *v.* to see to beforehand.
Prov'ident, *a.* providing for.
Prov'ender, *n.* food for cattle.
Prov'idence, *n.* forethought.
Provis'ion, *n.* victuals; food.
Provi'so, *n.* something that provides against.
Pru'dent, *a.* cautious; wise.
Pur'vey, *v.* to provide.
Purvey'or, *n.* a provider.
Revise', *v.* to examine again.
Review', *n.* a critical examination.
Supervise', *v.* to overlook.
Survey', *v.* to view carefully.

Vi'duo—to Deprive Of; to Part.

Avoid', *v.* to keep clear from.
Devoid', *v.* destitute of.
Void, *a.* empty.
Divide', *v.* to separate.
Div'idend, *n.* a share.
Individ'ual, *n.* a single person.

Vig'or—Strength.

Vig'or, *n.* strength; energy.
Vig'orous, *a.* full of strength.
Invig'orate, *v.* to strengthen.
Vig'orously, *ad.* with force.

***Vig'ilo*—to WATCH; to KEEP AWAKE.**

VIG'IL, *n.* a watching. | VIG'ILANT, *a.* watchful.

***Vi'lis*—of LITTLE WORTH; CHEAP; VILE.**

VILE, *a.* base; mean; wicked. | VIL'IFY, *v.* to defame; to abuse.
VILE'LY, *ad.* basely; meanly. | REVILE', *v.* to vilify again and again.

***Vin'co, vic'tum*—to CONQUER; to OVERCOME.**

CONVINCE', *v.* to satisfy by evidence. | INVIN'CIBLE, *a.* unconquerable.
CONVICT', *v.* to prove guilty. | PROV'INCE, *n.* a subject country; a division of a country.
CON'VICT, *n.* one found guilty.
CONVIC'TION, *n.* the state of being convicted or convinced; belief. | VAN'QUISH, *v.* to conquer.
| VIC'TOR, *n.* a conqueror.
EVINCE, *v.* to show clearly. | VIC'TORY, *n.* conquest.
VIC'TIM, *n.* a living being sacrificed.

***Vin'dex, vin'dicis*—a DEFENDER or AVENGER.**

VIN'DICATE, *v.* to defend; to justify. | REVENGE', *v.* to return an injury.
VINDIC'TIVE, *a.* revengeful. | AVENGE', *v.* to punish for an injury.
VEN'GEANCE, *n.* recompense of evil.

***Vi'num*—WINE.**

VINE, *n.* the plant which produces grapes. | VIN'EGAR, *n.* sour wine.
| VIN'TAGE, *n.* the crop of grapes.
VI'NOUS, *a.* having the qualities of wine. | VINE'YARD, *n.* a plantation of grape vines.

***Vir*—a MAN.**

VI'RILE, *a.* masculine. | VIRA'GO, *n.* a turbulent woman.

***Vi'rus*—POISON.**

VIR'ULENCE, *n.* malignity. | VIR'ULENT, *a.* full of poison.

***Vi'tium*—a VICE; a FAULT.**

VICE, *n.* a fault; a blemish. | VI'CIOUS, *a.* wicked; sinful.
VI'TIATE, *v.* to deprave; to spoil.

***Vi'to*—to SHUN; to ESCAPE.**

INEV'ITABLE, *a.* that cannot be avoided. | INEV'ITABLY, *ad.* certainly.

***Vit'rum*—GLASS.**

VIT'REOUS, *a.* resembling glass. | VIT'RIFY, *v.* to change into glass.

***Vi'vo, vic'tum*—to LIVE.**

CONVIV'IAL, *a.* gay; jovial. | VICT'UALS, *n.* food; provisions.
REVIVE', *v.* to live again. | VI'TAL, *a.* necessary to life.
SURVIVE', *v.* to outlive. | VIVAC'ITY, *n.* liveliness.
VI'AND, *n.* an article of food. | VIV'ID, *a.* active; bright.
VIV'IFY, *v.* to animate.

LATIN ROOTS AND DERIVATIVES. 303

Vo'co, voca'tum—to CALL.

AD'VOCATE, *n.* a pleader.
AVOCA'TION, *n.* a calling or employment.
CONVOCA'TION, *n.* an assembly.
CONVOKE', *v.* to call together.
EQUIV'OCAL, *a.* doubtful.
EQUIV'OCATE, *v.* to use doubtful expressions.
EVOKE', *v.* to call forth.
INVOCA'TION, *n.* a solemn address or prayer.

INVOKE', *v.* to implore.
REVOKE', *v.* to call back.
IRREV'OCABLE, *a.* not to be recalled.
PROVOKE', *v.* to irritate.
PROVOCA'TION, *n.* a cause of anger.
VOCAB'ULARY, *n.* a list of words.
VO'CAL, *a.* relating to the voice.
VOCIF'ERATE, *v.* to cry out loudly.
VOCA'TION, *n.* a business.
VOICE, *n.* sound from the mouth.
VOUCH, *v.* to attest; to affirm.

VOW'EL, *n.* a simple sound.

Vo'lo, vola'tum—to FLY.

VOL'ATILE, *a.* easily evaporated; gay; fickle.

VOL'LEY, *n.* a flight of shot.

Vo'lo, voli'tum—to WILL; to WISH.

BENEV'OLENCE, *n.* good will.
MALEV'OLENCE, *n.* ill will.
VOLI'TION, *n.* the power of willing.

VOL'UNTARY, *a.* acting from choice.
VOLUNTEER', *n.* a voluntary soldier.
INVOL'UNTARY, *a.* not willing.

Volup'tas—PLEASURE.

VOLUP'TUOUS, *a.* full of pleasure.

VOLUP'TUARY, *n.* one given up to pleasure.

Vol'vo, volu'tum—to ROLL.

CIRCUMVOLU'TION, *n.* a rolling round.
DEVOLVE', *v.* to deliver over.
EVOLVE', *v.* to unroll; to unfold.
EVOLU'TION, *n.* act of unfolding.
INVOLVE', *v.* to envelop.

REVOLT', *v.* to throw off subjection.
REVOLVE', *v.* to roll in a circle.
REVOLU'TION, *n.* an entire change.
VOL'UBLE, *a.* rolling; fluent.
VOL'UME, *n.* a roll; a book.

VOLU'MINOUS, *a.* great size; bulky.

Vo'ro, vora'tum—to EAT GREEDILY.

DEVOUR', *v.* to eat up greedily.
VORAC'ITY, *n.* greediness of appetite.
VORA'CIOUS, *a.* eating very greedily.

CARNIV'OROUS, *a.* eating flesh.
OMNIV'OROUS, *a.* eating all things.
OSSIV'OROUS, *a.* eating bones.

PISCIV'OROUS, *a.* eating fish.

Vo'tum—a VOW; a WISH.

AVOW', *v.* to declare openly.
DEVOTE', *v.* to set apart.
DEVO'TION, *n.* piety; affection.
DEVOUT', *a.* earnest; sincere.

VO'TARY, *n.* one who has vowed.
VOTE, *n.* a wish expressed.
VO'TIVE, *a.* given by vow.
VOW, *n.* a solemn promise.

Vulca'nus—the GOD OF FIRE.

VOLCA'NO, *n.* a burning mountain.

VOLCA'NIC, *a.* relating to a volcano.

Vul'gus—the COMMON PEOPLE.

DIVULGE', *v.* to make public.
VUL'GAR, *a.* common; unrefined.
VUL'GARISM, *n.* a vulgar expression.

VULGAR'ITY, *n.* coarseness; meanness.
VUL'GATE, *n.* an ancient Latin version of the Bible.

GREEK ROOTS AND DERIVATIVES.

Acade'mia, (ἀκαδημία,)—a GROVE NEAR ATHENS, WHERE PLATO TAUGHT PHILOSOPHY.
ACAD'EMY, *n.* a place of instruction. | ACADEM'IC, *a.* relating to an academy.

Ak'me, (ἀκμή,)—the SUMMIT.
AC'ME, *n.* the top; the highest point.

Acou'o, (ἀκουω,)—to HEAR.
ACOUS'TIC, *a.* relating to hearing. | ACOUS'TICS, *n.* the science of sounds.

Ac'ron, (ἀκρον,)—SUMMIT; EXTREMITY.
ACROP'OLIS, *n.* the summit of a city; a citadel. | ACROS'TIC, *n.* a kind of poem.

A'er, (ἀηρ,)—the AIR.
AE'RIAL, *a.* consisting of air. | A'EROLITE, *n.* a meteoric stone.
A'ERONAUT, *n.* one who sails in the air.

A'go, (ἀγω,)—to LEAD.
DEM'AGOGUE, *n.* a factious or seditious leader. | PED'AGOGUE, *n.* a schoolmaster.
| SYN'AGOGUE, *n.* a Jewish church.

A'gon, (ἀγων,)—a COMBAT; a CONTEST.
AG'ONY, *n.* struggle under severe pain. | AG'ONIZE, *v.* to afflict with agony.
| ANTAG'ONIST, *n.* an opponent.

Al'gos, (ἀλγος,)—PAIN.
CEPH'ALALGY, *n.* the headache. | ONDONTAL'GIA, *n.* the toothache.

Alle'lon, (ἀλληλων,)—ONE ANOTHER; EACH OTHER.
PAR'ALLEL, *a.* equidistant at all points. | UNPAR'ALLELED, *a.* unequaled.

Al'los, (ἀλλος,)—ANOTHER.
AL'LEGORY, *n.* a figurative narration. | ALLEGOR'ICAL, *a.* not literal.

Al'pha, (ἀλφα,)—the FIRST LETTER IN THE GREEK ALPHABET.
AL'PHABET, *n.* the letters of a language. | ALPHABET'ICAL, *a.* in the order of the alphabet.

GREEK ROOTS AND DERIVATIVES. 305

Ang'elos, (αγγελος,)—a MESSENGER; a BRINGER OF TIDINGS.

AN'GEL, *n.* a spiritual messenger.
ARCHAN'GEL, *n.* a chief angel.
EVAN'GEL, *n.* good tidings; the gospel of Christ.

EVAN'GELIST, *n.* a preacher of the gospel.
EVANGEL'ICAL, *a.* contained in the gospel.

EVAN'GELIZE, *v.* to teach the gospel to.

An'thos, (ἀνθος,)—a FLOWER.

ANTHOL'OGY, *n.* a discourse on flowers.

POLYAN'THUS, *n.* a plant with many flowers.

HELIAN'THUS, *n.* the sun-flower.

Anthro'pos, (ἀνθρωπος,)—a MAN; a HUMAN BEING.

MIS'ANTHROPE, *n.* one who hates the human race.
MISAN'THROPY, *n.* hatred of the human race.

PHILAN'THROPIST, *n.* one who loves mankind.
PHILAN'THROPY, *n.* love of the human race.

Ar'che, (ἀρχη,)—the BEGINNING; GOVERNMENT.

AN'ARCH, *n.* an author of confusion.
AN'ARCHY, *n.* want of government.
ARCH, *a.* chief; principal; shrewd.
ARCHBISH'OP, *n.* the chief bishop.
ARCHDUKE', *n.* a chief prince.

AR'CHITECT, *n.* one skilled in the art of building.
AR'CHIVES, *n.* records.
MON'ARCH, *n.* a sovereign; a king.
PA'TRIARCH, *n.* the head of a family.

AR'CHETYPE, *n.* the original.

Arc'tos, (ἀρκτος,)—a BEAR; the NORTH.

ARC'TIC, *a.* northern. | ANTARC'TIC, *a.* southern.

NOTE.—Literally relating to the constellation of the Bear.

Ar'gos, (ἀργὸς,)—SLUGGISH; INACTIVE.

LETH'ARGY, *n.* morbid sleepiness. | LETHAR'GIC, *a.* dull; sluggish.

Aris'tos, (ἀριστος,)—NOBLEST; BLEST.

ARISTOC'RACY, *n.* the government of the nobles.

ARIS'TOCRAT, *n.* one who favors an aristocracy.

Arith'mos, (ἀριθμος,)—a NUMBER.

ARITH'METIC, *n.* the science of numbers.

ARITHMETI'CIAN, *n.* a master of arithmetic.

Aro'ma, (ἀρωμα,)—any SEASONING; SPICE; SWEET HERB.

ARO'MA, *n.* a pleasant odor.
AROMAT'ICS, *n.* fragrant spices.

AROMAT'IC, *a.* spicy; fragrant.
ARO'MATIZE, *v.* to scent with spices.

At'mos, (ἀτμος,)—VAPOR; AIR.

AT'MOSPHERE, *n.* the air, etc., above us.

ATMOSPHER'IC, *a.* relating to the atmosphere.

Ath'los, (ἀθλος,)—a COMBAT.

ATH'LETE, *n.* a wrestler. | ATHLET'IC, *a.* strong of body.

As'tron, (ἀστρον,)—a STAR.

AS'TERISK, *n.* a mark, like a star.
AS'TRAL, *a.* star-like.
ASTROL'OGY, *n.* the science of foretelling by the stars.
| ASTRON'OMY, *n.* the science of the stars.
DISAS'TER, *n.* a bad or evil star; misfortune.

Au'los, (ἀυλος,)—a PIPE.

HYDRAU'LIC, *a.* relating to water pipes. | HYDRAU'LICS, *n.* the science of the motion and force of fluids.

Authen'teo, (ἀυθεντεω,)—to HAVE AUTHORITY.

AUTHEN'TIC, *a.* genuine; true. | AUTHENTIC'ITY, *n.* genuineness.

Au'tos, (ἀυτος,)—ONE'S SELF.

AU'TOCRAT, *n.* a sole ruler.
AU'TOGRAPH, *n.* one's handwriting.
AU'TOPSY, *n.* ocular evidence.
| AUTOM'ATON, *n.* a self-moving machine.

Bal'samum, (βαλσαμον,)—a FRAGRANT RESIN; an OINTMENT.

BALM, *n.* a fragrant ointment. | BAL'SAM, *n.* a soothing ointment.

Bap'to, (βαπτω,)—to DIP; to WASH.

BAPTIZE', *v.* to immerse. | BAP'TISM, *n.* a Christian sacrament.

Ba'sis, (βασις,)—the BASE or FOUNDATION.

BASE, *n.* the bottom. | BASE, *a.* mean; vile.
DEBASE', *v.* to degrade; to lower.

Bib'los, (βιβλος,)—a BOOK.

BI'BLE, *n.* the Holy Scriptures. | BIB'LICAL, *a.* pertaining to the Bible.

Bi'os, (βιος,)—LIFE.

AMPHIB'IOUS, *a.* living in two elements. | BIOG'RAPHY, *n.* an account of one's life.

Blap'to, (βλαπτω,)—to INJURE.

BLASPHEME', *v.* to speak impiously. | BLAS'PHEMY, *n.* impiety of speech

Bo'leo, (βαλλω,)—to SHOOT; to THROW.

EM'BLEM, *n.* a picture.
EMBLEMAT'IC, *a.* using emblems.
HYPER'BOLE, *n.* an exaggeration.
SYM'BOL, *n.* a sign; an emblem.
| PAR'ABLE, *n.* a similitude.
PROB'LEM, *n.* a question proposed
PROBLEMAT'ICAL, *a.* uncertain.

GREEK ROOTS AND DERIVATIVES. 307

Bot'ane, (βοτανη,)—an HERB; a PLANT.

BOT'ANY, *n.* the science of plants. | BOTAN'ICAL, *a.* relating to plants.

Bron'chos, (βρογχος,)—the WIND-PIPE.

BRON'CHIAL, *a.* belonging to the wind-pipe. | BRONCHI'TIS, *n.* inflammation of the wind-pipe.

Can'on, (κανων,)—a RULE.

CAN'ON, *n.* a rule; a law. | CAN'ONIZE, *v.* to declare one a saint.

Car'dia, (καρδια,)—the HEART.

CAR'DIAC, *a.* relating to the heart.
CARDIAL'GIA, *n.* the heartburn. | PERICAR'DIUM, *n.* a membrane enclosing the heart.

Caus'ticus, (καυστικος,)—BURNING.

CAUS'TIC, *a.* burning; corroding. | CAU'TERY, *n.* a burning or searing.

Cen'trum, (κεντρον,)—the CENTER.

CEN'TER, *n.* the exact middle.
CEN'TRAL, *a.* relating to the center.
ECCENTRIC'ITY, *n.* irregularity.
ECCEN'TRIC, *a.* irregular. | CONCEN'TRIC, *a.* having a common center.
CONCEN'TRATE, *v.* to bring together.

Ceph'ale, (κεφαλη,)—the HEAD.

CEPHAL'IC, *a.* pertaining to the head. | HYDROCEPH'ALUS, *n.* dropsy of the head.

Cha'os, (χαος,)—CONFUSION.

CHA'OS, *n.* a confused mass. | CHAOT'IC, *a.* confused; without order.

Charac'ter, (χαρακτηρ,)—DISTINCTIVE MARK.

CHAR'ACTER, *n.* reputation; quality.
CHARACTERIS'TIC, *a.* indicating character. | CHARACTERIS'TIC, *n.* a distinctive mark.
CHAR'ACTERIZE, *v.* to give a character.

Cha'ris, (χαρις,)—GRACE; JOY.

CHAR'ITY, *n.* good affection; alms.
EU'CHARIST, *n.* the Lord's Supper. | CHAR'ITABLE, *a.* kind; bountiful.

NOTE.—EUCHARIST, literally the act of giving thanks.

Chimæ'ra, (χιμαιρα,)—a FABULOUS MONSTER.

CHIME'RA, *n.* an absurd notion. | CHIMER'ICAL, *a.* wild; fanciful.

Cheir, (χειρ,)—the HAND.

CHIROG'RAPHY, *n.* handwriting. | CHIRUR'GEON, *n.* a surgeon.

Cho'le, (χολη,)—BILE; ANGER.

CHOL'ERA, *n.* a disease.
CHOL'ER, *n.* anger; rage.
CHOL'ERIC, *a.* irascible.
COL'IC, *n.* a pain in the bowels.
MEL'ANCHOLY, *n.* sadness; gloom.

Chor'da, (χορδη,)—a GUT; a STRING.

CHORD, *n.* the string of a musical instrument.
CORD, *n.* a small rope.
CORD'AGE, *n.* a quantity of cords.
ACCORD', *v.* to correspond in sound.

Chris'tos, (Χριστος,)—the "ANOINTED."

CHRIST, *n.* the Messiah.
CHRIST'EN, *v.* to baptize and name.
CHRIS'TIAN, *n.* a disciple of Christ.
CHRIST'MAS, *n.* the festival of Christ's nativity.
CHRISTIAN'ITY, *n.* the religion of Christ.

Chro'ma, (χρωμα,)—COLOR.

CHROMAT'IC, *a.* relating to colors.
ACHROMAT'IC, *a.* destitute of color.

Chron'os, (χρονος,)—TIME.

CHRON'IC, *a.* of long duration.
CHRON'ICLE, *n.* a record.
CHRONOL'OGY, *n.* the science of time.
CHRONOM'ETER, *n.* a time piece.
ANACH'RONISM, *n.* an error in dates.

Chy'mos, (χυμος,)—a JUICE; a LIQUID.

CHEM'IST, *n.* one who is versed in chemistry.
CHEM'ISTRY, *n.* the science of the nature and properties of bodies.
CHEM'ICAL, *a.* concerning chemistry.

Cle'ros, (κληρος,)—a LOT; a PORTION.

CLER'GY, *n.* the body of divines.
CLER'ICAL, *a.* relating to the clergy.
CLER'ICAL, *a.* relating to a writer.
CLERK, *n.* a secretary or bookkeeper.

Co'mos, (κωμος,)—a JOVIAL MEETING.

COM'EDY, *n.* an amusing dramatic piece.
COM'IC, *a.* raising mirth.
ENCO'MIUM, *n.* praise.

Cos'mos, (κοσμος,)—ORDER; ORNAMENT; the WORLD.

COSMET'IC, *a.* beautifying.
COSMET'IC, *n.* a wash to beautify the skin.
COS'MICAL, *a.* relating to the world.
COSMOP'OLITE, *n.* a citizen of the world.
MI'CROCOSM, *n.* a little world.

Cri'tes, (κριτης,)—a JUDGE.

CRIT'IC, *n.* a judge in literature or art.
CRITE'RION, *n.* something to judge by.
CRI'SIS, *n.* the deciding point.
CRIT'ICISE, *v.* to judge; to censure.
HYPERCRIT'ICAL, *a.* critical beyond reason.
HYPOCRIT'ICAL, *a.* like a hypocrite.
HYP'OCRITE, *n.* one who falsely assumes the appearance of virtue or piety.

GREEK ROOTS AND DERIVATIVES.

Cra'nium, (κρανιον,)—the SKULL.

CRA'NIUM, *n.* the skull.
CRANIOL'OGY, *n.* the science of skulls.
PERICRA'NIUM, *n.* the membrane which covers the skull.

Crystal'lus, (κρυσταλλός,)—CONGEALED LIKE ICE; TRANSPARENT.

CRYS'TAL. *n.* a hard transparent substance.
CRYS'TALLINE, *a.* bright; clear.
CRYS'TALLIZE, *v.* to form into crystals.

Cy'clus, (κυκλος,)—a CIRCLE.

CY'CLE, *n.* a circle or period of time.
CY'CLOID, *n.* a curve.
CYCLOPE'DIA, *n.* the circle of sciences.
ENCYCLOPE'DIA, *n.* the circle of sciences.
ENCYC'LICAL, *a.* in a circle.

Cylin'drus, (κυλινδρος,) –a ROLLER.

CYL'INDER, *n.* a roller.
CYLIN'DRICAL, *a.* like a cylinder.

Cy'on, (κυων,)—a DOG.

CYN'IC, *n.* a surly person; a snarler.
CYN'IC, *a.* snarling; satirical.
CYN'ICAL, *a.* like a dog; snarling.
CYN'OSURE, *n.* the dog's tail.

NOTE.—CYNOSURE, figuratively, signifies anything that attracts general notice or admiration.

De'ca, (δεκα,)—TEN.

DEC'ADE, *n.* the number ten.
DEC'ALOGUE, *n.* the ten commandments.
DEC'AGON, *n.* a figure with ten angles.
DEC'IMAL, *a.* numbered by ten.
DEC'IMATE, *v.* to take the tenth.
DECEM'BER, *n.* the twelfth month.

NOTE.—Among the ancient Romans, March was taken as the first month, consequently September would be the *seventh,* October the *eighth,* November the *ninth,* and December the *tenth* month.

De'mos, (δημος,)—the PEOPLE.

DEMOC'RACY, *n.* a popular government.
ENDEM'IC, *a.* peculiar to a place.
DEM'OCRAT, *n.* one who favors democracy.
EPIDEM'IC, *n.* a prevailing disease.

Despo'tes, (δεσπότης,)—a MASTER or LORD.

DES'POT, *n.* a tyrant; an absolute ruler.
DES'POTISM, *n.* unlimited monarchy.

Didas'co, (διδασκω,)—to TEACH.

DIDAC'TIC, *a.* instructive.
DIDAC'TICS, *n.* the art of teaching.

Dis, (δις,)--Two.

DILEM'MA, *n.* a difficult or doubtful choice.
DIPH'THONG, *n.* a union of two vowels in one sound.
DISSEV'ER, *v.* to part in two.

Dox'a, (δοξα,)—an OPINION; GLORY.

HET'ERODOX, a. holding erroneous opinions.
OR'THODOX, a. correct in opinion.
DOXOL'OGY, n. words of glory to God.
PAR'ADOX, n. something apparently absurd but actually true.

Dra'ma, (δραμα,)—an ACTION; a PLAY.

DRA'MA, n. a poem written for the stage.
DRAMAT'IC, a. relating to plays.
DRAM'ATIST, n. a writer of plays.

Dyn'amis, (δυναμις,)—POWER; FORCE.

DYNAM'ICS, n. the science of forces.
DY'NASTY, n. power or government.
DYNAM'IC, a. pertaining to power.

Dys, (δυς,)—DIFFICULTY; PAIN.

DYS'ENTERY, n. a disease.
DYS'PEPSY, n. difficulty of digestion.

Elec'trum, (ηλεκτρον.)—AMBER.

ELEC'TRIC, a. of or like amber.
ELEC'TRIFY, v. to make electric.
ELECTRIC'ITY, n. a subtile fluid evolved by friction, first observed in amber.

Ec'eo, (οικεω, from οικος, a HOUSE; a HOUSEHOLD;)—to DWELL.

DI'OCESE, n. a bishop's jurisdiction.
DI'OCESAN, a. pertaining to a diocese.
ECON'OMY, n. frugality.
ECONOM'ICAL, a. frugal.
PAR'ISH, n. an ecclesiastical district.
PARO'CHIAL, a. pertaining to a parish.

Elegi'a, (ελεγεια,)—a MOURNFUL POEM.

EL'EGY, n. a funeral song.
ELEGI'AC, a. mournful.

E'meo, (εμεω,)—to VOMIT.

EMET'IC, a. causing to vomit.
EMET'IC, n. a medicine.

Epicu'rus, (Επικουρος,)—a SENSUAL PHILOSOPHER.

EP'ICURE, n. one given to luxury.
EPICURE'AN, a. luxurious.

Ep'os, (επος,)—a WORD; a SPEECH; a POEM.

EP'IC, a. narrative; heroic.
ORTHO'EPY, n. correct pronunciation.

Er'emos, (ερημος,)—LONELY; ALONE.

ER'EMITE, n. one who lives in seclusion.
HER'MIT, n. one who lives in seclusion.

Er'gon, (εργον,)—a WORK.

EN'ERGY, n. action or activity within.
MET'ALLURGY, n. the art of extracting metals from their ores.

Eth'os, (εθος,)—a CUSTOM.

ETH'ICS, n. the science of morals.
ETH'ICAL, a. relating to morals.

Eth′nos, (ἔθνος,)—a PEOPLE.

ETH′NICAL, *a.* relating to the races of mankind.

ETHNOL′OGY, *n.* a description of races.

Et′ymon, (ἔτυμον,)—the TRUE MEANING OF A WORD.

ET′YMON, *n.* a primitive word.

ETYMOL′OGY, *n.* the derivation of words.

Eu, (εὐ,)—WELL.

EU′LOGY, *n.* praise.
EU′LOGIZE, *v.* to commend; to praise.

EULO′GIUM, *n.* praise.
EU′PHONY, *n.* agreeable sound.

Ga′lax, (γάλαξ,)—MILK.

GAL′AXY, *n.* the milky way; a splendid assemblage.

Ga′meo, (γαμεω,)—to MARRY.

AMAL′GAMATE, *v.* to mix metals.
POLYG′AMY, *n.* plurality of wives.

BIG′AMY, *n.* the crime of having two wives at once.

Gas′ter, (γαστήρ,)—the BELLY; the STOMACH.

GAS′TRIC, *a.* belonging to the stomach.

GASTRON′OMY, *n.* the art of good living.

Ge, (γη,)—the EARTH.

GEOG′RAPHY, *n.* a description of the earth's surface.
GEOL′OGY, *n.* the science of the structure of the earth.
GEOM′ETRY, *n.* the science of magnitude.

GEOPON′ICS, *n.* agriculture.
AP′OGEE, *n.* greatest distance from the earth.
PERI′GEE, *n.* nearest approach to the earth.

Ge′nea, (γενεα,)—BIRTH; ORIGIN.

GENEAL′OGY, *n.* an account of one's descent.

GEN′ESIS, *n.* origin; creation.

Glos′sa, (γλωσσα,)—the TONGUE.

EPIGLOT′TIS, *n.* a cartilage near the root of the tongue.

GLOSS′ARY, *n.* a limited dictionary.
POL′YGLOT, *a.* having many languages.

Gly′pho, (γλύφω,)—to CURVE or ENGRAVE.

GLYPH, *n.* a kind of ornament in sculpture.

HI′EROGLYPH, *n.* a mystical character or symbol.

Go′nia, (γωνια,)—a CORNER; an ANGLE.

DIAG′ONAL, *n.* a line from angle to angle.
DEC′AGON, *n.* a figure having ten angles.

PEN′TAGON, *n.* a figure having five angles.
POL′YGON, *n.* a figure of many angles.
TRIGONOM′ETRY, *n.* the measuring of triangles.

Gno'mon, (γνωμων,)—Something that Makes Known; a Pointer.

Gnome, *n.* an imaginary being.
Gno'mon, *n.* the hand of a sun-dial.
Physiog'nomy, *n.* countenance.
Prognos'tic, *n.* that which foreshows.

Graph'o, (γραφω,)—to Write.   ***Gram'ma,*** (γραμμα,)—a Writing.

Au'tograph, *n.* one's own handwriting.
Di'agram, *n.* a figure; a drawing.
Engrave', *v.* to mark or scratch in.
Ep'igram, *n.* a short, witty poem.
Gram'mar, *n.* the science of language.
Graph'ic, *a.* well delineated.
Graph'ite, *n.* plumbago.
Lithog'raphy, *n.* the art of drawing on and printing from stone.
Par'agraph, *n.* a distinct part of a discourse.
Stenog'raphy, *n.* short-hand.
Tel'egraph, *n.* a machine for conveying intelligence by signals.
Tel'egram, *n.* intelligence by telegraph.
Topog'raphy, *n.* a description of a place.
Typog'raphy, *n.* the art of printing.

Gym'nos, (γυμνος,)—Naked.

Gymna'sium, *n.* a place for athletic exercises.
Gymnas'tic, *a.* pertaining to athletic exercises.

Gy'rus, (γυρος,)—a Circle.

Gyra'tion, *n.* a whirling round.
Gy'ral, *a.* whirling.

Harmo'nia, (ἁρμονία,)—Harmony.

Har'mony, *n.* musical concord; agreement.
Harmon'ic, *a.* musical.
Har'monize, *v.* to cause to agree.
Harmo'nious, *a.* musical; peaceful.

He'lios, (ἥλιος,)—the Sun.

Aphe'lion, *n.* the point farthest from the sun.
Perihe'lion, *n.* the point nearest the sun.
Parhe'lion, *n.* a mock sun.
He'liotrope, *n.* a plant that turns to the sun.

He'ma, (αἷμα,)—Blood.

Hem'orrhage, *n.* a flow of blood.
Hem'orrhoids, *n.* bleeding tumors.

He'mera, (ἡμερα,)—a Day.

Ephem'eral, *a.* lasting but a day.
Ephem'eris, *n.* a kind of almanac.

Hem'isus, (ἥμισυς,)—Half.

Hem'isphere, *n.* half a globe.
Hem'icycle, *n.* a half circle.

Hep'ta, (ἑπτα,)—Seven.

Hep'tagon, *n.* a figure having seven angles.
Hep'tarchy, *n.* a government by seven persons.

Her'esis, (αἵρεσις,)—an Opinion.

Her'esy, *n.* false doctrine.
Her'etic, *n.* one guilty of heresy.

Het′eros, (ἑτερος,)—OTHER; DIFFERENT; CONTRARY.

HET′ERODOX, *a.* heretical. | HETEROGE′NEOUS, *a.* unlike each other.

Hex, (ἑξ,)—SIX.

HEXAM′ETER, *n.* a verse of six metrical feet. | HEX′AGON, *n.* a figure of six angles.
| HEXAG′ONAL, *a.* having six angles.

Hi′eras, (ἱερος,)—SACRED.

HI′ERARCHY, *n.* ecclesiastical government. | HIEROGLYPH′IC, *n.* a sacred character or symbol.

Hip′pos, (ἱππος,)—a HORSE.

HIPPOPOT′AMUS, *n.* the river horse. | HIP′PODROME, *n.* a circus.

Ho′los, (ὁλος,)—the WHOLE; ALL.

CATH′OLIC, *a.* relating to the whole. | CATHOL′ICISM, *n.* adherence to the Catholic-church.

Hom′os, (ὁμος,)—UNITED; LIKE.

HOMOGE′NEOUS, *a.* of the same kind. | HOMOL′OGOUS, *a.* proportional to each other.

Ho′ra, (ὡρα,)—an HOUR.

HO′RAL, *a.* relating to an hour.
HOR′OLOGUE, *n.* an instrument that marks the hour. | HOROL′OGY, *n.* the art of making time-pieces.
| HOR′OSCOPE, *n.* aspect of the plants at the hour of birth.

Hori′zo, (ὁριζω,)—to BOUND; to FIX A LIMIT.

HORI′ZON, *n.* the line bounding the view.
APH′ORISM, *n.* a maxim; a precept. | HORIZON′TAL, *a.* parallel to the horizon.
| APH′ORIST, *n.* a writer of aphorisms.

Hy′dor, (ὑδωρ,)—WATER.

HY′DRA, *n.* a water snake.
HY′DRANT, *n.* a pipe for discharging water.
HYDRAU′LICS, *n.* the science of the motion and force of fluids.
HYDROCEPH′ALUS, *n.* water in the head. | HY′DROGEN, *n.* a gas which combined with oxygen produces water.
| HYDROPHO′BIA, *n.* a dread of water.
| HYDROSTAT′ICS, *n.* the science of the weight and equilibrium of fluids.
| DROP′SY, *n.* a disease.
| CLEPSY′DRA, *n.* a water clock.

Ide′a, (ἰδεα,)—a MENTAL IMAGE.

IDE′A, *n.* an image of the mind.
IDE′AL, *a.* pertaining to an image of the mind; imaginary. | IDE′ALIZE, *v.* to form ideas.
| IDOL′ATRY, *n.* the worship of images.
| I′DOLIZE, *v.* to love to excess.

Id'ios, (ἰδιος,)—PRIVATE; PECULIAR.

ID'IOM, *n.* a peculiarity of speech.
ID'IOCY, *n.* want of understanding.
ID'IOT, *n.* a fool.
IDIOMAT'ICAL, *a.* containing an idiom.
IDIOSYN'CRASY, *n.* peculiar temperament.

Iro'nia, (εἰρωνεια,)—IRONY.

I'RONY, *n.* a mode of speech in which the meaning is contrary to the words.
IRON'ICAL, *a.* derisive; mocking.
IRON'IC, *a.* derisive.

La'os, (λαος,)—the PEOPLE.

LA'ITY, *n.* the people as distinguished from the clergy.
LAY, *a.* not clerical.
LAY'MAN, *n.* one who is not a clergyman.

Lep'ra, (λεπρα,)—LEPROSY.

LEP'ER, *n.* one who has the leprosy.
LEP'ROUS, *a.* full of leprosy.
LEP'ROSY, *n.* a disease of the skin.

Le'the, (ληθη,)—FORGETFULNESS; OBLIVION.

LETHE'AN, *a.* inducing forgetfulness.
LETH'ARGY, *n.* morbid sleepiness.
LETHAR'GIC, *a.* sleepy by disease.

Li'thos, (λιθος,)—a STONE.

A'EROLITE, *n.* a meteoric stone.
LITH'ARGE, *n.* the scum of lead.
LITHOG'RAPHY, *n.* drawing on and printing from stone.
CHRYS'OLITE, *n.* a precious stone.

Lo'gos, (λόγος,)—a SPEECH, ACCOUNT, or DESCRIPTION.

ANAL'OGY, *n.* agreement throughout.
APOL'OGY, *n.* a warding off by words.
CAT'ALOGUE, *n.* a list.
CHRONOL'OGY, *n.* the science of dates.
CONCHOL'OGY, *n.* the science of shells.
DI'ALOGUE, *n.* a conversation.
DEC'ALOGUE, *n.* the ten commandments.
DOXOL'OGY, *n.* words of glory to God.
EULO'GIUM, *n.* praise.
EU'LOGIZE, *v.* to commend.
EP'ILOGUE, *n.* the speech at the end of a play.
LOG'IC, *n.* the art of reasoning.
PRO'LOGUE, *n.* a preface to a play.
SYL'LOGISM, *n.* a form of reasoning.

NOTE.—The termination or suffix *logy*, which is found in many words, is from λόγος, and denotes *art, science, description*, etc.

Ly'sis, (λύσις,)—a LOOSING or DISSOLVING.

ANAL'YSIS, *n.* an entire separation of a body into its elemental parts.
AN'ALYZE, *v.* to make an analysis.
PAL'SY, *n.* a privation of motion.
PARAL'YSIS, *n.* palsy.
PARALYT'IC, *n.* one affected with palsy.
PAR'ALYZE, *v.* to affect as with palsy.

Ma'nia, (μανια.)—MADNESS; INSANITY.

MA'NIAC, *n.* an insane person.
MA'NIA, *n.* madness.

Mar'tyr, (μαρτυρ,)—a WITNESS; a MARTYR.

MAR'TYR, *n.* one put to death for adherence to a cause.
MAR'TYRDOM, *n.* the death of a martyr.

GREEK ROOTS AND DERIVATIVES. 315

Mathe'ma, (μαθημα,)—LEARNING; SCIENCE.

MATHEMAT'ICS, *n.* the science of quantity.

MATHEMAT'ICAL, *a.* relating to mathematics.

Mechan'ao, (μηχαναω,)—to CONTRIVE; to INVENT.

MACHINE', *n.* a contrivance.
MACHINA'TION, *n.* a contriving.
MECHAN'ICS, *n.* the science of machines.

MECH'ANISM, *n.* the construction of a machine.

Mel, mel'lis, (μελι,)—HONEY.

MELLIF'EROUS, *a.* yielding honey.
MELLIF'LUENT, *a.* sweetly flowing

OX'YMEL, *n.* a mixture of vinegar and honey.

Mel'os, (μελος,)—a SONG or POEM.

MELO'DIOUS, *a.* agreeable to the ear.
MEL'ODY, *n.* sweetness of sound.

MEL'ODRAME, *n.* a drama containing songs.

Metal'lum, (μεταλλον,)—a METAL.

MET'AL, *n.* a hard fossil substance.
MET'ALLOID, *n.* a substance resembling metal.

METALLIF'EROUS, *a.* producing metals.
MET'ALLURGY, *n.* the art of working metals.

Meteo'ra, (μετεωρα,)—FLYING LUMINOUS BODIES IN THE AIR.

ME'TEOR, *n.* a shooting star.
METEOR'IC, *a.* bright and transient.

METEOROL'OGY, *n.* the science of meteors.

Me'ter, (μητηρ,) *me'tros*—a MOTHER.

METROP'OLIS, *n.* the largest or chief city of any country.

METROPOL'ITAN, *a.* of, or pertaining to, a metropolis.

Met'rum, (μετρον,)—a MEASURE.

ME'TER, *n.* a measurer.
ME'TER, *n.* measure as applied to verse.
BAROM'ETER, *n.* an instrument to measure the weight of the atmosphere.

MET'RICAL, *a.* pertaining to meter.
CHRONOM'ETER, *n.* a time measurer.
DIAM'ETER, *n.* measure through.
GASOM'ETER, *n.* a gas measurer.
THERMOM'ETER, *n.* a heat measurer.
SYM'METRY, *n.* due proportion of parts.

Mic'ros, (μικρος,)—LITTLE; SMALL.

MI'CROCOSM, *n.* the little world.

MI'CROSCOPE, *n.* an instrument for viewing the smallest objects.

Mon'os, (μονος,)—ONE; ALONE.

MON'AD, *n.* an atom.
MON'ARCH, *n.* a sole ruler.
MON'ASTERY, *n.* a convent.
MONAS'TIC, *a.* pertaining to monks.

MONK, *n.* one living in a monastery
MONOP'OLIZE, *v.* to engross the whole
MONOT'ONY, *n.* sameness of sound.
MONOT'ONOUS, *a.* wanting variety.

Mi'sos, (μισος,)—HATRED; ENMITY.

MISAN'THROPY, *n.* hatred of mankind. | MIS'ANTHROPE, *n.* a hater of mankind.

Mor'phe, (μορφη,)—FORM; SHAPE.

AMOR'PHOUS, *a.* without form. | METAMOR'PHOSE, *v.* to change the form of.

Mu'sa, (μουσα,)—a SONG or POEM.

AMUSE', *v.* to divert.
MUSE, *v.* to meditate deeply.
MU'SIC, *n.* harmony; melody.
MUSE'UM, *n.* a collection of curiosities.

Mys'tes, (μυστης,)—HIDDEN; SECRET.

MYS'TERY, *n.* something secret. | MYS'TIC, *a.* obscure; secret.
MYSTE'RIOUS, *a.* full of mystery.

My'thos, (μυθος,)—a WORD; a FABLE.

MYTH, *n.* a work of fiction.
MYTH'IC, *a.* fabulous.
MYTHOL'OGY, *n.* a system of fables, respecting heathen deities.

Nar'ce, (ναρκη,)—NUMBNESS; STUPOR.

NARCIS'SUS, *n.* the daffodil. | NARCO'SIS, *n.* stupefaction.
NARCOT'IC, *a.* soporific; causing sleep.

Nec'tar, (νεκταρ,)—the DRINK OF THE GODS; HONEY.

NEC'TAR, *n.* the feigned drink of the gods. | NEC'TARY, *n.* the place where the honey is secreted in a flower.

Ne'os, (νεος,)—NEW.

NEOL'OGY, *n.* new science or philosophy. | NE'OPHYTE, *n.* a new convert; a novice.

Neu'ron, (νεὐρον,)—a NERVE; a SINEW.

NERVE, *n.* an organ of sensation.
EN'ERVATE, *v.* to weaken.
NEURAL'GIA, *n.* a diseased state of the nerves.

No'mos, (νομος,)—a LAW; a REGULATION.

ANOM'ALY, *n.* deviation from rule.
ECON'OMY, *n.* good management.
ECONOM'ICAL, *a.* using economy.
ECON'OMIZE, *v.* to practise economy.

O'de, (ὠδη,)—an ODE; a HYMN.

ODE, *n.* a short poem or song.
MEL'ODY, *n.* sweetness of sound.
COM'EDY, *n.* an amusing drama.
PAL'INODE, *n.* a recantation.
PAR'ODY, *n.* a humorous imitation.
PROS'ODY, *n.* the laws of versification.
RHAP'SODY, *n.* a rambling composition.
RHAP'SODIST, *n.* one who writes rhapsodies.
PSALM'ODY, *n.* the singing of sacred songs.

GREEK ROOTS AND DERIVATIVES

O'dos, (ὁδός,)—a ROAD or WAY.

EX'ODUS, *n.* a departure.
METH'OD, *n.* a manner; a way.
SYN'OD, *n.* a church assembly.
EP'ISODE, *n.* an incidental narrative.
PE'RIOD, *n.* a circuit.

NOTE.—EXODUS, (ἐξοδος, a going out,) particularly, the departure of the Israelites from Egypt.
SYNOD, from συν, *together,* and ὁδὺς, *a way;* and signifies a journeying or coming to meet one another.

On'oma, (ὀνομα,)—a NAME.

ANON'YMOUS, *a.* without name.
METON'OMY, *n.* a change of names.
PATRONYM'IC, *n.* a name derived from a father.
SYN'ONYM, *n.* a word of the same meaning with another.
SYNON'YMOUS, *a.* conveying the same idea.

Op'to, (οπτω.)—to SEE; to LOOK.

OP'TICS, *n.* the science of seeing.
OP'TICAL, *a.* pertaining to sight.
OPTI'CIAN, *n.* one skilled in optics.
AU'TOPSY, *n.* ocular evidence.
SYNOP'SIS, *n.* a viewing together.
SYNOP'TICAL, *a.* affording a general view.
THANATOP'SIS, *n.* a view of death.

Ora'ma, (ὁραμα,)—a SIGHT; a SPECTACLE.

DIORA'MA, *n.* an optical machine.
PANORA'MA, *n.* a complete view.

Os'teon, (ὀστεον,)—a BONE.

OSTEOL'OGY, *n.* the science of the bones.
PERIOS'TEUM, *n.* a fibrous substance which invests the bones.

Ox'ys, (ὀξυς,)—SHARP; SOUR; ACID.

OXAL'IC, *a.* pertaining to sorrel.
OX'YGEN, *n.* the gas which generates acids.
OX'YDIZE, *v.* to combine with oxygen.
OX'IDE, *n.* a substance combined with oxygen.
PAR'OXYSM, *n.* temporary violence of a disease.

Pa'pas, (παπας,)—a FATHER.

PA'PACY, *n.* the office of the pope.
PA'PAL, *a.* pertaining to the pope.
POPE'DOM, *n.* papal jurisdiction.
POPE, *n.* the head of the Roman Catholic Church.

Pas, (πας,) or, Pan—ALL; the WHOLE.

PANACE'A, *n.* a universal medicine.
PANEGYR'IC, *n.* a eulogy.
PAN'OPLY, *n.* complete armor.
PAN'THEISM, *n.* the doctrine that the universe is God.
PAN'THEON, *n.* a temple dedicated to all the gods.
PAN'TOMIME, *n.* an imitation of all kinds of action, etc., without speaking.

Pen'te, (πεντε,)—FIVE.

PEN'TAGON, *n.* a figure having five angles.
PEN'TATEUCH, *n.* the five books of Moses.

Pa'ter, (πατηρ,)—a FATHER.

COMPA'TRIOT, *n.* a fellow countryman.
EXPA'TRIATE, *v.* to banish from one's country.
PAR'RICIDE, *n.* the murder of a parent.
PATER'NAL, *a.* fatherly.
PATRI'CIAN, *n.* a nobleman.

PA'TRIARCH, *n.* the father and ruler of a family.
PAT'RIMONY, *n.* an inherited estate.
PA'TRIOT, *n.* a lover of his country.
PA'TRON, *n.* a supporter.
PAT'RONIZE, *v.* to support.

Pa'thos, (παθος,)—FEELING; AFFECTION; DISEASE.

ANTIP'ATHY, *n.* aversion.
AP'ATHY, *n.* want of feeling.
APATHET'IC, *a.* without feeling.

PA'THOS, *n.* passion; warmth.
PATHET'IC, *a.* exciting emotion.
PATHOL'OGY, *n.* the science of diseases.

SYM'PATHY, *n.* fellow feeling.

Pep'to, (πέπτω,)—to BOIL; to CONCOCT.

DYSPEP'SY, *n.* bad digestion.
DYSPEP'TIC, *a.* having bad digestion.

EUPEP'SY, *n.* good digestion.
EUPEP'TIC, *a.* having good digestion.

Pet'alon, (πεταλον,)—a FLOWER LEAF.

PET'AL, *n.* a flower leaf.

PET'ALED, *a.* having petals.

APET'ALOUS, *a.* without petals.

Pe'tra, (πετρα,)—a ROCK; a STONE.

PE'TER, *n.* a man's name.
PETRES'CENT, *a.* turning to stone.
PET'RIFY, *v.* to convert into stone.

PETRIFAC'TION, *n.* the process of turning to stone.
SALTPE'TER, *n.* a mineral salt.

Pha'no, (φαινω, à φαω,)—to ENLIGHTEN; to SAY or TELL.

BLAS'PHEMY, *n.* impious language.
EM'PHASIS, *n.* stress laid upon a word.
EMPHAT'IC, *a.* forcible.
EPIPH'ANY, *n.* the manifestation.
PHAN'TOM, *n.* an apparition.

PHAN'TASM, *n.* a fancied appearance.
PHASE, *n.* an appearance.
PHENOM'ENON, *n.* an appearance.
PROPH'ECY, *n.* a foretelling.
PROPH'ET, *n.* a foreteller.

SYC'OPHANT, *n.* a low flatterer.

NOTE.—EPIPH'ANY, the manifestation of Christ to the Gentiles.

Phar'macon, (φαρμακον,)—a MEDICINE or DRUG.

PHAR'MACY, *n.* the art of preparing medicines.

PHARMACEU'TIC, *n.* relating to pharmacy.

Phe'ro, (φερω,)—to CARRY; to BRING.

MET'APHOR, *n.* a short similitude.
METAPHOR'ICAL, *a.* figurative.
PERIPH'ERY, *n.* circumference.

PHOS'PHORUS, *n.* a luminous substance.
PHOSPHORES'CENT, *a.* shining.

Pho'ne, (φωνή,)—a SOUND.

EU'PHONY, *n.* agreeable sound.

EUPHON'IC, *a.* agreeable in sound.

SYM'PHONY, *n.* harmony of sounds.

Phi'los, (φιλος,)—a Friend or Lover.

PHILADEL'PHIA, *n.* brotherly love.
PHILAN'THROPIST, *n.* one who loves mankind

PHILOL'OGIST, *n.* a student of language.
PHILOS'OPHY, *n.* the study of general laws.

NOTE.—PHILOS'OPHY, literally, the love of wisdom.

Phra'sis, (φρασις,)—a Saying; a Speech.

PHRASE, *n.* a short sentence.
PER'IPHRASE, *n.* a speaking round.
PAR'APHRASE, *n.* a more clear and ample explanation.

PHRASEOL'OGY, *n.* expression in words.
PERIPHRAS'TIC, *a.* expressing by more words than are necessary.

Phren, (φρην,)—the Mind.

PHRENOL'OGY, *n.* the science of the mind as connected with the brain.

FREN'ZY, *n.* madness; delirium.
FRAN'TIC, *a.* violently delirious.

Phys'is, (φυσις,)—a Bringing Forth; Nature.

PHYS'ICS, *n.* the science of nature.
PHYSIOL'OGY, *n.* the science of animals and plants.
PHYSI'CIAN, *n.* a doctor.

PHYS'ICAL, *a.* natural; bodily.
METAPHYS'ICS, *n.* the science of the mind.

Pla'ne, (πλανη,)—a Wandering About.

PLAN'ET, *n.* a wandering star.

PLAN'ETARY, *a.* pertaining to the planets.

Plas'so, (πλασσω,)—to Mould or Shape; to Smear.

PLAS'TIC, *a.* capable of being moulded; soft.

CAT'APLASM, *n.* a poultice.
PLAS'TER, *n.* lime to cover walls.

Pneu'ma, (πνευμα,)—a Breath; a Blast.

PNEUMAT'ICS, *n.* the science which treats of the air.
PNEUMAT'IC, *a.* pertaining to air.

PNEUMO'NIA, *n.* inflammation of the lungs.
PNEUMON'IC, *a.* relating to the lungs.

Po'leo, (πωλεω,)—to Sell.

MONOP'OLY, *n.* exclusive sale.

MONOP'OLIZE, *v.* to engross the whole.

Po'ly, (πολυ,)—Many.

POL'YGLOT, *n.* having many languages.
POL'YGON, *n.* a figure having many angles.

POLYNE'SIA, *n.* a division of the earth consisting of many islands.
POL'YPUS, *n.* an insect having many feet.

Po'ros, (πορος,)—a Passage or Way.

PORE, *n.* a small passage in the skin. | POROUS, *a.* having pores.
POROS'ITY, *n.* porousness.

Po'lis, (πολις,)—a CITY; a TOWN.

METROP'OLIS, *n.* the chief city.
POLICE', *n.* the government of a city.
POL'ITY, *n.* the form of government.
POL'ITIC, *a.* prudent; wise.
POL'ITICS, *n.* the science of government.
POLIT'ICAL, *a.* relating to politics.
POL'ICY, *n.* management of public affairs.
POL'ISH, *v.* to smooth; to brighten.
POLITE', *a.* refined; genteel.
IMPOLITE', *a.* rude; uncivil.

Pous, po'dus, (πους,)—a FOOT.

ANTIP'ODES, *n.* those who stand feet to feet.
TRI'POD, *n.* a seat with three feet.

Prac'tos, (πρακτος,)—DONE. *Prag'ma,* (πραγμα,)—a DEED.

PRAC'TICE, *n.* habit; use.
PRAC'TICABLE, *a.* that may be done.
PRAGMAT'ICAL, *a.* meddling.
IMPRAC'TICABLE, *a.* that cannot be done.
PRAX'IS, *n.* a form to teach practice.

Pro'tos, (πρωτος,)—FIRST.

PRO'TOCOL, *n.* a record or registry.
PROTHON'OTARY, *n.* a register.
PRO'TOTYPE, *n.* a model.
PROTOX'YD, *n.* the first oxyd.

Psalm'a, (ψαλμα,)—a SACRED SONG.

PSALM, *n.* a sacred song.
PSAL'TER, *n.* the book of psalms.
PSALM'ODY, *n.* a singing of psalms.
PSAL'TERY, *n.* a harp.
PSALM'IST, *n.* a writer of psalms.

Psy'che, (ψυκη,)—the BREATH; the SOUL.

METEMPSYCHO'SIS, *n.* the transmigration of souls.
PSYCHOL'OGY, *n.* the science of the nature of the soul.

Pyr, (πυρ,) *Py'ros*—FIRE.

EMPYR'EAL, *a.* formed of pure fire.
PYRE, *n.* a funeral fire.
PYROLIG'NEOUS, *a.* produced from smoke.
PYROTECH'NICS, *n.* the art of making fireworks.

Rhe'o, (ρεω,)—to FLOW; to SPEAK.

CATARRH', *n.* a discharge of mucus from the nose.
DIARRHE'A, *n.* a flux; a purging.
HEM'ORRHAGE, *n.* a flow of blood.
RHEUM, *n.* a thin, watery humor.
RHEU'MATISM, *n.* a painful disease.

Sarx, (σαρξ, σαρκος,)—FLESH.

SAR'CASM, *n.* a keen reproach.
SARCAS'TIC, *a.* keen; severe.

NOTE.—SAR'CASM, literally, a cutting or tearing of the flesh.

Scep'tomai, (σκεπτομαι,)—to LOOK ABOUT; to DOUBT.

SKEP'TIC, *n.* one who doubts.
SKEP'TICISM, *n.* a state of doubting.
SKEP'TICAL, *a.* doubting.

GREEK ROOTS AND DERIVATIVES.

Sce'na, (σκηνη,)—the STAGE; a REPRESENTATION.

SCENE, *n.* an appearance. | SCE'NERY, *n.* a collection of scenes.

Schis'ma, (σχισμα,)—a SPLITTING ; a DIVISION IN THE CHURCH.

SCHISM, *n.* a division in the church. | SCHISMAT'IC, *a.* promoting schism.

Scho'la, (σχολη,)—LEISURE; a SCHOOL.

SCHOOL, *n.* a place of instruction. | SCHOLAS'TIC, *a.* pertaining to the schools.
SCHO'LAR, *n.* a man of learning.
SCHO'LIAST, *n.* a commentator.

Sco'peo, (σκοπεω,)—to WATCH ; to OBSERVE NARROWLY.

EPIS'COPAL, *a.* governed by bishops. | TEL'ESCOPE, *n.* a glass for viewing distant objects.
EPIS'COPATE, *n.* a bishopric.
SCOPE, *n.* view; design; space.

Si'tos, (σιτος,)—WHEAT ; FOOD.

PAR'ASITE, *n.* one who earns his welcome by flattery. | PARASIT'ICAL, *a.* fawning for bread or favors.

So'phia, (σοφια,)—WISDOM.

PHILOS'OPHY, *n.* the love of wisdom. | UNSOPHIS'TICATED, *a.* not acquainted with evil; pure.
SOPH'ISM, *n.* a fallacious argument.
SOPH'ISTRY, *n.* fallacious reasoning.

Spas'ma, (σπασμα,)—a CONVULSION.

SPASM, *n.* a violent contraction. | SPASMOD'IC, *a.* convulsive.

Sta'sis, (στασις,)—a STANDING ; a WEIGHING.

APOS'TASY, *n.* a departure from one's religion. | HYDROSTAT'ICS, *n.* the science of the weight, motion, and equilibrium of fluids.
EC'STASY, *n.* excessive joy.
ECSTAT'IC, *a.* rapturous. | SYS'TEM, *n.* regular method.

Stel'lo, (στελλω,)—to SEND.

APOS'TLE, *n.* a messenger. | EPIS'TLE, *n.* a letter sent.

Sten'os, (στενος,)—SHORT.

STENOG'RAPHY, *n.* the art of writing in shorthand. | STENOG'RAPHER, *n.* a shorthand writer.

Stichos, (στιχος,)—a LINE ; a ROW.

ACROS'TIC, a kind of poem. | DIS'TICH, *n.* a couplet.

Stig'ma, (στιγμα,)—a MARK OF INFAMY.

STIG'MA, *n.* a blot; a reproach. | STIG'MATIZE, *v.* to disgrace; to censure.

Stro'phe, (στροφη,)—a TURNING ROUND.

APOS'TROPHE, *n.* a figure of speech.

CATAS'TROPHE, *n.* an unfortunate accident; a final event.

Tac'tos, (τακτος,)—PUT IN ORDER.

SYN'TAX, *n.* the construction of sentences.

TAC'TICS, *n.* the art of directing movements.

Ta'phos, (ταφος,)—a TOMB.

CEN'OTAPH, *n.* a monument for one buried elsewhere.

EP'ITAPH, *n.* an inscription upon a tomb.

Tech'ne, (τεχνη,)—ART; SKILL.

TECH'NICAL, *a.* belonging to an art.
TECHNOL'OGY, *n.* a discourse upon the arts.

POLYTECH'NIC, *a.* embracing many arts.
PYR'OTECHNY, *n.* the art of making fireworks.

Tec'ton, (τεκτων,)—an ARTIST; a BUILDER

AR'CHITECTURE, *n.* the science of building.

AR'CHITECT, *n.* a builder.

The'os, (θεος,)—GOD.

A'THEIST, *n.* one who denies the existence of a God.

THEOC'RACY, *n.* government directed by God.

THEOL'OGY, *n.* the science of God and divine things.

The'sis, (θεσις,)—a PLACING or PUTTING.

ANATH'EMA, *n.* an ecclesiastical curse.
ANTITH'ESIS, *n.* opposition of words.
EP'ITHET, *n.* a descriptive word.
HYPOTH'ESIS, *n.* a supposition.

SYN'THESIS, *n.* a putting together.
SYNTHET'ICAL, *a.* relating to synthesis.
THEME, *n.* a subject.
THE'SIS, *n.* a position

NOTE.—EP'ITHET, something placed upon. HYPOTH'ESIS, a placing under.

To'mos, (τομος,)—a CUTTING.

ANAT'OMY, *n.* the art of dissecting.
AT'OM, *n.* an indivisible particle.

EPIT'OME, *n.* an abridgement.
TOME, *n.* a volume.

NOTE.—ANAT'OMY, literally, a cutting up. TOME, a section or part cut off.

To'nos, (τονος,)—a STRETCHING; a SOUND.

ASTON'ISH, *v.* to surprise.
ASTOUND', *v.* to strike dumb.
ATTUNE', *v.* to put in tune.
DET'ONATE, *v.* to explode.

INTONA'TION, *n.* manner of sounding.
TONE, *n.* vigor; sound.
TON'IC, *a.* giving tone.
TUNE, *n.* sound; harmony.

Top'os, (τόπος,)—a PLACE; a TRACT OF COUNTRY.

TOP'IC, *n.* a subject of discourse.
TOP'ICAL, *a.* local.

TOPOG'RAPHY, *n.* a description of a place.

Trop'os, (τροπος,)—a TURNING.

TROPE, *n.* a figure of speech.
TRO'PHY, *n.* a monument of victory.
TROP'IC, *n.* the point at which the sun appears to turn again towards the equator.

Ty'pus, (τυπος,)—a TYPE; a MARK.

TYPE, *n.* an emblem; the model or form of a letter.
TYP'ICAL, *a.* symbolical.
TYP'IFY, *v.* to represent by figure.
TYPOG'RAPHY, *n.* the art of printing.
STE'REOTYPE, *n.* solid type.

Zo'on, (ζωον,)—an ANIMAL.

ZOOL'OGY, *n.* the science of animals.
ZO'DIAC, *n.* a broad circle in the heavens.
ZO'OPHYTE, *n.* a body which partakes of the nature of both an animal and a vegetable.

THE END.

Composition and Rhetoric

Butler's School English
    Cloth, 12mo, 272 pages . . . . 75 cents

A brief, concise and thoroughly practical manual for use in connection with the written English work of secondary schools. It has been prepared specially to secure definite results in the study of English, by showing the pupil how to review, criticise, and improve his own writing.

Quackenbos's Practical Rhetoric
    Cloth, 12mo, 477 pages $1.00

This book develops, in a perfectly natural manner, the laws and principles which underlie rhetorical art, and then shows their use and application in the different processes and kinds of composition. It is clear, simple, and logical in its treatment throughout, original in its departure from technical rules and traditions, copiously illustrated with examples for practice, and calculated to awaken interest and enthusiasm in the study. A large part of the book is devoted to instruction and practice in actual composition work, in which the pupil is encouraged to follow and apply genuine laboratory methods.

Waddy's Elements of Composition and Rhetoric
    Cloth, 12mo, 416 pages $1.00

A complete course in Composition and Rhetoric, with copious exercises in both criticism and construction. It is inductive in method, lucid in style, orderly in arrangement, and clear and comprehensive in treatment. Sufficiently elementary for the lower grades of high school classes and complete enough for all secondary schools.

Copies of the above books will be sent prepaid to any address, on receipt of the price, by the Publishers:

American Book Company

New York   •   Cincinnati   •   Chicago

For the Study of Literature

Matthews' Introduction to the Study of American Literature
By BRANDER MATTHEWS, Professor of Literature in Columbia University. Cloth, 12mo, 256 pages $1.00
A text-book of literature on an original plan, admirably designed to guide, to supplement and to stimulate the student's reading of American authors.

Watkins's American Literature (Literature Primer Series).
By MILDRED CABELL WATKINS.
Flexible cloth, 18mo, 224 pages . . . . . 35 cents
A text book of American Literature adapted to the comprehension of pupils in common and graded schools.

Seven American Classics, containing choice literary selections from Irving, Cooper, Bryant, Hawthorne, Longfellow, Whittier, Holmes.
Cloth, 12mo, 218 pages . . . . . . 50 cents

Brooke's English Literature (Literature Primer Series). By the Rev. STOPFORD BROOKE, M. A. New edition, revised and corrected.
Flexible cloth, 18mo, 240 pages . . . . 35 cents
Equally valuable as a class-book for schools or as a book of reference for general readers.

Seven British Classics, containing choice literary selections from Addison, Scott, Lamb, Campbell, Macaulay, Tennyson, Thackeray.
Cloth, 12mo, 217 pages . . . . . . 50 cents

Smith's Studies in English Literature, containing complete selections from Chaucer, Spenser, Shakespeare, Bacon and Milton, with a History of English Literature from the earliest times to the death of Dryden in 1700. By M. W. SMITH, A. M.
Cloth, 12mo, 427 pages $1.20

Cathcart's Literary Reader. A manual of English Literature containing typical selections from the best British and American authors, with biographical and critical sketches, portraits and fac-simile autographs. By GEORGE R. CATHCART.
Cloth, leather back, 12mo, 541 pages $1.15

Copies of any of the above books will be sent prepaid to any address, on receipt of the price, by the Publishers:

American Book Company

New York • Cincinnati • Chicago

Eclectic English Classics for Schools

This series is intended to provide selected gems of English Literature for school use at the least possible price. The texts have been carefully edited, and are accompanied by adequate explanatory notes. They are well printed from new, clear type, and are uniformly bound in boards. The series now includes the following works:

Arnold's (Matthew) Sohrab and Rustum	20 cents
Burke's Conciliation with the American Colonies	20 cents
Carlyle's Essay on Robert Burns	20 cents
Coleridge's Rime of the Ancient Mariner	20 cents
Defoe's History of the Plague in London	40 cents
DeQuincey's Revolt of the Tartars	20 cents
Emerson's American Scholar, Self-Reliance, and Compensation	20 cents
Franklin's Autobiography	35 cents
George Eliot's Silas Marner	30 cents
Goldsmith's Vicar of Wakefield	35 cents
Irving's Sketch Book—Selections	20 cents
Tales of a Traveler	50 cents
Macaulay's Second Essay on Chatham	20 cents
Essay on Milton	20 cents
Essay on Addison	20 cents
Life of Samuel Johnson	20 cents
Milton's L'Allegro, Il Penseroso, Comus, and Lycidas	20 cents
Paradise Lost—Books I. and II.	20 cents
Pope's Homer's Iliad, Books I., VI., XXII. and XXIV.	20 cents
Scott's Ivanhoe	50 cents
Marmion	40 cents
Lady of the Lake	30 cents
The Abbot	60 cents
Woodstock	60 cents
Shakespeare's Julius Cæsar	20 cents
Twelfth Night	20 cents
Merchant of Venice	20 cents
Midsummer-Night's Dream	20 cents
As You Like It	20 cents
Macbeth	20 cents
Hamlet	25 cents
Sir Roger de Coverley Papers (The Spectator)	20 cents
Southey's Life of Nelson	40 cents
Tennyson's Princess	20 cents
Webster's Bunker Hill Orations	20 cents

Copies of any of the Eclectic English Classics will be sent prepaid to any address, on receipt of the price, by the Publishers:

American Book Company

New York   •   Cincinnati   •   Chicago

An Introduction to the

Study of American Literature

BY

BRANDER MATTHEWS

Professor of Literature in Columbia University

Cloth, 12mo, 256 pages · · · Price, $1.00

A text-book of literature on an original plan, and conforming with the best methods of teaching.

Admirably designed to guide, to supplement, and to stimulate the student's reading of American authors.

Illustrated with a fine collection of facsimile manuscripts, portraits of authors, and views of their homes and birthplaces.

Bright, clear, and fascinating, it is itself a literary work of high rank.

The book consists mostly of delightfully readable and yet comprehensive little biographies of the fifteen greatest and most representative American writers. Each of the sketches contains a critical estimate of the author and his works, which is the more valuable coming, as it does, from one who is himself a master. The work is rounded out by four general chapters which take up other prominent authors and discuss the history and conditions of our literature as a whole; and there is at the end of the book a complete chronology of the best American literature from the beginning down to 1896.

Each of the fifteen biographical sketches is illustrated by a fine portrait of its subject and views of his birthplace or residence and in some cases of both. They are also accompanied by each author's facsimile manuscript covering one or two pages. The book contains excellent portraits of many other authors famous in American literature.

Copies of Brander Matthews' Introduction to the Study of American Literature will be sent prepaid to any address, on receipt of the price, by the Publishers:

American Book Company

New York • Cincinnati • Chicago

Webster's School Dictionaries

REVISED EDITIONS

Webster's School Dictionaries in their revised form constitute a progressive series, carefully graded and especially adapted for Primary Schools, Common Schools, High Schools, Academies, etc. They have all been thoroughly revised, entirely reset, and made to conform in all essential points to the great standard authority—Webster's International Dictionary.

WEBSTER'S PRIMARY SCHOOL DICTIONARY . . . 48 cents
   Containing over 20,000 words and meanings, with over 400 illustrations.

WEBSTER'S COMMON SCHOOL DICTIONARY . . . 72 cents
   Containing over 25,000 words and meanings, with over 500 illustrations.

WEBSTER'S HIGH SCHOOL DICTIONARY . . . 98 cents
   Containing about 37,000 words and definitions, and an appendix giving a pronouncing vocabulary of Biblical, Classical, Mythological, Historical, and Geographical proper names, with over 800 illustrations.

WEBSTER'S ACADEMIC DICTIONARY $1.50
   Abridged directly from the International Dictionary, and giving the orthography, pronunciations, definitions and synonyms of the large vocabulary of words in common use, with an appendix containing various useful tables, with over 800 illustrations.

The Same, Indexed $1 80

SPECIAL EDITIONS

Webster's Condensed Dictionary. Cloth . . .	$1.44
The Same, Indexed	1.75
Webster's Condensed Dictionary. Half calf . .	2.40
Webster's Handy Dictionary. Cloth . . .	15 cents
Webster's Pocket Dictionary. Cloth . . .	57 cents
In Roan Flexible	69 cents
In Roan Tucks	78 cents
Webster's American People's Dictionary and Manual .	48 cents
Webster's Practical Dictionary. Cloth . . .	80 cents
Webster's Countinghouse Dictionary. Sheep, Indexed .	$2.40

Copies of any of Webster's Dictionaries will be sent prepaid to any address, on receipt of the price, by the Publishers:

American Book Company

New York • Cincinnati • Chicago

Pupils' Outline Studies

IN THE

HISTORY OF THE UNITED STATES

BY

FRANCIS H. WHITE, A.M.

Paper, Square Octavo, 128 pages • • Price, 30 cents

This is a book of Outline Studies, Maps and Blanks, intended for use in connection with the study of United States History. It contains an original and systematic combination of devices consisting of outline maps, graphic charts, and blanks for historical tables and summaries, for the reproduction of pictures, for biographical sketches, for studies in civil government, etc. It also contains valuable suggestions to teachers and pupils, and carefully selected lists of historical books and authorities for collateral reading and reference.

Its use will encourage the pupil to observe closely, to select the leading and salient facts of history, to classify his knowledge, to investigate for himself, and to carry his investigations up to recognized authorities and even to original sources. It also furnishes opportunity and material for the best exercises and training in English Composition.

The book is conveniently arranged for either class or individual instruction and may be used in connection with any text-book on United States History.

Copies of White's Pupils' Outline Studies will be sent prepaid to any address, on receipt of the price, by the Publishers:

American Book Company

New York • Cincinnati • Chicago

(28)

An Advanced English Grammar

FOR THE USE OF

HIGH SCHOOL, ACADEMY AND COLLEGE CLASSES

BY

W. M. BASKERVILL

Professor of the English Language and Literature in Vanderbilt University, Nashville, Tenn.

AND

J. W. SEWELL

Of the Fogg High School, Nashville, Tenn.

Cloth, 12mo, 349 pages . . . . 90 cents

This new Grammar is designed for advanced students who desire to extend their studies in English beyond the course ordinarily pursued in Common or Grammar Schools. In this work, grammar is treated as a science based on *facts and principles* derived from the actual use of the language and not from technical rules and traditions.

Its aim is to lead the pupil to deduce for himself grammatical rules from the best examples of construction and style to be found in English literature and to acquire skill in their use. For this purpose abundant and apposite quotations from standard authors are given to illustrate each grammatical relation and construction and to show the student that he is dealing with the *facts* of the language and not with the *theories* of the grammarians.

While the book represents original and advanced methods it is at the same time conservative in treatment, and aims to preserve what is good in the older methods.

Copies of Baskervill and Sewell's English Grammar will be sent prepaid to any address, on receipt of the price, by the Publishers:

American Book Company

New York • Cincinnati • Chicago

Halleck's Psychology and Psychic Culture

By REUBEN POST HALLECK, M.A. (Yale)

Cloth, 12mo, 368 pages. Illustrated . . . . Price, $1.25

This new text-book in Psychology and Psychic Culture is suitable for use in High School, Academy and College classes, being simple and elementary enough for beginners and at the same time complete and comprehensive enough for advanced classes in the study. It is also well suited for private students and general readers, the subjects being treated in such an attractive manner and relieved by so many apt illustrations and examples as to fix the attention and deeply impress the mind.

The work includes a full statement and clear exposition of the coördinate branches of the study—physiological and introspective psychology. The physical basis of Psychology is fully recognized. Special attention is given to the cultivation of the mental faculties, making the work practically useful for self-improvement. The treatment throughout is singularly clear and plain and in harmony with its aims and purpose.

"Halleck's Psychology pleases me very much. It is short, clear, interesting, and full of common sense and originality of illustration. I can sincerely recommend it."

WILLIAM JAMES,
Professor of Psychology, Harvard University.

Copies of Halleck's Psychology will be sent prepaid to any address on receipt of the price by the Publishers:

American Book Company

New York • Cincinnati • Chicago

Fisher's Brief History of the Nations

AND OF THEIR PROGRESS IN CIVILIZATION

By GEORGE PARK FISHER, LL.D.
Professor in Yale University

Cloth, 12mo, 613 pages, with numerous Illustrations, Maps, Tables, and Reproductions of Bas-reliefs, Portraits, and Paintings. Price, $1.50

This is an entirely new work written expressly to meet the demand for a compact and acceptable text-book on General History for high schools, academies, and private schools. Some of the distinctive qualities which will commend this book to teachers and students are as follows:

It narrates in fresh, vigorous, and attractive style the most important facts of history in their due order and connection.

It explains the nature of historical evidence, and records only well established judgments respecting persons and events.

It delineates the progress of peoples and nations in civilization as well as the rise and succession of dynasties.

It connects, in a single chain of narration, events related to each other in the contemporary history of different nations and countries.

It gives special prominence to the history of the Mediæval and Modern Periods, — the eras of greatest import to modern students.

It is written from the standpoint of the present, and incorporates the latest discoveries of historical explorers and writers.

It is illustrated by numerous colored maps, genealogical tables, and artistic reproductions of architecture, sculpture, painting, and portraits of celebrated men, representing every period of the world's history.

Copies of Fisher's Brief History of the Nations will be sent prepaid to any address, on receipt of the price, by the Publishers :

American Book Company

New York •:• Cincinnati • Chicago

Handbook of Greek and Roman History

BY

GEORGES CASTEGNIER, B.S., B.L.

Flexible Cloth, 12mo, 110 pages.   •   •   Price, 50 cents

The purpose of this little handbook is to assist the student of Greek and Roman History in reviewing subjects already studied in the regular text-books and in preparing for examinations. It will also be found useful for general readers who wish to refresh their minds in regard to the leading persons and salient facts of ancient history.

It is in two parts, one devoted to Greek, and the other to Roman history. The names and titles have been selected with rare skill, and represent the whole range of classical history. They are arranged alphabetically, and are printed in full-face type, making them easy to find. The treatment of each is concise and gives just the information in regard to the important persons, places, and events of classical history which every scholar ought to know and remember, or have at ready command.

Its convenient form and systematic arrangement especially adapt it for use as an accessory and reference manual for students, or as a brief classical cyclopedia for general readers.

Copies of Castegnier's Handbook of Greek and Roman History will be sent prepaid to any address, on receipt of the price, by the Publishers:

American Book Company

New York   •   Cincinnati   •   Chicago

(44)

Milne's Elements of Algebra

A COURSE FOR BEGINNERS

By WILLIAM J. MILNE, Ph.D., LL.D.

President of New York State Normal College

Cloth, 12mo, 199 pages • • Price, 60 cents.

This book has been prepared to meet the demand for a text-book sufficiently elementary for pupils commencing the study of Algebra in Intermediate or Grammar Schools, as well as in High Schools. It is intended to thoroughly instruct the student in the fundamental principles of the science and to lay a sound foundation for more advanced work in the study.

Some of the distinctive qualities and features which particularly adapt this book for beginners are:

The natural arrangement and simple treatment of the elementary facts of the science.

The easy and natural transition from arithmetical to algebraic processes,—the early steps being exceedingly simple, clear, and progressive.

The large number and judicious selection of examples for practice, insuring a thorough understanding of each principle as presented; complex problems and mere puzzles being carefully excluded.

The early introduction and practical use of the equation,—which is made the keynote of the book.

The use of the same methods of presentation, exemplified in the other books of Milne's Mathematical Series, which have met with such general approval by the teachers.

Copies of Milne's Elements of Algebra will be sent prepaid to any address, on receipt of the price, by the Publishers:

American Book Company

New York •• Cincinnati • Chicago

Important New School Books

READING

Baldwin's School Readings by Grades.

First Year	$0.25	Sixth Year	$0.50
Second Year	.35	Seventh Year	.50
Third Year	.45	Eighth Year	.50
Fourth Year	.45	Combined Fourth and Fifth Years	.70
Fifth Year	.45	Combined Sixth and Seventh Years	.80

SPELLING

Patterson's American Word Book 25

ARITHMETIC

Baird's Graded Work in Arithmetic   Four Books.
Milne's Mental Arithmetic 35

GEOGRAPHY

Natural Elementary Geography 60
Natural Advanced Geography . . . . .

ENGLISH

Metcalf and Bright's Language Lessons. Part I. . . .35
   The Same. Part II. 55
Metcalf's Elementary English 40
Metcalf's English Grammar for Common Schools . . .60

HISTORY

McMaster's School History of the United States . . 1.00

PENMANSHIP

Spencerian Penmanship, Vertical Edition.
   Shorter Course, Nos. 1 to 7 . . . . Per doz., .72
   Common School Course, Nos. 1 to 6 . . " .96
Curtiss's Vertical Copy Books, 6 numbers . . " .96
Ward's Graded Lessons in Penmanship and Spelling.
   Small Numbers, 1 to 6 . . . . Per doz., .72
   Large Numbers, 1 to 6 . . . . " .96

MUSIC

Natural Advanced Music Reader 1.00
Betz's Gems of School Songs 70

Copies of any of the above books will be sent, prepaid, to any address on receipt of the price by the Publishers:

American Book Company

NEW YORK   •   CINCINNATI   •   CHICAGO

www.ingramcontent.com/pod-product-compliance
Lightning Source LLC
Chambersburg PA
CBHW021149230426
43667CB00006B/320